AND MUHAMMAD IS HIS MESSENGER

AND MUHAMMAD IS HIS MESSENGER

THE VENERATION OF THE PROPHET IN ISLAMIC PIETY

ANNEMARIE SCHIMMEL

THE UNIVERSITY OF NORTH CAROLINA PRESS

CHAPEL HILL AND LONDON

Manufactured in the United States of America

Library of Congress Cataloging in Publication Data

Schimmel, Annemarie.
And Muhammad is his messenger.

(Studies in religion)
Translation of: und Muhammad ist sein Prophet.
Bibliography: p.
Includes indexes.
1. Islamic poetry—History and criticism. 2. Muhammad, d. 632, in literature. 3. Muḥammad, d. 632—Cult.
I. Title. II. Series: Studies in religion (Chapel Hill, N.C.)
PJ827.S3313 1985 809.1'9351 84-17374
ISBN 0-8078-1639-6
ISBN 0-8078-4128-5 (pbk.)

Designed by Naomi P. Slifkin

The original German edition of *Und Muhammad Ist Sein Prophet* by Annemarie Schimmel was published in 1981 by Eugen Diederichs Verlag, Düsseldorf/Köln.

The calligraphic motif at the opening of each chapter, which reads "Muhammad is the Messenger of God," is a modern rendition, by Wasmaa Chorbachi, from a manuscript (40.164.2a) in the Metropolitan Museum, New York.

کافر ہوں کہ مومن ہوں خدا جانے میں کیا ہوں   میں بندہ ہوں ان کا جو ہیں سلطانِ مدینہ

Be I infidel or true believer—
God alone knows, what I am!
But I know: I am the Prophet's servant,
Who Medina's ruler is.

Sir Kishan Prasad Shad
Hindu Prime Minister of Hyderabad State

CONTENTS

ILLUSTRATIONS

PREFACE

This book is the fruit of an interest in the figure of the Prophet of Islam that has developed over more than four decades. I was first introduced to and deeply moved by the concept of the "mystical Muhammad" when I was a teenager, busying myself with the study of Arabic under the guidance of Dr. Hans Ellenberg. During those formative years, the books of Syed Ameer Ali, *The Life and Teachings of Muhammad, or The Spirit of Islam*, and Tor Andrae's masterful study *Die person Muhammads in lehre und glaube seiner gemeinde* were among my favorites, and Andrae's book remains a source of inspiration to this day. During my student days at Berlin University I enjoyed reading Suleyman Chelebi's *Mevlûd-i sherif*, a simple, touching poem that tells of the miracles at Muhammad's birth in images very similar to popular Christian Christmas carols, but little did I know then that I would attend many *mevlût* in the five years I spent in Turkey as professor of Comparative Religion in the Islamic faculty of theology in Ankara. In that period, I learned much about the popular veneration of the Prophet among Turkish Muslims. A deepening interest in the poetical and mystical literature of the Indo-Pakistani subcontinent then led me to realize how much love of the Prophet had colored the work of Muhammad Iqbal, the poet-philosopher of this century. The study of Sindhi folk literature added new facets to the picture. My fascination with the development of the veneration of the Prophet and its reflection in literature, especially poetry, resulted in a number of articles pertaining to prophetology as perceived by Iqbal, reflected in Sindhi poetry, and theoreticized by a reformist Muslim mystic like Mir Dard in eighteenth-century Delhi, and other topics. The material thus collected and combined with that culled from other sources formed the basis of one of the lectures I delivered in 1980 to the American Council of Learned Societies (published as chapter 5 of my book *As Through a Veil*). My German publisher, Ulf Diederichs, then encouraged me to enlarge that chapter into a book about the veneration of the Prophet, which appeared in 1981. It is this book that is offered here to anglophone readers, but in a form that has outgrown the space limits of the German edition. We have also omitted the illustrations from that edition here, for although they belong to the medieval Islamic tradition, modern Muslims tend to be offended by representations of the Prophet other than the verbal description.

Many people have had their share in the growth of this book: *qawwāls* in India and Pakistan who sang the praise of the Prophet in unforgettable tunes; theologians who sometimes objected to the "mystical" interpretation of the person of the Messenger of God; old women in the villages of Turkey and Pakistan, whose whole life was permeated by a deep, trusting love of the Beloved of God; and students both in the Islamic countries and in the United States, who asked questions and tried to learn more about a phenomenon that is so little known in the West.

In particular, I have to thank my friends and colleagues Professors William A. Graham of Harvard and Peter J. Awn of Columbia University. Dr. Graham read the whole manuscript and made some valuable suggestions, especially for the classical period and *hadīth*; Dr. Awn generously helped resolve editing problems with the Press during my absence in Europe and Asia. My research assistant Ali S. Asani located many bibliographical items. The copy editor for The University of North Carolina Press, Laura Oaks, skillfully polished a manuscript that was written and typed in part at Harvard, in part at Bonn, and gently removed inconsistencies. My gratitude is due to all of them.

Cambridge, Massachusetts
Spring 1984

AND MUHAMMAD IS HIS MESSENGER

INTRODUCTION

A manuscript copy of the Koran, written probably in the twelfth century in eastern Iran in a rather simple, late Kufic hand, has one notable peculiarity: the whole of Sura 112, the profession of God's Unity, is written in unusually interlaced, powerful letters, and on another page, the words *Muḥammad rasūl Allāh*, "Muhammad is the messenger of God," are likewise distinguished by their eye-catching calligraphic form from the rest of the page.[1] The unknown scribe has expressed, in a tangible way, the central position of the Prophet in the religion of Islam. Indeed, the passage he has chosen to celebrate comprises the second half of the Muslim profession of faith, *Lā ilāha illā Allāh, Muḥammadun rasūl Allāh*, "There is no deity save God, [and] Muhammad is the messenger of God." By this position in the profession of faith, Muhammad defines the borders of Islam as a religion.

In an article on Ibn ʿArabi's prophetology, Arthur Jeffery wrote: "Many years ago . . . the late Shaikh Mustafa al-Maraghi remarked on a visit to his friend, the Anglican bishop in Egypt, that the commonest cause of offence, generally unwitting offence, given by Christians to Muslims, arose from their complete failure to understand the very high regard all Muslims have for the person of their Prophet."[2] This comment from the Egyptian theologian hits the mark precisely. Misunderstanding of the role of the Prophet has been, and still is, one of the greatest obstacles to Christians' appreciation of the Muslim interpretation of Islamic history and culture. For, more than any other historical figure, it was Muhammad who aroused fear, aversion, and hatred in the medieval Christian world. When Dante in his *Divine Comedy* sees him condemned to eternal pain in the deepest abyss of Hell, he expresses the feelings of innumerable Christians of his era who could not understand how after the rise of Christianity another religion could appear in the world, a religion that—even worse!—was active in this world, and politically so successful that its members occupied large parts of the formerly Christian Mediterranean areas.

This is not the place to discuss in detail the deformation of the image of Muhammad as found in medieval and even rather modern European literature. There is scarcely any negative judgment that the Western world has not passed upon this man who had set in motion one of the most successful religious movements on earth; and the study of his image as reflected in history, drama, poetry, and last but not least scholarship would require a voluminous work of its own.[3]

In our day the new self-consciousness of the Muslims has come as a great surprise in the West, where Islam has been so long regarded as moribund. This new self-consciousness, however, has forced the West to reconsider some of the basic religious and social ideas of Islam in order to reach a better understanding of the values that have been and still are central for the Muslims. This may justify our attempt to depict how pious Muslims have seen the Prophet Muhammad through the centuries, even though their picture was not always historically correct. Certainly it reflects his enormous influence over their lives, and the non-Muslim reader will perhaps understand from the witness of theologians and poets, of Arabs, Persians, and Turks, of Muslims in India and in Africa, how deep the Muslims' love for him, how warm their trust in him are, how widely he has been venerated and called upon throughout the ages, and how he has been surrounded with the most glorious epithets. He will find that Muhammad indeed constitutes the exemplar and model for every Muslim believer, who is called to imitate him in all, even seemingly insignificant, actions and habits, and he will likely be amazed by the way in which the mystics developed the doctrine of Muhammad's primordial light and accorded to him, in his position as The Perfect Man, an almost cosmic status and function. For Muhammad, the last in the long chain of prophets beginning with Adam the father of mankind, is the one who brought the final revelation that comprehended all earlier revelations and at the same time recapitulated them in their pristine purity.

Wilfred Cantwell Smith is right when he states that "Muslims will allow attacks on Allah; there are atheists and atheistic publications, and rationalistic societies; but to disparage Muhammad will provoke from even the most 'liberal' sections of the community a fanaticism of blazing vehemence."[4] Indeed, when in late 1978 in Pakistan the principle of *Niẓām-i Muṣṭafā*, the Order of the Chosen One (that is, the Prophet), was introduced as a guideline for all actions and some voices critical of this notion were heard, the leading daily newspaper of the country published in response an announcement nearly half a page long by one Mohammad Ismail from the Karachi area, with the title "A fantastic fallacy."[5] In this piece, the writer attacked those who wanted to define the status of the Prophet before entering a discussion about the principles taught by him. The central paragraphs read:

> Who can measure and define the greatness of the Holy Prophet? We will not be surprised if such insolent persons, for their own ulterior motives, go even a step further and start saying that the status of Almighty Allah should also be determined before speaking about Islam in Pakistan, presupposing that crores [500,000s] of Muslims of Pakistan are ignorant of God and the Holy Prophet.
>
> It is an acknowledged and undisputed fact that the status of the Holy Prophet comes next to God, who alone knows the glory of His Prophet which He has bestowed on him. It has been very well expressed by the famous poet and saint Shaikh Saadi: *Baʿad Az Khuda Buzurg Tuee qissa Mukhtasar*, "In short, after God you are the greatest."

In Europe, where Muhammad has at times been understood as an idol-worshiper or transformed into Mahound, the Spirit of Darkness, his historical biography was studied from the eighteenth century onward, and although he was generally depicted as a kind of Antichrist or a Christian heretic and arch-schismatic, he also appeared to some philosophers of the Enlightenment period as representative of a rational religion, one devoid of speculations about Trinity and Redemption and, even more importantly, a religion without a powerful clergy.[6] From the nineteenth century onward Western scholars began to study the classical Arabic sources, which henceforward slowly became available in Europe. However, even during that period biographies of the Prophet were often marred by prejudices and in no way did justice to the role of the Prophet as seen by pious Muslims. It is understandable that the Muslims reacted with horror to the European image of their beloved Prophet, with which they became acquainted, particularly in India, through British educational institutions and missionary schools. Small wonder that they as Muslims loathed this Christian attitude, which contrasted so markedly with the veneration they were wont to show to Jesus, the last prophet before Muhammad, and to his mother the Virgin.[7] This encounter with such a distorted image of the Prophet is one of the reasons for the aversion of at least the Indian Muslims to the British.

It was as a consequence of this confrontation that the Muslims, reacting to works like William Muir's *Life of Mohamet*, began to study the historical role of the Prophet.[8] For in the course of the centuries his historical personality had almost disappeared behind a colorful veil of legends and myths; the bare facts were commonly elaborated in enthusiastic detail, and were rarely if at all seen in their historical perspective. The new interest in the study of the life of Muhammad, which runs almost parallel, in Muslim India, with the emergence of interest in the *Leben-Jesu-Forschung* (the quest for the historical Jesus) in the Protestant West, resulted in a number of serious, but also numerous superficial, purely apologetic writings. Syed Ameer Ali's *Life and Teachings of Muhammad, or The Spirit of Islam*, published in 1897, showed the direction in which modern Islamic biographies of Muhammad were to develop in the following decades.

At the moment there are available in Western languages a considerable number of biographies of the Prophet or discussions of his pivotal role in Islamic life and culture that have been written by Muslim authors and hence reflect different approaches to his personality in the Muslim community. An important introduction is Muhammad Hamidullah's *Le Prophète d'Islam*, which, based on his lifelong penetrating studies into the original Arabic sources and his deep personal piety, depicts the life of the Prophet as it appears to a devout Muslim who has received his academic training mostly in Western universities. Similarly, Emel Esin's beautiful book *Mecca the Blessed, Medinah the Radiant* contains a fine account of the Prophet's biography and, more importantly, an excellent description of the feelings of a highly cultured modern Turkish lady at the threshold of the Rauda (mausoleum) of the Prophet in Medina. Martin Lings's *Muhammad*, a life of the Prophet as depicted in the oldest sources, is an excellent introduction to the subject and very well written. These are only three typical examples from a large number of publications.

On the non-Muslim side, biographies of the Prophet Muhammad written during recent years by European scholars are certainly much more objective than the works of earlier generations and try further to do justice to his personality. W. Montgomery Watt's *Muhammad, Prophet and Statesman* is perhaps the best known of these studies. We may also mention here as one of the latest, and certainly most controversial, attempts the book by Günther Lüling, *Die Wiederentdeckung des Propheten Muhammad*, in which Muhammad is presented as the *Engelsprophet* (Angelic Prophet) who continued the unmitigated, pure tradition of Semitic, that is, Judaeo-Christian religion as contrasted to the hellenized Christianity that (according to Lüling's claims) was prevalent in Mecca. Adolf von Harnack's remark, based on centuries-old deprecatory Christian allegations, that Islam was essentially a Christian heresy is thus again revived, although now with a more favorable attitude toward the Prophet.

Some years ago Maxime Rodinson, himself a biographer of the Prophet, provided a very useful survey of the various approaches to the Prophet among Western students of Islam.[9] But of these scholars only one has tried specifically to depict Muhammad's role in Islamic piety. Even today Tor Andrae's *Die person Muhammads in lehre und glaube seiner Gemeinde* (1918) remains the standard work in this area, unsuperseded by any other major study, though complemented by random remarks in numerous modern works on Sufism. It is, however, unfortunately too little known even among Islamicists. Shortly before Andrae's masterly study appeared, the German scholar Max Horten published his *Die religiöse Vorstellungswelt des Volkes im Islam*, which also has fallen almost completely into oblivion; relying upon classical and contemporary sources, he gives numerous poignant examples of the veneration of the Prophet in popular religion. Almost half a century later, Hermann Stieglecker described the role of Muhammad in theology and, to a lesser extent, piety in his dogmatic handbook *Die Glaubenslehren des Islam* (1964).

Among works in English, Constance E. Padwick's *Muslim Devotions* (1960) leads the reader into the very heart of Muslim piety, namely the life of prayer, in which the Prophet Muhammad occupies a truly sublime position. This book on Muslim religious life is equally knowledgeable and lovable and contains abundant material about the veneration of the Prophet, culled from prayerbooks and devotional literature of the entire Islamic world. It is, to my feeling, the best introduction to the topic. Good translations of the most crucial classical Arabic accounts of Muhammad's life and work are offered by Arthur Jeffery in his *Reader on Islam*.

However, none of these authors has devoted himself to the study of the area in which love of the Prophet is expressed most beautifully and most eloquently: the poetry of the Islamic peoples. Not only is poetry in the classical languages of Arabic, Persian, and Ottoman Turkish worthy of attention here, but even more the popular verses in the various vernacular Islamic languages. These are the poems through which children imbibe the love of the Prophet from early childhood, poems that have helped to form and shape the image of the beloved Prophet, the intercessor on Doomsday and luminous Seal of the Prophets, in the hearts of the Muslim masses. To this day Muslim children like to write little poems, using traditional imagery, to express their love of and trust in the Prophet.[10] Their elder relatives may interpret the Prophet's words as the message of change and dynamism, of social justice, of democracy, or of intellectual progress.

The different facets of the image of the Prophet offer the historian of religion rich material for comparative studies, as James E. Royster has shown in a critical article.[11] Parallels to the lives of the other major founders of religious traditions are evident, and in the mystical veneration of the Prophet one can detect influences from or similarities to Christian or Hellenistic-Gnostic ideas. The phenomenologist of religion as well as the psychologist will discover that Islam offers highly interesting examples of loving devotion to the Prophet. All will agree that the personality of Muhammad is indeed, besides the Koran, the center of the Muslims' life; the Prophet is the one who forever remains the "beautiful model" (Sura 33:21) for the life of all those who acknowledge in the profession of faith that he is truly "the messenger of God."

ONE

BIOGRAPHICAL AND HAGIOGRAPHICAL NOTES

Muhammad's life is known to us from different sources. The Koran contains allusions to events in his life and the life of the young Muslim community.[1] Furthermore, his sayings and reports about his actions were carefully preserved and collected to form, in the course of the first centuries, a large compendium, showing how his community saw him. Another early source is the poems of Hassan ibn Thabit, who joined the Prophet in Medina and sang of the important events in the life of the Muslim community, praising Muhammad and derogating his enemies. Also very early are the various descriptions of the Prophet's wars and raids (*maghāzī*) and of the spread of Islam in the Arabian Peninsula. All this constituted raw material for his *sīra*, his biography. The *sīra* composed by Ibn Ishaq (d. ca. 768) and then edited by Ibn Hisham (d. ca. 830) became the basis of all later biographies.[2] It goes without saying that numerous legends crystalized around a nucleus of factual material; but the charisma of a true religious leader can be better recognized from such legends than from the dry facts of his life, facts that are always likely to be interpreted by the biographer according to his peculiar viewpoint.

Muhammad's biographical dates have always been considered the best-known among those of all great religious founders, but even in earliest Islam a "sacred biography," which nonetheless certainly kept in mind the major external events of his life, including the dates, developed among the Muslims and has remained intact to our day. It was elaborated in the various Islamic languages and retold in prose and verse, sometimes (as in Ottoman Turkey) even adorned with illustrations,[3] and as late as a few years ago a Turkish poet composed a series of sixty-three "pictures" from the Prophet's life in simple verse.[4] "The quest for the historical Muhammad" is, as the innumerable studies of his life show,[5] a seemingly impossible undertaking, but without attempting to divest Muhammad's biography of the luminous haze of legends, we can sketch his historical life approximately in the following way.

Muhammad was born in the Hashim branch of the clan Quraish, which ruled at the beginning of the seventh century over Mecca, a great center of commerce in Arabia. He is generally believed to have been born about A.D. 570, or, as M. Hamidullah has computed, in June 569.[6] According to Muslim tradition a foreign army was besieging Mecca in the year of his birth; suddenly it turned away (as told in the Koran, Sura 105). This was later interpreted as a miracle pointing to Muhammad's coming.[7] His father, called ʿAbdallah son of ʿAbdul Muttalib, died before his birth; his mother, Amina, when he was about six years old.[8] Like other boys among the city-Arabs, the infant Muhammad was handed over to a nurse, Halima. It is told that she owned a lame old donkey, which had great difficulty in reaching Mecca from the countryside. But when the animal had to carry Muhammad on the way back, it suddenly became swift-footed and fresh. This was one of the first signs of the child's future greatness.[9]

The report that the young boy once got lost (without harm) from Halima is taken by later mystical poets as another marvelous witness to his future role as leader of man and djinn.

> Do not worry—he is not lost to you!
> It is he, in whom the whole world will be lost![10]

Thus tells the poet and mystic, Jalaluddin Rumi (d. 1273), interpreting the voice from the Unseen that consoled the worried woman. According to some biographers, the miracle of the Opening of the Breast (see chapter 4) took place during this absence. And according to a late tradition, when Amina died she spoke a few verses in which she foretold her son's destiny:

> You are sent to mankind
> by the Mighty and Kind Lord . . .

After her death, the djinn were heard as they sang threnodies for the mother of the last Prophet.[11]

From his birth Muhammad was placed under the protection of his grandfather, ʿAbdul Muttalib, who died, however, about two years after Muhammad's mother, Amina. The young orphan was then entrusted to his uncle Abu Talib, whose son, ʿAli, was to become one of the first to believe in his message. His being an orphan, *yatīm*—as pointed out in Sura 93—was to inspire many later poets to compare him to a *yatīma*, a unique (literally, "orphan") pearl.

Like many other Meccans, Muhammad too became engaged in trading.

As a mere boy, "the gifted orphan" is said to have accompanied his uncle to Syria. On the way they met the monk Bahira',[12] who recognized the "seal of prophethood" between the child's shoulders and thus acclaimed him as the future prophet whose arrival had been foretold in the Johannine Gospel: all the signs mentioned in the ancient books fitted him.[13] Muhammad was at that time about twelve years old. His early profession gave trading an honored place in Islamic life; even now a Sindhi children's song from the beginning of our century admonishes the boys to learn trade, "for the Prophet himself has occupied himself with it, and has made it important with all his energy."[14]

When Muhammad had reached the age of approximately twenty-five years, the woman for whom he had been carrying out business and who was impressed by his honesty and sincerity (he was called *al-Amīn*, the Faithful One) married him. Her name was Khadija, and though she was considerably senior to him, their marriage proved very happy. The couple had four daughters, and one or two sons who died in infancy. A popular Ottoman *mathnawī*, a modern Egyptian strophic poem, and quite a few other folk ballads in various languages describe the marriage of Khadija with the Prophet,[15] and she has been highly praised by both Sunnis and Shiites as a noble woman:

> Khadija, Khadija, great and pure,
> Mother, dearer to us than our own mother . . .[16]

She was Muhammad's greatest support when his life suddenly changed at the age of about forty years. Pensive and searching for something higher and purer than the traditional religious forms, Muhammad sometimes went to the cave of Hira in the hills near Mecca, and it was there that a first Divine revelation overwhelmed him—a revelation in which he was ordered to "recite" (Sura 96). A period of "spiritual dryness" followed the first overwhelming experiences, and poets in later times have dramatically described "how Muhammad wanted to throw himself from Mount Hira"[17] until inspiration came again and he realized, full of awe, that it was God Himself who revealed Himself to him—that one and unique God, who ordered him to call his compatriots to absolute faith in Him.

The Prophet often suffered when exposed to the revelations, and various of his symptoms are recorded. Even his camel became restless and knelt down when a revelation came while the Prophet was riding. Tradition quotes Muhammad on the experience: "Revelation sometimes comes like the sound of a bell; that is the most painful way. When it ceases I have remembered what was said. Sometimes it is an angel who talks to me like a human, and I remember what he says."[18]

The Meccans venerated a number of deities, many of whose statues and pictures were enshrined in their city sanctuary, the Kaʿba. Lately the theory has been propounded that these pictures may well have been Christian icons, for it is reported that a picture of the Virgin and Christ was found among them.[19] A strong influence from Hellenistic Christianity upon Meccan and western Arabian ideas cannot be excluded here; the pre-Islamic Bedouin religion most probably revered no images but rather worshiped stones, trees, and other objects, and the ancient Arabs seem to have been content, beyond that cult, with a more general belief in an all-pervading Fate. The pilgrimages to the Kaʿba, which were connected with fairs and meetings (as is usual in the case of pilgrimages) formed an important part of the Meccan economic system. Otherwise one does not get the impression that the Meccans or the Bedouins led a very active or highly spiritual religious life. The strong vein of fatalism, which is palpable in the poems of pre-Islamic Arabia, is not surprising in a society where the hardship of desert life inspired the best poets.

There were also some Jewish settlements in the Arabian peninsula; not all of them belonged to the orthodox Jewish tradition, and "heretic" trends were well represented. The influence of Christianity was quite strong, for the areas adjacent to the peninsula (Syria, Mesopotamia, and Egypt) were largely inhabited by Christians of various confessional loyalties, so that the Arabs came to know, more or less intimately, Monophysites, Nestorians, and other Christian sectarians. It seems that some spiritual seekers among the Arabs were in search of a purer and more satisfying faith than that generally practiced. The Koran calls them *ḥunafā* (singular, *ḥanīf*) and Muhammad knew them through Khadija's relative Waraqa ibn Naufal. In the Koran the *ḥunafā* appear as representatives of the pristine religion of Abraham before its bifurcation into different religions such as Judaism and Christianity, and they may well have been members of old Judaeo-Christian groups.

The revelations that descended upon Muhammad from about 610 onward spoke primarily of God the One, Who is both the Creator of the world and its Judge. He will call mankind before His judgment unless they follow the commands to love their neighbors, to do justice, and to act honestly. In the early, short suras, as the chapters of the Koran later came to be called, the terrors of the Day of Judgment are depicted in brief and powerful, rhyming sentences that follow each other like sharp lightning and roaring thunder. The Meccans did not find this message very convincing; in particular, the idea of the resurrection of the dead did not make much sense to them. But the revelations Muhammad repeatedly received to counter such doubts argued that even the earth, seemingly dead in winter, could bring forth fresh greenery in the spring, and that the miracle of conception and birth is not less than that of the resurrection of the flesh.[20] The leading Meccans were, however, not easily won over even by this, and the tensions between them and Muhammad's small group of followers grew worse from year to year. One group of these followers therefore emigrated to Abyssinia because the Christian faith as practiced there seemed to be closest to the ideals preached by the Prophet. (They returned later at various times.)

In the year 619 Muhammad lost his faithful wife Khadija, who had been his strongest support in times of affliction and near-despair. In the same year his uncle Abu Talib also died, a man who had never ceased protecting his nephew although not converted to the new religion—which was called *Islām*, "Surrender," that is, the complete trust in and acknowledgment of the One Supreme God.

Two years after the death of Khadija and Abu Talib, in a time of increasing difficulties, a delegation from the city of Yathrib, an oasis north of Mecca, came to perform the pilgrimage. They asked Muhammad to join them and solve some of the social and political problems that were caused by frictions between the different groups of people living in their city. The Muslims (that is, "those who practice Islam"), as Muhammad's followers were called, migrated to Yathrib. Muhammad followed last, along with his friend Abu Bakr. Together the two set out from Mecca, but the Meccans were keen to apprehend them. Legend tells how they sought shelter in a cave over which a spider spun its web and pigeons hurriedly built their nests—so that the Meccans in their pursuit did not imagine that anyone could be hiding in that place (cf. Sura 9:40). The Persian expression that is used for Abu Bakr in this situation, *yār-i ghār*, "friend of the cave," denotes the closest possible friendship between two men,[21] and according to the tradition of the Naqshbandiyya order, it was in the cave that the Prophet taught Abu Bakr the secrets of silent remembrance of God, the *dhikr-i khafī*.

Muhammad reached Yathrib in September 622, and that year marks the beginning of the Muslim era, which is calculated from the Hegira (*hijra*, "separation, leaving") of the Prophet. The calendar opens with the first month of the Arabic lunar year in June 622, and proceeds in pure lunar years of 354 days without intercalation.

The city of Yathrib soon became known as *Madīnat an-nabī*, the City of the Prophet, in short, Medina. Muhammad was called to find a solution for the communal tensions in this city, and he succeeded in drawing up a kind of constitution that governed not only the different tribes living in Medina, most of whom were considered to be in the category of the *anṣār*, or "helpers" of the Muslims, but also those who accompanied him in his emigration, the *muhājirūn* from Mecca. Though fully implemented only for a brief span of time, the document remained a basis and model for later Muslim communal administration.[22]

In March 624 a major confrontation between Muslims and Meccans occurred at Badr, near Medina. Though the Muslims found themselves suddenly confronted with an army much stronger than they had expected, the victory in the ensuing battle was theirs. This victory at Badr was perhaps the most important miracle for the young community, a miracle that helped them find their identity and that has continued to be remembered as the event that changed early Islamic history. According to tradition it seems that a handful of pebbles, which the Prophet cast symbolically against the Meccans, proved a decisive factor in the victory. The Koran states concerning this event: "Not you cast when you cast, but God cast" (Sura 8:17). This sentence became the foundation of numerous mystical speculations about the Prophet, whose hand was, as it were, God's hand.[23] Thus the very name Badr became the cipher for the undeniable proof of Muhammad's God-given role as leader of his community, and of God's never-failing help for His servants.

One year later, in 625, a similar encounter took place near Mount Uhud but with considerably less success. Some of the best Muslim fighters were killed, including the Prophet's uncle Hamza, whose name looms large in popular tales all over the East. The Prophet's foot was injured, and he lost two teeth during this battle, a fact that inspired later poets to compose extremely involved verses about the "pearls" that turned "into rubies" (because his white teeth were stained with red blood).[24]

In 627, the Meccans tried to conquer Medina. According to tradition, the Persian Muslim Salman al-Farisi suggested to the Medinans that they dig a trench for defense. The Meccans, not used to siege warfare, lifted the siege without having achieved tangible success.

In the following year, Muhammad set out to perform the pilgrimage to the Meccan precincts, which had become the center of his religious aspirations shortly after the Hegira. The Muslims at Medina had originally prayed in the direction of Jerusalem, the sanctuary of the two earlier prophetic religions, but in 623 or 624 they had been instructed (Sura 2:134–35) to turn toward the Kaʿba at Mecca. From that time onward the conquest of Mecca and the Kaʿba, the central sanctuary of the ancient religion of Abraham, said to have been built by him and his son Ishmael, began to form an important aspect of Muhammad's strategy. Even though the Meccans did not permit him to enter his native city on this visit in 628, he succeeded in concluding a treaty with them in which he was acknowledged as an equal negotiant; it further guaranteed that he might perform the lesser pilgrimage, *ʿumra*, in the following year.

During the years in Medina, Muhammad's attitude toward the Jewish community hardened. The Jews in Medina refused to acknowledge his revelations as the completion of the Torah, and it seems that some of them

Koran Sura 33:45, calligraphy by the Ottoman sultan Mahmud II, ca. 1830

belonged to the *munāfiqūn*, the hypocrites, whose lukewarm attitude sometimes endangered the young community. For various reasons, and at different points in time, the Jewish clans in the environments of Medina were forced to leave; other Jewish groups in northwest Arabia surrendered and agreed to pay tribute.[25] The conquest of the Jewish stronghold Khaibar, in which ʿAli ibn Abi Talib, the Prophet's cousin and husband of his youngest daughter, Fatima, played a key role, forms a recurrent theme in later religious poetry and is often alluded to in other connections as well.

The Meccans realized that Muhammad's power had increased immensely, and when he conquered his native city in 630, no resistance was offered. Even some of his most bitter opponents embraced Islam and were generously rewarded. The Kaʿba was completely divested of all idols and icons and remained from that time onward the center of the Muslim cultus, without image and effigy. It is in the direction of the Kaʿba that faithful Muslims all over the world still turn five times a day in prayer, and it is the Kaʿba that they circumambulate during the *ḥajj*, the great annual pilgrimage in the last month of the lunar year, in which every devout Muslim hopes to participate, if only once in a lifetime.

Muhammad did not stay long in Mecca after conquering it. He returned to Medina, where his family was living. After Khadija's death he had married several times. Among his wives only ʿAʾisha, the daughter of his friend Abu Bakr, a mere child still playing with her dolls, was a virgin when she was married to him; he was apparently particularly fond of the young woman. Other wives were widows of soldiers who had been killed in battle, and one, Zainab, was the ex-wife of his adopted son Zaid. A Coptic slave girl who was given to the Prophet bore him a son who, however, died before he was two. Although the Koran restricts the number of legal wives to four, Muhammad himself was granted the right to exceed this number, and allusions to some of his marital problems and to tensions among his wives are found in some later suras of the Koran. His wives were respectfully called "the mothers of the faithful" (Sura 33:6) and were subject to some special restrictions; after his death, for example, they were not allowed to remarry (Sura 33:53).

The Divine revelations to Muhammad continued throughout his life. During the first years of his career they dwelt mainly upon the horrors of the Last Judgment and upon the omnipotence of the one and solely adorable God and His marvelous work in creating and sustaining the world. In the middle period, during the times of crises and persecutions, they often spoke of the suffering and afflictions that were showered upon earlier prophets who, like Muhammad, did not meet with any understanding among their compatriots and were tried hard until God gave them victory over their enemies.[26] These revelations certainly helped Muhammad to continue on his chosen path despite the growing hostility of the Meccans. In Medina, Islam became institutionalized, and the contents of the Prophet's later revelations, correspondingly, often concern civic problems and treat politically and socially relevant questions such as emerged from Muhammad's activity as leader of a political community. The revelations in this period show Muhammad as the "beautiful model" (*uswa ḥasana*, Sura 33:21); the faithful are admonished to follow him and imitate his example, for "to obey him means to obey God" (Sura 4:80). The community was also informed that the Prophet was sent *raḥmatan lil-ʿālamīn*, "as a Mercy for the worlds" (Sura 21:107),[27] and that God and the angels pronounced the blessing over him (Sura 33:56).

Western scholars have often asked what the sources of the Prophet's revelations might have been, and whence came the apparently disjunct material of the Koran. They have wondered why the Koran mentions figures from the Judaeo-Christian tradition, like Moses and Jesus, Joseph, and David and Solomon, in contexts that differ considerably from the biblical stories, whereas the great prophets of Israel are not mentioned at all. A vast body of literature about the Prophet's "borrowing"—wittingly or unwittingly—from Christian (Nestorian and Monophysitic) and/or Jewish sources has been written during the last 125 years, with different, and partly conflicting, conclusions.[28] Many scholars would agree with Johann Fück that in the end, "the means of rational science will never suffice to unveil the secret of the personality of this man, and we will never be able to establish, by analysis, which *Erlebnisse* moved his soul until he finally reached the certainty—after painful struggle—that God had elected him to be a warner and messenger."[29]

For the Muslims, the differences between the biblical and the Koranic versions of certain stories are nothing but further proof that the Koran is indeed God's word. The Prophet Muhammad, being *ummī* (a word generally interpreted in the Islamic tradition as "unlettered, illiterate"), could not read, and hence could not know the contents of the biblical stories: how could he have utilized them if they were not directly inspired? But contrary to the traditional acceptance of Muhammad's ignorance concerning the earlier sources, the German scholar Günther Lüling claims that the Prophet was well aware of the Judaeo-Christian tradition, which he then utilized ingeniously. Whatever the explanation may be, the stories of earlier prophets, beginning with Adam, serve in the Koran as paradigms for the life of Muhammad, and he was confirmed in his faith time and again by the thought that just as earlier nations had been doomed to perish because they refused to believe their prophets and persecuted them, so too would the Meccans suffer the same fate unless they accepted the message of the Lord as revealed to and preached by Muhammad.

In the year 632, Muhammad again made the pilgrimage to Mecca, and this performance remained forever a binding example for the Muslims who undertake the *ḥajj*. It was during this "farewell pilgrimage," Muslim traditions affirm, that the final revelation came upon him, which is noted down in Sura 5:5: "Today I have perfected your religion for you and completed My favor unto you, and have chosen for you Islam as religion."[30]

A few weeks later, on 8 June 632 (A.H. 11),[31] Muhammad died, in the apartment of ʿA'isha, who was then about eighteen years old and on whose authority a good number of his sayings and stories about him are told. Muhammad could well apply to himself, as Fück writes in a perceptive article, the Koranic word of Sura 6:162: "Lo, as for me, my Lord has guided me unto a straight path, a right religion, the community of Abraham, the upright, who was no idolater. Say: Lo, my worship and my sacrifice and my living and my dying are for God, Lord of the worlds."[32]

Even though some more rigorous theologians like Ibn Taimiyya in the fourteenth century and the Wahhabis in the late eighteenth and the nineteenth centuries raised their voices in protest against the visits of pilgrims to the Rauda (Garden), as his mausoleum is called, Muhammad's last resting place in Medina became a center of pious veneration. By custom, the pilgrim who stands in front of the Rauda will say, referring to the end of Muhammad's farewell sermon:

> I bear witness that thou art the Apostle of God. Thou hast conveyed the message. Thou hast fulfilled the trust. Thou hast counselled the community and enlightened the gloom, and shed glory on the darkness, and uttered words of wisdom.[33]

Muhammad did not leave any rules for his succession. Of his four daughters, Zainab, Ruqayya, Umm Kulthum, and Fatima,[34] only Fatima, called *az-Zahrā'*, "Luminous," "the Radiant," survived him. She was married to her father's cousin ʿAli, and died soon after the Prophet. The legendary figure of this ailing woman was soon adorned with miracles, especially in the Shia tradition:[35] her birth was surrounded by light; she was absolutely pure and had no menstruation, and her sons were born through her left thigh. Thus she was honored with the title *batūl*, "virgin," and later she assumed also the position of a true Mater Dolorosa after the death of her younger son Husain. That she was called as well *Umm abīhā*, "her father's mother," gave rise to high-soaring speculations about her cosmic role in God's *Heilsgeschichte*.

In the confusion that set in after Muhammad's death, his father-in-law Abu Bakr made the poignant remark to the Muslims who mourned him that "If someone has worshiped Muhammad, Muhammad is dead. If someone has worshiped God, He is alive and never dies."[36] Abu Bakr, called *aṣ-Ṣiddīq*, "the most trustworthy," was elected the first caliph (*khalīfa*, successor, substitute) of the Prophet.[37] After his death in 634, another father-in-law of the Prophet, ʿUmar ibn al-Khattab, followed him. ʿUmar, called *al-Fārūq*, "he who distinguishes truth from falsehood," and said to have converted at a rather early stage when listening to the recitation of a passage from the Koran, was probably the most imposing personality among the early Muslims.[38] From a grim enemy of the Prophet he turned into the fiercest and most active fighter for the true faith. His name is connected in literature and piety with the virtue of absolute justice, which spared not even members of his own family, and his role in the organization of the Islamic community and the implementation of law and order has been compared, in the West, to that of Saint Paul in Christianity,[39] but he appears even more bound to puritanic application of the Koranic revelation. The Shiites hate him intensely for his supposedly harsh treatment of Fatima after her father's death.

ʿUmar was assassinated by a Persian slave in 644, and a member of the old Meccan aristocracy, ʿUthman ibn ʿAffan, became his successor, although not undisputed: too many pious Muslims remembered the opposition of his family to the Prophet's message in earlier days. ʿUthman had been married, successively, to two of Muhammad's daughters, Ruqayya and Umm Kulthum, and is therefore called *Dhū' n-nūrain*, "the owner of the two lights" (hence the proper name ʿOthman, Turkish Osman, is usually combined with the epithet *Nūruddīn*, abbreviated Nuri or Nur). ʿUthman ibn ʿAffan is credited with having commanded the redaction of the Koran into the form known to the present day, which is divided in 114 suras, arranged roughly according to descending length. The first sura, *Al-Fātiḥa*, "The Opening," is a short prayer that has been compared, more or less correctly, to the Lord's Prayer.[40] After the short confession of God's absolute Unity, Sura 112, follow two short suras, *Al-Muʿawwidhatān*, in which man is taught to take refuge with God from various evils.

ʿUthman too was assassinated, in 656, and was succeeded by ʿAli ibn Abi Talib, Muhammad's cousin and son-in-law, who was, according to the opinion of one faction of the Muslims, the legitimate successor of the Prophet. Those who adhered to him and claimed that he should have been the first caliph are known as the *shīʿat ʿAlī*, "ʿAli's party," or briefly, the Shia.[41] ʿAli as well as his wife Fatima (see above), along with their two sons Hasan and Husain, are the central figures of Shiite piety. Indeed, in some strands of Shia Islam, they occupy a truly mythical place, ʿAli being, on occasion, even more important than the Prophet himself. ʿAli, Fatima, and their sons together with the Prophet form the *Panjtan*, the Five People, or the *ahl al-kisā*, the People of the Cloak, because Muslim tradition affirms that Muhammad once took them under his robe in order to show that he cared for them in a very special way. They are usually also equated with the *ahl al-bait*, the People of the House, the closest family of the Prophet, as mentioned in Sura 33:33.

The veneration of the family of the Prophet is important not only from the religious viewpoint (although Shia piety is on the whole much more colorful and variegated than the general "Sunni" orientation); it also developed into a decisive factor in the political history of Islam. The Shia presented from the very beginning the view that ʿAli alone was the legitimate caliph, and they refused to accept the first three caliphs, especially ʿUthman, condemning them in more or less outspoken words. The Sunnite Muslims, however, always maintained the excellence of the *khulafāʾ ar-rāshidūn*, "the rightly guided caliphs," or the Four Friends (*chār yār*), as they are called in Persian, even though they might allot to ʿAli a special place in their hearts. According to the Shia, during the last year of his life, on 18 Dhu'l-hijja, Muhammad had invested ʿAli as his successor at a gathering at the pond Ghadir Khum. When ʿAli was assassinated in 661 by a member of a dissenting faction, the Kharijites, two extreme views about the Prophet's succession clashed. Against the legitimist Shia, the "democratic" Kharijites defended the idea that only the worthiest member of the community, "even though he be an Abyssinian slave," should lead the Muslims. But the extremist, puritan Kharijites were soon overcome by the majority of the

Muslims, who were proud of being *ahl as-sunna waʾl-jamāʿa*, "those who adhere to the Prophetic tradition and belong to the community," that is, the Sunnis. Only a scattering of small groups of Khariji Muslims—for instance, the Ibadis in North Africa—are extant today.

After ʿAli's death the Umayyad house, descendants of the Meccan aristocracy and hence unacceptable to more extreme Shiites, came to power and made Damascus their capital. Hasan, ʿAli's elder son from Fatima, was bribed by the first Umayyad caliph, Muʿawiya, to abandon his claim and died somewhat later (according to Shiite tradition, from poison). His younger brother, Husain, the third *imām* (literally, leader of the prayer; generally, religious leader of the community) of the Shia after ʿAli and Hasan, tried once more to fight against the Umayyads after Muʿawiya's death in the fall of 680. He and his followers moved from their headquarters in Kufa (Iraq) to Kerbela, where the majority were killed in battle on 10 Muharram (10 October) 680. This event is the vantage point for a very special sort of piety typical of Shia circles, a kind of "passion piety" that has been expressed since early days in heartrending poems and touching prose pieces and also developed in later times, particularly in Iran, into dramatic representations of the suffering of Imam Husain and his family. A whole genre of Persian and Urdu literature, the *marthiya*, or dirge, is devoted to the tragic fate of the martyrs of Kerbela, which is conceived as the turning point of world history.[42] Weeping for Husain opens the gates to Paradise, and Fatima, like Mary the mother of Jesus, will intercede for those who shed tears for her son.

Numerous branches developed within the Shia in the course of time. The *Ithnāʿashariyya*, or Twelvers, continue the line of imams to the twelfth one, who mysteriously disappeared in 873 and has since ruled the world from the Unseen; this branch was made the state religion of Iran in 1501 and also has many followers in India, particularly in the Lucknow and Hyderabad/Deccan areas. Another branch stops the line as early as the fifth imam, Zaid, son of the only surviving son of Husain after the battle of Kerbela. These Zaidites, representing a theological trend rather close to that of the Sunnites, ruled in Yemen till 1964, and they also had some smaller kingdoms in medieval Iran.

The Shia groups that follow the seventh imam, Ismaʿil, are known by different names; one branch founded the Fatimid kingdom in Egypt, where after 1094 a split occurred that resulted in the present groups known as the Nizaris, or followers of the Aga Khan, and the Bohoras. The Ismailis, dreaded and maligned as "Assassins" during the Middle Ages in Iran and the Near East, have developed recently into a progressive modern community; their highly interesting, esoteric religious literature is slowly becoming known and reflects their comprehensive system of philosophical thought as much as their poetic tendencies, especially in their Indian environment.

But not only the Shia, the Sunnites too (that is, the people of the Prophetic tradition, *sunna*, and the community, *jamāʿa*) deeply venerate the Prophet's family; for as the great Sunni mystic Hallaj said: "God has not created anything that is dearer to him than Muhammad and his family."[43] The descendants of ʿAli and Fatima (called *sayyid*, plural *sādāt*; or *sharīf*, plural *ashrāf*, *shurafāʾ*), especially the children of Husain, still enjoy great prestige: how could a *sayyid*'s daughter marry a non-*sayyid*?! Many mystics are said to be of *sayyid* ancestry, even though critical scholars feel that "this occurs too frequently to be indisputable."[44] Veneration was, and still is, shown to the descendants of impoverished *sayyid* families; a maidservant from such a family will not be allowed to do any dirty or lowly work in the house, as I was recently told in the Deccan. The feeling underlying the veneration of these people is that some of the Prophet's *baraka*, his power of blessing, is still alive in his descendants and that they therefore deserve at least part of the honor owed to their ancestor.

While the important, often even politically important, role of the *sayyid* families has continued to our day, other figures in the environment of the Prophet have been transformed into symbols of certain spiritual attitudes or adopted as representatives of ideologies. Abu Lahab, Muhammad's uncle and archenemy, who is cursed in the Koran (Sura 111), has become, along with his wife, the exemplar of the infidel who refuses with all his strength to accept the new order and who does everything to block the Prophet's way. He is thus the typical antagonist in the drama of a prophet's life. The poet Rumi, who puns on the meaning of the name *Abū Lahab*, Father of the Flame, thinks that its bearer was probably the only person never to be touched by the flame of Divine love:

> I have not seen, lacking Thy fire, anyone but Abu Lahab![45]

Among the positive symbolic figures is Bilal ibn Rabah, Muhammad's Abyssinian muezzin, who was sometimes asked by the Prophet, "Bilal, refresh us with the call to prayer!"[46] For ritual prayer reminded the Prophet of his heavenly journey when he could speak to God without a veil. Bilal was an Ethiopian slave who had adopted Islam very early and was tortured on that account by his Meccan owner until Abu Bakr bought and freed him. In popular tradition he became the symbol of the black people who embraced Islam and were taken into the community without hesitation, since Islam knows no differentiation of races. Sana'i, around 1100, goes so far as to sing,

Bilal's sandal is better than two hundred Rustams—[47]

that is, the black slave, freed by his acceptance into the Islamic community, is by far superior to even the greatest hero of pre-Islamic Persian legendary history. Bilal became the patron saint of many Black African and Abyssinian Muslim groups and is often cited as a model of piety.[48] Hence his name is now used not infrequently as a proper name for boys, especially in India and Pakistan, where Iqbal's two poems on the poor Bilal who was honored through Islam have made this name very popular.[49] Lately, the Black Muslims have adopted the term "Bilalian" for themselves; their journal is now called *Bilalian News*, and one also hears of a Bilalian College and of Bilalian journalists.

Abu Dharr, a Companion of the Prophet, was noted for his attempts to remind the wealthy of the Koranic injunction to give up their treasures and concentrate on God and the Otherworld. He therefore has become a prototype of early ascetic Sufism.[50] Louis Massignon has called him, perhaps somewhat too idealistically, "un socialiste avant la lettre."

Of special importance is the role of Salman al-Farisi, often called in the Persian tradition *Salmān-i pāk*, Salman the Pure.[51] Western scholars have devoted a number of studies to this follower of the Prophet.[52] A Persian barber who embraced Islam, Salman became in the later esoteric interpretation of early Islamic history the symbol of the Persians who had been adopted into Islam, and thus a model of all foreigners who enter the Islamic world and bring with them their own knowledge and capacities, so that the Muslims may use them and enrich their lives. Salman, it will be remembered, is credited with inventing the trench that saved the Medinans from the Meccan siege. Being a barber, he had the privilege of touching the Prophet's hair; later he became the patron saint of barbers, and sometimes of other craftsmen, and can be considered the first saint of an artisans' guild in Islam.[53]

Finally one has to mention Uwais al-Qarani, because his name plays a role in the mystical biography of the Prophet. Uwais lived in Yemen and converted to Islam without ever meeting the Prophet. Muhammad reportedly said about him, "Verily I feel the *nafas ar-raḥmān*, the breath of the Merciful, coming to me from Yemen!"[54] In the mystical tradition Uwais is the model of those who enter the mystical path without being initiated by a living master: an *uwaisī* (Turkish *veysi*) mystic has no special teacher but is guided directly by God on the mystical path, or has been initiated by the mysterious prophet-saint Khidr.

There are of course many more *ṣaḥāba* (singular, *ṣaḥābī*) or Companions of the Prophet, who are remembered as fighters, as traditionalists, as faithful servants, or among *al-ʿashara al-mubashshara*, "the ten who were promised Paradise,"[55] but the abovementioned figures have remained so much alive in the tradition of the Islamic countries that even in our century an Urdu poet could compare his heart, which is completely devoted to the Prophet, and his loving soul, to Bilal and Uwais.

TWO

MUHAMMAD THE BEAUTIFUL MODEL

One must always keep in mind that Muhammad never claimed to possess any superhuman qualities. He was, and wanted to remain, "a servant to whom revelation has come" (Sura 41:5), and when he was challenged by the Meccans to perform miracles he used to say that the only miracle in his life was that he had received the Divine revelation in clear Arabic language, which was proclaimed through him as the inimitable Koran. He knew that he was only a mediator, and when his compatriots asked him to substantiate his message by performing miracles it was revealed to him: "Say: If men and djinn would unite to bring something like this Koran, they could not bring it, even if they would support each other" (Sura 17:90; cf. Sura 6:37). As eloquent as the Arabs might be, and as perfect as their highly refined traditional poetry might be, even they would not be able to produce a single sentence that could be compared in form and content to the Koran.

This central position of the Koran in the Islamic *Heilsgeschichte* stands, phenomenologically, parallel to the position of Christ in Christianity: Christ is the Divine Word Incarnate, the Koran is (to use Harri Wolfson's apt term) the Divine Word Inlibrate. It is therefore these two manifestations of the Divine Word that should be compared, for neither in theological nor in phenomenological terms can Muhammad be likened to the Christ of Christianity—hence the Muslims' aversion to the term "Muhammadans," which seems to them to imply a false parallel to the concept of "Christians." *Muḥammadī*, as in "the Muhammadan Path," is used in specific connections, usually by mystics who try to emulate the Prophet's example even more than others. As a medieval mystic, Shams-i Tabrizi, said: "A *muḥammadī* is he who has a broken heart . . . , who has reached the heart, and can utter the *Anā'l-ḥaqq-i muḥammadī*, the Muhammadan 'I am the Truth.' "[1]

Muhammad knew, and was repeatedly reminded by the Koranic revelation, that he was only a human being, a man, whose only prerogative was that he was granted a revelatory experience. As Sura 6:50 admonishes him: "Say: I do not say: 'With me are the treasures of God' and I do not know the Invisible, and I do not say that I am an angel—I follow only that which is revealed to me." He was also reminded that only the Lord was able to guide mankind: "You cannot guide on the right path whom you want. It is God who guides!" (Sura 28:56). What had been revealed to him is that "Your God is One God" (Sura 37:4), and thus he was called to preach the message of uncompromising monotheism, of absolute surrender to the One God who is Creator, Sustainer, and Judge.

Muhammad felt that whatever happened to him was nothing but God's inexplicable grace, which he did not deserve and which had elected him as its vessel. For God admonished him: "Verily if We wanted We would take away what We have revealed to you, and then you would not find for yourself a defendant against Us" (Sura 17:88). He knew that he could never have hoped that such a Koran would be given to him "save by the mercy of your Lord" (Sura 28:86). And when the Meccans ridiculed him, asking persistently when the hour of Judgment would arrive—an hour of whose horrors he had been speaking in such terrifying words—he had to repeat again that he too was not informed about its arrival, that he was nothing but "an evident warner" (Sura 29:49), awakening the hearts of those who are in fear of this "Hour" (Sura 20:15, 79:42, and others).

Yet there are some passages in the Koran that point to Muhammad's exceptional role. As God "taught Adam the names" (Sura 2:30), thus He taught Muhammad the Koran (Sura 96:3). For Muhammad was sent "as a Mercy for the worlds," *raḥmatan lil-ʿālamīn* (Sura 21:107), and God and His angels utter blessings over him (Sura 33:56). He is "verily of noble nature" (Sura 68:4). In several places one finds the Divine command "Obey God and obey His messenger" or similar formulations. Such Koranic sentences formed the basis of a veneration of Muhammad that soon far surpassed the respect normally accorded to a prophet, and even now the pious Muslim will never mention anything belonging to or relating to the Prophet without adding the attribute *sharīf*, "noble." In the course of time, then, short Koranic remarks were elaborated and spun out into long tales and wondrous legends, which slowly illuminated the outlines of the historical Muhammad with an array of color.

The obedience due to the Prophet seems to have played an important, perhaps the central role in the development of Islamic piety.[2] Does not Sura

3:29 state: "Say: if you love God, follow me, then God will love you and forgive your sins. Verily God is forgiving, merciful" (cf. Sura 33:30)?

In the bipartite profession of faith, *lā ilāha illā Allāh, Muḥammadun rasūl Allāh*, "There is no deity save God, [and] Muhammad is the messenger of God," the second half, which defines Islam as a distinctive religion, constitutes, as Wilfred Cantwell Smith rightly says, "a statement about God" in his activity in the world rather than about the Prophet's person.[3] For by sending His prophet, who proclaims His word, God reveals Himself to the world: the Prophet is, according to Nathan Söderblom, "an aspect of God's activity."[4] Muhammad is singled out by God; he is truly the Chosen one, *al-Muṣṭafā*, and for this reason his *sunna*, his way of life, became the uniquely valid rule of conduct for the Muslims. As the Prophet says: "Who follows me, belongs to me, and who does not love my *sunna*, does not belong to me."[5] For Muhammad is indeed, as the Koran states, an *uswa ḥasana*, "a beautiful model" (Sura 33:21).

In the understanding of classical Islamic religious theory, Muhammad's *sunna* consists of his actions (*fiʿl*), his words (*qaul*), and his silent approval of certain facts (*taqrīr*). His well-attested way of behavior—or at least the way that was considered well enough attested to be historically true—attained a normative value for subsequent generations from at least as early as the second century of Islam. Because of the importance of the Prophet's noble example, the science of *ḥadīth* came gradually to occupy a central place in Islamic culture.

A *ḥadīth* (narrative, tradition; specifically a Prophetic tradition) is a report that contains a remark about a saying or an action of the Prophet as it is told by one of his trustworthy Companions who related it to someone in the next generation. The *ṣaḥāba*, Muhammad's Companions, are thus the most important source for Prophetic traditions. A *ḥadīth* may treat a ritual problem; it can discuss details of faith and doctrine, tell about the punishment in the next world, or simply describe the Prophet's behavior while eating, sleeping, or giving advice. To the chain of transmitters, the *isnād*, every generation added new members, until long lines of traditionists developed, each link connected with the previous one, in a well-established relationship. In the third Islamic century (ninth century of the Christian era), during which the most important "canonical" collections of *ḥadīth* were compiled, a typical *ḥadīth* looked like this: *A said: I heard B say that he had heard C telling that D told him that E stated: F said that G transmitted: I have heard from Abu Huraira that the Prophet did this or that.*

One of the most important branches of scholarship was the examination of traditions, because they contained the exposition of the Prophet's behavior and thus formed the source for all aspects of human behavior. However, the scrutinization of *ḥadīth* was primarily geared not toward the text of the tradition, but rather toward the reliability of the chain of traditionists by whom a certain text was transmitted. Careful study was devoted to ascertaining which of them was a trustworthy person, whether he could have been in touch with the person whom he mentions as his source, or was too young when that person died, or had never visited the latter's hometown. After all such formal criteria for trustworthiness had been met, the *ḥadīth* in question was considered to be *ṣaḥīḥ*, "sound, immaculate." The best and most reliable traditions, the number of which understandably increased in the course of time in spite of all scholarly scrutiny, give in a certain way a picture of the development of theological and practical problems that the Muslim community faced during the first centuries of its history. The most trustworthy *ḥadīth* were put together in the middle of the ninth century by a series of scholars, in large collections, among which the works of Bukhari and Muslim are usually called *aṣ-ṣaḥīḥān*, "the two sound ones," although four others (which four differs from list to list) are also regarded as having great authority. The *ṣaḥīḥān* are so highly esteemed in Muslim circles that Bukhari's *Ṣaḥīḥ* was often regarded as second in importance only to the Koran. From these works the Muslims obtained the necessary information about the customs of the Prophet, about his outward appearance as about his ethical ideals. Sometimes in later centuries the whole *Ṣaḥīḥ* of Bukhari, which contains some seven thousand traditions, was read out during the month of Ramadan (thus in Mamluk Egypt), and the *khatm al-Bukhārī*, the completion of such a reading, was solemnly celebrated.[6] Sometimes an individual scholar who had completed the study of Bukhari would invite his friends to celebrate this auspicious event.[7]

On the basis of the "six books" of greatest authority later scholars compiled other, handier collections of *ḥadīth*, which generally left out the chain of transmitters. These were studied throughout the Islamic world, for they formed the pivot of theological studies in the colleges, *madrasa*s, together with the Koran. Among the *ḥadīth* collections that were favorites in somewhat later times we may mention Baghawi's *Maṣābīḥ as-sunna* (The Lamps of the *Sunna*), with 4,719 *ḥadīth*, and, following it, Tabrizi's *Mishkāt al-maṣābīḥ* (The Niche for Lamps), called in India *Mishkāt-i sharīf* (The Noble Lamp). Its very title implies an allusion to the Light verse of the Koran (Sura 24:35), which was often interpreted as pointing to the Prophet, through whom the Divine light radiates into the world (see chapter 7 below). Persian and later Urdu translations of these works became popular in Muslim circles and were among the first books ever printed in India.[8] In the sixteenth century ʿAli al-Muttaqi, a scholar from Burhanpur in central India, used his long sojourn in Mecca to organize the most important and best-attested *ḥadīth* in his *Kanz al-ʿummāl* (The Treasure of the Workers), a book that gained wide fame because of its practical arrangement.

Other pious scholars and poets extracted sets of *ḥadīth* concerning certain problems, such as predestination or the peculiarities of the days of the week, or sayings about fasting or pilgrimage; still others collected *arbaʿīn*, groups of forty *ḥadīth* that usually comprised traditions of which they were particularly fond or which they found most useful.[9] Later, such *arbaʿīn* were often versified in Persian and Turkish, and the most famous of these collections, written by the great Persian poet and mystical scholar Jami in the late fifteenth century, has been penned by the masters of calligraphy in exquisite forms,[10] for such a book carries the blessing of the Prophet's word with it. Indeed, in later times, especially in the Turkish tradition, it became a general practice to inscribe *levha*s, single pages, with Prophetic traditions, in which the two cursive styles, the small *naskh* and the larger, impressive *thuluth*, were very elegantly combined to form a "calligraphic icon."

Frequently, pious medieval scholars would set out on long journeys in the hope of finding some new reliable *ḥadīth* or in order to listen to a renowned scholar of traditions; indeed, to travel "in search of knowledge" in the form of *ḥadīth* was essential for a good traditionist in early times.[11] Scholars would sit at the master's feet, for it was necessary to learn one's *ḥadīth* from a master. Even though small collections of traditions already existed in writing at an early point in history,[12] the ideal remained to collect one's *ḥadīth* from the mouth of a teacher who, in turn, had acquired his knowledge from another authority, thus maintaining the living chain which led back to the Prophet.[13] Incidentally, one finds quite a number of female traditionists in the chain of transmitters, the first one being Muhammad's young wife ʿA'isha. One of these learned ladies, Karima of Mecca (d. 1069), was able to teach the whole *Ṣaḥīḥ* of Bukhari in only five days![14]

Such sessions of *ḥadīth* were days of great importance. For just as the faithful Muslim feels that when reading the Koran or listening to its recitation he is listening to God Himself, he also feels that occupation with Prophetic traditions brings him in close contact with the Prophet, so that, as it were, he sees him and hears his voice. For this reason the teaching of *ḥadīth* was understood as a great responsibility, and the teacher would prepare very carefully for the occasion. He would undertake such teaching of *ḥadīth* with great awe, and only in a state of perfect ritual purity. It is told of Malik ibn Anas (d. 795), the founder of the Malikite school of jurisprudence and one of the great *ḥadīth* transmitters, that "when he intended to sit down to recite *ḥadīth*, he performed the ablution, donned new garments, put on a new turban, took his place on the platform, in awe, reverence, and great seriousness. As long as the lecture continued, incense was constantly burned. His reverence to *ḥadīth* was so great that it happened in one session that a scorpion stung him sixteen times, and he did not show any sign of disturbance."[15]

The Prophetic tradition can also be regarded as the first step in the interpretation of the Koranic revelation, for it reflects what the earliest generations had retained from the Prophet, who was necessarily the prime exegete of the revelations he brought. Certainly Muhammad must have been himself the paradigm for his companions even before formal *ḥadīth* developed, as Fazlur Rahman has pointed out; "for whatever new material was thought out or assimilated was given as an interpretation of the principles of the Koran and the *sunna*."[16] Thus the living tradition continued and spiritually nourished the Muslim community. In fact, it became so important that one could call it "the highest normative instance," *as-sunna qāḍiyatun ʿalā' l-Qur'ān*.[17] A modern interpreter of Islam in the mystical tradition puts the importance of the *sunna* in the following words:

> It is inconceivable that these virtues [of the *sunna*] could have been practiced through the centuries down to our time if the founder of Islam had not personified them in the highest degree; it is also inconceivable that they should have been borrowed from elsewhere—and one cannot imagine from where since their conditioning and their style are specifically Islamic. For Muslims the moral and spiritual worth of the Prophet is not an abstraction or a supposition; it is a lived reality, and it is precisely this which proves its authenticity retrospectively.[18]

However, despite the deep veneration for the Prophet's *sunna*, a number of problems posed themselves during the study of *ḥadīth*. Could conflicting *ḥadīth* really stem in their entirety from the Prophet? Did not every political and theological group in Islam come up with relevant traditions by which they tried to defend their attitude? Were the *ḥadīth* collected in the six canonical books, or at least those contained in Muslim's and Bukhari's work, *all* absolutely binding for the Muslim? All these questions have been discussed for centuries, and from early times there were those who favored exclusive reliance on the Koran as the safest way.

The question of the authenticity has, however, been brought in the foreground especially in modern times when the confrontation of the Muslims with Western science and technology, but also customs and habits, threatened their time-honored way of life. European scholarship since Ignaz Goldziher is extremely critical of the traditions. But such criticism is rejected by pious Muslims as an attempt to shake if not destroy the very foundations of Islam. S. H. Nasr, one of the leading Muslim thinkers of our day, educated at Harvard, writes in his thought-provoking book *Ideals and Realities of Islam*, in the chapter "The Prophet and Prophetic Tradition":

> Purporting to be scientific and applying the famous—or rather should one say the infamous—historical method which reduces all religious truths to historical facts, the critics of *ḥadīth* have come to the conclusion that this literature is not from the Prophet but was 'forged' by later generations. What lies behind the scientific façade presented in most of these attacks is the *a priori* assumption that Islam is not a Divine revelation. . . . Were the critics of *ḥadīth* simply to admit that the Prophet was a prophet, there would be no scientifically valid argument whatsoever against the main body of *ḥadīth*.[19]

However, in the modern Muslim world itself we find most widely differing attitudes toward *ḥadīth*. In the second half of the nineteenth century, among the Indian Muslims the very orthodox Ahl-i hadith accepted without questioning all that is written in the classical collections, while at the same time the modernists, led by Sir Sayyid Ahmad Khan, advocated a more selective method in the use of *ḥadīth*: it should be binding in religious matters but not for details of social behavior or political and other worldly affairs. And yet one should not forget that Sayyid Ahmad himself in a rather early work, which remained the basis for his later thinking, meditated upon the Prophet's word "O my son, the one who has cherished my *sunna* without doubt he has cherished me and he who cherishes me will be with me in Paradise" and exclaimed:

> O Muslims, reflect a little; even if a thousand souls would sacrifice themselves for this word "with me," it would still be little! To be together in Paradise with the Apostle of Allah is such glad tidings that verily both worlds have no value whatsoever in comparison with that reality! What a good fortune the person enjoys who is granted to be with the Prophet Muhammad! Alas, where do you err wandering around? Whatever gracious gift there is, it is in the *sunna* of the Prophet, by God, in nothing else, in nothing else, in nothing else![20]

But among the followers and collaborators of Sir Sayyid in later days, *ḥadīth* were viewed more critically, and one of his friends, Chiragh Ali, was almost more radical in his critique of the traditions than Goldziher, who wrote shortly after him in Hungary. Chiragh Ali expresses the opinion that "the vast flood of traditions soon formed a chaotic sea. Truth and error, fact and fable, mingled together in an undistinguishable confusion."[21]

The situation is not much different today: while one wing of orthodoxy in

Pakistan strictly clings to the Prophetic traditions, Ghulam Parvez, a modernist thinker in the same country, rejects *ḥadīth* in toto and accepts only the Koran (which he interprets in a very idiosyncratic way) as the sole source of moral and ethical values.[22] Again, Fazlur Rahman caused much discussion and bitter antagonism with his interpretation of the "living *sunna*." To be sure, even in the Middle Ages the question had been posited (by the Ashʿarite theologian al-Baqillani) whether complete submission to the model of the Prophet was absolutely necessary. Was it perhaps only meritorious, or even without special religious value? This discussion of course dealt not with the religious contents of the *ḥadīth* but only with ethically indifferent questions such as manners of eating or dressing and the like. However, the majority of Muslims preferred to follow the motto of the first caliph, Abu Bakr, who said: "I do not omit anything of the things the Messenger of God has done, for I am afraid that if I should omit it, I could go astray."[23] This careful and loving imitation of the Prophet's example would be, for them, the true *dīn-i muḥammadī*, as particularly the Sufis emphasized it.[24]

Such an approach was on the one hand the basis for the loving veneration of Muhammad, who appears often as a kind of paternal figure (he himself is quoted as saying, "Verily I am like a father to you"),[25] a father or a deeply respected elder in the family to whom one would turn in full trust because one was absolutely certain that he knew the right answer to all questions, and the solution of all problems for those who belonged to him.[26] But it could also lead to an absolutely tradition-bound attitude, even in the minutest externals, as it is expressed by the great medieval theologian al-Ghazzali, who devotes to the Prophet the twentieth, that is, the central, chapter of his *Iḥyāʾ ʿulūm ad-dīn* and clearly states:

> Know that the key to happiness is to follow the *sunna* and to imitate the Messenger of God in all his coming and going, his movements and rest, in his way of eating, his attitude, his sleep and his talk. I do not mean this in regard to religious observance, for there is no reason to neglect the traditions which were concerned with this aspect. I rather mean all the problems of custom and usage, for only by following them unrestricted succession is possible. God has said: "Say: If you love God, follow me, and God will love you" (Sura 3:29), and He has said: "What the messenger has brought—accept it, and what he has prohibited—refrain from it!" (Sura 59:7). That means, you have to sit while putting on trousers, and to stand when winding a turban, and to begin with the right foot when putting on shoes. . . .[27]

And yet Ghazzali, "the scholar among the inhabitants of the world," was accused by mystics like Maulana Rumi of lacking true love (as manifested in his younger brother Ahmad Ghazzali) and of not having found "the secret of the Muhammadan proximity"![28]

The *imitatio Muhammadi* is, as Armand Abel has stated, an imitation of the Prophet's actions and activity, whereas the *imitatio Christi* is rather the imitation of Christ's suffering. But it was through this imitation of Muhammad's actions as transmitted through the *ḥadīth* that Islamic life assumed a unique uniformity in social behavior, a fact that has always impressed visitors to all parts of the Muslim world. It is also visible, for instance, in the hagiography of Muslim saints.[29] For, as Frithjof Schuon says: "This 'Muhammadan' character of the virtues . . . explains the relatively impersonal style of the saints; there are no other virtues than those of Muhammad, so they can only be repeated in those who follow his example; it is through them that the Prophet lives in his community."[30] Even the introduction of a good *sunna* is, according to one *ḥadīth*, a laudable act, and the person who introduces it will be given the reward of someone who acts accordingly, as he who introduces a bad *sunna* will be equally punished.[31] The Muslim willing to devote himself completely to the imitation of the *nūr al-hudā*, the Light of Right Guidance, that is, the Prophet, may express his feelings in this prayer:

> We ask Thee for that for which Thy servant and messenger Muhammad has asked Thee, we take refuge with Thee from that from which Thy servant and messenger has taken refuge with Thee.[32]

THE *SHAMĀ'IL* AND *DALĀ'IL* LITERATURE

Veneration of the Prophet and the interest in even the smallest details of his behavior and his personal life grew in the same measure as the Muslims were distanced from him in time. They wanted to know ever more about his personality, his looks, and his words in order to be sure that they were following him correctly. The popular preachers enjoyed depicting the figure of the Prophet in wonderful colors, adding even the most insignificant details (thus, that he had only seventeen white hairs in his beard).[33] One sometimes sympathizes with more sober theologians who were not too happy when listening to these pious, well-meant exaggerations. But it was this very genre of literature, these treatises containing *qūt al-ʿāshiqīn*, the Nurture of the Lovers, as Makhdum Muhammad Hashim of Thatta called his collection of Prophetic traditions and legends in rhyme, that remained favorite with readers and listeners.[34] This *Qūt al-ʿāshiqīn*, written in the Sindhi language in the early eighteenth century, was one of the first Sindhi books ever printed in Bombay (ca. 1868), and its narratives, developed out of simple *ḥadīth*, enchanted and uplifted the masses and inspired the folk poets to elaborate them in ever more imaginative detail.

In early days, the forerunner of such collections was a genre called *dalā'il an-nubuwwa*, "proofs of Prophethood," complemented by that of the *shamā'il*, literary expositions of the Prophet's lofty qualities and outward beauty. Two of the earliest *dalā'il* and *shamā'il* works were composed by Abu Nu'aim al-Isfahani (d. 1037), mystic and historian, and by al-Baihaqi (d. 1066). Both are more or less biographies of the Prophet, studded with evidentiary miracles—those that happened before and after Muhammad's birth as well as before and after his call to prophethood, and those that pointed to his exalted status as the last Prophet. Both sources speak of his noble genealogy and his qualities and indulge in telling many of the miracles through which men and animals recognized him as God's special messenger. Such tales formed the bases for legends and poems in which popular views about Muhammad were to be reflected throughout the centuries.[35]

Almost two hundred years before Baihaqi, the traditionist Abu 'Isa at-Tirmidhi (d. 892) compiled the first basic book about the *shamā'il al-Muṣṭafā*, in which the Prophet's external form as well as his moral superiority was described in great detail.[36] Muhammad appears here as the model of moral perfection, and it is not surprising that Tirmidhi's collection was used as a source by that medieval author who composed a most extensive work about the greatness of the Prophet, Qadi 'Iyad. He was a stern Malikite theologian, noted enemy of the Sufis, and much-feared judge in Ceuta and Granada. His *Kitāb ash-shifā' fī ta'rīf ḥuqūq al-Muṣṭafā*, however, has been used by nonmystics and mystics alike. In fact, it is perhaps the most frequently used and commented-upon handbook in which the Prophet's life, his qualities, and his miracles are described in every detail. The *Shifā'* was so highly admired in medieval Islam that it soon acquired a sanctity of its own and was even used as a talisman,[37] protecting the house of its owner: "If it is found in a house, this house will not suffer any harm, and a boat in which it is, will not drown [*sic*]; when a sick person reads it or it is recited for him, God will restore his health."[38] For surely a book that is exclusively devoted to the admiring description of the noble Prophet partakes of the Prophet's *baraka*. Its very name, *shifā'*, "cure, healing," points to its healing power.

From Qadi 'Iyad's book an even more extensive work about the same subject was derived, the *Al-mawāhib al-laduniyya* of Qastallani (d. 1517), and the literature in this area grew incessantly. Thus the last great collector of *dalā'il*, *shamā'il*, and poems in honor of the Prophet, the indefatigable

Yusuf an-Nabhani (early twentieth century), mentions in one place the twenty-fifth (!) volume of a *shamā'il* work that he had used for his compilation.[39]

THE PROPHET'S PHYSICAL BEAUTY

Descriptions of the physical beauty of the Prophet are found scattered in early traditions. Among them, the story of Umm Maʿbad can serve as a proof for the Prophet's impressive presence (see chapter 4 below). For as the Prophet was the most beautiful of mankind in character, so he was the most handsome in his looks. The oldest descriptions in Tirmidhi's *Kitāb shamā'il al-Muṣṭafā* (the one quoted here is by ʿAli) show him like this:

> Muhammad was middle-sized, did not have lank or crisp hair, was not fat, had a white circular face, wide black eyes, and long eyelashes. When he walked, he walked as though he went down a declivity. He had the "seal of prophecy" between his shoulder blades. . . . He was bulky. His face shone like the moon in the night of full moon. He was taller than middling stature but shorter than conspicuous tallness. He had thick, curly hair. The plaits of his hair were parted. His hair reached beyond the lobe of his ear. His complexion was *azhar* [bright, luminous]. Muhammad had a wide forehead and fine, long, arched eyebrows which did not meet. Between his eyebrows there was a vein which distended when he was angry. The upper part of his nose was hooked; he was thick-bearded, had smooth cheeks, a strong mouth, and his teeth were set apart. He had thin hair on his chest. His neck was like the neck of an ivory statue, with the purity of silver. Muhammad was proportionate, stout, firm-gripped, even of belly and chest, broad-chested and broad-shouldered.[40]

A special mark of the Prophet was the "seal of prophethood," which documented his position as the final herald of the Divine revelation (see Sura 33:40). The seal is described by all sources unanimously as a fleshy protuberance or kind of mole the size of a pigeon's egg, of blackish color with some yellow, which was located between his shoulders. It is said that the Christian monk Bahira' in Syria recognized young Muhammad by this very mark as the promised last prophet, the Paraclete of the Johannine gospel.

The Prophet's hands are described as cool and fragrant, "cooler than ice and softer than silk," and in all traditions the fragrance that exuded from him is duly emphasized. Some of the women close to him allegedly collected his perspiration to use as perfume.[41]

Out of the belief in the Prophet's lovely fragrance a delightful legend developed: during his heavenly journey, when he was on his way into the Divine presence, some drops of his sweat fell on the ground, and from them, the first fragrant rose appeared. Thus the believer can still experience the Prophet's scent from the fragrance of the rose, as Rumi sings in his great poem in honor of the blessed mystical rose:

> Root and branch of the roses is
> the lovely sweat of Mustafa,
> And by his power the rose's crescent
> grows now into a full moon.[42]

Pashto popular poetry, on the other hand, mentions that the rose's petals blushed from shame when the radiantly beautiful Messenger entered the garden, so that the flower's color is derived from his beauty.[43] In later times narratives of this kind have led to extravagant statements that, for instance, the Prophet was so pure and fragrant that flies did not sit on him, or that thanks to his pure, luminous nature he did not cast a shadow. And ʿA'isha was told that "the earth swallows up the excrements of the prophets so that they are not seen."[44]

Muhammad becomes the archetype of all human beauty because the noblest spiritual qualities are also manifested in him somatically. He is, as a contemporary Urdu poet says,

> Beauty from head to toe, Love embodied.[45]

Similarly, a modern Arabic source mentions that the perfection of faith consists in the conviction that "God has created Muhammad's body in such unsurpassable beauty as had neither before him nor after him been seen in any human being. If the whole beauty of the Prophet were unveiled before our eyes, they could not bear its splendor."[46] Poets in all Islamic languages have expressed this conviction, inventing ever new images to express the praise for this marvelous beauty.

> Your light was in Joseph's beauty, o Light of God;
> It healed Jacob's blind eye so that it became well,

sings the Urdu poet Dagh at the end of the nineteenth century.[47] He takes up with these words a favorite topic of earlier writers: not only is the wisdom of all prophets contained in Muhammad but also their beauty. And while Yusuf (Joseph) is generally accepted as the paragon of human beauty, a *ḥadīth* makes Muhammad say: "Yusuf was beautiful but I am more handsome (*amlaḥ*)."[48] Perhaps one should also consider the famous *ḥadīth* "Verily God is beautiful and loves beauty,"[49] which has inspired so many artists, in connection with the beauty of the Prophet, the beloved of God.

It is natural that in a religion that prohibits the representation of living beings, particularly of saintly persons, no picture of the Prophet could be legitimately produced. (One proof of the totally wrong ideas of medieval Christians is that, confusing Islam with the paganism of antiquity, they spoke in their poetry and *chansons de geste* of "the golden images, or statues, of Mahomet."[50] To be sure, we find representations of the Prophet in quite a number of miniature paintings in the Turkish, Persian, and even Indian traditions. In later times his face is usually veiled, although early fourteenth-century paintings show him unveiled as well, a practice that today is vehemently attacked as heresy by Muslim fundamentalists and even by large parts of the intelligentsia.[51] But the Muslims found another way to make him present before their eyes: the so-called *ḥilya*.

Tirmidhi, in the late ninth century, quotes a *ḥadīth* in which the Prophet promises: "For him who sees my *ḥilya* after my death it is as if he had seen me myself, and he who sees it, longing for me, for him God will make Hellfire prohibited, and he will not be resurrected naked at Doomsday." The *ḥilya* (literally, "ornament") consists of short descriptions of the Prophet's external and internal qualities, drawn from early Arabic sources. It is told that the Abbasid caliph Harun ar-Rashid bought such a description from a wandering dervish, rewarding him lavishly; the following night he was honored by a vision of the Prophet, who promised him eternal blessings.[52] According to other popular traditions, the Prophet himself advised his "four friends," the first four caliphs, before his death to remember his *shamā'il-nāma*,[53] that is, the description of his looks and qualities. One who stitches the *ḥilya* in his shroud will be accompanied on his last way by a thousand angels who will recite the funeral prayer for him and ask forgiveness on his behalf until Doomsday.[54]

Out of the simple, sonorous Arabic descriptions of Muhammad's qualities more artistic forms developed. It seems that veneration of the *ḥilya* was especially widespread in Ottoman Turkey. There the calligraphers developed a peculiar style of writing it during the sixteenth century, which was perfected by Hafiz Osman, the master calligrapher of the late seventeenth century. These *ḥilya*, often imitated, are round, and beneath the circular frame that contains the description of the Prophet, the line "Mercy for the worlds" is written in large letters.[55] Even today, the *ḥilya* is usually printed according to the model set by Hafiz Osman and his disciples, and is kept in homes as a picture of the Virgin might be in a Catholic home, to convey blessings upon the inhabitants. To execute a *ḥilya* in fine calligraphy was considered a work of great merit: one Turkish woman, widowed and childless, said she regarded the nine she had completed during her lifetime as a substitute for nine children, hoping that they would intercede for her at Doomsday.[56]

Poets also transformed the short, pithy Arabic sentences describing the

The ḥilya *of the Prophet, in* nastaʿlīq *script*
by the Turkish calligrapher Yesarizade Mustafa ʿIzzat, 1830

The ḥilya *of the Prophet, in traditional Turkish* naksh *calligraphy by Ahmet Kâmil Efendi, for his graduation as calligrapher, 1882*

Prophet into long-winded verse.[57] The Turkish *Ḥilya* by Khaqani, a poet of the late sixteenth century, is especially worthy of mention. The poet tells extensively the blessings contained in the *ḥilya*: not only will its owner be safe from punishment in the Otherworld, but Satan will not enter his house; his recompense will be equal to the manumission of a slave and a pilgrimage to Mecca, "and the citadel of his body will not be impaired and he will not be afflicted by maladies."[58] Then the poet ingeniously describes the Prophet and his beauty. His white complexion is explained in images like this:

> He with a heart like the ocean was an incomparable pearl—
> No wonder that [his color] was inclined toward white![59]

His harmoniously arched eyebrows serve the whole world as *qibla*, direction of prayer, for they resemble a beautifully arched prayer-niche; but even more, they remind the spectator of the secret of *qāba qausain*, "two bows' length" (Sura 53:9), that is, the mystery of Muhammad's close presence before God during his heavenly journey.[60] His nose, again, was "as if it were the bud of a white rose."

Khaqani also devotes long descriptions to the clothing of the Prophet, for not only his figure and his face were topics for the traditionists and poets but also his garments, which the believer should strive to imitate. He preferred white or green clothing, but owned, according to classical description, only one piece of each kind. Khaqani then extends his verse to the various colors in which the Prophet appeared, each of them fitting for one of his aspects:

> In white, he looked like a pearl, in red, like a rose.

Indeed, for him "who is beautiful like the rose" the Pathan folksinger is willing to sacrifice his life.[61] On the whole, however, the color red is rarely connected with the Prophet.

It is interesting to note that a modern Egyptian narrative ballad deals with an incident concerning the Prophet's shirt. Since he had no cash to help a starving beggar, Muhammad gave him his only shirt, which was then auctioned until a Jew bought it for an enormous sum; the Jew's blindness was cured by this very shirt and he, of course, embraced Islam. The motif of Joseph's fragrant shirt, which healed his father's blindness, is here applied to the Prophet.[62] The same idea has also been expressed in Sindhi popular verse.[63]

The precious relic of the *khirqa-i sharīf*, or *burda*, the noble coat of the Prophet,[64] is found in several mosques, among them one in Khuldabad in the northern Deccan, and in the treasury of the Topkapu Seray in Istanbul. Another *khirqa-i sharīf*, preserved in Qandahar, Afghanistan, in a building that non-Muslims may not even approach, inspired Muhammad Iqbal in 1933 to compose a deeply felt, mystically tinged poem (see p. 243).[65]

The Prophet wore a special kind of sandal, the two strings of which were drawn between the toes. These sandals, *naʿl*, became likewise an amulet full of *baraka*, particularly strong against the evil eye.[66] Were they not worthy of all admiration and veneration, for the Prophet had touched the Divine Throne with them during his heavenly journey, so that they became "the vertex of the crown of the Throne"?[67] Popular poetry in the various Islamic languages has often included mention of this aspect of the sandals. The fifteenth-century Persian mystical poet Jami, for example, writes that all heavenly beings rubbed "the forehead of their intention" on Muhammad's "Throne-rubbing sandals."[68] He also claims that the heavenly tree Tuba had rubbed its head at the Prophet's sandals and thus reached highest honor,[69] and he repeatedly expresses the feeling that "the thread of the soul" is nothing but the string of Muhammad's sandals and that the cheek of the longing lover resembles the fine Ta'ifi leather of which these sandals were made: do the lover's cheeks not hope to be touched by the Prophet's feet and thus to obtain every conceivable bliss?[70]

The relic itself was first mentioned in the thirteenth century in Damascus. But pictures of these sandals were apparently quite common in the later Middle Ages, especially in the western Islamic world, for around them a whole poetical genre developed. The poets, many of them from North Africa and Spain, described these sandals or expressed their longing for them. Thus an Andalusian poetess, Saʿduna Umm Saʿd bint ʿIsam al-Himyariyya (d. 1242), begins one of her poems with the words

> I shall kiss the image if I do not find
> A way to kiss the Prophet's sandal.
> Perhaps the good fortune of kissing it
> Will be granted to me in Paradise in the most radiant place,
> And I rub my heart on it so that perhaps
> The burning thirst which rages in it may be quenched.[71]

The North African historian al-Maqarri (d. 1644) devoted a voluminous book to the subject of the Prophet's sandals;[72] its more than five hundred pages contain not only prose and poetical texts but also drawings of the sandals as they were used by people as a protective talisman, for "it protected one's house from fire, caravans from hostile attacks, ships from disaster at sea and property from loss." Around the turn of the present century, Yusuf an-Nabhani, the collector of eulogies for the Prophet, sang in one of his poems:

> Verily I serve the image of the sandal of Mustafa
> So that I may live in both worlds under its protection.[73]

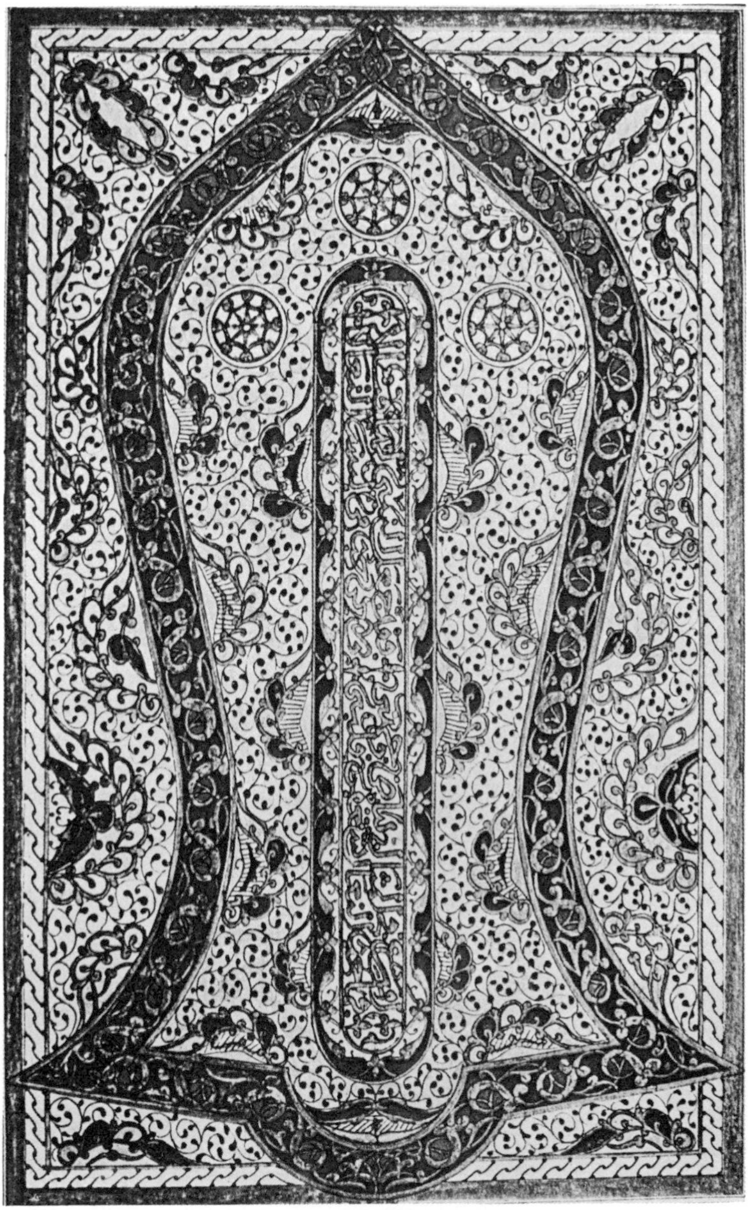

The sandal of the Prophet,
from the Dhakhīra *of the Sharqawa*
(Reprinted by permission of Dr. Mohammed Sijelmassi)

Popular songs in honor of the *niʿāl sharīfa*, the "noble sandals," have persisted down to the present, according to an Iraqi friend who remembers such songs from her childhood in Baghdad.

In addition to the sandals, another relic that became widely accepted was the impression of the Prophet's foot.[74] According to legend, Muhammad's foot left a trace on the rock in Jerusalem where he alighted during his night journey before ascending into the Divine Presence. The Dome of the Rock was built to honor and protect the site, which is greatly revered. At various times and places other large stones have been found with an impression in them that came to be regarded as the trace of the Prophet's foot, and hence worthy of veneration. When visiting such a footprint one touches the stone and then passes one's hand over the upper part of one's body, beginning with the head, in order to obtain some of the stone's *baraka*. That this custom goes back to a rather early period is shown by the fact that in the year 1304, the reformist theologian Ibn Taimiyya, who tried to remove such a stone in Damascus to stop the superstitious practices connected with it, was driven away by the enraged masses and even accused of impiety.[75] One also poured water over such *qadam rasūl* stones, which was then used for its acquired *baraka*.

From the Middle Ages onward such stones were brought to India by credulous pilgrims. One of the first known instances is connected with the name of the great Suhrawardi saint Makhdum Jahaniyan from Ucch, who deposited such a *qadam rasūl* in Delhi.[76] It must have been this very *qadam sharīf*, "the noble footprint," that Sultan Feroz Tughluq placed on his son's tomb. As late as the early nineteenth century "an annual fair [was] held on the 12th Rabiʿ al-awwal (that is, the Prophet's birthday)" at that site; one observer ca. 1840 reported that "thousands of *malang faqīrs* assemble and perform ecstasies in front of its gate."[77] Soon a number of places between Narayanganj (Bangladesh), Gaur (West Bengal), and Gujarat boasted of owning such a relic. (Shia sanctuaries, incidentally, sometimes preserve a footprint of ʿAli in stone, for instance at Maulali near Hyderabad/Deccan.)

The veneration for the *qadam rasūl* was so deeply rooted that even the Moghul emperor Akbar waited upon such a stone that one of his grandees had brought back from his pilgrimage to Mecca in 1589. Because this happened after the ruler had promulgated the *dīn-i ilāhī*, his eclectic religious order, the critical chronicler Badaoni notes the event with great amazement: how was such respect for the Prophet's footprint compatible with the ruler's otherwise so "un-Islamic" attitude?[78]

Late Urdu poets loved to sing of the glory of the Prophet's footprint, for, as they felt,

> The trace of his foot has the rank of Mount Sinai,[79]

that is, it is the place where the Divine Light becomes visible, and therefore,

> Mustafa's footprint is the place where the bearers of the Divine Throne prostrate themselves.[80]

Even more than the *qadam rasūl*, hairs from the Prophet's beard became a most valued relic. The beauty of his beard was always emphasized,[81] and as hair and beard are considered to be endowed with special power, the oath "by the Prophet's beard" was considered extremely powerful. The Prophet is said to have given hairs to his faithful followers, and understandably, the pious strove to acquire at least some of them. Khalid ibn al-Walid, the victorious hero of the battle of Yarmuk, kept some of the Prophet's hairs in his headgear and claimed, as tradition has it, "Whosoever does so, will be victorious."[82] Over the centuries, a number of sacred places in Islamic countries have been fortunate enough to possess such a relic,[83] which is usually preserved in a small precious vessel. Veneration remains strong even today: only recently the beautiful Hazrat-bal Mosque in Srinagar was built in the place of another, older mosque in order to give "the most venerable hair" (*hażrat bāl*) a worthy abode. Non-Muslims are very rarely allowed to see the relic; on one occasion the Alaettin Mosque in Konya (Anatolia) did permit my mother and me to view the sacred hair, preserved in a very fine glass bottle. Usually it is well guarded, to be exhibited on certain festive days; in Rohri, Pakistan, for instance, the jewel-studded vessel is displayed once each year, in March. Sometimes only men, not women, are admitted into the presence of such a valuable relic, as we discovered in the Athar Mahal in Bijapur (Deccan) in 1979 and 1980. And the theft—or alleged theft—of such a hair can still cause extensive rioting, as was the case some years ago in Kashmir.

Besides the veneration of relics connected with the Prophet's bodily presence, the Muslims carefully studied the way in which he cared for his body, because in this respect too, he was taken as the paradigm of behavior. According to ʿA'isha, he never woke up without using the *miswāk*, a piece of twig that serves as a toothbrush. Therefore the *miswāk* plays an important role in Muslim life—so much so that an Indian mystical writer of the eighteenth century, Nasir Muhammad ʿAndalib, praised the use of the toothbrush as a special sign of Divine grace by which the Muslims are distinguished from all other peoples.[84] Whether the Prophet used antimony to blacken his eyes or not, whether or not he daubed his hair and beard with henna[85]—all manner of details constituted problems whose appropriate solution was critically important to generations of pious Muslims who had never seen him in the flesh but wanted to remain faithful to his *sunna* even in the externals.

And there are other issues as well: most importantly, that the Prophet began every work with the right hand (or the right foot), and used exclusively the right hand for eating. Thus the first three fingers of this hand are to be employed when obtaining food; the left hand should be used only for the purification after urinating and defecation. Even today a traditional Muslim would never touch food with the left hand; when dining with fork and knife (the use of which was violently debated in pious circles in the late nineteenth century), many prefer to take the fork in the right, the knife in the left hand.

Even the food that the Prophet liked and disliked is carefully recorded. Although the sources usually stress his modesty, his prolonged periods of fasting, and, at times, his starving, they still agree that he liked certain foodstuffs better than others, for instance the foreleg of lamb, milk, and dates. Sweets, particularly honey, were among his favorites. Such details were taken over in the descriptive poetry written about him. Composed at the turn of the present century, Nabhani's *Hamziyya*, a biographical poem of many hundred verses, sings not only of the spiritual greatness of the Prophet and of his miracles, but also tells how

> He liked all permitted food
> And he particularly loved *ḥalwā*.
> He liked cream and dates very much, and other things
> That he liked were melon and squash . . .[86]

Anas ibn Malik, who served the Prophet for many years and thus became acquainted with his habits, is reported to have said: "Once I saw the Messenger of God fetch pieces of squash (*kūsa*) from the kettle, and from that day I have always loved squash."[87] A famous example of the tradition-bound attitude of pious Muslims is connected with Sayyid Ahmad Khan, who in 1850, when he was in his early thirties, discussed with Azurda, the Mufti of Delhi, the permissibility of eating mangoes and ended the conversation with the emphatic statement: "By God, who holds my life in His hands! If a person refrains from eating mangoes for the sole motive that the Prophet did not eat them—the angels will come to his deathbed to kiss his feet."[88] To eat this favorite fruit of Indian Muslims was thus for him certainly "doubtful": it was "better to leave it." Sayyid Ahmad, who was to become the reformer of Indian Islam, here followed exactly the attitude manifested by the great mystic Bayezid Bistami a thousand years before him: according to legend, this saint did not eat melons for sixty years, because he did not know how the Prophet cut that fruit.[89]

While the favorite foods of the Prophet have been lovingly adopted by the Muslims, they are not bound to follow his aversion to garlic and onion—although they should avoid consuming those vegetables before going to the mosque.[90] The Prophet disliked their smell and thought that the archangel Gabriel might be offended by it when descending to bring him another revelation.

The Prophet's attitude toward medicine should also be mentioned briefly. He said: "God did not send any illness unless he sends a medicine for it."[91] The water with which he had washed himself was often reused by the pious as a medicine because of its *baraka*—a custom well known in the history of religions. Likewise, and for the same reason, his saliva could serve for healing purposes, and it is often told that he cured ʿAli's sore eyes by putting some of his saliva on them.[92] It seems that he attributed special importance to cupping and also recommended the use of purgatives, for he apparently considered the stomach to be an important source of many ailments; from his sketchy remarks in this field a special science developed, called *aṭ-ṭibb an-nabawī*, "Prophetic medicine," which is still practiced even today in some places. His own success in healing—of which some popular stories give examples—was part of the *baraka* that accompanies the saintly person and that enables him sometimes to perform healing miracles by merely touching a person or breathing upon him.[93] Many Muslims have also experienced that Muhammad's apparition in a dream cured them, and it is believed that prayers "by the honor of the Messenger of God" will definitely help an ailing person to get well soon.

Muhammad is often called *ṭabīb*, "physician," for the prophets are, as Ghazzali says, "the physicians of the soul," who can recognize the ailments of the human heart and can heal them by their teaching and preaching. Thus the Prophet appears frequently—especially in poetry—as the *ṭabīb* and *ḥabīb*, physician and beloved friend, and it is under this twofold aspect that his community trusts in him and loves him. As Maulana Rumi sings in a lovely little Arabic poem:

> *Hādhā ḥabībī, hādhā ṭabībī, hādhā adībī, hādhā dawāʾī . . .*
> This is my friend, this is my physician, this is my tutor, this is my remedy . . .[94]

THE PROPHET'S SPIRITUAL BEAUTY

Muhammad is considered, as we have already mentioned, the paragon of physical beauty. His face was, as later poets often claimed, "the Koran copy, *muṣḥaf*, of beauty," and the dark "down" on his cheeks the "text of the sent-down revelation."[95] But this external beauty was but a mirror of his interior beauty, for God had created him perfect in nature and moral qualities, *khalqan wa khulqan*. When ʿA'isha, his favorite young wife, was once asked about his character she simply stated: "His character was the Koran—he liked what the Koran liked, and grew angry when the Koran was angry."[96]

The Western reader, raised in a centuries-old tradition of aversion to Muhammad, will probably be surprised to learn that in all reports the quality that is particularly emphasized in the Prophet is his humility and kindness. Qadi 'Iyad, one of the best representatives of the reverent admiration of the Prophet so typical of Muslim piety, writes:

> God has elevated the dignity of His Prophet and granted him virtues, beautiful qualities and special prerogatives. He has praised his high dignity so overwhelmingly that neither tongue nor pen are sufficient [to describe him]. In His book He has clearly and openly demonstrated his high rank and praised him for his qualities of character and his noble habits. He asks His servants to attach themselves to him and to follow him obediently. It is God—great is His Majesty!—who grants honor and grace, who purifies and refines, He that lauds and praises and grants a perfect recompense . . . He places before our eyes his noble nature, perfected and sublime in every respect. He grants him perfect virtue, praiseworthy qualities, noble habits and numerous preferences. He supports his message with radiant miracles, clear proofs, and apparent signs.[97]

All reports speak of Muhammad's friendly, kindly but serious attitude and point out that he did not often laugh. (One famous Prophetic tradition, frequently quoted by the early ascetics, says: "If you knew what I know you would cry much and laugh little.")[98] However, he is also said to have had a most winning smile that never failed to enchant his followers, and Ghazzali even mentions his tendency to laugh.[99] His softspoken humor is palpable from some early Islamic stories, such as the following: "One day a little old woman came to him to ask whether old wretched women would also go to Paradise. 'No,' answered the Prophet, 'there are no old women in Paradise!' And then, looking at her grieved face, he continued with a smile: 'They will all be transformed in Paradise for there, there is only one youthful age for all!' "[100] And his practical wisdom in dealing with his companions is nicely revealed in his remark to Abu Huraira, who had the habit of visiting him too often: *zur ghabban tazdid ḥubban*, "Visit rarely, then you'll be loved more!"[101]

The sources praise Muhammad's concern for the weak, and his kindliness is always highlighted: "He did not beat a servant, nor a maid servant, and none of his wives," says the tradition. Tirmidhi describes him as follows: "He was well acquainted with sorrow, much absorbed in thought, had little rest, was silent for long periods and did not talk without cause. He began and finished his talk with the formula 'In the name of God.' His talk was pithy, neither too long nor too short, not coarse, but also not too playful or light. He honored each of God's signs of grace, even though it might be small, and never found blame in anything."[102]

Practical advice to his people is not lacking either. When a Bedouin asked him whether, since he trusted in God and His protection, he could let his camel roam loose, the Prophet answered briefly: *Iʿqilhā wa tawakkal*, "First tether it, and then trust in God."[103] The importance of activity in this world, as contrasted to an unhealthy fatalism that leads in the long run to a lack of responsibility, is expressed best in the oft-repeated *ḥadīth*: "This world is the seedbed for the next world";[104] every action upon which man embarks here will bring its fruits—good or bad—in the next world, at the day of Resurrection. Furthermore, every faithful Muslim should be reminded to appropriate the Prophet's short prayer "Oh Lord, increase my knowledge!" The devout should likewise imitate his way of dealing with his contemporaries and behavior in society. Was he not even blamed in the Koran (Sura 80:1) for frowning when a blind visitor interrupted him in an important conversation?[105] This Divine blame led him to a well-balanced kindness toward everyone: "When someone came with a request he was not sent off before it had been granted or before he had at least received a friendly word. The Prophet's friendliness and largesse encompassed everyone; he was like a father for his companions."[106]

To illustrate such brief remarks, long and touching legends easily grew up over the centuries. Among them is one told by Rumi in his *Mathnawī*: An infidel visited the Prophet and, as is the infidels' custom, "ate with seven stomachs." After stuffing himself overmuch he lay down in the guest room, where he soiled the linen, and leaving the room dirty, slipped out secretly before dawn. However, he had to return to seek an amulet that he had forgotten in his room, and found the Prophet washing the sullied linen with his own hands. Of course he immediately became a Muslim, put to shame by such humility and generosity.[107] Such stories cannot have been invented without any basis; they may go back to early historical nuclei, having been elaborated in later times to make the ideals of Muslim ascetic-mystical circles conform with the example of the Prophet.

Along these lines, Muhammad's poverty and the destitute situation of his family members form an essential theme of popular tradition. His bread, it is said, was made from unsifted barley, and some reports describe how he and his family, especially his beloved daughter Fatima, suffered from hunger many a night. In fact, the Prophet always fastened a stone on his stomach to suppress the feeling of hunger,[108] and the misery of Fatima has been told in heartrending stories (mainly in the Shiite tradition). It is even related that after the Prophet had returned from his most sublime experience, the heavenly journey, the next morning he had to borrow some barley from an unsympathetic Jewish merchant in order to assuage his hunger. ʿUmar ibn al-Khattab, destined to become Muhammad's second successor, once wept when looking at the Prophet's miserable household; upon being asked the reason for his tears, he replied that he could not bear the idea that Khosroes and Caesar, the rulers of Iran and Byzantium, lived in luxury while the Prophet of God was near starvation in his poverty. "They have this world, and we the next one," answered the Prophet, consoling him.[109] Had not God offered him the keys of all treasures on earth? Yet he had refused them because he wanted to stay with his Lord, "Who feeds me and gives me to drink."[110] Did not God want to make him a king-prophet like David and Solomon, though he preferred to be a servant-prophet? "I eat as a slave eats, and sit as a slave sits, for I am a slave [of God]." His prayer, which became a favorite with mystics and ascetics, was: "Oh Lord, keep me hungry one day and satiated one day. When I am hungry I pray to you, and when I am full I sing your praise."[111] And the sufferings inflicted upon him by the unfeeling Meccans resulted in his remark that "those most afflicted are the prophets, then the saints, and then the others according to their position."[112]

It is told that someone came to the Prophet and said: "I love you, O Messenger of God!" To which he replied: "Be ready for poverty!"[113] Hence love of the poor became a sign of love for the Prophet: to honor the poor and to associate with them means not only to follow his example but, in a certain sense, to honor him in them. The Prophet's admonition concerning the treatment of slaves—"Let them wear what you wear, and let them eat what you eat"—was quite popular in later centuries, as several anecdotes prove.[114]

In later times Muhammad's saying *faqrī fakhrī*, "My poverty is my pride," became the motto of the mystical seekers.[115] Poverty was now understood not merely as destitution but rather as a spiritual stage that consists in man's knowledge of his own lowliness and poverty before God, the One Who Has No Need (*al-ghanī*); for it is said in the Koran: "He is the Rich, and you are the poor!" (Sura 35:16). Thus the Prophet became the model for the *nihil habentes, omnia possedentes* of Islam. Part of this mystical concept of poverty is gratitude. The words of Job, "The Lord has given, the Lord has taken away—praised be the name of the Lord!" express the Muslims' ideal of acceptance. It was this kind of gratitude that the Prophet practiced, and his saying "I cannot account the praise due to Thee" has been central to mystical reflection upon gratitude and praise of God.[116]

Muhammad's lovingkindness extended over all beings. He was noted for his love of children, and used to greet them in the street and play with them. Later folk ballads tell in touching verses how his two grandsons Hasan and

Husain—often simply called al-Hasanain, the Two Hasans—climbed on "Gran' Dad Prophet's" back while he was performing his prayer,[117] and he was not at all disturbed by the lively boys, who were "the earrings of the heavenly Throne."[118] For the Prophet had been informed by Gabriel about their future sad fate: the angel had brought a green robe for Hasan and a red one for Husain to indicate that the former would die from poison, whereas his younger brother would be slain in battle.[119] The Prophet therefore had a special attachment to these grandchildren, and it is told that when one of his companions saw him kiss Hasan, and remarked with disdain, "I have ten boys but have never kissed any of them," the Prophet thereupon replied: "He who does not show mercy will not receive mercy."[120]

Muhammad was also known for his love of animals. He once promised Paradise to a sinful, evil woman who had saved a dog from death by fetching water for it. But he had a special liking for cats. Did he not cut the sleeve from his coat when he had to get up for prayer and yet did not want to disturb the cat that was sleeping on the sleeve? One of his cats even gave birth to kittens on his coat, and special blessings were extended to Abu Huraira's cat, who killed a snake that tried to cheat the Prophet and sting him despite the kindness he had shown it. Because he petted this cat's back, cats never fall on their backs; and because his five fingers left a mark on her forehead, every cat has some black stripes over her eyes.[121] (One is reminded of the black lines on the petals of a fragrant yellow flower that blooms in spring near the Khyber Pass, called by the Pathans *paighāmbar gul*, "the Prophet's flower.")[122] Remembering the Prophet's fondness for cats, one *ḥadīth* claims that "love of cats is part of faith."[123] Such traditions have led to the formation of many charming legends in the Muslim world, and the individual creatures that were promised Paradise (among them Abu Huraira's cat) have even become part of German literature since Goethe introduced them in his *West-Östlicher Divan* as *Begünstigte Tiere*, Preferred Animals.

One aspect of the Prophet's life has always puzzled, bothered, even shocked, non-Muslim students of Islam: his attitude to women. At the end of his life he was married to nine wives. Someone raised in the Christian tradition, with its ascetic ideal of the celibate Jesus and its stress on monogamy, will of course have difficulty acknowledging that a true prophet could have been married, nay, even polygamous. Indeed, one of the most frequently reiterated attacks against Muhammad from the early Middle Ages to this day has been the charge of lasciviousness and sexual vice. The Muslim, on the other hand, feels that the capacity of the Prophet to combine the worldly and the spiritual spheres is a special proof of his high rank. (The Koranic restriction of polygamy to four wives, who must be treated with absolutely equal justice according to specific scriptural orders, was in fact a great improvement on pre-Islamic customs.) Islamic apologetics constantly emphasize that Muhammad married some of his wives in later years with the intention of giving a new home to the widows of fighters for the faith. Besides, the numerous wives and concubines of Solomon and David, the two kings of Israel who appear in the Koran as prophets and thus precursors of Muhammad, make the number of Muhammad's marriages after Khadija's death look quite modest. One often forgets that Muhammad was married, for the better part of his life, only to one wife, Khadija, who was considerably senior to him. Only in his last thirteen years did he contract several other marriages, and even so, as noted earlier, Khadija remained so much his ideal after her death that the young ʿA'isha never ceased being jealous of her.

Muhammad set an example for his community in his treatment of his wives, who were by no means always united in harmonious love. "To marry is my *sunna*": this word was related from him in early times, and therefore Islam does not cultivate the ideal of celibacy. "There is no monkery in Islam," as another *ḥadīth* has it. Certainly, some ascetics preferred celibacy, but even among them one finds saintly people who thanks to a vision of the Prophet in their dreams were finally animated to get married—suffice it to mention Ibn Khafif of Shiraz (d. 982) and Maulana Rumi's father, the noted theologian Baha'uddin Walad (d. 1231).[124]

Some of the most important traditions concerning Muhammad's private life are reported on the authority of ʿA'isha, who was still a child playing with dolls when she became betrothed to her father's friend. It is ʿA'isha who stresses the modesty and bashfulness, *ḥayā'*, of the Prophet, a quality that the believer is expected to possess in large measure. ʿA'isha is the authority of numerous *ḥadīth*.[125] It was she who heard Muhammad say, "My eyes are asleep but my heart is awake,"[126] and thus learned that the Prophet was spiritually awake even during the times that he shared her bed and seemed to slumber, because he never lost the spiritual connection with his Lord. And sometimes he would tenderly call her: *Kallimīnī yā Ḥumairā*, "Talk to me, you little reddish girl!"[127]

Muhammad was human enough to recognize the weak spots in human beings, including women. In Goethe's *West-Östlicher Divan* we find a poetical transformation of the *ḥadīth* according to which God "has created woman from a crooked rib; if her husband wants to use her let him use her as crooked because if he tries to straighten her she will break, and her breaking is divorce."[128] That does not sound like the equal rights of women's liberation, in the modern sense, but it was a great step forward from a social system in which newborn daughters had sometimes been buried alive because the parents were afraid that they would be unable to feed and rear them.

Naturally, Muslim exegetes have considered the problem of the Prophet's many marriages. Although they admit that in general women are able to distract men and divert them from God and from their preoccupation with spiritual goals, they are convinced the case is different with the Prophet: "His wives have never diverted him from God, rather, it was an increase in his piety that he kept them chaste and made them participate in his merits and his guidance. Although marriage is, for others, an affair of this world he rather sought the other world with his marriages."[129] This statement, by a medieval theologian, is echoed by a writer in the twentieth century: "The multiple marriages of the Prophet, far from pointing to his weakness towards 'the flesh,' symbolize his patriarchal nature and his function, not as a saint who withdraws from the world, but as one who sanctifies the very life of the world by living in it and accepting it with the aim of integrating it into a higher order of reality."[130]

In this connection one should not forget the high veneration shown by the Prophet to mothers. It is told that "when the Prophet was informed once that the monk Juraij did not care for his mother, who wanted to see him, Muhammad said: 'If Juraij were a learned, knowing monk he would have known that it is part of the service of God to answer one's mother's call.' "[131] Tradition also ascribed to him the beautiful saying "Paradise lies beneath the feet of the mothers."[132]

One has to beware of deriving later developments in Islamic societies, such as purdah or the veiling of women, from Muhammad's own example. He ordered only certain restrictions for his own wives, "the mothers of the faithful"; in general the Koran speaks merely of a required decent covering for women, and tradition calls for the covering of the head, not the face. The example of ʿA'isha shows that women in early Islamic days participated actively in social life and communal affairs. In advanced age, long after the Prophet's death, she herself even went out into the battlefield.

As much as the Islamic ascetics derogated women as dangerous, deceptive, and unintelligent creatures,[133] they could not completely blacken the feminine image, for the Koran repeatedly speaks of the pious and faithful men and women, *al-muʾminūn waʾl-muʾmināt*, and of the Muslim women, *al-muslimāt*, who have the same religious duties as men and will receive equal recompense for their performance. The Prophet's love for his wives and his daughters, especially Fatima, itself excluded any completely negative judgment. Indeed one of the most frequently repeated sayings of Muhammad states: "God has made dear to me from your world women and fragrance, and the joy of my eyes is in prayer." The great medieval mystical theologian Ibn ʿArabi made this saying the center of an extended meditation designed to evoke sublime thoughts about the mysteries of the Prophet of Islam.[134] Astonishing as it sounds to a non-Muslim, this *ḥadīth* allows us a glimpse into the twofold function of the Prophet, who knew how to combine this world and the next and, if we follow the Islamic interpretation, how to sanctify both.

Another aspect of the Prophet's biography that may appear repellent to Western tastes and is correspondingly difficult to assess correctly is his blending of religion and politics, of *dīn wa daula*. The normal pattern according to which the non-Muslim judges Muhammad, namely that he was "prophet and statesman," usually implies that while he began as a sincere religious seeker, after his migration to Medina he became an unscrupulous politician and the cunning leader of a fast-growing armed community. The Muslim, understandably, sees this development from a completely different angle: the message of Christ, with its emphasis on otherworldliness and withdrawal, seems incomplete and, despite its admirable traits, defective; surely a successful prophet should also use worldly means to propagate the message that God entrusted to him. What seems to the non-Muslim a contradiction, that is, Muhammad's role as prophet *and* statesman, is according to the Muslim's conviction the very proof of Muhammad's unique role as God's messenger, evidencing his greatness and the truth of his message. How could it happen that God, who sent him, should not grant him ultimate success and inspire him to guide his community well?

The battle of Badr, in which "not you cast when you cast, but God cast" (Sura 8:17), had given the Muslims who had migrated to Medina for the first time the feeling that the heavenly hosts were with them, supporting them in their struggle, and even the skirmishes of later years, the fights and negotiations that led to the reconquest of Mecca after a comparatively short span of time, were interpreted by them as signs of Divine succor. The irresistible spread of Islam over the Arabian Peninsula during the Prophet's lifetime and, even more, the incredibly fast expansion of Islamic rule in the first century after Muhammad's death left no room for doubt: this victorious religion was indeed *the* true religion, and he who had preached it was the true Prophet of God. Who but such a person could have brought the final and all-comprehensive revelation? He was clearly sent not only to the Arabs but to "the Red and the Black," that is, to all peoples and races.

Even in early times the proof of the truth of Muhammad's message was derived from the success of Islam. This argument has been used even more pointedly in modern times. If a Western observer, brought up in the liberal tradition of post-Enlightenment thought, claims that religion and politics (in the widest sense of the word) should be separated and that religion is a personal, interiorized, and exclusively private affair, a matter of the heart alone, the traditional Muslim will explain to him that, rather, religion and state belong together like the two sides of a coin. If Muhammad—as it was said at some point in Islamic history—is the axis around which the *Heilsgeschichte* of the human race is revolving, then the political and social aspects of life too belong to that process. Muhammad's political acumen, his battle for social improvement in Mecca and even more in Medina, his "constitution" of Medina, which is praised today as a model of modern democratic institutions, and his activities in the economic sector—all these appeal to the modern Muslim as examples by which he too should shape his life and that of his community. There is no room in Islam for the dualism of a good spiritual realm and an evil material sphere: this world too has been created by God, and He has made it subservient to man. That is one reason why orthodox Muslims have often turned against certain mystical currents that have reviled this world in favor of the other world and urged the abandonment of worldly activities for the hope of eternal beatitude: "The spirituality of Islam of which the Prophet is the prototype is not the rejection of the world but the transcending of it through its integration into a Centre and the establishment of a harmony upon which the quest of the Absolute is based."[135] The kingdom of God, which Muhammad announced, was also of this world. Therefore the mystic who, completely submerged in the vision of God, wants to stay forever in the realm of spirit without returning hither to the material sphere, has been frequently contrasted in Islamic thought with the Prophet, who returned to this world after his ineffable dialogue with God, in order to ameliorate the world and to implement the fruits of his inspiration for the betterment of society.

Part of the picture is the *jihād*, the so-called Holy War, which is interpreted as a war against infidelity for the sake of bringing near all-embracing peace, the Pax Islamica.

> The Prophet embodies to an eminent degree this perfection of combative virtue. If one thinks of the Buddha as sitting in a state of contemplation under the Bo-tree, the Prophet can be imagined as a rider sitting on a steed with the sword of justice and discrimination in his hand and galloping at full speed, yet ready to come to an immediate halt before the mountain of Truth. . . . His rest and repose was in the heart of the holy war itself and he represents this aspect of spirituality in which peace comes not in passivity but in true activity. Peace belongs to one who is inwardly at peace with the Will of Heaven and outwardly at war with the forces of disruption and disequilibrium.[136]

It is in this deeper sense of *jihād* that the Prophet declared, in a famous *ḥadīth*, that "the greatest *jihād* is that against the *nafs*, the base instincts,"[137] those instincts and evil qualities that should be subdued and transformed into something positive. Muhammad thus embodies the quality that has been termed (by Nathan Söderblom) the "Prophetic No," the distinctive feature of prophetic religiosity, as contrasted with the all-inclusive "mystical No."[138]

Differences in the interpretation of the Prophet's sociopolitical activities can easily arise among the Muslims. The material at our disposal is many-sided and often contradictory, and the very history of early Islam poses numerous problems to the faithful as to how to implement the Prophet's ideals. Herein lies one reason for the difficulties that modern nations face when they attempt to create a truly "Islamic" state based on the teachings of the Koran and the Prophetic *sunna*.

One should not forget that some aspects of the Prophet's political career have provided the Muslims with a special terminology. His Hegira, for example, became the model of the *hijra* of pious men and women who left their countries in search of a home under Islamic rule. One such *hijra* occurred after the extension of British rule in India, and those who left India for Pakistan in the wake of partition are called, like the Prophet's Companions who settled with him in Medina, the *muhājirūn*, a word that gives their emigration a distinctly religious flavor.

In war and peace, at home and in the world, in the religious sphere as in every phase of working and acting, the Prophet is the ideal model of moral perfection. Whatever he did remains exemplary for his followers. Thus his prayers have become formulas that the Muslims, hoping for Divine response, repeat constantly. Koranic sentences of which he was particularly fond are also very dear to the Muslims, who try to use them in the same manner as did the Prophet. For instance, when going to bed, one should remember what ʿA'isha told: "When [the Prophet] went to bed he would put his two hands together and recite *al-Ikhlāṣ* (Sura 112) and the *muʿawwidhatān* (Suras 113–14), then blow into his hands and pass them over as much of his body as he could reach, beginning with his head and face and the nearer parts. And this he would do three times. To copy him in this is approved."[139] This *ḥadīth* is only one instance of many model prayer usages of the Prophet. Every standard work of Islamic religious education contains chapters with numerous useful formulas and prayers, first used by the Prophet, that are still very much alive in the community of the faithful.

In these prayers, the Messenger's humility and trust in God is especially evident. He always appears aware of his own need for forgiveness: "I ask forgiveness from God seventy [sometimes, one hundred] times a day."[140] Even though such an expression seems to contradict the long-standing doctrine of his prophetic *ʿiṣma*, that is, freedom from sins and defects, it is usually interpreted as his effort, whatever his own excellence, to provide an example for his sinful community so that they might pray in awareness of their human weakness. Here his role as teacher of his followers comes to the fore. He is, after all, quoted as saying: "I have come to perfect the noble habits."

The ethical norms that are handed down from him breathe the same spirit as those taught by all great religious leaders. Asked "What is virtue?" he answered: "Ask your heart for a *fatwā* [legal decision]. Virtue is when the soul feels peace and the heart feels peace, and sin is what creates restlessness in the soul and rumbles in the bosom."[141] And when asked "What is the best Islam?" he replied: "The best Islam is that you feed the hungry and spread peace among people you know and those you do not know."

The imitation of the noble actions and thoughts that Muhammad, the "beautiful model," had taught his community by his personal example was meant to form each and every Muslim, as it were, into a likeness of the Messenger. This is so that each, like him, should give witness of God's unity through his or her whole being and existence. Therefore, as it is said in the *Dalā'il al-khairāt*, the pious Muslim should pray: "I ask Thee, O our Lord, to employ us in his [Muhammad's] usages, to cause us to die in his community, to number us in his band, under his banner, and to make us his companions, to supply us from his reservoir, to give us to drink from his cup, and to give us the boon of his love."[142]

It is this ideal of the *imitatio Muhammadi* that has provided Muslims from Morocco to Indonesia with such a uniformity of action: wherever one may be, one knows how to behave when entering a house, which formulas of greeting to employ, what to avoid in good company, how to eat, and how to travel. For centuries Muslim children have been brought up in these ways, and only recently has this traditional world broken down under the onslaught of the modern technological culture. Awareness of the danger that now confronts Islamic tradition has certainly contributed to the sudden growth of Muslim fundamentalism that came as such a surprise to the unprepared Western world.

But one must keep one thing in mind: it would be unthinkable that such a tradition could have developed if Muhammad had not been blessed by an unusual charisma. As Johann Fück aptly says, "Still today we see in true Muslim piety a reflection of that *Gotteserlebnis* [experience of the divine] which forced—1,300 years ago—Muhammad son of 'Abdallah to come forward and to preach of God and the Last Judgment."[143] And we certainly agree with Tor Andrae, who in 1917 wrote in his study of the role of the Prophet in Muslim doctrine and piety: "We have all reason to believe that Muhammad indeed knew the art of winning hearts to a rare degree."[144]

THREE

MUHAMMAD'S UNIQUE POSITION

One important chapter in Islamic prophetology concerns the *ʿiṣma* of the Prophet. This term means basically "protection or freedom (from moral depravity)" and connotes virtually automatically not only perfect moral integrity but even impeccability. For, as Islam teaches, God protects His prophets from sin and error lest His Divine word be polluted by any external stain upon its human bearer.[1]

To understand the concept of *ʿiṣma* correctly one has to recall the character of Islamic prophetology in general. The Koran states in Sura 10:48 that every people has been sent a messenger; further, in Sura 14:8 it is said that God did not send any messenger who did not speak the language of the people who were entrusted to him. The Muslim holds that God never left Himself without a witness in history, and beginning with Adam, the first man and first prophet, Divine messengers have continued to instruct mankind about God's will until God finally addressed Muhammad as *Yā ayyuhā'n-nabī*, "O you prophet!" (Sura 33:1), and destined him to be the *khātam al-anbiyā'*, the Seal of the Prophets. However, the *nabī*, "prophet," is not charged with proclaiming a new law in the world; this is the duty of the *rasūl*, or "messenger"; and while the number of *anbiyā'* (plural of *nabī*) is unknown, that of the legislator prophets can be defined more exactly.[2] According to a widespread tradition, Muhammad himself mentioned 124,000 prophets and 313 messengers.[3] The Koran contains the names of twenty-eight of them, but nothing has hindered the Muslim in acknowledging as well prophets who are not mentioned by name in the Koran but might perhaps have appeared before Muhammad in China or South America to teach the people of that area the ways of God and His laws.

Among the great messengers five are usually singled out to form the category of the *ūlū'l-ʿazm*, "those with firm resolution" (Sura 46:34): Muhammad, Abraham (the father of the three "Abrahamic religions," Juda-

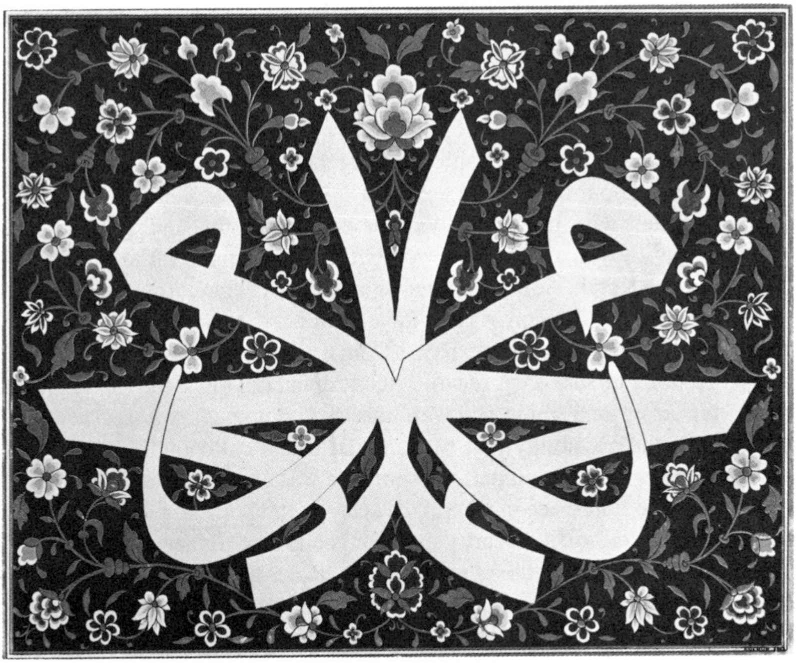

Twofold Muhammad, Turkey, eighteenth century, from a design in the Türk-Islam Eserleri Müzesi, Istanbul

ism, Christianity, and Islam), Moses, Jesus, and Noah. Abraham occupies the highest rank after Muhammad, and theologians have discussed for some time the problem whether Muhammad is a *khalīl Allāh*, a "close friend of God," as the Koran defines Abraham, or whether he is, as the Sufis love to claim, rather the *ḥabīb Allāh*, "God's beloved friend." In later times his position as *ḥabīb Allāh* has been generally accepted in Muslim piety, while *khalīl Allāh* is used exclusively for Abraham, as is *kalīm Allāh*, "the one to whom God spoke," for Moses.[4] In fact, from Muhammad's role as *ḥabīb Allāh* one could derive the conclusion (as Ibn ʿArabi and his followers did) that Islam is "the religion of Love," for "the station of perfect love is appropriated to Muhammad beyond any other prophet."[5]

The theological manuals exactly define the qualities of a prophet. Thus one reads in the *Sanūsiyya*, a widely used handbook of dogmatics from the later Middle Ages: "The prophet has four necessary attributes: he must be truthful (*ṣidq*) and trustworthy (*amāna*); he has definitely to proclaim the Divine Word (*tablīgh*) and has to be sagacious and intelligent (*fatāna*). It is impossible that he should lie (*kidhb*), be faithless or treacherous (*khiyāna*), should conceal the Divine message (*katmān*), or be stupid (*balāda*). One possible trait is that he may be subject to accidental human weaknesses."[6] The doctrine of the *ʿiṣma*, "being protected from error and sin," must be seen in connection with such definitions. Qadi ʿIyad writes of the prophets in general that "they have been protected by God and have been taken care of by free choice and acquisition." That holds obviously a fortiori for Muhammad, The Prophet par excellence.[7]

In the oldest days no official doctrine concerning the sinlessness of the Prophet was known, and there are conflicting trends in the earliest interpretations of the Koran. Some commentators would declare him free from all moral defects; but this leaves open the question, what was his status before he was called to be a prophet, nay, *the* final prophet? There is the embarrassing remark in Sura 93:7, in which the Prophet is addressed: "Did He not find you erring and guide you?" Some early commentators see here an allusion to the possibility that Muhammad in his childhood followed the religion of his Meccan compatriots before he was guided to the true worship of the One God; in this connection the story of the "opening of the breast" and the cleansing of his heart gains its special importance when used to signal his call to prophethood (see below, chapter 4).[8]

But simultaneously the commentators increasingly strove to prove that Muhammad had always avoided the idolatrous practices of the Meccans. Even as a young boy he is said to have refused to participate in the games of his companions, and there was nothing he hated more than the Meccan idols. Abu Nuʿaim's *Dalāʾil* mentions a number of instances in which the young Muhammad was protected from sinful pursuits, or even minor defects in his boyhood.[9] Zamakhshari clearly states in his commentary on Sura 93: "If one claims that Muhammad had lived for forty years exactly like his companions, and that he was lacking, like them, in those sciences that one can learn by instruction, that is fair. But if one intends to say that he lived according to the religion and infidelity of his tribal companions—God forbid!"[10]

The often discussed tradition according to which Satan once urged Muhammad to accept the three major Meccan goddesses Al-Lat, Al-ʿUzza, and Manat as *gharānīq* (evidently meaning they were mediators in some sense between man and God), slowly fell into oblivion. As mentioned earlier, in numerous *ḥadīth* Muhammad is seen praying for forgiveness, and these traditions are bound up with the question of his sinlessness:

> The Apostle of God used to say when he stood up for the prayers: "Thou art my Lord, I Thy servant. I have wronged myself and I confess my sin. Forgive me then all my sins, for there is none that forgiveth sins save thee!"[11]

Such prayers, which could be taken as proof of Muhammad's very human feeling of weakness and sinfulness, were later regarded as intended to instruct the believers, who thus would receive a paradigm for their own prayers of contrition. For as the Spanish Arabic theologian Ibn Hazm said in the eleventh century: "If disobedience were possible in the prophets it would be permitted to us all as well since we have been asked to imitate their actions, and thus we would not know whether our faith were all error and infidelity and perhaps everything that the Prophet did, disobedience."[12] This argument has remained valid to our day; indeed, the absolute obedience owed to the Prophet is meaningful only if Muhammad was free from any faults and could thus constitute an immaculate model even for the most insignificant details of life.

Some remarks, for instance that the light of Muhammad shone brightly through his body, can in a certain way be interpreted as pointing to the materialization of his luminous spiritual qualities: there was nothing grossly material about him, so that sin could stain him. Here, as in the whole development of the doctrine of the impeccability of the Prophet, Shiite influences have certainly played a role, for the *ʿiṣma* of the imams was always maintained, and elaborated in detail, by the Shiite scholars; there could be no question that the imams' great ancestor, the Prophet, had to be exempt from sin and error and to be the pure bearer of the Divine light.

Certain religious groups, again, considered it possible that a prophet could commit sins, even grave ones, for did not the Koran mention some sinful or at least faulty acts by earlier prophets? Other early exegetes regarded at least minor sins as possible in a messenger of God. Thus, the outstanding historian and commentator on the Koran, at-Tabari (d. 923) interprets the beginning of Sura 48 in the following manner:

> "Verily We have given you an apparent victory [as a sign] that God forgives you your previous and later sins. . . ." God informs His prophet that the great victory that He has given him and the grace that He has completed, should awaken his gratitude and spur him to ask forgiveness, and by this request God will grant him the forgiveness of those sins which he had committed before the victory and after the victory. . . . For otherwise the order to ask for forgiveness, which is also given in later passages of the Koran, would be meaningless, and so would be his pious exercises of this kind.[13]

Tabari was evidently convinced that the Divine mercy that the Prophet experienced led to an intensification of gratitude that resulted in his increasing approximation to God. This viewpoint appears frequently in the doctrine of the mystics, with the difference that this wholesome gratitude is not only a distinctive attribute of the Prophet alone but rather a spiritual duty of every believer.

Some interpreters, particularly in the early Muʿtazilite school, thought that the Prophet could commit sins out of negligence, but that even the smallest inadvertence of a prophet weighs more heavily than the sin of another human being, and his foibles are therefore more severely blamed. In later Muʿtazilite teaching, however, it is maintained that the Prophet cannot sin at all, either from negligence or from obliviousness. The ethical teachings of this school, which are based on stern moralism and the postulate of God's absolute justice, could not admit that the Prophet could have sinned in any possible manner: the principle of the "most useful," which is applied by God to everything on earth, requires that the proclaimer of His message be perfectly free from blemish and moral stain.

A different viewpoint was defended by the early Ashʿarite school. Their greatest theologian, al-Baqillani, held that the *ʿiṣma* of the prophets means mainly that they are Divinely protected from intentionally lying when proclaiming their message, and from "major abomination and gross, deadly sins," as Baqillani's theological adversary, Qadi ʿIyad, writes with palpable dismay.[14] To appreciate Baqillani's position one has to remember that he is well known for having given the Koran the central position in his theological thought. It is the Divine Word, the pivot of Muslim life, that matters; the one who proclaimed it is of lesser importance. Of course, says Baqillani, the Prophet too has given certain rules that must be followed, but these concern only the sayings he uttered, as it were, *ex cathedra* about religious problems, not every minute detail of his life and behavior as related in *ḥadīth*.[15] Baqillani's view is rather similar to that of some modernist theologians (like Sir Sayyid Ahmad Khan and his collaborators) who have wanted to restrict the Muslims' duty to imitate the Prophet's example only to religious matters.

But in general the doctrine of the absolute sinlessness of the Prophet prevailed. As Qadi ʿIyad writes: "Thus we cling to the opinion, which is supported by the consensus of the faithful, that a wrong pronouncement in the proclamation of the Divine revelation and while informing [his listeners] about his Lord—be it willingly or unwillingly, in good cheer or in wrath, in health or in illness—is not possible in his [Muhammad's] case."[16] And if the Prophet did err in a worldly matter, as for instance in his remark about the fertilization of palm trees, he was able to correct such a mistake.

The Sufis certainly had a most important share in the development of the doctrine of the Prophet's absolute freedom from sin. The "overcloudings of the heart" that are mentioned in a well-known *ḥadīth* have been interpreted by the mystics as pertaining to the Prophet's continuous traveling through ever new veils of light on his way to God. They explain these "overcloudings" as the changing spiritual states that the wayfarer experiences while drawing closer and closer to God.[17] But the Sufis found also another Prophetic tradition that offered them, again, a model for their own spiritual education in the *imitatio Muhammadi*. When the Prophet was asked once about the *shaiṭān*, the base faculties and carnal appetites of man, he answered at the end of the discussion: *Aslama shaiṭānī*, "my *shaiṭān* has handed himself over to me completely [or, has become a Muslim], and does only what I order him."[18] That means, the perfected man has tamed his instincts and passions in such a way that he uses them in the end exclusively for positive, godly works, obeying the will of God in every moment of his life in thought and action. This is for the Sufis the secret of the "greater Holy War," namely, the constant struggle with one's negative tendencies and lowly passions, which should not be obliterated but rather overcome and transformed into positive values. The Prophet's saying about his "defeated *shaiṭān*" points to a very important psychological truth, and it became therefore not only an example for the mystics but also for some of the modernists: Iqbal has placed it at the center of his thoughts about the relation between man and the "satanic" powers. The Prophet is, in this case, seen not as completely sinless by nature but as having been transformed by constant spiritual growth in the grace of God.

It is this constant growing toward Divine proximity that constitutes for Maulana Rumi the true proof of Muhammad's superiority over others. When Shams-i Tabrizi asked why Bayezid Bistami, who exclaimed, *Subḥānī*, "Glory be to me!" was not greater than Muhammad, who confessed to God that "we do not know You as we ought to," Maulana answered that Bayezid had stopped at a station where he considered himself filled with God, whereas the Prophet "saw every day more and went farther" into the Divine proximity, and was aware that no one could ever fathom God's greatness.[19]

But if one asks how Satan could at all approach the Prophet—for the *ḥadīth* states that "Satan flies from the shadow of ʿUmar" (ibn al-Khattab, the second caliph)—Maulana Rumi again has an answer: "Muhammad was an ocean, and ʿUmar a cup. One does not protect the ocean from a dog's saliva, for an ocean is not polluted by a dog's mouth, but a cup is; for a small vessel's contents are changed to the worse from the licking of a dog." Thus, whatever seemingly "impure" matter touches the Prophet can never change the purity of his ocean-like personality.[20]

Muhammad's position as the final prophet, the Seal of all those who preceded him, leads the Muslim quite naturally to discuss also how he relates to the previous messengers. The Koran had warned the Muslims: "We do not distinguish between the prophets!" (Suras 2:130, 3:84). There exists also one *ḥadīth* that prohibits *tafḍīl*, "preference," that is, preferring Muhammad to another God-sent messenger: "Do not place me above Yunus ibn Matta, and do not make any comparisons or preferences among the prophets, and do not prefer me to Moses."[21] But at almost the same time other *ḥadīth* were circulated that seem to express the Prophet's self-consciousness and explain his superiority above the others by his willingness and capacity to intercede for his community:

> I am the messenger of God, without boasting. I shall bear the banner of praise on the Day of Resurrection. I am the first to intercede and the first whose intercession will be granted. I am the first to move the knocker at the gate of Paradise. God will open it for me and will lead me into it, and with me the poor among the faithful. Thus I am the most honored one among the leaders of the earlier and the later [generations].[22]

Najmuddin Razi Daya gives the tradition in a somewhat different form:

> The Prophet, upon whom be peace and blessings, said: "I have been granted excellence over the other prophets in six things: the earth has been made a mosque for me, with its soil declared pure; booty has been made lawful for me; I have been given victory through the inspiring of awe at the distance of a month's journey; I have been given permission to intercede; I have been sent to all mankind; and the prophets have been sealed with me."[23]

But Razi has an even more beautiful explanation for Muhammad's activity in the world: "From the age of Adam to the time of Jesus, each of the prophets kneaded the dough of religion in a different fashion, but it was to Muhammad, upon whom be peace, that the glowing oven full of the fire of love belonged." In this "oven of love" the "bread of religion" was baked for twenty-three years; "then he brought it forth from the oven of love and hung over the door of his shop a proclamation saying, 'I have been sent to the Red and the Black.'" It is this bread that satiated the hungry and "became the object of delight" of those who belong to Muhammad's *umma*.[24] And yet all these prerogatives and graces did not induce the Prophet to take pride in them; he was so detached that all these wonderful qualities notwithstanding, he could say: "Poverty is my pride."

The ninth-century historian Ibn Saʿd calls Muhammad *sayyid al-mursalīn*, "the lord of the messengers," an epithet that became deeply rooted in Islam. In the fourteenth century, the Hanbalite theologian Ibn Qayyim al-Jauziyya formulated the important principle that the status of the Prophet of Islam is doubtless superior to that of Moses: Moses fainted at the manifestation of the Divine attributes in the Burning Bush, but Muhammad, during his heavenly journey, could immediately speak to God without even trembling.[25] This comparison was also a favorite with the mystics from early days (see chapter 9 below).

The poets constantly meditated how to praise Muhammad's superiority. Not all of them went so far as ʿUrfi at the Moghul court in India, who addressed the Prophet with contrived hyperbole typical of his Persian poetical style:

> Jesus is a fly, while your speech
> Is sweetmeat from the shop of creation.

ʿUrfi refers to flies again in another context: the *sabʿ mathānī*, the "seven double ones" (probably "seven Koranic verses," Sura 15:87) are "the flies of the Prophet's honey."[26] But centuries before him, Khaqani in Iran had already mentioned that the two immortal prophets Jesus and Idris will come down from their heavenly abode when they see the leftover victuals on Taha's (Muhammad's) table in order to carry them home[27]—an inverted allusion to the relation of Jesus to the miraculous table mentioned in Sura 5.

Rumi expresses similar thoughts in more poetical and attractive images:

> Jesus is the companion of Moses, Jonah that of Joseph;
> Ahmad sits alone, which means: "I am distinguished."
> Love is the ocean of inner meaning, everyone is in it like a fish;
> Ahmad is the pearl in the ocean—look, that is what I show![28]

ʿIraqi, in the thirteenth century, described the Prophet with a formulation that became commonplace in Persianate poetry:

> A pinch of his noble being
> was placed in Jesus' breath,
> And from the radiance of the candle of his countenance
> Moses' fire was lighted.[29]

Here, we are already confronted with the mystical idea that all previous prophets were nothing but partial aspects of the light of Muhammad, which became so common in the mystical trends under the influence of Ibn ʿArabi. Jami, a major protagonist of this idea, poetically sings of Muhammad's greatness compared to the other prophets: while Solomon touched the Queen of Sheba's throne with his hand, Muhammad's foot touched the apex of the Divine Throne, and Gabriel served him as the hoopoe had served Solomon. . . .[30]

This elevation of metaphor is of course also reflected in Muslim prayers. Dirini describes the Prophet as follows:

> Adam knew him and made petition through him, and he took a covenant from all the prophets to himself. He took the purity of Adam, the

> lamentation of Noah. Part of his teaching contains the knowledge of Idris. Included in his ecstatic experiences is the grief of Jacob. Within the mystery of his ecstasy is the endurance of Job. Enfolded in his bosom is the weeping of David. A part only of the riches of his soul exceeds the wealth of Solomon. He gathered into himself Abraham's friendship with God. He attained the converse of Moses, God's interlocutor, and was more exalted than the highest kings. He excels the prophets as the sun excels the moon, the ocean the drop.[31]

Muhammad's superiority over Moses and Jesus is most frequently mentioned:

> Certainly, Adam is God's special friend, Moses the one with whom God spoke,
> Jesus is even the spirit of God—but you are something different![32]

Thus an Indian Muslim poet sang some time ago. For Muhammad combines the qualities of the two great prophets whose followers are still active in the world: he does not rely exclusively on God's justice and on the law as did Moses, nor does he concentrate only on God's lovingkindness and on otherworldliness as did Jesus. His path is the sound middle path between the extremes, uniting all that is valid from the teaching of the previous prophets. Amir Mina'i in India in the late nineteenth century expressed his blessings upon the Prophet with the words

> God bless him and give him peace,
> The leader of Moses, the guide of Jesus![33]

His compatriot Ismaʿil Meeruthi wrote, at about the same time:

> The message of which God's sign through Abraham consisted
> And his good tidings through Jesus,
> That was the appearance of Ahmad.[34]

And in the piety of ordinary Muslims, who do not delve into the intricacies of legal works or deep speculations about the *ḥaqīqa muḥammadiyya*, the "archetypal Muhammad," as the mystics did, there is no question whatever that Muhammad is greater and higher than all the prophets before him. Besides, it is firmly believed, and repeated in apologetic writings over and over again, that the pre-Islamic sacred books contain numerous passages that foretell Muhammad's arrival in more or less clear terms.[35]

This sublime and unique position of the Prophet had of course to be protected against slander, contempt, and defamation. The legal scholars in Islam therefore discussed at great length the problems connected with a lack of reverence for the Prophet. Especially in the western Islamic countries the theologians had an extremely strong opinion about the respect and deference due him.[36] Theological writers like Qadi ʿIyad remarked that it is a sign of bad taste and lack of reverence to use comparisons with the Prophet in mundane panegyrics for kings and princes—as, for instance, when the notorious poet Abu Nuwas had seemingly placed "Ahmad the messenger" and Ahmad Amin, the son of the Abbasid caliph Harun ar-Rashid, on the same level in one of his encomia for the prince.[37]

This warning was certainly not always heeded by Persian poets, for in the Persian literary tradition one often finds daring allusions to the Prophet when a person by the name of Muhammad is being eulogized and when normal hyperboles seemed too weak to the poet. "Orthodox" Islam, however, regarded such an eccentric use of the name of the Prophet (which, after all, has a sanctity and blessing power of its own) as a dangerous development that could even lead to the defamation of the Prophet. And this offense was regarded by the earliest legal authorities in Islam, such as the Iraqi Abu Hanifa (d. 767) as something almost equaling apostasy. For how could one defame or slander a person whose name is mentioned close to that of God in the second half of the profession of faith? If someone should commit this sin, he has to be asked to return to Islam; if he refuses, he has to be put to death. Other authorities went even farther: the slanderer of the Prophet was declared to deserve immediate capital punishment, which could not be averted even by contrition. And indeed Islamic historians now and then report that someone was either executed legally or lynched by an enraged mob when he had been overheard slandering the Prophet.[38] It is ironic that one of the greatest theologians in Islamic history, the medieval reformist Ibn Taimiyya, was sentenced to heavy punishment because of his alleged "lack of veneration" for the Prophet when he spoke up against certain unhealthy exaggerations in the popular cult of the Prophet in Damascus, such as the veneration of his footprint.

The problem is more complicated in the case of the *ahl al-kitāb*, the religious communities who possess a revealed book and are placed under the protection of the Muslims by a special covenant, *dhimma*, and the payment of a certain tax. These include Jews, Christians, Sabians, Zoroastrians, and in India the Hindus as well. Certainly, a Christian may say that Muhammad has nothing to do with his own religion, but as soon as he pronounces an insult against the Prophet, his covenant of protection is invalidated, according to the opinion of several jurists, and he can save his life only by converting to Islam. This explains some extant accounts—especially from medieval Spain—of Christians who intentionally and openly insulted the Prophet and thus were granted martyrdom for their faith, for which they had yearned so intensely.[39]

Reports of Muhammad's own reactions to slander and insult are contradictory. Many *ḥadīth* emphasize the Prophet's mildness and generosity in such cases; others found it necessary to give a much harder picture of his reactions. An example of the latter is Ibn Taimiyya—once himself accused of lack of reverence for the Prophet!—who composed a special work with the telling title *Aṣ-ṣārim al-maslūl ʿalā shātim ar-rasūl* (The Sword Drawn against the Vilifier of the Prophet), in which he states that "whoever vilifies a prophet is to be killed and whoever vilifies his Companions is to be flogged." The latter sentence is of course directed against the Shiites, who curse the first three caliphs and other Companions. Slightly later, Ibn Taimiyya's work was followed by a similar book (with much the same title) by the Egyptian scholar Taqiuddin as-Subki.

The problem still continues to excite and annoy the Muslims, as is evident from an incident that happened in the late 1920s in India. A Hindu published a book with the upsetting title *Rangēlā Rasūl* (The Pleasure-loving Prophet). After some time he was killed by two young Muslims who could not bear such a calumny of their beloved Prophet.[40] Although they were found guilty of murder and sentenced to death, the sympathies of the large majority of Indian Muslims were with them. Some years later, in 1935, Iqbal inquired about the punishment for defamation of the Prophet in some other connection and was informed that it could indeed be punished by the death sentence.[41] And during the 1950s, in the course of a revival of Islam in Turkey, the Turkish press also published extended debates about the same problem. Everyone who has lectured in a Muslim environment knows that even a remark that may be intended perfectly innocently can be misinterpreted by the audience, who are hypersensitive when it comes to the person of their beloved Prophet.

FOUR

LEGENDS AND MIRACLES

According to tradition the Prophet himself refused the claim that he had produced or would produce any miracle to attest the truth of his message, with the one exception of the Koran, which was given to him by his Lord.[1] Najmuddin Daya Razi therefore states rightly that "the miracle of each prophet is confined to his own age; but the special property of the religion of Muhammad is that one of his miracles, namely the Koran, has survived him and will remain until the end of the world."[2] Even so, the Holy Book itself contains allusions not only to Muhammad's noble qualities and actions but also to some mysterious events in his life that point to his special status among men. It was here that the commentators, still more the popular preachers (*quṣṣāṣ*), and most of all the mystics and poets found sufficient material to develop longwinded and often fanciful legends and miracle stories that became, in the course of time, an ingredient of almost all biographies of the Prophet and inspired numerous poetical works.

Prophetic miracles are called *muʿjizāt*, "deeds that render [others] unable to match them." They are different from the miracles performed by saints, which are termed *karāmāt*, "charismata." In later times, especially in non-Arab environments, miraculous actions performed by the Prophet, his Companions, family members, and great saints also came to be known by the general term *manāqib*, "heroic deeds."

The meaning of the Prophet's mission and the related problem of the necessity of miracles were often discussed in later centuries, especially among Muslim modernists who saw the danger of too strong a reliance upon the "miraculous" aspect of prophetship and therefore tried to demythologize the Prophet's biography.[3]

Among the legends connected with Muhammad's career the Opening of the Breast became a central feature of all biographies.[4] Sura 94 begins with the Divine address to the Prophet: "Did We not open [or, expand] your breast?" This was interpreted to mean God's special cleansing of Muhammad's breast endowed the Prophet with a unique degree of purity, so that he could convey the divine message without defect. An early tradition quotes the Prophet's own words about this experience:

> While I was thus for some time with my friends, there came to me a group of three. One of them had a silver pitcher in one hand, and in the other hand a vessel of green emerald, filled with snow. They took me and hurried with me to the top of the mountain and placed me very softly on the mountain. Then he [the first of them] split my breast to the abdomen while I was looking at them, but I did not feel anything; it was not painful. Then he sank his hand into the hollow space in my abdomen, took out the intestines and washed them with that snow, cleansing them very carefully. Then he put them back. Now the second one rose and said to the first one: "Go away, you have done what God has ordered you." Then he approached me and sank his hand in the cavity of my body and pulled out my heart, split it and took out of it a black speck filled with blood, threw it away, and said: "That is Satan's part in you, O beloved of God." Then he filled it with something that he had with him and put it back in its place, then he sealed it with a seal of light, and I still feel the coolness of the seal in my veins and joints. Then the third one rose and said: "Go away, both of you, for you have done what God has ordered you." Now the third one approached me and passed with his hand from my breast bone to the pubic region. Then the angel said: "Weigh him against ten of his community." They weighed me, and I was heavier than all of them. Then he said: "Leave him, for even if you weigh him against his entire community, he would still be heavier than them." Then he took me by the hand and helped me descend carefully, and they bowed down upon me, kissed my head and between my eyes, and said: "O beloved of God, verily you will never be frightened, and if you knew what good has been prepared for you, you would be very happy." And they let me sit on this my place, and then they set off to fly away and entered the skies, and I watched them, and if you want I will show you where they have gone.[5]

In the sources, this story is told by the child Muhammad to his nurse Halima who had been worried when he had disappeared suddenly. The story presents a typical initiation rite in which the young boy is being prepared to receive divine revelation. For this reason the biographers sometimes place the event not in Muhammad's childhood but rather before his heavenly journey. In such accounts the Prophet says:

"Muhammad is the Messenger of God,"
Turkish wall painting, nineteenth century

> They came to me while I was with my family, and I was brought to the well Zamzam, and my breast was opened and washed with water from Zamzam; then I was brought a golden vessel, full of faith and wisdom, and my breast was filled with it. Then the angel rose with me heavenward.[6]

Then follows the heavenly journey and Muhammad's meeting with the former prophets (see below, chapter 9). Here again the story serves clearly as an initiatory preparation for his prophetic calling and mission, which the heavenly journey then sets in motion in this particular legend cycle.

If the Opening of the Breast is connected with the Prophet's initiation into the spiritual world, another favorite miracle of later generations is seen as proof of his truthfulness. This is the Splitting of the Moon, *shaqq al-qamar*, which is derived from the beginning of Sura 54: "The hour approached, and the moon was split."[7] Even in early traditions this sentence is explained not as an eschatological sign but rather as pertaining to a miracle performed by the Prophet in order to convince the doubting Quraish of the truth of his message: he split the moon into two halves, between which Mount Hira could be seen. To convince those who do not believe in this miracle, Qadi ʿIyad argues that

> It has not been said of any people on earth that the moon was observed that night such that it could be stated that it was *not* split. Even if this had been reported from many different places, so that one would have to exclude the possibility that all agreed upon a lie, yet, we would not accept this as proof to the contrary, for the moon is not seen in the same way by different people. . . . An eclipse is visible in one country but not in the other one; in one place it is total, in the other one only partial.[8]

Living in Ceuta, Qadi ʿIyad of course did not know the Indian tradition. He would have been delighted to learn that it is told in that part of the world that one King Shakrawati Farmad in southern India had indeed watched the Splitting of the Moon, and when he learned from reliable witnesses what had happened in Mecca on that very night, he embraced Islam. Accordingly, the first Muslim settlements in the Indian subcontinent are supposed to have resulted from this very miracle. This story must have been rather well known in southern India and was recounted there in the later Middle Ages in an Arabic text.[9] It is interesting to note that even as late as the mid-nineteenth century a miniature painted at the Rajput (Hindu) court of Kotah shows the Splitting of the Moon with all its details.[10]

Because Muhammad is equated in poetical language with the sun or the morning light, it is natural for the poets that "the sun should split the moon in two," as Sana'i expressed it in the early twelfth century,[11] and popular poetry—be it in Sindhi, Panjabi, Swahili, or other languages—has always loved to retell this miracle and to embellish it with charming details. More rationalistic thinkers had, understandably, some difficulties when it came to explaining the Splitting of the Moon, and they sometimes tried to demythologize that event and other preternatural phenomena. The Indian reformist theologian Shah Waliullah of Delhi wrote in the mid-eighteenth century that the Splitting of the Moon may have been a kind of hallucination, or was perhaps caused "by a smoke, by the swooping down of a star, a cloud, or an eclipse of the sun or the moon which might have given the impression that the moon was actually split in two."[12] However, in the Arabic poetry he wrote in honor of the Prophet, Shah Waliullah too, in unison with hundreds of pious writers, has lovingly spoken of this miracle that proves Muhammad's greatness. For the believers know that he who is completely devoted to the Prophet splits the moon with Mustafa's finger,

as Rumi sings in one of his lyrical poems.[13]

To be split by the Prophet's finger is indeed the greatest bliss the lowly moon can hope for.[14] This idea of Rumi's was elaborated in a highly complicated way by Jami, who plays, as he loves to do, with the shapes and numerical values of the Arabic letters. The full moon, resembling a circular *m* م with the numerical value 40, was split by the Prophet so that it became like two crescent shaped *n*'s ن ن, whose numerical value is 50 each—which proves that the moon has indeed increased in value thanks to this miracle![15]

The astronomer who believes in this miracle
  should laugh at his own profession as well as at sun and moon,
As everyone who has attended the school of Ahmad the *ummī*
  may ridicule knowledge and art.[16]

In this verse, Maulana Rumi combines two miraculous aspects of the Prophet: the Splitting of the Moon, which shows the futility of man's scientific approach to nature, and the fact that the Prophet was *ummī*, "illiterate." He is described by that epithet in Sura 7:157–58. The word also occurs in Suras 2:74, 3:74, and 62:2 and seems to refer there to the *umma*, or "community," that is, in this context, the Arabic community, which unlike the Christians or the Jews had not yet been blessed with a prophet before Muhammad's appearance. In that sense *ummī* would be an equivalent of the concept of "Gentile" in the biblical sense, or "ethnic."[17] But in the Islamic tradition, particularly the mystical sectors of it, this word is generally understood to mean "not knowing how to read and to write, unlettered."

Though European scholars are divided concerning whether Muhammad could read or write (even two of his wives were literate!),[18] Muslim theologians and especially mystics found in the concept of *ummī* as "illiterate" a marvelous proof for the truth of Muhammad's message and its true inspiration. For how could he, who was unable to write or to read, have knowledge of so many events of the past and the future as are noted down in the Koran? Does not this very quality of *ummī* indeed guarantee that the Koran was God's true word, His pure, untainted revelation? How should an orphan from Arabia have gained all the scientific and historical information that the believer finds on every page of the Koran? The mystics have seen in this word *ummī* an expression of the mystery of Muhammad's extremely close relationship with God: he was not only the cupbearer who offered the world the wine of Divine wisdom and guidance, but rather he was, as Rumi says, the vessel through which this wine was offered to mankind.[19] As in Christian dogmatics Mary must be a virgin so that she can immaculately bear the Divine Word to its incarnation, thus Muhammad must be *ummī* so that the "inlibration," the revelation of the Divine Word in the Book, can happen without his own intellectual activity, as an act of pure grace; for as Hallaj (d. 922) says in his comparison of the Prophet with Iblis: "He withdrew from his own power by saying: 'In thee I turn and in Thee I walk.' "[20]

Nizami poetically interpreted the term *ummī* as consisting of the *a* of Adam and the *m* of *masīḥ*, "messiah," and thus comprising all previous prophets.[21] But Jami has invented an even more ingenious pun to explain the word: the Prophet was nourished by the grace of the *Umm al-kitāb*, the Mother of the Book, the primordial prototype of the Koran; hence he was truly an *ummī*, "belonging to the mother, *umm*."[22]

Rumi, who sings in his *Mathnawī* that

> A hundred thousand books full of poetry
> Became ashamed before the *ummī*'s word,[23]

elaborated that topic in his prose work *Fīhi mā fīhi*:

> Muhammad . . . is called "unlettered" not because he was incapable of writing and learning; he is called "unlettered" because with him writing and learning and wisdom were innate, not acquired. He who inscribes characters on the face of the moon, is such a man unable to write? And what is there in all the world he does not know, seeing that all men learn from him? What then, pray, should appertain to the partial intellect that the Universal Intellect does not possess?[24]

Thus in a rather rare philosophical mood he equates, as it were, Muhammad with the Universal Intellect from which all human knowledge is derived—an idea that was developed in detail in certain mystical circles during his time.

The poets have always mentioned the quality of *ummī* when they wish to highlight the Prophet's mystical propensities:

> An orphan who never learned to read
> Washed off [the texts in all] the libraries of many lands,[25]

says the Persian poet Saʿdi in the thirteenth century, and some 350 years later, Faizi writes in Moghul India:

> With *sharīʿa* and Divine Book, a splendid light;
> With sword and with tongue, a cutting proof;
> From dust, and yet descending on the apex of the Throne,
> Illiterate, but a library in his heart.[26]

A few years after him, around 1600, Naziri goes even farther:

In the library of mystery he knew by heart the Koran on the day
When the Universal Intellect could not yet discern *a* and *b* in the alphabet.[27]

Other Indo-Persian poets play with the terminology of Islamic calligraphy:

Without knowing [the calligraphic styles of] *naskh* and *taʿlīq*,
He drew the line of abrogation (*khaṭṭ-i naskh*) over everything before him.[28]

That is, after the unlettered Prophet appeared, the earlier books of revelation such as the Torah, the Psalms, and the Gospels were no longer valid. And as in Rumi's example, the Prophet's quality of *ummī* was often combined with the miracle of the Splitting of the Moon: he who drew a line across the moon, why should he take a pen in his hand?[29]

For the mystics, Muhammad the *ummī* became the exemplar of all those who, without bookish learnedness, have been inspired solely by Divine grace, those who, in poetical parlance, do not know from the alphabet anything but the first letter, *alif*. That letter is, in mystical interpretation, the cipher of God, the One and Unique, and therefore contains "the meaning of the four sacred books" in itself. For

If perfection were in reading or writing,
Why then was the *qibla* of the universe illiterate?[30]

as Jami asks. For this reason many Sufis have claimed to be illiterate like the Prophet. *Ummī* has therefore been used, among other things, as a surname by a whole group of Turkish mystical folk poets (Ümmi Kemal and Ümmi Sinan for example), who felt that their work was inspired and did not rely upon traditional sources of learning.

This immediate knowledge of God, called in the Koran *ʿilm ladunī*, "a knowledge from Me" (Sura 18:65) enabled the Prophet to know everything in the world, even the future. Qadi ʿIyad relates, on the authority of the Prophet's companion Hudhaifa, that "once the Prophet rose and talked, and on this occasion he did not leave anything unmentioned that would happen to the Day of Judgment. Those who kept it in their memory, remember it; those who forgot it, forgot it. My companions have known it. When something happens [that he mentioned] I remember it as one remembers the face of a person when he is absent so that one recognizes him when one sees him again."[31] This idea contradicts the Koranic statement that even Muhammad could not boast of the knowledge of future events (Sura 6:50), but it shows that even in comparatively early times it was taken for granted by his admirers that his knowledge surpassed by far the limits of human acquisition. Endowed with such knowledge, Muhammad could become the alleged founder of all branches of science, and just as the Sufis trace their chain of initiation back to him, so have calligraphers and historians, scientists and physicians, discovered that he had set the example for their respective fields.

Though miracles like the Opening of the Breast or the Splitting of the Moon as well as Muhammad's role as *ummī* can be derived from the Koran, as can his heavenly journey and to a certain degree his role as intercessor at Doomsday, numerous other miracles that are ascribed to him appear to be based on motifs widespread in folklore.

In order to show that Muhammad too was able to infuse life into dead matter as Jesus did according to the Koranic report, it is told in a popular Pashto ballad that when the Prophet was asked to produce a bird from a stone, indeed a bird with feet of agate, eyes of lapis lazuli, a neck of crystal, and a golden beak appeared to attest Muhammad's veracity.[32] Though this is a type of miracle of which the Indo-Muslims were apparently particularly fond, others are more frequently mentioned. In oriental countries miracles connected with the production of rain occupy a special place in hagiography. Since the prayer for rain in a long period of drought (*istisqā*) is counted among the official prayers, it is only natural that the Prophet is mentioned as the first to utter an efficient prayer for rain.[33] Thus his are the words that should be used by the faithful when they perform this special rite. His appellation as *raḥmat*, "mercy," and the connection between *raḥmat* and "rain" in oriental languages may have helped to strengthen faith in the efficacy of using his prayer. Closely related to rainmaking is the miracle of producing water, which Muhammad caused to gush forth from between his fingers. As late as in the sixteenth century the Turkish poet Fuzuli was inspired by that event to compose a highly artistic eulogy for the Prophet, which is distinguished by the *radīf* (continuing rhyme) *ṣū*, "water." He refers to Muhammad's miracle and expresses the hope that "the water of his kindness will extinguish hellfire." Keeping the metaphor consistent, he closes his long poem in style with the request that

> The fountain of union may grant water to my eyes
> Which are thirsty for the vision [of the Prophet].[34]

Other miracles are connected with food, which is very important in a society where hospitality is regarded as one of the highest virtues.[35] Among the food miracles the oldest and best attested is probably the story of Umm Maʿbad. A group of Companions of the Prophet passed by Umm Maʿbad's tent in the desert and tried to buy some meat and dates from her, but she had absolutely nothing edible with her. Then the Prophet pointed to her only sheep, which was lying in a corner, and asked:

"Has it milk?"

She said: "It is too weak."

He asked: "Will you permit me to milk it?"

She said: "You who are dearer to me than father and mother, if I had seen any milk in it I would have milked it before."

Then the Messenger of God called the sheep and passed his hand over its udder and called to God and prayed for her and her sheep. Suddenly the sheep spraddled its legs toward him, and milk began to flow. He called for a vessel to hold the milk, and milked a plentiful quantity into it. Then he gave her to drink until she was satisfied, and he gave his companions to drink until they were full, and he drank the last. When they had quenched their thirst he milked it once more until the vessel was full, and he left it with her and took leave, and they continued their journey.

Somewhat later her husband, Abu Maʿbad, arrived, driving a few miserable-looking hungry goats whose marrow had almost dried up. When he saw the milk he was amazed and asked her: "Where have you got this milk, Umm Maʿbad? For the sheep is barren and there are no milking cattle in the house."

She said: "True, but a blessed man has passed by who was so and so."

He said: "Describe him to me, Umm Maʿbad!"

She said: "I saw a man who was very cleanly, with bright face, of fine manner. Neither did leanness disfigure him nor did baldness make him despicable; graceful and elegant; his eyes deep black, with curved eyelashes, in his voice a neighing and in his neck luminosity, in his beard thickness, with beautifully arched eyebrows. When he was silent, dignity surrounded him, and when he spoke he was towering, and radiance surrounded him. The most beautiful and radiant of men from a distance, and the sweetest and loveliest one from nearby. . . ."[36]

This legend also seems to form the basis for the descriptions of the Prophet's looks, such as one finds in the poetry of Hassan ibn Thabit. Its wording was taken over by later poets who sometimes added more details.

There are more food miracles in later traditions: a single sheep sufficed to feed a thousand people, or small quantities of food proved sufficient for a large crowd of unexpected guests. Very frequently quoted is the story of the roast lamb that a Jewish woman in Khaibar offered to the Prophet, whereupon he remarked: "This lamb's leg tells me that it is poisoned." Hence the legend eventually developed that the roasted lamb really "got up on its four legs"[37] and addressed itself to the Prophet to warn him of the danger.

In addition, animals often appear to attest the sincerity of the Prophet. Abu Nuʿaim and Baihaqi, for instance, mention in their respective *Dalāʾil an-nubuwwa* how camels and wild beasts prostrated themselves before him and how the gazelle, the wolf, and the lizard proclaimed that he was indeed the messenger sent by God.[38] Trees and stones also bear witness that Muhammad is the Messenger of God, and thus contribute to the conversion of infidels.[39] Pebbles that he held in his hand praised him,[40] of which Jami many centuries later sings:

> A little stone, smaller than a rosary's bead
> Recited in his hand with eloquent words the praise of God,
> And those eloquent ones whose hearts were black as stone,
> Were unison in silence.[41]

Even the doors and walls of a house are said to have given the "Amen" to his prayer,[42] and when he went out in scorching heat a cloud wandered with him to protect him from the sun.

It is natural that Muhammad's companions should have used his washing water as medicine, as is common in the veneration of a powerful leader, for everything that touches his body participates in his *baraka*. A similar concept underlies the cases in which the Prophet healed someone by the application of his saliva, another substance that bears strong blessing powers.[43] In later days, ʿAbdul Qadir Gilani was blessed by a vision of the Prophet's putting some of his saliva onto his tongue to enable him to preach successfully;[44] such initiatory visions are not rare among Sufis.

Not only human beings but also animals—for instance, a weak camel—were cured by the Prophet's hand, and it is this kind of miracle that has been repeated again and again in popular songs, for Bedouins and villagers appreciate such miraculous acts better than others. For this reason not all miracles enumerated in Abu Nuʿaim's and Baihaqi's works are equally popular, and other legends not found in their lists have quite often incited the imagination of theologians and, even more, of poets. The learned, American-educated Muslim editor of the Sindhi Folklore Series, Dr. N. A. Baloch, rightly reminds modernists who regard such miraculous stories as outdated leftovers from primitive societies that "it is a psychological truth that it is natural to exaggerate in the description of the beloved because [such an exaggeration] comes from the heart."[45] Nothing is wonderful and beautiful enough to give an adequate impression of the personality of the beloved Prophet, and thus the legends and verses that have grown up around the rather simple life story of Muhammad are true reflections of people's deep and sincere love for him. Ahmad al-ʿArusi, a Spanish-Arabic poet of the late Middle Ages, offers a model of the innumerable invocations addressed to the Prophet when he sings in a long poem:

Is it not you who has been sent as mercy to mankind?
Is it not you whom the pebbles praised
And whom the lizard in the desert addressed, and the wolf too?
Is it not you for whom the full moon in the sky was split?[46]

One story in particular has been a favorite with the poets and has been repeated with deep affection through the ages: the tale of the *ḥannāna*, the sighing palm trunk. Muhammad used to put his hand on a palm trunk while preaching, but when finally a pulpit was erected for him, the palm trunk became superfluous.[47] Full of grief and longing, the piece of wood sighed heavily because it longed for the touch of the Prophet's hand—and the Prophet, taking pity on it, had it brought into his presence to console it. On this cue, Rumi asks:

Should we then be lower than the sighing palm trunk?"[48]

If even a soulless piece of wood feels longing for the Prophet, how much more should a person endowed with heart and intellect long for him whose virtues and elevated rank he can understand!

The folk poets were also fond of the story of a gazelle that had been caught by a cruel huntsman.[49] (According to some traditions, the culprit was the son of Muhammad's archenemy, Abu Jahl.)[50] As the Prophet passed by, he found the animal weeping because her two kids in the desert were dying from thirst. This has been a wonderful topic for popular singers, who like to describe the plight of the poor creature in dramatic or touching verse. Thus one of the thirteen Sindhi poets who have elaborated this story tells in simple rhymes:

Her call was heard by the Prince—
    Ahmad came close to her.
He said: "Why do you call for help—
    What happened to you, O gazelle?"
She said: "Lord, I have left hungry
    my two kids in the desert.
Help me, poor me, please,
    be my bailsman, O Ahmad!
I'll go, I'll come back very soon,
    Just give them a little milk!"
The excellent lord, with his noble hands
    opened quickly the snare,
And the gazelle ran swiftly away
    to where her kids were waiting.
Then came the stupid hunter back
    and asked the Messenger:

"Look, I have done this cruelty
because I've fun in hunting—
Why did you tear apart the snare?
Why did you send off the gazelle?
Who are you, where do you come from,
and what is your name? Tell me that!
Either you'll produce the gazelle,
or give an answer to me!"
The Messenger rose before the man,
the lord of patience full:
"Muhammad Amin, the faithful, I'm called—
That is my proper name.
The gazelle promised me to return
and to offer herself to you,
But I am in any case for you
her bailsman here in her place,
And when the gazelle does not return
I shall be her substitute . . ."

In the meantime the gazelle has reached her kids, who inquire what has happened. She tells them that the Prophet has made himself her bondsman; then she asks them to accompany her. All of them fall down and kiss his feet; the hunter, confronted with this miracle, immediately embraces Islam.[51] The faithful gazelle is then set free to return to her native hills along with her kids. In a later version of the same legend, the theologically well-trained animal even says to the Prophet, alluding to Sura 108, *Al-Kauthar*:

For you the Kauthar flows,
in my teats the milk flows too.
Let mankind drink the Kauthar,
I would like to give [my kids] a drink of milk![52]

In another tale, an eagle that snatches the Prophet's slipper does so because a poisonous snake is hidden in it; to protect him he carries the slipper to the desert mountains, where he drops the venomous animal.[53] In much the same way, Abu Huraira's cat saves the Prophet from a snake that takes advantage of his kindness and tries to strangle him. The kerchief with which Muhammad has wiped his face does not get burnt when it is cast in the fire, for it is impregnated with the light of prophethood, which is stronger than fire.[54] Did not Hellfire itself address the true believer who follows the Prophet with the words "Your light has extinguished my fire"?

Even the greatest classical poets in the Arabic and Persianate tradition, like Busiri in his *Hamziyya* and Jami in his lyrical and his epic verse, describe in lively words all the miracles of the Prophet, because of the firm popular conviction that these stories carry in themselves a *baraka*, a blessing power, that extends to both the teller and the listener.[55] Thus a Sindhi poet promises endless recompense on the Day of Resurrection to everyone who recites his poem about the Miracle with the Snake in the night before a Friday.[56] South Indian poets have made similar promises when reciting poetical legends or encomia.

The faithful believe that by composing or listening to such traditional legends one is able to establish a very personal relationship with the Prophet. They are certain that though buried in Medina, he yet lives in God's presence and is able to be present everywhere, especially in places where his name is lovingly mentioned, as in the *dhikr*-meetings of dervish orders when blessings upon him are recited (the Tijaniyya order has made this almost part of the fundamental belief; see chapter 5), or during the recitation of a *maulid* that tells the miracles connected with his birth.[57]

Blessings for the Prophet and the loving repetition of legends connected with him may also grant the faithful Muslim the greatest boon one can hope for in this life, the vision of the Prophet in a dream. Such dreams play an extraordinary role in Islamic piety to this day.[58] They are always true, for Satan can never assume the Prophet's form. These dreams console the faithful; they can bring healing in cases of illness or melancholia. To dream of the Prophet might be an initiatory experience for the Sufi, or it might help someone to solve a theological problem. A medieval Sufi, Ibn Khafif of Shiraz, when he learned that the Prophet had performed the ritual prayer on tiptoe because his foot had been wounded in the battle of Uhud, tried to imitate him without success; he was then instructed by Muhammad in a dream that this kind of prayer was reserved for the Prophet alone and that the average believer was not bound to imitate this special style.[59] In Sufi lore, the Prophet appears to chastise theologians who have no faith in a certain mystic,[60] or to honor a Sufi leader.[61] Maulana Rumi's friend and successor, Husamuddin Chelebi, even saw him holding Rumi's *Mathnawī* in his hands, reading it and boasting of the presence of such a saint among his community.[62] This the Prophet also did, according to another source, with Al-Ghazzali.[63] Sometimes practical problems were solved by his appearance in dreams. One early mystic, on the point of starvation, went to the Prophet's tomb, claimed to be his guest, and in a dream was given bread, half of which he ate; the other half he found on his mat upon awakening in the morning.[64] Even *ḥadīth* could be transmitted through apparitions of the Prophet in dreams; but these *ḥadīth* were, as Shah Waliullah clarified, valid only for the dreaming person, not for others. Some Sufis recommended a special prayer, Jami's poem with the rhyme-word *Muḥammad*, for inducing a vision of the Prophet.[65] But it seems that impostors sometimes took advantage of pious people's firm belief in such apparitions, using alleged visions in which the Prophet recommended them to do this or that, or to teach the community certain formulas of prayer or blessing. We find Hamadhani dealing satirically with this topic in his *Maqāmāt* by the early eleventh century,[66] and some Sufis saw in their friends' boasting of such visions "imaginings on which the infants of the Path are nurtured."[67]

A lovely story told by as-Suyuti about an earlier mystic shows well what the dream apparition of the Prophet means for the pious, loving Muslim:

> One night I fulfilled the number of blessings of the Prophet and I fell asleep. I was dwelling in a room and, lo, the Prophet had come to me in through the door, and the whole room was lighted up by him. Then he moved towards me and said: "Give me the mouth that has blessed me so often that I may kiss it." And my modesty would not let him kiss my mouth; so I turned away my face, and he kissed my cheek. Then I woke trembling from my sleep and my wife who was by my side awoke, and lo, the house was odorous of musk from the scent of him, and the scent of musk from his kiss remained on my cheek about eight days. My wife noticed the scent every day.[68]

In another instance, a Turkish calligrapher was told in a dream by the Prophet to spend the rest of his life in writing the *Dalā'il al-Khairāt*,[69] a book whose contents—prayers for the Prophet—lead us to another aspect of Muhammad's miraculous activities and the Muslims' reaction to it: that is, his intercession for his community and the Muslims' calling down of blessings upon him.

FIVE

MUHAMMAD THE INTERCESSOR, AND THE BLESSINGS UPON HIM

The title of a book published some years ago, *Muhammad: A Mercy to All the Nations*, expresses very well the Prophet's position in theology and faith.[1] The traditions that highlight the Prophet's mildness and kindness could always rely on the Koranic statement that Muhammad was sent "as a Mercy for the worlds" (Sura 21:107). "He was clothed," as Najm Razi says, "in the cloak-of-honor of the Attribute of Mercy. Then, as mercy endowed with form, he was sent down to creation."[2] The believer can therefore trust him without reservation; he knows that the Prophet can quicken dead hearts and protect those who love him.[3]

Oriental poets have found a wonderful image to describe this special quality of the Prophet: that of the "cloud of mercy" or "rain of mercy." In Anatolia and the eastern countries of Islam rain is still called, in rural areas, *raḥmat*, "mercy," because in arid zones the fertility of the land and a good harvest, as well as the well-being of the cattle, entirely depend upon the right amount of rainfall. It was therefore a logical development that the merciful Prophet was symbolized as a beneficent rain cloud that sails over all lands and revives with its showers the unfeeling hearts, which are similar to dried-up fields. Jami has praised this cloud of mercy which, pouring down its rain from the "sphere of generosity" saturates the thirsty lovers,[4] and the Indo-Muslim poet Ghalib called his didactic poem in honor of the Prophet *Abr-i gauharbār* (The Jewel-carrying Cloud). One can easily draw a parallel here with the Buddha, who is described in the *Saddharma Pundarika* as the great merciful rain cloud. The image of rain for an act of Divine grace was in fact common all over the East,[5] and can be observed in the Sufi tradition first in the writings of an-Nuri around 900.[6] An Urdu poet, Rasikh, went so far as to compare the coarse black rug on which the Prophet used to sleep, to the dark cloud of mercy.[7] Long before him Rumi sang about this cloud, which manifests Divine grace:

O you Mercy for the worlds! Out of the ocean of certitude
Do you grant pearls to the dustborn, peace to the fishes![8]

Perhaps the most beautiful description of the cloud of mercy is found in "Sur Sārang," one of the chapters in the *Risālō* of the Sindhi poet Shah ʿAbdul Latif (d. 1752). He tells in realistic images of the approaching clouds and of the longing of humankind, animals, and plants for their arrival, and he describes poetically the life-giving downpour of the rain. In the final lyrical song of the chapter he suddenly turns to the praise of the "cloud of mercy," that is, the Prophet:

Today there is a north wind, and
    the cuckoo does complain.
The farmer takes his plough out,
    the herdsman does rejoice:
Today my friend has donned
    the garment of the clouds.

Today there is a north wind, and
    the clouds: black like his hair,
Red garments like my bridegroom—
    each flash of lightning wears!
Thus brings the rainy air
    My friend from far away.

For the clouds have come from the Rauda, the mausoleum of the Prophet, and it is from there that the lightning turns toward the thirsty desert of Sind.

O cloud—please show kindness
    to the thirsty, for God's sake!
Collect water in the ponds,
    O, make the grain cheap,
    Make fertile the land,
That happy be the farmer!

They all think of the rain clouds,
    gazelle, man, buffalo,
Wild ducks await the cloud, and
    the frog complains.
The oyster in the ocean
    looks out for it all day—

O, fill the water tanks,
That happy be the farmer!

The clouds come in rows,
the lightning begins to flash
The blissful cloud
fills the dried-up riverbeds.

The clouds come in rows,
the lightning begins to flash—
The lightning made me happy
in the black clouds,
The rain's gentle drizzling
washes the dust of grief from the hearts.

My prince will protect me—therefore I trust in God
The beloved will prostrate, will lament and cry—
therefore I trust in God.
Muhammad, the pure and innocent, will intercede there for his people . . .
When the trumpet sounds, the eyes all will be opened . . .
The pious will gather, and Muhammad, full of glory . . .
Will proceed for every soul to the gate of the Benefactor . . .
And the Lord will honor him, and forgive us all our sins—
therefore I trust in God!

Another canto of the same "Sur Sārang" ends with an even more poetical description of the cloud of grace, which is said to extend from Istanbul to Delhi and Jaisalmer; the poet implores it to pour special blessings upon his country, the province of Sind.[9]

But in the poem Shah Latif leads his listeners from the merciful character of the Prophet to another important—perhaps even more central—aspect of prophetology as it developed from early days: Muhammad's role as intercessor for his community, which ultimately is the concomitant of his mercifulness. To be sure, it is difficult to derive this role directly from the Koran.[10] In the Throne verse (Sura 2:256) it is stated that no one can intercede with God "except with His permission"; but one could interpret this to mean that the Prophet was granted this special permission, for Sura 17:79 speaks of his "praiseworthy rank," which might point to his power to intercede for his community. Again, Sura 40:7 mentions that those (the angels) who carry the Divine Throne and surround it ask constantly for forgiveness for the faithful.

There is also belief in other possible intercessors. One very commonly held idea is that the Koran itself will appear at Doomsday as an intercessor for those who have studied it lovingly and devotedly. This hope is often expressed in certain prayers that are uttered after one completes a recitation or reading (*khatm*) of the Holy Book; these are sometimes found, especially in manuscript copies, at the end of the text. Furthermore, the pious works of the faithful, or the profession of faith that they have repeated again and again, may also intercede for them at Doomsday. Martyrs, too, can act as intercessors for certain persons, just as children who have died in infancy are believed to intercede on behalf of their parents. But these are only peripheral possibilities; intercession, *shafāʿa*, in its fullness is the prerogative of the Prophet of Islam alone. He is the *shafīʿ*, as one of his epithets states, and thus Muslim boys, especially in India, are often called Muhammad Shafiʿ, or even Shafaʿat.

The idea of intercession by the Prophet began early in Islam. Some verses by Muhammad's eulogist Hassan ibn Thabit contain allusions to the Muslims' hope for his intercession.[11] But it is mainly the story concerning the Day of Judgment, as found in various redactions in the oldest collections of *ḥadīth*, that has supplied believers with the basis for their hope in Muhammad's very special role on that day of horrors.[12] On the Day of Judgment, so the tradition has it, God gathers all mankind on a hill. The sun draws closer to them and they are overwhelmed by fear and grief. Finally they agree to seek someone who could intercede with God on their behalf. They come to Adam and say:

> "You are the father of mankind. You have been created by God's own hand and He has breathed into you from His spirit. He has made the angels prostrate themselves before you. Intercede for us with your Lord! You see how worried we are!"
>
> But Adam replies: "Today my Lord is angry as he was never before and will never be again. He had prohibited me [to eat from] the tree, and I have disobeyed him—*nafsī, nafsī*: I myself, I myself, [have to fear]."

They then proceed to ask each and every prophet, but each remembers one act of disobedience or sin, with the exception of Jesus. But even he says: "I myself, I myself!" They then come to Muhammad and say: "O Muhammad, you are the Messenger of God, the Seal of the Prophets! God has forgiven you your previous and later sins—intercede for us with your Lord!" And Muhammad consents:

> Thus I shall go and come before the Throne. He reveals Himself to me and inspires in me such a glorification and praise as He has never inspired in anyone before that.

> Then He says: "O Muhammad, lift your head, ask, and you will be given; intercede, and you will be granted [what you ask]!"
>
> I lift my head and say: "O Lord, *ummatī, ummatī*: my community, my community!"[13]
>
> And God says: "O Muhammad, lead into Paradise those from your community who need not undergo reckoning, through the right gate. But in what is beyond that they shall be equal to those that enter through the other gates."

This *ḥadīth* and its variations have been a source of consolation for Muslims ever since, although it has been debated at times exactly for whom the Prophet would intercede. His own answer in *ḥadīth* is clear: "My intercession is for those from my community who have committed grave sins."[14] And how few may have felt completely free from grave sins!

In a strange anecdote, Maulana Rumi refers to this tradition and tells his listeners that the reason for the execution of the great mystic Hallaj was that he exclaimed: "If I could get hold of Muhammad I would have taken him to task!" For he minded that the Prophet restricted his intercession to the believers and did not intercede for everyone on earth. The Prophet, of course, defended himself against Hallaj's complaint in a vision, and the mystic had to suffer for his preposterous remark.[15]

To be sure, the theological school of the Muʿtazilites in the ninth century did not agree with the growing emphasis on Muhammad's role as intercessor, which they felt contradicted one of the two central principles of the cosmic order, namely God's absolute justice. But on the whole the belief in his intercession became pivotal in Muslim religious life. This belief reflects the conviction that Divine mercy manifests itself in and through the Prophet; his intercession is in a certain way a result of his position as "Mercy for the worlds." Abu ʿAbdallah at-Tirmidhi in his *Nawādir al-uṣūl* remarks aptly that other prophets had been sent to their communities as an *ʿaṭiyya*, that is, a gift of mercy that the Lord sends his servants when He sees them weak, meek, and helpless. Muhammad, however, is more than that: he is a *hadiyya*, a gift of love, which the Lord gives His servants to honor them and to win their hearts. The first kind of gift puts its recipient under an obligation; the second one gratifies him.[16]

The importance of the sublime rank of Muhammad is also indicated in that the Muslims, in some of their prayers, have implored God specifically to confirm this high position of the Prophet and make him the truly accepted intercessor. Thus it is said:

> O God, I ask Thee by his position with Thee, and his confidence in Thee, and his yearning for Thee, to appoint him a Mediator to whom

> is given the task of intercession for me and for my parents and for all who believe in Thee.[17]

One of the most widely used handbooks of blessings for the Prophet, the *Dalā'il al-khairāt* by the Moroccan Sufi al-Jazuli, mentions the following prayer formula:

> O God, appoint our lord Muhammad as the most trusted of speakers and the most prevailing of requesters and the first of intercessors, and the most favoured of those whose intercession is acceptable, and cause him to intercede acceptably for his nation and his people, with an intercession in which the first and the last are included![18]

The most striking aspect of the early tradition concerning the *shafāʿa* is not that a single individual is selected to become the recipient of a special grace, but rather that Muhammad's intercession embraces his entire community. One tradition expresses this conviction with words that have been repeated frequently:

> God wrote a script a thousand years before the creation of the world. Then He put it on His Throne and exclaimed: "O community of Muhammad, look, My mercy precedes My wrath. I give you before you ask, and forgive you before you ask my forgiveness. Everyone of you who meets Me and says: 'There is no deity save God, and Muhammad is the messenger of God'—I shall lead him to Paradise!"[19]

Like other basic facts and early narratives about the Prophet, the tradition concerning the intercession was elaborated as time passed. One of its most important ingredients is the idea, again expressed in a *ḥadīth*, that Muhammad will carry the Flag of Praise, *liwā' al-ḥamd*. Later poets love to mention this banner, under which the faithful will gather to be protected from the horrors of Doomsday, and it has also been said that all the previous prophets are under Muhammad's banner.[20] (One thinks here of Goethe's description of the prophetic message, in which he says that the prophet tries to gather people around him "as around a banner"—an intuitive grasping of the Islamic idea of the *liwā' al-ḥamd*.)[21]

The Muslims have never ceased inventing moving words and touching sentences to implore the Prophet not to withhold his intercession from them:

> Thou are the Intercessor whose mediation is hoped for on the narrow path when footsteps slide.
> Then be my Intercessor when I am in the tomb, and have become Thy guest, for a guest is respected![22]

Learned scholars and ecstatic mystics, popular minstrels and cunning statesmen, have uttered countless verses to express their hope of Muhammad's intercession, sometimes using artistic rhymes and other times simple words like sighs, or recalling the traditional oriental hospitality (as does the prayer quoted just above). They claim to be the guest of the Seal of the Prophets, hoping for a sip from his blissful fountain, the *Kauthar*.[23] It is understandable that some standard formulas occur wherever such verses were written, and one may find a certain monotony in these constant repetitions of sighs and cries. Yet few branches of Islamic religious poetry are so warm, so sincere, and often so touching as the verses in which the Prophet, the best of all creatures, is asked for his mediation at the terrible moment when every soul has to meet the Eternal Judge, or those that express the poet's gratitude that he is a member of the *umma marḥūma*, the community to which mercy has been granted.[24] It is trust in Muhammad's intercession that makes death easy for the believer:

> My wish is this, that when I die
> I still may smile,
> And while I go, Muhammad's name
> be on my tongue,

sings Shakil Badayuni, an Indian Muslim poet of our day.[25]

In this connection theologians have frequently discussed the problem whether it is permitted to address the Prophet with *Yā rasūl Allāh*, "O Messenger of God!" or *Yā ḥabīb Allah*, "O beloved of God!" or similar personal addresses that imply that he is indeed alive, *ḥāżir u nāẓir*, "present and watching," as it is said. Though stern traditionists reject this kind of address, a large number of theologians have permitted it, and the *fatwā* given in South Africa in 1982 about this question offers numerous examples from classical and postclassical sources in which the authors, whose piety is undoubted, address the Prophet in the second person singular. Not only are the poets from the Middle Ages (among them Maulana Rumi in his *Naʿt-i sharīf*) cited but also numerous theologians of the school of Deoband.[26] And indeed, there are few poems in which the Prophet is either blessed or implored for help and intercession, in which this very personal form of address is not used: it evokes the feeling that he is close to those who love him.

There is scarcely any author, be he poet or scholar, "heretic (*bidʿatī*), drug-addict (*bhāngī*), or wine-bibber,"[27] who has not entreated the Prophet's intercession and, to use Jami's poetical term, did not "sow the seed of blessing for the Prophet in the soil of asking for forgiveness."[28] Some of them, who felt particularly close to the Prophet, went rather far in their requests, as when Ahmad at-Tijani made the supplication "I beg the favor of our master, the Messenger of God, that he guarantee me admission to Paradise without being brought to any account or undergoing any punishment," extending this wish also to his whole family, his ancestors, and his followers.[29] But on the whole, the heart of the request is to obtain forgiveness of sins. The great North African philosopher of history, Ibn Khaldun, asks the Prophet:

> Grant me by your intercession, for which I hope,
> A beautiful page instead of my ugly sins![30]

Writing a century before him, the mystic ʿAfifuddin at-Tilimsani, suspected by the orthodox Muslims for his extreme, "pantheistic" utterances, desperately calls to the Prophet in a long poem:

> I have sins, abundant—but perhaps
> Your intercession may save me from Hellfire . . .

and closes his cry for mercy with:

> I have called you, hoping for an act of grace from you—
> God forbid, God forbid, that you would be called and would not answer![31]

Shah ʿAbdul Latif in Sind begins his poetical *Risālō* with the statement:

> When those who say "He is God alone without companions"
> Venerate Muhammad the intercessor out of love in their hearts,
> Then no one is doomed
> To [reach] a bad landing place.[32]

Slightly later the greatest lyrical poet of Urdu, Mir Taqi Mir (d. 1810), sings at the beginning of his second *Dīwān*:

> Why do you worry, O Mir, thinking of your black book?
> The person of the Seal of the Prophets is a guarantee for your salvation![33]

And a poet of our day in the mountains of Chitral (Pakistan) likewise closes his encomium for the Prophet in his native tongue, Khowar, with the line

> This sinner awaits your intercession![34]

Rulers in the Islamic world, who were anything but paragons of piety, also turned to the Prophet in their verses. Among them is the Mamluk Sultan Qaitbay of Egypt (d. 1496), who sings in a very simple Turkish strophic poem:

This is God's beloved,
The physician for all pains—
Look, this noble, one, unique,
In the midst of the field of intercession![35]

In the *dhikr* meetings of certain dervish orders the request for intercession is sometimes used as a litany, as among the North African beggar order of the Heddawa, who constantly repeat the exclamation "O Mulay Muhammad, pray for us!"[36] The numerous refrains of popular poetry that express the poets' hope for the Prophet's intercession may have developed from this custom. In Turkish religious poetry, this device has been used frequently from the days of Yunus Emre (d. ca. 1321), whose verses were primarily sung in the meetings of dervishes. Likewise, the repeated line in poems in Sindhi, Panjabi, or Urdu, which is usually sung in chorus in a distinct rhythm, often contains the same call:

The worlds long for you—
Muhammad, intercede for us![37]

It also occurs in other poetical forms, such as the *musaddas*, a six-line stanza in which the last line of each stanza may contain a call for mercy. A good example from the regional tradition is a *musaddas* in Panjabi with the telling title "The Pain-filled Search for Refuge of the People of God [*Allāhwālūn*] in the Presence of the Leader of Creatures, the Pride of Existent Things, Ahmad Mujtaba Muhammad Mustafa," in which the repeated line says:

O Hazrat, in the two worlds I have no one but you![38]

Sometimes popular poets of later times go slightly too far in their descriptions of the gracious Prophet: the Balochi poet Hammal Faqir Laghari (d. 1872), a devotee of the branch of the Naqshbandi order centered in Lunwari Sharif in Sind, has enumerated in his Sindhi eulogy for the Prophet no fewer than 141 places in which the Prophet's power is at work; these extend from Ingrez (England) to Kathiawar, from Sibi in Upper Sind to Lucknow, from Poona to Kanaan, and all these names are connected by puns and the constant use of alliteration, each rhyming stanza capped with a repeated plea for the mercy of the Prophet. For example:

Your drum is there in Turan,
Persians, Arabs, and Iran,
Mecca, Misir [Egypt], and Multan—
    Mustafa, be kind to me!

Clouds are raining on Bulghar,
Ghazna, Ganja, and Girnar,
Masqat, Mambay [Bombay], Malabar—
    Mustafa, be kind to me!

In Babal, Bukhara, and Balkh,
In Khiwa, Khorasan, and Khalkh
You are obeyed by ant and *malkh* [locust]—
    Mustafa, be kind to me!

And at the end of the poem, which comprises 81 stanzas of this kind, the Prophet is finally asked once more to intercede on behalf of the poet at the Day of Judgment.[39]

In India even Hindus took up the custom of imploring the Prophet for his intercession. Thus sings, in the early twentieth century, the Sindhi folk poet, Sufi Bhai Asuram:

Save me from unbelief's darkness,
Help me, O Prophet of God!
You are the luminous light,
Friend, sweetest, of the Most High,
No second or third is like you—
    Be merciful, Prophet of God . . .[40]

His contemporary and coreligionist, the noted Urdu poet Kaifi, exclaims triumphantly:

My protector, he whom I praise, is the intercessor for the peoples of the world—
O Kaifi, why should I be afraid of the Day of Reckoning?[41]

The faithful imagine time and again how they will look for shelter under the protective banner of the Prophet on the Day of Judgment:

In the place of resurrection at Doomsday
    Muhammad arrives with his green banner.
The pious tell each other the good tidings:
    Muhammad arrives with his green banner![42]

And they know what will happen then:

"Oh my dear community, my community!"
    thus cries Muhammad.[43]

The same feeling that is expressed in these lines by the medieval Turkish poet Yunus Emre is shared by Muslims in Africa. In religious poetry in Swahili the Prophet appears above all as the intercessor under whose banner the believers will triumphantly enter Paradise,[44] and this faith in Muhammad's *shafāʿa* and protection, as manifested in his "green banner of praise" helps them to keep their hopes up.

The recitation or composition of verses that radiate hope and trust has a talismanic power of its own. When Ghani of Thatta, in the Indus Valley around 1700, composed the Persian lines

> Here is my hand and the pure hem of Muhammad—
> Here is my eye and the collyrium of the dust of Muhammad,

the poem was "accepted extremely well by the tongues of old and young and served as a means for those who wanted to achieve their goals."[45] In other words, the reader felt that simply by reciting this verse, he had as it were already grasped the protective hem of the Prophet's robe and used the dust of his blessed feet as a healing salve for his eyes. Examples of this kind of poetry are frequently found, as for instance in a popular Pashto ballad that has the refrain

> On the day of Resurrection, O Prophet,
> My hand [is on] your skirt![46]

Poets even expressed the hope that their eulogies might serve as a kind of mediator between them, sinful creatures, and the Prophet, who can "wash off the author's sins with the water of the cloud of kindness."[47] Muhsin Kakorawi, the greatest panegyrist of the Prophet in modern Urdu, even has the angel Gabriel recite the poem he has written, closing it with these daring lines:

> In the rows of Resurrection your panegyrist will be with you,
> In his hand this enthusiastic *ghazal*, this *qaṣīda*,
> And Gabriel will say with a hint: "Now, In the name of God:
> 'From the direction of Benares went a cloud toward Mathura . . .' "

The poet hopes that this poem, which is indeed unusually impressive thanks to his skillful use of two different stylistic levels, will move the Prophet to administer special kindness to his servant who has praised him so eloquently.[48] Is not the poem praising the Prophet "a flag of forgiveness, a candle on one's tomb?"[49]

But besides writing beautiful poems and prayers or litanies, the pious have sought various other ways to ensure that their sins will be forgiven, and have sometimes resorted to charms inspired, as they believe, by the Prophet himself. Among these is the Seal of Prophethood, about which the caliph Abu Bakr allegedly said: "Whosoever puts it in his shroud or his grave will never experience the pain of the grave, and God will forgive all his sins, great and small, and will fill his grave with light."[50]

يا رحيم	يا رحمن	يا الله
يا قيوم	يا حى	يا كريم
يا ديان	يا منان	يا حنان
يا برهان	يا سلطان	يا سبحان

The so-called Seal of Prophethood, as given in the Jawāhir al-auliyā

Though thousands of prayers and poems speak of the Muslims' hope of Muhammad's intercession for themselves and their families,[51] there is one means to this end that is much more powerful than anything else: to implore God to bless Muhammad and his family. The Koran itself says (Sura 33:56) that God and His angels "pray upon," that is, bless the Prophet. Could the believer do anything better than follow the example given by the Lord Himself? In fact, Rumi explains that "these acts of service and worship and attention do not come from us and we are not free to perform them. . . . They belong to God; they are not ours, but His."[52] The blessing formula *ṣallā Allāhu ʿalaihi wa sallam*, "God bless him and give him peace," known as the *taṣliya, aṣ-ṣalāt ʿalā Muḥammad* or (in the plural) *ṣalawāt sharīfa*, has been used from earliest times, and the pious Muslim will never mention the Prophet's name or refer to him without adding those words. In print, they are either stated in full or abbreviated with a siglum over or after the name: صلى الله عليه وسلم ; in English, often (Ṣ). A very old variant of this blessing formula, "O God, bless Muhammad and his family as You have blessed Abraham and his family," connects the Prophet of Islam with the venerated prophet who erected the Kaʿba in Mecca and who is, through Ishmael, the ancestor of the Arabs. Related formulas have been used frequently through the centuries in more or less elaborate wording.[53]

Numerous *ḥadīth* remind the Muslims of the importance of this blessing, for God Himself, as it is reported, once addressed the Prophet with the words, "Do you approve, O Muhammad, that nobody from your community utters the formula of blessing for you [even] once but I bless him ten times, and nobody from your community greets you [even] once but I greet him ten times?"[54] This Divine promise was later expressed in more detailed form: for every blessing upon the Prophet, man is elevated by ten degrees, and ten good actions are credited to him, and so on in steady progression. The Prophet himself said, as the *ḥadīth* has it, "Whosoever utters the blessing for me, he is blessed by the angels as often as he utters the blessing, be it often or rarely."[55]

It is therefore not surprising that the *taṣliya* has been accorded since earliest times a fixed position in ritual prayer. One should also utter it at certain other times, for instance while the call to prayer is recited (the earliest attested mention of this custom is from the year 710). A *ḥadīth* admonishes the faithful to bless the Prophet often on Friday, "for your greetings are put before me that day."[56] The blessing has also been regarded as a necessary condition for the granting of a prayer of petition: "The personal supplication (*duʿā*) remains outside [the heavens] until the praying person utters the blessings upon the Prophet."[57] Or, as the Sufi Ibn ʿAta (d. 922) says: "Prayer has supports, wings, means for being granted, and special times. . . . The means for being granted are the blessings for the Prophet."[58]

In the beginning, the *ṣalāt ʿalā Muḥammad* was probably considered to be a kind of prayer intended to add to the Prophet's glory, but as time passed it was increasingly regarded as praise that the Prophet, alive near God, could enjoy. The attendant problem, that is, where the Prophet would have to be in order to really enjoy the blessings, has been discussed in detail. According to some traditions, the prophets are all alive in their graves (the Prophet can thus answer from the Rauda to the greetings of his visitors); according to others, at least Muhammad lives close to God, and Ibn ʿAsakir states that if Muhammad can reply to the *salām* from his grave, he can do the same from everywhere. But however the prophets' life after death is imagined, there seems no doubt possible that they are, in a mysterious way, alive in their tombs, nourished by Divine signs of grace.[59] How could the Prophet of Islam not be alive, argues Ibn Hazm, since one says "Muhammad *is* the messenger of God" and not "has been the messenger of God"?[60]

This firm belief in the living presence of the Prophet, whose ubiquity was felt with increasing strength by the believers, led to ever more beautiful embellishments of the formula of blessing. One finds at the beginning of literary works after the long, poetically elaborated formula "In the name of God," blessings for the Prophet that are written in equally artistic verse, full of sublime eulogies. These became so developed as to form a special genre in Persian, Turkish, and Urdu epic poetry.

Theologians have occasionally discussed the problem whether the blessing upon the Prophet might be superfluous, because he is already perfect and perfected in every conceivable manner, so that even the blessing of the faithful cannot add anything more to his honor. The reply to this would be, "There is no perfection, but there is a greater one existing with God."[61] These are the words of Shah Waliullah, the Indian reformist theologian of the eighteenth century, rebuking those who considered the *taṣliya* unnecessary. In so doing, he felt, and most likely reflected the opinion of the majority of believers, that the blessing for the Prophet was still possible, even necessary. To defend his view he quoted from Busiri's *Burda*:

> Verily the Prophet's greatness has no limit,
> so that anyone who speaks with his mouth could express it.[62]

Ultimately most Muslims would probably agree with Rumi, who saw in the *ṣalawāt* a means to draw closer to the beloved Prophet.[63] As a folk poet in the Indus Valley sings:

> Your *dhikr* [remembrance] is essential for the peace of the soul—
> Lord, the *ṣalawāt* for you cure grief and pain.[64]

Thus in the mystical fraternities and the popular piety that developed under their influence, as well as in high poetry, the *ṣalawāt-i sharīfa* or, as they say in Indo-Pakistan, *durūd-i sharīf* became an important ingredient of the *dhikr* and is still repeated hundreds and thousands of times by the faithful, who often sing it to beautiful tunes. The Shadhiliyya order, for example, uses in the *dhikr* the well-known *ṣalawāt al-mashīshiyya*, a prayer that goes back to the medieval Moroccan saint Ibn Mashish; these blessings are recited every day after the morning and the sunset prayers. Such litanies are regarded as extremely efficacious in many orders and are therefore widely used.

In poetry the blessing formula occurs frequently, again—as with the prayer for intercession—mainly as a refrain, so that poem acquires to a certain extent the character of a true litany. The wording of the *durūd* varies according to the exigencies of meter and rhyme. A typical example is the Arabic refrain of an Urdu poem by the pioneer of Indo-Muslim historiography, Maulana Shibli Nuʿmani (d. 1914):

> Bless, O Lord, the best Prophet and messenger!
> Bless, O Lord, the noblest among djinn and men![65]

Innumerable formulas from the Koran and *ḥadīth* have been collected and elaborated in the course of the centuries in order to recite these blessings in increasingly artistic and at the same time memorable forms.[66] Pious collectors often mention the future recompense for reciting this or that formula at a certain moment, or a specific number of times. Among the many handbooks that contain such prayers and invocations the *Dalāʾil al-*

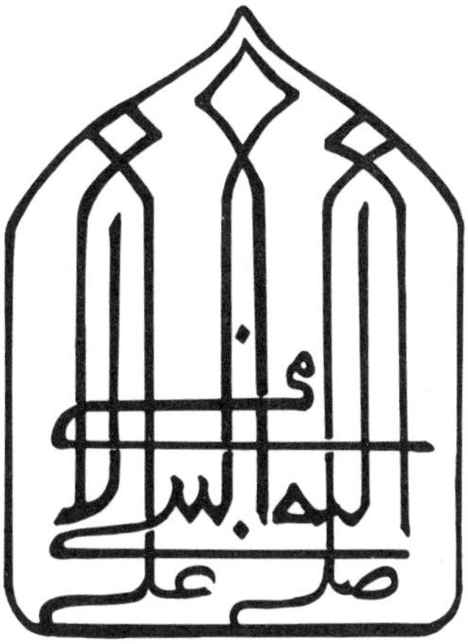

"May God bless the unlettered Prophet,"
tughrā *calligraphy by the author*

khairāt by al-Jazuli has been a favorite of the devout from the fifteenth century onward and is still being used by millions, from its Moroccan homeland to Malaysia and Indonesia.[67] It invokes blessings over the Prophet in highly poetical language whose beauty is unfortunately lost even in the best translation. In it, Muhammad is described, inter alia, as

> The man of the stalwart staff
> The man who wore sandals
> The man of argument
> The man of sound reason
> The man of power
> The wearer of the turban
> The hero of the Night Ascent . . .
> He of whom the gazelles sought intercession in articulate speech
> He to whom the lizard spoke at an open conference of the most learned

The devoted evangelist
The brilliant lamp . . .
He who was pure and yet purified
The light of lights . . .
The spreading dawn
The brilliant star
The trusty handle
The monitor of the people of the earth[68]

There was even a sort of brotherhood in Marrakesh, called Ashab ad-dala'il, whose essential function was the recitation of this celebrated collection of prayers. The *Dalā'il* commonly functions as a sort of talisman and is often carefully calligraphed or preserved in silver or embroidered leather cases.[69]

In other formulas, God is asked to bless the hero of faith, who bears innumerable beautiful names and surnames, and who deserves blessings

> to the number of the rolling clouds and the sweeping winds, from the Day when Thou didst create the world to the Resurrection Day . . . to the number of drops that rain from Thy heavens on Thy earth, and that will rain till the Resurrection Day . . . to the number of breezes of the wind and the movement of trees and leaves and field crops, and all that Thou hast created in desert or cultivated land, from the day of Creation till the Resurrection.[70]

Constance E. Padwick, who has collected these invocations with great care, is right in maintaining that "the *taṣliya* has become an essential, sometimes it would seem, *the* essential of the life of salvation and devotion,"[71] and her fine analysis of this type of piety is doubtless the best introduction to the loving veneration of the Prophet Muhammad.

"If a man brings on the Day of Resurrection as many good works as those of all people in the world and does not bring with them the calling down of blessing on the Prophet, his good works are returned to him, unacceptable."[72] Thus says ʿUthman al-Mirghani, the founder of a Sufi brotherhood noted for its extreme veneration of the Prophet, and in one of his poems he sings:

May God the Most high bless—ala ah Ahmad!
The elected, chosen Prophet—ala ah Ahmad!
We constantly yearn for you—ala ah Ahmad!
We fly from joy toward you—ala ah Ahmad!
We lead our camels to you—ala ah Ahmad!
We wail in longing for you—ala ah Ahmad! . . .[73]

"Muhammad is the Messenger of God—may God bless him and give him peace!"
by the Turkish calligrapher Nasih Efendi, 1852

But there are much earlier stories that show that the *taṣliya* was considered central for man's salvation. In one tale recounted in the fifteenth century,

> One of the saints saw in his sleep a hideous form, and he said, "Who art thou?"
> It answered, "I am thy misdeeds!"
> He said, "And how can I be delivered from thee?"
> It said, "By much calling down of blessing on the Prophet!"[74]

The Muslims have trusted that even though their sins might be as manifold as the foam on the ocean, they will be forgiven by virtue of this blessing. And if one has repeated the *ṣalawāt* often enough, the grave will become wide and spacious, a garden of serenity, and the scales at Doomsday will be heavy in one's favor. But even more important is the belief that the formula of blessing can bring the believer closer to the Prophet and can also help him to see the beloved Muhammad in his dream. That is why many authors finish their works with blessings on or greetings to the Prophet:

> I have finished it in a blessed hour—
> Thousands of greetings to the Prophet Muhammad![75]

says Ghawwasi, the author of the Dakhni epic *Saiful Mulūk* in seventeenth-century Golconda, to mention only one typical example. And the *taṣliya* can also be used for practical purposes, for instance, to avert the evil eye, even "when looking in the mirror."[76]

Handbooks that teach such formulas of blessing still appear frequently; recently some of them have begun to be published in transcription in Roman letters, or with an English translation of the Arabic text for those who have not yet learned Arabic (as often with recent converts) or have grown up in an environment with a different language and script (as in India).[77]

The formula of blessing had definitely become an integral part of the daily ritual by about 1200, but probably much earlier. The great saint Abu Hafs ʿUmar as-Suhrawardi (d. 1234) provides a good example of this constant use of the *taṣliya* in his *ʿAwārif al-maʿārif* (The Gifts of Spiritual Perceptions), a book on religious etiquette (as one may describe it) that was widely studied wherever mystically inclined pious Muslims were found. In the following passage, the author instructs the novice in the correct performance of the ablution for lesser impurity before the ritual prayer:

> During the ritual ablution one begins with the toothbrush, then one turns toward Mecca and begins with the ablution, starting with "In the name of God the Merciful, the Compassionate" and saying: "O Lord, I seek refuge with Thee from the instigations of the devils, and I seek refuge with Thee from their visitations." While washing his hands, the believer says: "God, I ask Thee for happiness and blessing and I seek refuge with Thee from misfortune and disaster." While rinsing his mouth he says: "My God, bless Muhammad and help me to recite Thy book and to remember Thee often." While taking the water into the nostrils one says: "O my God, bless Muhammad and let me experience the fragrance of Paradise while Thou art content

> with me." While blowing out the water one says: "My God, bless Muhammad! I take refuge with Thee from the stench of Hellfire and the evil abode." While washing one's face one says: "My God, bless Muhammad and make my face white on the day on which the faces of Thy friends become white, and do not blacken my face on the day when the faces of Thy enemies turn black." While washing his right hand and lower arm: "My God, bless Muhammad and give me my book in my right hand and reckon with me with an easy reckoning." While washing his left hand and lower arm: "My God, I take refuge with Thee from [the possibility] that Thou givest me my book into my left hand or from behind." While passing the hand over the head: "My God, bless Muhammad and cover me with Thy mercy, send down something from Thy blessing and protect me under the shade of Thy Throne on the day when there is no shade but the shade of Thy Throne." While rinsing the ears one says: "My God, bless Muhammad and make me one of those who listen to the word and follow the best of it. My God, let me hear the call of the herald of Paradise along with the pure." While washing one's neck one says: "My God, save my neck from Hellfire. I take refuge with Thee from chains and fetters." While washing the right foot one says: "My God, bless Muhammad and make firm my foot on the Sirat-bridge along with the feet of the faithful." While washing the left foot one says: "My God, bless Muhammad! I take refuge with Thee from [the possibility] that my foot slide on the Sirat-bridge on the day when the feet of the hypocrites slide."[78]

Here one sees that almost every movement during the ablution is introduced by a blessing over the Prophet; the same holds true for the other ritual acts that have to be performed throughout the day and the year.

ʿUmar as-Suhrawardi was the organizer of one of the most successful Sufi orders, the Suhrawardiyya, and the *taṣliya* has indeed become a distinctive feature of some Sufi fraternities. It is told that Maulana Rumi, when whirling around in ecstatic dance (*samāʿ*), sometimes uttered the blessing formula in the rhythm of the music.[79] Of certain Sufis in the Sudan it is said that "this blessing isolates them from everything worldly, be it good or evil, because it is a prayer out of love for the Prophet for his own sake, not out of hope for his intercession or fear lest he withhold it—nay, purely out of love for him."[80] That is certainly an important aspect of the *taṣliya*, but it cannot be denied that even in Sufi orders a more "magical" quality of the *ṣalawāt sharīfa* was well known. In some North African circles one attends *ṣalawāt* meetings in which one indulges in congregational prayers for the Prophet and hopes that a request made in such a meeting will soon be granted. Among the formulas used there, one finds the so-called Cordovan Prayer of Consolation, which should be recited 4,444 times in one session in order to obtain one's wish "as fast as fire." It goes like this:

> O God, bless with a perfect blessing our lord Muhammad by whom difficulties are solved, sorrows consoled, affairs completed, through whom the longed-for object is obtained and from whose noble countenance the clouds ask for rain, and [bless] his family and his companions.[81]

Members of the contemporary Hamidiyya Shadhiliyya order may pray for the Prophet Muhammad for two hours each night.[82] But even more remarkable are the prayers of the Tijaniyya order, whose founder, Ahmad at-Tijani, claimed that he had been instructed in these litanies by the Prophet himself. A brief prayer, the *ṣalāt al-fātiḥ*, was held in particular esteem:

> O God, bless our master Muhammad, who opened what had been closed, and who is the seal of what had gone before; he who makes the Truth victorious by the Truth, the guide to Thy straight path, and bless his household as is the due of his immense position and grandeur!

Short as it is, the prayer is considered to have

> merits of eight categories . . . : He who reads it once is guaranteed the bliss of the two abodes; also reciting it once atones for all sins and is equivalent to six thousand times all prayers of glorification to God, all *dhikr* and *duʿā*, long or short, which have occurred in the universe. He who recites it ten times acquires recompense greater than that due to a *walī* [saint] who lived ten thousand years but did not say it. Saying it once is equivalent to the prayers of all angels, human beings, and djinn from the beginning of their creation to the time when it was uttered, and saying it a second time is like it [i.e., equivalent to the recompense of the first] plus the recompense of the first and the second, and so on.[83]

Even more exalted is the *Jauharat al-kamāl*, which the Prophet himself taught to Tijani, and which he and the four first caliphs of Islam will attend when it is recited seven times.[84] Tijani saw nothing unusual in his close constant relationship with the Prophet, for the latter's death "meant merely that he was no longer visible to all human beings, although he retained the appearance which he had before his death and became ubiquitous; and he appeared in dream or daylight to those whom he especially favored."[85]

Orthodox Muslims, however, rebutted the claim of Ahmad at-Tijani and his followers, for if the Prophet in person had taught him certain special formulas it would mean that Muhammad had "died without completely delivering his prophetic message, and [to believe] this is an act of infidelity, *kufr*."[86]

Though such exaggerated claims of Sufi leaders about their familiarity with the Prophet have always been viewed with mistrust in more orthodox circles, the Sufi poets spread the glad tidings of Muhammad's kindness and of the necessity of *durūd* for him over the whole Muslim world. For example, the singers in the Indian subcontinent, the *qawwāl*s, often take up the theme of the blessing for the Prophet in their songs. Then the listeners' ardor is aroused; they recite or murmur the words together with the singer, or hum the soft, rhythmical melodies full of delight, placing the right hand on their heart as a sign of veneration.

> O heart, call blessings on him with blackened eye—
> On the Day of Resurrection he will be your helper in the terror![87]

This is the beginning of a popular Arabic epic poem in honor of the Prophet. Even in the puppet theater the *taṣliya* is not lacking, irreligious as the contents of the piece may be.[88]

The medieval Turkish poet ʿAshiq Pasha reminds his compatriots of the primordial existence of Muhammad, which became such an important facet of mystical prophetology:

> Adam was still dust and clay—
> Ahmad was a prophet then,
> He had been selected by God—
>   Utter blessings over him![89]

A Sindhi folk poet of our century sings, very similarly, in his "Golden Alphabet" under the letter *l*:

> Lovely is and pure Muhammad,
> King of *laulāk* is Muhammad!
> Leads you to the goal, Muhammad,
> Leaves nobody grieved, Muhammad—
>   Bless him always, O my God![90]

And one of his compatriots, a simple shepherd from the Indus Valley, offers his blessings for the Prophet in the style of plain children's songs. In more than fifty verses he addresses all the prophets mentioned in the Koran and the Bible and reminds them, as he reminds everything created, that their blessings are all due to the Prophet:

O you Chosen of the Lord!
    Master, blessings upon you!
Hour and hour and place and place
    Master, blessings upon you!
Khidr's blessing, Abraham's,
Elijah's and Ismaʿil's,
Elisa's and Israʾil's—
    Master, blessings upon you!
On the move and during rest,
Be it daytime, be it night,
Morning, noon, and evening
    Master, blessings upon you!
As the drops in all the rains,
As the hairs on all the beasts,
And as sands in desert wide
    Master, blessings upon you![91]

For the folk poets know that "water, fire, wind and earth, nay rather heaven and earth recite the *ṣalawāt* without tongue day and night."[92]

The importance of the *durūd-i sharīf* in popular piety becomes evident from a charming little Sindhi ballad whose theme, as far as I know, does not occur in classical Arabic literature; allusions to it are, however, found in both the Turkish and the Indo-Muslim tradition. It is the story of the bee. Around 1300, Yunus Emre in Anatolia had mentioned that the bee, when entering the beehive, hums the blessings for the Prophet.[93] This remark is particularly interesting because it is widely reported that the Prophet was indeed fond of honey and had praised the bees, which are also mentioned in the Koran as examples of God's inspiration working in animals (Sura 16:68–69). The Prophet's fondness for the wholesome honey inspired medieval Muslims in North Africa to call his birthday the "honey feast" because much honey was used during the celebrations. On the other hand, several miracles of ʿAli tell of his special relations with the useful insect.[94] One Sindhi poet, who flourished around 1920, celebrated in plain verses, all rhyming in *ā*, a marvelous event that happened one day in Medina:

In the books there is written
    Such a lovely tale:
One day in the noble mosque
    the heroes assembled were,
Coming as Muhammad's guests
    they were full of cheer,
And they greeted the leader there
    with great sincerity.

"And upon you be peace!" thus said
now the sweet Muhammad,
And he conversed friendly with them—
how happy they were there!
Quickly he ordered eggs and bread
to be made for the guests—
But there was nothing to eat with it
which could be offered to them.
When they discovered this mistake,
they were completely confused!
Suddenly there came a little bee,
whirling around them a bit.
"Why did you come?" thus asked now
Muhammad the little bee.
And in front of Muhammad the prince
the bee explained everything:
"I have come here this time for you
on order of the Lord—
Give me a special servant now
to go along with me!"
The sweet Muhammad now presently
pointed to ʿAli Shah,
And the bee flew ahead and then
there followed her ʿAli Shah.
In a hurry they reached a certain tree
which is not far from Medina,
And with a stick he then took down
the beehives altogether.
He brought them and gave them to the guests
who ate them happily.
Then Prince Muhammad asked the bee
to explain the strange event.
"How happened such a grace to you,
tell honestly the tale!"
In front of Prince Muhammad now
the bee explained it well:
"Whatever honey bees there be,
I am the leader of all;
We fly and we graze in the woods and trees,
bitter be they or sweet,
And we collect all this flower sap
in hives high in the trees,

But the sap will never, never be sweet—
  it serves us only as food.
But when we speak, O Prophet dear,
  the blessings for you with love,
Then our honey becomes so sweet
  by virtue of this word.
Thus you too speak the blessings now
  For Muhammad with great love,
And become, thanks to this blessing, then
  as sweet as honey is!"[95]

This little folk ballad leads us back to the numerous miracle stories about the Prophet, from which our discussion of the *shafāʿa* began.

SIX

THE NAMES OF THE PROPHET

It is a well-known fact in the history of religions that a person's name contains a very special power. It is connected with the named one in a mysterious way: to know someone's name means to know him himself. That is why God "taught Adam the names" (Sura 2:30) to make him the master of everything created. For the same reason the lover is not allowed to reveal his beloved's name, for he does not want anyone to have access to the secrets of his love. Since the name is part, and a very important part indeed, of a thing or a person, it carries *baraka*, blessing power, with it, and when someone is endowed with special power or occupies a particularly lofty rank, his name too can work in a mysterious way on people who are given the same name (hence the numerous Marys, Johns, and Peters in the Christian tradition). It is therefore not surprising that Muslims have always ascribed a very special *baraka* to the Prophet's name.[1] These feelings are summed up in an invocation by the Anatolian minstrel Yunus Emre, written ca. 1300:

> Please pray for us on Doomsday—
> Your name is beautiful, you yourself are beautiful, Muhammad!
> Your words are accepted near God, the Lord—
> Your name is beautiful, you yourself are beautiful, Muhammad![2]

It appears that this veneration of the name of Muhammad may even go back to the lifetime of the Prophet, for Qadi ʿIyad quotes a verse by Hassan ibn Thabit, the Prophet's poet, which could easily have formed the basis for all later speculations about Muhammad's name. In these lines, the famous Arab poet points to the relation between the name Muhammad and one of the Divine attributes, *maḥmūd*:

[God] derived for him, in order to honor him, part of His name—
Thus the Lord of the Throne is called *maḥmūd*, and this one
muḥammad.[3]

That is, *muḥammad* is the passive participle of the second form of the verb *ḥamada*, "to praise, to laud," and means "[he who is] worthy of praise, [the one] often praised." *Maḥmūd* is the passive participle of the first form of the same verbal root, "[he who is] praised, to whom praise is due." Because the first sura of the Koran begins with the words *Al-ḥamdu lillāh*, "Praise be to God," God is the "Praiseworthy," the *maḥmūd* par excellence. This simple grammatical connection between the Divine attribute and the name of the Prophet was especially emphasized by the mystics and then elaborated in various ways.[4] The nineteenth-century Urdu poet Tapish goes so far as to claim in this connection that

When the Pen wrote the name of God,
It wrote [also] the name of the Messenger of God [Muhammad].[5]

This remark can also be interpreted differently, for the Muslims have always dwelt upon the fact that the Prophet's name is mentioned in the profession of faith directly after the name of God: *Lā ilāha illā Allāh, Muḥammadun rasūl Allāh*. This combination has long served to remind the Muslims of the Prophet's unique position, and not only have the theologians pondered this mysterious connection and its implications, but poets never tire of alluding to it, as for instance Naziri did in the early seventeenth century in India:

In the *shahāda* He has spoken Mustafa's name along with His own
name
And has thus made manifest the final goal of Adam.[6]

The poet takes up this very idea a few pages later in the same poem and adds an important detail:

God has made his [Muhammad's] name in the *shahāda* the sequence
of His own name,
And by mentioning him has separated the believer from the
Christian.[7]

These lines reveal the return to a more orthodox viewpoint after Akbar's religious latitudinarianism.

The ninth-century collector of Prophetic traditions, ad-Darimi, wrote in the preface to his work on *ḥadīth* some words that were taken over, six centuries later, by the Egyptian theologian Jalaluddin as-Suyuti to explain the mystery of Muhammad's name:

> His name is Muhammad and Ahmad; his people are the people of praise (*ḥamd*)—and his prayer rite and the prayer rite of his people is opened with praise (*ḥamd*). In the Preserved Tablet in God's abode it was written that his Caliphs and his Companions in writing the Sacred Volume, should open it with praise (Sura 1:1). And in his hand on the Resurrection Day will be the banner of praise. And when he then prostrates himself before God in intercession on our behalf and it is accepted he will praise the Lord with a new song that shall then be revealed to him, for his is the heavenly Station of Praise (*al-maqām al-maḥmud*, Sura 17:79)—and when he rises up in that Station all the assembly shall praise him, Muslims and misbelievers alike, the first and the last, and all meanings and modes of thankful praise shall be gathered up and offered to him.[8]

In other words, the very name Muhammad prefigures all the praise that will be his share and that of his followers in this world and the next. This name has existed from the beginning of time and will forever resound in Paradise. As Sana'i exclaims:

> On the Throne of the revolving spheres, you see his place assigned;
> On the base of the Divine Throne you see his name![9]

A mystical handbook elaborates this theme:

> And by that name Adam named him and through him interceded, and blessings were called down upon him in the nuptials of Eve . . . and by that name 'Isa will name him in the other world when he indicates him for mediation; and by that name Gabriel addressed him in the tradition (*ḥadīth*) of the *miʿrāj*. And by that name Abraham also called him in the tradition of the *miʿrāj*. And the Angel of the Mountains addressed him by that name, and with that name the Angel of Death ascended weeping when he bore his soul away, crying: "Oh me! Muhammad, Ah!" And by that name he called himself to the Guardian of Paradise, when he asked for its opening and it was opened to him.[10]

In addition, the mystics discovered by applying the method of *ishtiqāq kabīr* (the derivation of a certain meaning from each letter of a word) that his name consists of the *m* of *majd*, "glory"; the *ḥ* of *raḥma*, "mercy"; the *m* of *mulk*, "kingdom"; and the *d* of *dawām*, "everlastingness."[11]

The Prophet himself is credited with the saying "Do you not wonder how God averts from me the abuse and the curse of the Quraish? They insult me as 'blameworthy' (*mudhammam*) and curse me as a blameworthy one, but I am a praiseworthy one (*muḥammad*)."[12] In another early *ḥadīth* the

Prophet mentions as his names, besides Muhammad, Ahmad (derived from the same root, *ḥamd*); *al-māḥī*, "he through whom God effaces (*maḥw*) infidelity"; *al-ḥāshir*, "he at whose feet mankind will gather at Doomsday"; and finally *al-ʿāqib*, "the last," because there will be no other prophet after him.[13]

Among these names, Ahmad has gained a very special importance in Islamic theology. Sura 61:5 states that God "will send a prophet by the name of Ahmad" or "of highly praiseworthy name." This sentence was regarded by the Muslims from early days as a reference to the Paraclete, whose advent was foretold in the Christians' Gospel of John. The reading of *paracletos* as *pericletos*, which could be interpreted as "most praiseworthy," made such an interpretation possible, and thus Ahmad was generally accepted as the Prophet's name in the Torah and the Gospel.[14] Rumi says in the first book of his *Mathnawī* that some Christians of old used to kiss the name Ahmad in the Gospel and were saved from persecution thanks to the blessing power of that name.[15] Ahmad is also Muhammad's heavenly name, around which there grew up a complex mystical literature, as we shall see presently. As his "spiritual" name it is at the same time the name of all prophets (who are part of his primordial light).[16]

Najm Razi Daya invents a very odd description of the different names given to Muhammad: "When the egg of the human state of the Prophet had not yet been laid by the hen of ʿAbdallah, God called him Ahmad (Sura 61:5)," that is, Ahmad is his primordial name; "but when that egg had come into being nurtured with prophethood and messengerhood under Gabriel's wing," he was called Muhammad (Sura 3:144), and when the bird finally began to fly "in the station of *qāba qausain*, He called him bondsman (*ʿabduhu*) (Sura 53:10)."[17]

According to Ibn Ishaq, Muhammad was called during his early youth *al-Amīn*, the faithful and trustworthy one, for his friends were impressed by his noble qualities and reliability. That explains the frequent use of Amin as a proper name in Islamic lands.

Besides the names mentioned by the Prophet himself the Muslims developed a plethora of names for him that they claimed to have discovered either in the Koran or in the tradition. Those taken from the Koran remained of course essential. Besides Muhammad and Ahmad we find *ʿAbdallāh*, "God's servant," or *ʿAbduhu*, "His servant" (derived from Suras 17:1 and 53:10, both verses referring to his exalted rank during his heavenly journey). The mysterious unconnected letters at the beginning of Sura 20 and Sura 36, *Ṭāhā*[18] and *Yāsīn*, were likewise understood as names of the Prophet. Sura 20 begins: "*Ṭāhā*—did We not send down the Koran upon you?" The letters *Yāsīn* at the beginning of Sura 36 (which is called "The Heart of the Koran") are interpreted as *Yā insān*, "Oh man!"—which is again an address to the Prophet.[19] Therefore Taha and Yasin became proper names among the Muslims, and many writers have pondered their secret meanings, reading *Ṭāhā*, for instance, as an abbreviation of *ṭāhir*, "pure," and *hādī*, "guiding." The Turkish poet Khaqani sings in his *Ḥilya* that

> That walking cypress came with the *ṭūgh* of Taha,
> Swinging like a banner did he come.[20]

(The *ṭūgh* is an imperial standard made of a yak's tail.) And Amir Khusrau in India combined, three centuries earlier, the word *Yāsīn* with the interpretation of the letter *sīn* as "teeth":

> *Yāsīn* has spread out pearls from his mouth,
> His *Ṭāhā* has received *in yakādu*,

(that is, it is connected in some mysterious way with the last three verses of Sura 68, which are recited against the evil eye).[21] The use of these names is still common even in distant corners of the Muslim world, and just as the *qawwāl*s in Khuldabad (India) repeat time and again the Urdu refrain of their song:

> How God has surrounded you in the Koran with wonderful names!
> Sometimes He addressed you as Taha, sometimes as Yasin . . .

so too does the pious contemporary poet of Gilgit use these same epithets in a eulogy of the Prophet in his native language, Shina.[22]

In later times the letters *ḥā-mīm*, which are found at the beginning of Suras 40–46, have also been assumed to pertain to the Prophet, signifying *Ḥabībī Muḥammad*, "My beloved Muhammad." As such, they are sometimes developed in decorative calligrams. Muhammad's designation as *ḥabīb*, "beloved friend" of God, has likewise led to the formation of numerous proper names, such as Habibullah, "Beloved of God," or Habib ur-Rahman, "Beloved of the Merciful," which are nothing but equivalents of the name Muhammad.

A particularly important source for the veneration of the Prophet is Sura 33:45, in which Muhammad is called both *bashīr*, "bringer of good tidings," and *nadhīr*, "warner." Both epithets are frequently used as proper names, especially in the Indian subcontinent (Bashir Ahmad, Nadhir Ahmad, and the like). The next Koranic verse contains a description of Muhammad as *sirājun munīr*, "a shining lamp," and this too has inspired Muslim nomenclature: Siraj ud-din, Siraj ud-daula, Siraj ul-Islam, that is, Lamp of Religion, of the State, of Islam. Munir is used either alone or in combination (here again, frequently with Ahmad, as in Muniruddin Ahmad).

The Prophet is also called *al-muṣṭafā*, "the chosen one," and somewhat less frequently *al-mujtabā*, "the elected one";[23] both have become favorite proper names among Muslims. Divine addresses to the Prophet such as the introductory words of Sura 74, *Yā ayyuhā'l-mudaththir*, "O you covered one," and Sura 73, *Yā ayyuhā'l-mūzammil*, "O you enwrapped one," are used, particularly in India, as male names.[24]

In the fourteenth century the historian Safadi composed a rather long poem in which he enumerated all the names of the Prophet, and quite early the Muslims discovered that Muhammad too had no fewer than ninety-nine names, the *asmā' ash-sharīfa*, Noble Names, which are parallel to the ninety-nine *asmā' al-ḥusnā*, the Most Beautiful Names of God.[25] Whenever any of these names is mentioned, the *taṣliya* "May God bless him and give him peace" follows, as it must follow every mention of the Prophet in written or spoken discourse.[26] Among these ninety-nine names one finds two that are also among the Divine Names and that were granted, as tradition has it, to the Prophet as a sign of God's special grace: *ar-ra'ūf*, "the mild one," and *ar-raḥīm*, "the merciful one." Jami goes so far as to claim that "the Prophet's beauty is the mirror of the Greatest Name [of God]!"[27] Many modern printed copies of the Koran enumerate the ninety-nine Divine Names at the beginning and list the ninety-nine names of the Prophet on the final two pages. An annotated list appears in the Appendix of this volume.[28]

A seventeenth-century Suhrawardi mystic of Ucch (Pakistan) composed a work called *Jawāhir al-auliyā* (Jewels of the Saints), that contains an interesting chapter on the virtues and blessing powers of Muhammad's ninety-nine names.[29] These names, or some of them, were also used in talismans.[30] The author recounts various traditions connected with their use. ʿAbdul Qadir Gilani is reported to have said that a person who recites them once every day and every night will be preserved from all kinds of affliction, and his faith will always remain undisturbed. According to the author's ancestor, Makhdum Jahaniyan of Ucch, the recitation of these names after the dawn prayer will cause all sins, great and small, open and secret, to be forgiven, and Sultan Sayyid Mahmud Nasiruddin Bukhari is reported to have said that whoever recites them seven times after the noon prayer will never be harassed by birds or beasts. Another Sufi ascribed to their elevenfold recitation after the evening prayer an increase in knowledge, mildness, and gnosis. But the greatest reward, for someone who recites Muhammad's ninety-nine names twelve times after the night prayer, was revealed to Makhdum Jahaniyan by the Prophet himself during that Sufi's visit to Medina: Muhammad promised that he would definitely bring that person to Paradise, and would not enter it without him.[31]

But even ninety-nine names seemed insufficient for the Prophet. Soon

III
THE NAMES OF THE PROPHET

The "Muhammadan Rose," containing, left, *the Ninety-nine Names of the Prophet and,* right, *the Ninety-nine Names of God; the lower flowers bear the names of the Ten to whom Paradise was promised (Courtesy Staatsbibliothek Preussischer Kulturbesitz, Berlin)*

two hundred names were enumerated, later even a thousand.[32] Popular belief even holds that the Prophet is called a special name by each type of creature. For the fishes he is ʿAbdul Quddus, "Servant of the All Holy"; for the birds, ʿAbdul Ghaffar, "Servant of the All-Forgiving"; for the wild beasts, ʿAbdus Salam, "Servant of the Peace(maker)"; for the devils, ʿAbdul Qahhar, "Servant of the All-Powerful"; and so on.[33]

The poets too never tired of inventing new names for the beloved Prophet. In the report of Umm Maʿbad, whose barren sheep the Prophet had milked, Muhammad is described as *nasīm wasīm*, "graceful and elegant." These words were used, in an expanded form, in the mid–thirteenth century by Saʿdi in his famous poem at the beginning of his *Būstān*, where the Prophet is given, among others, the appellations

> *wasīmun qasīmun jasīmun nasīm*:
> Elegant, well shaped, noble, and graceful.

This mellifluous string of epithets, presented so prominently in what was to become one of the favorite books of the Persianate world, was soon known everywhere, and the attributes of the Prophet were then often used as proper names, either alone (Wasim, feminine Wasmaa), or in combinations, like Jasimuddin.

Later, especially among the non-Arab Muslims, the Prophet was frequently referred to with appellations pertaining to his native country and his family: Quraishi, Muttalibi (after his grandfather ʿAbdul Muttalib), Hashimi (from the clan Hashim), Makki, Madini, or simply ʿArab. Alluding to the places where the Prophet's earthly manifestations occurred, Nizami addresses him as "O you with a Medinan *burqaʿ* and a Meccan veil!" and asks him to "lift his head from the Yemenite cloak" because his community needs him so much in these evil days.[34] It seems that Jami, who elaborated such utterances in even more artistic form, is somewhat responsible for the frequent use of these appellations in later Persian and more especially in Indo-Persian and Urdu parlance, for his *naʿtiyya* poetry abounds in such terms as "O Idol of al-Batha!" (that is, of the area around Mecca)[35] and

> O you with a countenance like the moon, with the rising-place of Mecca,
> With the cradle of Medina, with a Yemenite veil!

He, "the envy of the sun," is "the moon of al-Batha and the luminary of Yathrib [Medina],"[36] and as such he can

> draw the Arabs' sword because eloquence is his,
> And can hunt the Persians because elegance is his.[37]

These ideas are repeated in thousands of verses. But whereas in Jami's lines such epithets apparently serve to emphasize the all-embracing power and beauty of the Prophet, in the Indian tradition they are often understood as reminders for the Muslims of the Arab homeland of their religion.

It would be a tempting project to collect all the loving and admiring epithets with which Muslim poets and prose writers, mystics and non-mystics, have surrounded Muhammad, who is often simply called *rasūl-i akram*, "the most noble Prophet," or in the Persianate tradition *risālat-panāh*, "the shelter of the prophetic office." He is, for example, the *sarwar-i kā'ināt*, "the leader of the universe," and the Nightingale of Love, the Sun of the world of monotheism, the Master of the Lovers, the Axis of the spheres of both worlds, the Rose of the meadows of prophethood—and on and on.[38] The poets and mystics carefully select appropriate names for him that are in consonance with the character of their work; in a heroic epic, for instance, his power and strength may be highlighted, in a love poem, his beauty and kindness.

Because Muhammad's name contains a very strong *baraka*, every boy should be called by it or at least by one of its derivatives or equivalents. A tradition related by Ja'far as-Sadiq, the sixth imam of Shiite Islam, holds that God will call out on the Day of Judgment: "Everyone who bears the name of Muhammad shall rise and enter Paradise!" In Morocco it is said: "If there lives a man by the name of Muhammad in a house or a tent, then there are angels always present, unless they are driven away by a black dog or a band of musicians and dancers."[39]

The Prophet has a special relationship with those who bear his name, as Busiri, the poet of the *Burda*, tells in his famous poem:

> For since I have been given the name of Muhammad, he has for me
> an obligation,
> He, who is most perfect in fulfilling all his duties among the
> creatures.[40]

A touching story, which shows the deep trust in the power of Muhammad's name, is connected with a poem composed by 'Abdur Rahim al-Bur'i, one of the greatest religious poets in the Arab world in the eleventh century. When his young son Muhammad was seriously ill, he turned to the Prophet, the great intercessor, and ended a long supplication with the lines

> And affliction has become aggravated on my son who is named after
> you:
> Have mercy upon his tears, which flow over his cheeks!

And indeed, "the boy was healed."[41] Similar examples from Persian, Turkish, and Indo-Muslim poetry could easily be quoted.

But the use of Muhammad's name for every boy also has another aspect.

It was rightly feared from the very first years of Islam that the Prophet's name might be desecrated by its constant use among the faithful. Of course, the Muslims also called their children by the names of earlier prophets, such as Musa, Sulaiman, or ʿIsa; but was it not outrageous when parents scolded their son Muhammad, calling him names, or when some Muhammad was called a liar or a fornicator? One way to overcome this difficulty was to add an honorific word when the Prophet was intended, such as *sayyidnā*, "our lord," *sīdī*, "lord," or *Hazrat*, "His Excellency," or always to add the *taṣliya* when mentioning him, or else simply to speak of him as The Noble Prophet. Another way to solve the problem was to pronounce the consonants of his name, *mḥmd*, with a different vocalization when applying them to ordinary mortals: thus in Morocco one finds personal names like Mihammad, Mahammad, or simply Moh and similar abbreviations.[42] In West Africa, forms like Mamado are in use. In Turkey the pronunciation Mehmet was generally accepted for private use, and the correct Muhammad was exclusively reserved for the Prophet. One may also shorten the name, especially in combination with other names, to an *M*, pronounced *Mim* (as in M. N. Rashid = Mim Nun Rashid), for *m* is the most important letter in the name of the Prophet. It can also be used as an abbreviation for Mustafa (as in M. Kemal). The Turkish Bektashi order developed a special *mīm duasī*, "prayer of *mīm*," that dwells upon the secrets of this letter.[43] By retaining the consonants of *mḥmd*, one preserves the *baraka* of the name; at the same time, by changing the vowels, one need not fear profaning the Prophet's noble name.

Like every Arab, Muhammad too has a *kunya*, a name that designates him as "father of so-and-so." This *kunya* was Abu'l-Qasim, and the problem has often been discussed, and never unanimously solved, whether a boy may be called by both the Prophet's proper name and his *kunya* (that is, Muhammad Abu'l-Qasim), or whether one should restrict the use to only one of the two names.[44] The combination Muhammad Amin, however, has frequently been used.

It is generally believed that the repetition of the Prophet's holy name conveys blessings upon the reciting person. The closing line of an old Urdu *charkhī nāma*, a poem in which the imagery of spinning is used to administer religious instruction, admonishes the pious:

> You are the maid servant in your dervish's house—
> Say Allah and the Prophet's name in every breath![45]

But on the other hand, poets and mystics often expressed their fear of not being worthy even to pronounce the holy, pure name of the Prophet. In the late sixteenth century in India, ʿUrfi wrote that

A thousand times I wash my mouth
  with musk and with rose water,
And still, to speak your name
  is absolute impudence.[46]

And Ghalib, almost three hundred years later, devoted a *qaṣīda* of 101 verses to the Prophet, describing toward its end how "etiquette" warned him lest he trespass the limits of decent behavior: a sinner like him should be silent and not address the Prophet at all—him, who was praised by God Most High![47]

The Sufis began very early to meditate upon the mystical and symbolic qualities of Muhammad's names. Hallaj was among the first to resort to letter mysticism.[48] Was not Adam, the prototype of humanity, created from the name Muhammad? His head is the round letter *m* ـمـ, his hand the *ḥ* ـحـ, his waist again a small *m* ـمـ, and the rest a *d* د—so that the entire human race emerges, as it were, from the name of the Prophet.[49] Ibn ʿArabi has probably given the most detailed explanation of this letter mysticism of the Prophet's name: >o>o.

> The first *mīm* is the head, and that is the world of the supreme Sovereignty (*ʿālam al-malakūt al-aʿlā*) and of the Greatest Intellect (*al-ʿaql al-akbar*). The breast and the arms are under the letter *ḥ*, and this is the Glorious Throne; its numerical value is 8, which is the number of the angels who carry the Throne. The second *m* represents the stomach, and that is the World of the Kingdom (*ʿālam al-mulk*). The hips, the legs and the feet are from the *d*, and that is the stable composition by means of the Eternal Writ.[50]

Similarly, in its calligraphic form Muhammad's name was interpreted to represent a human being in prostration: محمد.

By cabalistic devices one could find contained in his name the names of the 313 prophets who were messengers, plus the one who was a saint.[51] And even more: when Adam was created he saw that the name of Muhammad was written everywhere from pre-eternity. This is mentioned even in folk poetry, as, for example, in an eighteenth-century poem from the Indus Valley:

On the Throne, on the pinnacles
Muhammad's name is written as a *mantra* [magic formula];
On the trees, on leaf after leaf,
Muhammad's name is written as a *mantra*.[52]

The same idea occurs in Egyptian narrative ballads:

Your name, O Prophet, is the one chosen in majesty
Before the firmament, together with the highest heaven, was
founded.[53]

Among the early Persian poets, Nizami was most eloquent in his explanation of the name Ahmad: is not Ahmad

Straight like an *alif* in faithfulness to the covenant,
The first and the last of the prophets?[54]

This is a very clever pun, for the word *anbiyā*, "prophets," begins and ends with an *alif*, the first letter of Ahmad, so that Ahmad's twofold role is well attested even in a grammatical fact.

Apparently the great mystical poet of Iran, Fariduddin ʿAttar, was largely responsible for further speculations about the names of Muhammad. In his work (ca. 1200) there appear for the first time allusions to certain aspects of prophetology that became very popular in the following centuries. In his *Muṣībatnāma* ʿAttar claims that both worlds are created from the two *m*'s of the name of Muhammad, for the word *ʿālam*, "world," has only one *m* and thus the two *m*'s of *mḥmd* must refer to both worlds, this one and the next.[55] Three centuries later Jami took up this idea but elaborated it, as usual, through more complicated reasoning, by regarding the Prophet's name Ahmad (to which Nizami had referred so skillfully in his poem). The *alif*, the first letter of Ahmad, came into existence, he says, from the "dot of Unity" (as in calligraphy the initial dot is the measurement for all letters, and *alif* is the letter according to which the other letters are measured and shaped). This *alif* is upright like the diameter of a circle (⦶, again a traditional calligraphic form), and thus split the circle of the hidden Divine Ipseity into two: one half is the world of uncreatedness, of the unknowable Divine Essence, and the other is the world of contingency. The Prophet—or rather the *ḥaqīqa muḥammadiyya*—is the juncture between the two.[56] (Some later Naqshbandi mystics would even speak of the *ḥaqīqa aḥmadiyya* as the first and last manifestation of the Prophet, which expresses the closest possible approximation to Pure Love.)[57]

To return to ʿAttar: he also alludes to a tradition that was to become extremely important for the development of mystical thought in the eastern Islamic lands, and is connected with the name Ahmad. This is the *ḥadīth qudsī*, one of God's extra-Koranic revelations, *Anā Aḥmad bilā mīm*, "I am Ahmad without the *m*," that is, *Aḥad*, "One." "*Aḥmad* is the messenger of *Aḥad*," as ʿAttar repeatedly states,[58] and he knows that when

the radiance of the light of manifestation became evident,
the *m* of Ahmad became invisible,[59]

that is, only God the One remained.

Scarcely any other *ḥadīth qudsī* has been used so frequently in the Persianate parts of the Muslim world, even though it is not attested in the early collections of traditions and appears only in the twelfth century. It seems to prove that Ahmad-Muhammad is separated from God only by a single letter, the *m*. In the Arabic numeric system this letter has the value of 40, the number of patience, maturing, suffering, preparation. (Israel was for forty years in the desert; Jesus spent forty days in the desert; Muhammad was forty when his calling came; the forty days of Lent; the forty days of complete retirement as practiced by the Sufis, called *arbaʿīn* or *chilla*; these and other similar customs and traditions are expressions of this special role of the number 40.)[60] In Islamic mystical speculations 40 furthermore signifies the forty steps that man must pass on his way back to his origin—a topic elaborated by ʿAttar in his *Muṣībatnāma*, and later by numerous mystics in the Ibn ʿArabi tradition. The *m* of Ahmad points to all these mysteries; it is "the fountainhead of his teachings for which reason thirsts," as Jami says.[61] A later poet in the Panjab has called the *m* "the shawl of humanity,"[62] which the One God put on when he created Muhammad in his exemplary role. Amir Khusrau, in a different vein of thought, found that the circular form of this *m* revealed it as "the Seal of Prophethood,"[63] and it is often called the "letter of contingency." Maulana Rumi, who sings that "Ahmad is a veil" through which he wants to reach *Aḥad*,[64] dwells on the mystery of this *ḥadīth qudsī* in his prose musings, *Fīhi mā fīhi*: "Every addition to perfection is a diminution. . . . *Aḥad* is perfect, and *Aḥmad* is not yet in the state of perfection; when the *m* is removed it becomes complete perfection."[65]

Innumerable poets have followed ʿAttar in their love for the tradition of *Anā Aḥmad bilā mīm*—poets who, as Muhsin Kakorawi sings, "have the name of Ahmad on their tongue, the secret of 'without *mīm*' in their hearts." In the early sixteenth century the Uzbek ruler Shaibani used this Divine saying as much as modern Urdu poets do; Turkish folk poets love it as much as did the mystics of the Panjab or court poets in Iran. The Sindhi mystic Shah ʿAbdul Latif quotes the *ḥadīth qudsī*, as does, a century later, Mirza Ghalib, the elegant poet of Delhi.[66]

One of the poets who most indulged in speculations about the Prophet's name was Jami, who decided that the first *m* of *Muḥammad* forms the first ringlet of the word *mulk*, "kingdom," while the letter *ḥ*, with the numerical value 8, proves that the Prophet opened in this hexagonal world the eight windows toward the eight Paradises, and the footring of the *d* shows that the heads of the truly faithful (*dīnparwarān*, which begins with *d*) touch his feet.[67] He invents still other configurations with the letters of the Prophet's name: the *ḥ* between the two *m*'s looks to him like a houri's (begins with *ḥ*) face with two tresses, and the final *d* is connected with *dil*, "heart."[68] Even this is not enough: with a cabalistic trick probably inherited from Ibn ʿArabi,[69] Jami sees the first word of Sura 1, *al-ḥamd*, and the mysterious initial letters of Sura 2, *a-l-m*, as a wonderful combination: the *a-l* of Sura 2 are the same as the first letters of *al-ḥamd* and point to the *m*, the third constituent of the mysterious group of letters, so that the very name of Muhammad emerges from *al-ḥamd*. Thus, the Prophet's name forms, for those who know how to read, the very first word of the Koran.[70] On the other hand, the *a-l-m* of Sura 2:1 was often understood to signify the secret of love between God (*alif*) and Muhammad (*mīm*). The *l*, a cipher for the uniting power of love, could also be interpreted a sign of Gabriel, the angel of revelation.[71]

The mysterious qualities of the *m* in the Prophet's name continued to inspire the Muslims, particularly in India.[72] Ahmad Sirhindi, the Naqshbandi reformer in Northern India during the early seventeenth century, developed an entire reformative theology based upon the two *m*'s in the Prophet's name (see chapter 9 below).[73] And although the idea seems almost too far-fetched, one may even speculate whether the trust in the mystical qualities of the letter *m* may not have induced Busiri to select *m* as the rhyming letter of his most famous poem, the *Burda*, just as some of Sana'i's most glowing eulogies for the prophet use this same rhyme.

For the Sufis, the letter *d*, with which Muhammad's name ends, is equally meaningful. Its numerical value is 4, and it occupies the fourth position in the Prophet's name;[74] besides, the Prophet is mentioned by name four times in the Koran.[75] Mirza Ghalib, in nineteenth-century India, carries this kind of theological play even farther: from *Aḥmad* one reaches *Aḥad*, and when one then takes away the *alif*, the letter of Divine Unity, the letters *ḥ* and *d* remain; these have the numerical values 8 and 4 respectively, total 12, and thus refer to the twelve imams of the Shia. This shows that the name Ahmad contains in itself a complete dogmatic compendium.[76] Even so, Ghalib's scheme falls somewhat short of one devised by Ibn ʿArabi, who—as a good Sunni mystic—had not discovered the tenets of Imamiyya Shia theology in the Prophet's name, but evolved a numerological scheme of even more edifying sophistication: *d* (= 4) is half of *ḥ* (= 8), while *m* (= 40) is ten times *d*,[77] and, as we may continue, the two *m*'s (= 80) equal ten times the *ḥ*.

The veneration of the Prophet's name has influenced numerous aspects of Islamic culture. The peculiarities of the Arabic alphabet allow calligraphers to write it not only in elegant cursive forms but (even more often) in square Kufi, so that it can be featured on tiles and brick walls and in embroideries and weaving (often along with *Allāh* and, in Shia circles, with *ʿAlī*). Circular patterns or rosettes are also easily formed from the sacred name.

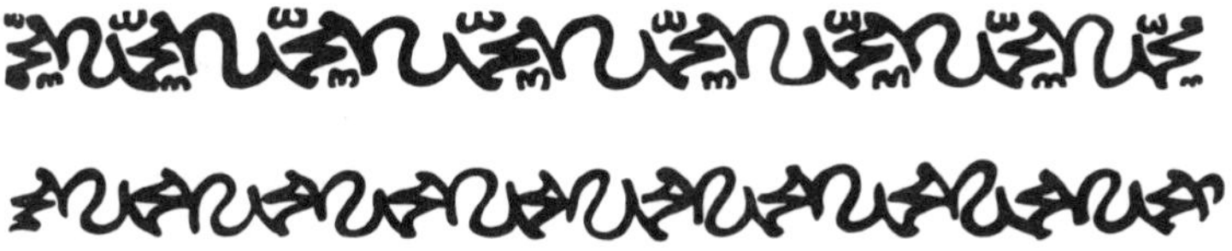

a.

b.

c.

Decorative motifs using the Prophet's name:
a. *Muhammad, contemporary linear motifs by Wasmaa Chorbachi;*
b. *twofold Muhammad in contemporary Kufi, by Wasmaa Chorbachi;*
c. *fourfold Muhammad, tilework pattern often used in architectural decoration*

Decorative motifs using the Prophet's name:
a. *eightfold Muhammad;* b. *eightfold Muhammad with eightfold ʿAli;*
c. *"Muhammad is the Messenger of God," in* tughrā *style*

When Iqbal in 1912 calls in his great Urdu poem *Jawāb-i Shikwā*:

> Light the world, too long in darkness,
> With Muhammad's radiant name,[78]

he is moved by the same feeling as the Qutubshahi king Muhammad-Quli, who sang around 1600 in the Deccan:

> The gates of both worlds are opened for a happy life
> To everyone who lowers his heart before the name of the Prophet![79]

Muhammad-Quli's own name in fact shows that in the later Middle Ages and to this day, the Muslims not only used the Prophet's different names for their male children, but also—especially in non-Arab areas—formed new names by calling them "servant of" or "slave of" Muhammad: Muhammad-Quli, "servant of Muhammad"; Paighambar Qul, "slave of the Prophet"; Ghulam Rasul, "servant of the Messenger"; Ghulam Sarwar, "servant of the leader"; Al-i Ahmad, "family of Ahmad"; Yar Muhammad, "Muhammad's friend"; Ghulam Yasin, "servant of Yasin"; and even ʿAbdun Nabi, "servant of the Prophet," and ʿAbdur Rasul or ʿAbdul Muhammad, although the use of *ʿabd* should be restricted to combinations with the names of God (one therefore also finds an ʿAbd Rabb an-nabi, "servant of the Lord of the Prophet").[80] Even Nur Muhammad, "Light of Muhammad," is found in Indo-Pakistan. On the other hand, masculine names like Nabibakhsh or Rasulbakhsh in Indo-Pakistan proclaim that the bearer was born as "a gift from the Prophet," whom the parents had implored for help. Thus, the name of the Prophet is indeed found in every house of the faithful.

In light of these many examples of the venerated names of the Prophet it seems fitting that we conclude this chapter—which could be extended almost infinitely—with the beginning of a *naʿt* from Ghawwasi's Dakhni version of the tale *Saiful Mulūk*; written in the simple "heroic" meter *mutaqārib* (⏑-- | ⏑-- | ⏑-- | ⏑-), the verses read:

> O truly Muhammad, O you Mustafa,
> You truly are Ahmad, you are Mujtaba;
> You Taha, you Yasin, you are Abtahi,
> You *ummī*, you Makki, you messenger true!
> The first and the last you, and you are the prince,
> You inward, you outward, you Prophet unique!
> The Hashimi Prophet, Quraishi are you—
> Whatever you say, God accepts it from you. . . .
> And you are the true lord of all the three worlds,
> The house of religion, it prospers through you . . .

The angels are moths all, surrounding your light,
The saints are the dust specks around you, the sun . . .[81]

And these last lines lead us to another important aspect of Islamic prophetology: the speculation about the *nūr Muḥammad*, the Prophet's luminous nature.

SEVEN

THE LIGHT OF MUHAMMAD AND THE MYSTICAL TRADITION

One of the central themes (if not *the* central theme) of mystical prophetology is that of the Light of Muhammad, *nūr Muḥammad*.[1] It is like the light of the sun around which everything revolves; it is that "light of the name" which Iqbal, as so many poets before him, mentions in his verse. The idea has colored every literary expression of mystical Islam, and has also featured widely in folk Islam, from early days to our own century.[2]

One of the most moving experiences a visitor to India or Pakistan can enjoy is a *qawwāli*, a gathering in which religious music is sung. The leading singer and the responding chorus slowly become excited and, like many of their listeners, seem to reach a state of near ecstasy. Among the songs most frequently heard at such occasions is a Persian *ghazal* ascribed to Amir Khusrau, the medieval Indian poet and musician, to whom Hindustani music owes if not its foundation then at least a very momentous impetus. The poem begins:

> *Namīdānam che manzil būd shabgāhī ki man būdam:*
> I do not know which place it was,
> the nightly place in which I was . . .

and after speaking of a mysterious nocturnal celebration in which God Himself appears as the cupbearer, the poet closes with the surprising line:

> *Muḥammad shamʿ-i maḥfil būd . . .*
> Muhammad was the candle there—
> the nightly place in which I was.[3]

The Prophet Muhammad is the candle of the assembly, *shamʿ-i maḥfil*, the light that illuminates the darkness of this world in which the listeners are gathered, the radiant candle around which human hearts throng like spellbound moths.

Among all the attributes and descriptions that have been woven around the Prophet's person to cover him with luminous veils of praise, those that speak of him as belonging to the sphere of light are most common. Indeed, the Koran itself (Sura 33:46), as we saw, calls the Prophet *sirājun munīr*, "a shining lamp," an expression taken over by Hassan ibn Thabit, who once described Muhammad as the one who brought light and truth in the darkness (as in Sura 5:15):

> There came to you from God a light and a clear book![4]

Furthermore, in the description of the battle of Badr, Hassan claims that the Prophet's face shone like the full moon, *badr*,[5] and in his threnody for the venerated Prophet he mentions also the radiant light that shone at Muhammad's birth, a topic repeated time and again in the literature:

> And he who is guided to the blessed light, is well guided.[6]

This poetical statement looks like a prelude to the mystical interpretation of the Light verse of the Koran as it was introduced by the theologian Muqatil in the eighth century. He seems to have been the first to interpret the words of this verse as referring to the Prophet:

> God is the Light of the heavens and the earth; the likeness of His light is as a niche wherein is a lamp—the lamp in a glass, the glass as if it were a glittering star—kindled from a Blessed Tree, an olive tree that is neither of the East nor of the West, whose oil wellnigh would shine, even if no fire touched it: Light upon Light; God guides to His Light whom He will. And God strikes similitudes for man, and God has knowledge of everything. (Sura 24:35)

It is the lamp, *miṣbāh*, that Muqatil sees as a fitting symbol for Muhammad. Through him the Divine Light could shine in the world, and through him mankind was guided to the origin of this Light.[7] The formula "neither of the East nor of the West" was then taken as a reference to Muhammad's comprehensive nature, which is not restricted to one specific people or race and which surpasses the boundaries of time and space.[8] To our day, one of the most common epithets of the Prophet is *nūr al-hudā*, the Light of Right Guidance. Did not Muhammad himself mention the light that penetrated him in one of his prayers, a prayer that has belonged to the most precious treasures of the faithful for century after century?

> O God, place light in my heart, and light in my soul, light upon my tongue, light in my eyes and light in my ears, place light at my right, light at my left, light behind me and light before me, light above me and light beneath me. Place light in my nerves, and light in my flesh, light in my blood, light in my hair and light in my skin! Give me light, increase my light, make me light![9]

Theories concerning Muhammad's luminous character began to develop, on the basis of Muqatil's exegesis, in the second half of the ninth century. It was an Iraqi Sufi, Sahl at-Tustari (d. 896), who first expressed the entire *Heilsgeschichte* in the terminology of the Light of Muhammad, and he too derived his ideas from the Light verse. As his modern interpreter, Gerhard Böwering, writes in his fundamental study of the Prophet's role in Tustari's theology:

> God, in His absolute oneness and transcendent reality, is affirmed by Tustari as the inaccessible mystery of divine light which yet articulates itself in the pre-eternal manifestation of the "likeness of His light," *mathalu nūrihi*, that is, "the likeness of the light of Muhammad," *nūr Muḥammad*. The origin of the *nūr Muḥammad* in pre-eternity is depicted as a luminous mass of primordial adoration in the presence of God which takes the shape of a transparent column, *ʿamūd*, of divine light and constitutes Muhammad as the primal creation of God. Thus, explaining the terminology of the Light-verse, Tustari says: "When God willed to create Muhammad, He made appear a light from His light. When it reached the veil of the Majesty, *ḥijāb al-ʿaẓamah*, it bowed in prostration before God. God created from its prostration a mighty column like crystal glass of light that is outwardly and inwardly translucent."[10]

Interestingly, Tustari also connects Sura 53 with the Light of Muhammad. He does not interpret this sura either as pertaining to the Prophet's initial vision or to his heavenly journey but claims instead that the words "And he saw Him still another time" (53:13) mean "at the beginning of time," when the column of the Light of Muhammad was standing before God,

> before the beginning of creation by a million years. He stood before Him in worship, *ʿubūdiyya*, with the disposition of faith, and [to him] was unveiled the mystery by Mystery Itself "at the Lote Tree of the Boundary" (Sura 53:14), that is the tree at which the knowledge of everyone comes to an end.[11]

Then, when creation began, God "created Adam from the light of Muhammad."

> The light of the prophets is from his, Muhammad's light and the light of the heavenly kingdom, *malakūt*, is from his light, and the light of this world and of the world to come is from his light.

Böwering continues with his interpretation of Tustari's doctrine:

> Finally when the emanation of the prophets and spiritual universe in pre-eternity was completed, Muhammad was shaped in the body, in his temporal and terrestrial form, from the clay of Adam, which however had been taken from the pre-eternal column of *nūr Muḥammad*. Thus the pre-eternal creation of light was perfected: the primal man was moulded from the crystallized light of Muhammad and took the corporate personality of Adam.[12]

That means, as Ibn ʿArabi was to state three centuries after Tustari, that the Prophet is "like the seed, *bidhr*, of the human race,"[13] and the poets have never tired of alluding to the paradox that Muhammad is prior to Adam in essence though outwardly his descendant.

Tustari's high-soaring speculations, which were to influence a large current in Sufi thought, were elaborated more poetically by his disciple Hallaj, who says in "Ṭāsīn as-sirāj" (Tasin of the Lamp), the first chapter of his *Kitāb aṭ-ṭawāsīn*:

> [He was] a lamp from the light of the Invisible . . . a moon radiating among the moons, whose mansion is in the sphere of mysteries; the Divine Truth [God] called him *ummī* because of the collectedness of his noble aspiration (*himma*). . . .
>
> The lights of prophethood—from his light did they spring forth, and their lights appeared from his light, and there is no light among the lights more luminous and more visible and previous to preexistence, than the light of this noble one.[14]

One must keep in mind that these words were written less than three hundred years after the Prophet's death. From this time the luminous Prophet appears everywhere in mystical and poetical works. He himself is credited with statements pertaining to his sublime rank, for instance "The first thing that God created was my light,"[15] and his remark "My companions are like the stars"[16] fits well with his role as the central sun or the full moon of Islam. Hallaj's friend, the somewhat eccentric Shibli, recited on his deathbed a verse that is still sung in *qawwālis*:

> Any house in which you dwell
> Does not need any lamps,
> And on the day when proofs are brought
> Then my proof is your face.[17]

Even though this verse may not originally have been meant as a eulogy for the Prophet (that would contradict Shibli's general attitude to him), it is telling that it has since been understood as an allusion to the Prophet's radiant face.

Again, Ibn ʿArabi is largely responsible for the central role of this light in later Sufism. "The first light appears out of the Veil of the Unseen, and from knowledge to concrete existence, it is the light of our Prophet Muhammad," he states in his Profession of Faith, and he goes on to compare Muhammad, the *sirāj munīr*, to the sun, inferring from this that "the intelligences, *ʿuqūl*, the spirits, *arwāḥ*, the intuitions, *baṣāʾir*, and the essences, *dhawāt*, are nourished by the luminous essence of Mustafa the Elect, who is the Sun of Existence."[18]

The ideas of Ibn ʿArabi and his interpreter ʿAbdul Karim al-Jili underlie a great many remarks in poetry throughout the Muslim world in which the Prophet is described in terms that sometimes sound surprising, if not shocking, to the outsider. Jili speaks, for instance, of the *ḥaqīqat al-ḥaqāʾiq*, the "innermost Reality," which is indeed the *ḥaqīqa muḥammadiyya* and which appears in pre-eternity as a white chrysolite, *yāqūta baiḍāʾ*. God looks at it, and it dissolves into waves and other watery substances, out of which the created world emerges.[19] But the tradition was much older. Thaʿlabi, in his *ʿArāʾis al-bayān*, written shortly after the year 1000, knew a colorful myth in which "a radiant pearl" plays the central role. In a less poetical vein, Najm Daya Razi, Ibn ʿArabi's contemporary but not his follower, offers a similar story of creation: the pearly drops of sweat that emerge from the Muhammadan Light are the substance from which the 124,000 prophets are created.[20] It is in this tradition that poets in Turkey and in Bengal sang of the wondrous role of the light of Muhammad, as does for instance Khaqani in his Turkish *Ḥilya*:

> God (*ḥaqq*) loved this light and said: "My beloved friend (*ḥabībī*)!"
> And became enamored (*ʿāshiq*) of this light . . .[21]

And then this primordial light, perspiring with awe and bashfulness, produced drops of perspiration, each of which was to become a prophet; then in degrees, an ocean, vapor, and the spheres emerged from this light.

The mystics before Ibn ʿArabi have lovingly used Tustari's vision of the pre-eternal column of light, and few passages in medieval Persian poetry convey a more impressive picture than ʿAttar's lines in the introduction of the *Manṭiq uṭ-ṭair*:

> What first appeared from out the Unseen's depth
> Was his pure light—no question and no doubt!
> This lofty light unfolded signs—the Throne,

The Footstool, Pen and Tablet thus appeared.
One part of his pure light became the world,
And one part Adam and the seed of man.
When this grand light shone up, it fell
Before the Lord, prostrate in reverence.
For ages it remained thus in prostration
And eras long in genuflection too,
And year by year it stood in prayer straight,
A lifetime in profession of the faith:
This prayer of the secret Sea of Light
Gave the community the prayer rite![22]

But not only the major learned poets speak of the luminous Muhammad; they are joined, even surpassed, by the popular minstrels. Thus Yunus Emre, in the late thirteenth century, has God say:

I created him from My own light,
And I love him yesterday and today!
What would I do with the worlds without him?
My, My Muhammad, My Ahmad of Light![23]

At about the same time, a Sufi in India wrote, in Persian:

This is the light of God (*ḥaqq*), which became embodied in the
Prophet's person,
Just as the moonlight is taken from the sun.[24]

The Kalhora prince Sarfaraz Khan of Sind, who composed a touching invocation of the Prophet during his imprisonment in 1774, affirms, like innumerable writers before him, that

There was no creation, no angels, neither heaven nor earth—
Your light was radiant before everything.[25]

Maulana Rumi too praised the wondrous qualities of the primordial light:

If only one branch of its millions of branches were unveiled,
Thousands of Christian ecclesiastics would immediately tear their
infidels' girdle.[26]

Likewise, as Jami sings, this light can change the conditions of the Muslims for the better:

Everyone on whom the light of your kindness [or, sun: *mihr*] shines,
Will become red-faced [honored] in the whole world like the dawn.[27]

And before him Rumi again had asked:

> How could we commit an error? For we are in the light of Ahmad![28]

It is this participation in the light of Muhammad by which the true believer is distinguished, and when he has submerged himself in this primordial light, Hell will tell him: "Your light has extinguished my fire."[29] For Hellfire, being created, is subject to extinction, whereas the Light of Muhammad is pre-eternal, and hence unchangeable.

On a different level the concept of Muhammad as the *nūr al-anwār*, "light of all lights" was connected with the legend that he did not cast a shadow.[30] As Najm Razi explains, "he was, from one point of view, the sun, and the sun has no shadow," just as he was, from another point of view, "the monarch of religion," and "the monarch is God's shadow on earth," and a shadow has no shadow.[31] It was also said that this light could work like a lamp in the dark night. Calligraphers found it natural that for this very reason none of the Prophet's original names Muhammad, Ahmad, Hamid, and Mahmud, nor his epithet *rasūl Allāh* has any diacritical marks in Arabic writing: his luminosity was not sullied by black spots when his name and status were written.[32]

In certain areas an entire mythology developed from the speculations about the *nūr Muḥammad*. The way in which a Bengali mystical poet of the fifteenth century, Shaikh Chand, describes the beginning of creation would certainly not be acceptable to a more orthodox and less poetically minded Muslim, but it is more or less a popularization of thoughts mentioned in the writings of Ibn ʿArabi and his successors:

> The Lord of *nūr* [light] with a stick in his hand, gazed to the east.
> The creation began with *nūr Muḥammad*,
> The Lord brought the *nūr* from his own heart.

After describing how *nūr Muḥammad* is endowed with consciousness, passion, intelligence, purpose, power, and also death, he continues:

> Then the Lord pronounced the word *kun* ["let there be"],
> *Kāf* and *nūn*, these two letters were created,
> And through combining these two letters, the Lord expressed
> Himself.
> *Kāf* representing *kalima* [profession of faith] and *nūn* representing
> *nūr* [light], from one of these two selves.
> Out of love for *nūr*, Allah created the universe,
> By seeing the beauty of *nūr*, he became enchanted
> And became attracted and gazed upon him . . .[33]

The similarity with Khaqani's description of the act of creation (mentioned above) is clear.

Cross-relations between the speculations of Sahl at-Tustari, Hallaj, and Ibn ʿArabi on the one hand and Shiite doctrines of the light of the imams on the other hand are highly probable, but it is difficult to assess their exact articulation. The same is true for the influence of Hellenistic-Gnostic ideas that may lie at the base of the entire mysticism of light as well as of other traditions in which the Prophet was elevated to an almost superhuman rank. Much research has been devoted to these aspects of mystical prophetology, but the full historical picture is still not completely clear.[34]

Along with the development of the idea that Muhammad is the original light in creation goes the desire to elevate the Prophet in every possible respect and give him a position far above the human rank. The growing tendency was ever to forget that some of the earliest Sufis—among them the first representative of love mysticism, Rabiʿa of Basra (d. 801)—had claimed that love of God had filled their souls so completely that there was no room left for a special love for the Prophet.[35] But a century later, when the mystic al-Kharraz gave the same answer to the Prophet, whom he saw in a dream, he received the reply: "He that loves God must have loved me!"[36] However, some later Sufis were still afraid of assigning the Prophet too elevated a position; Shibli, for example, addressed the Lord when he uttered the call to prayer (which contains the bipartite profession of faith): "If You had not commanded it I would not mention anyone besides You!"[37] But such doubts, which arose from the feeling that to mention the "messenger of God" in such a prominent place might impair the incomparable Unity of God, were erased by many later mystics. Hujwiri, speaking of Bayezid Bistami's heavenly journey, tells of the confused mystic's question: "What am I to do?" God answered: "O Abu Yazid, Thou must win release from the 'thou-ness' by following My beloved. Smear thine eyes with the dust of his feet and follow him continually."[38]

From at least Muqatil's days the mystical veneration of Muhammad grew rapidly. Numerous *ḥadīth* are now quoted to show that he was indeed the meaning and end of creation. In one he states: "I was a prophet while Adam was still between water and clay," that is, uncreated.[39] The Prophet is also reported to have said, "The first thing that God created was my spirit"; but one finds conflicting statements such as "The first thing that God created was the Pen" (which is "identical with the Muhammadan Spirit") or "the Intellect." Najm Razi skillfully combines all three seemingly contradictory *ḥadīth* by interpreting all of them as pertaining to the Prophet: "When God Almighty created the Muhammadan spirit and looked upon it with the gaze of affection, shame overcame it, and caused it to split in two"—one half of the Pen of God became the Spirit of the Prophet, the other half the Intelligence of the Prophet.[40]

Pivotal in this development was a *ḥadīth qudsī*, an extra-Koranic revelation, in which God said: *Laulāka mā khalaqtu'l-aflāka*, "If you had not been [i.e., but for your sake], I would not have created the spheres."[41] This tradition became so central, especially in poetical parlance, that Muhammad is often addressed as "the lord of *laulāka*." There is still another Divine word that was repeatedly quoted as proof of the Prophet's supreme rank, especially in the Indian tradition: "From the Throne to that which is beneath the dust everything seeks My satisfaction, and I seek your satisfaction, O Muhammad."[42]

Later mystics and poets did not hesitate to apply to the Prophet the *ḥadīth qudsī* that says *Kuntu kanzan makhfiyyan* . . . , "I was a hidden treasure and I wanted to be known; therefore I created the world."[43] God, longing in His pre-eternal loneliness to be known and loved, created Muhammad as the first mirror for His light and His beauty, a mirror in which He can look at Himself full of love. Therefore, the tradition that "Who has seen me, has seen *al-ḥaqq*" (has seen reality, the Truth, i.e., God)[44] was often interpreted to mean that Muhammad was indeed the perfect mirror of Divine Beauty, the locus of manifestation for all Divine names and attributes, through whose beauty one could understand the Divine Beauty and Perfection.[45] Ibn ʿArabi placed the tradition of the "hidden treasure" at the center of his system, and in his succession as in that of his poetical interpreter Jami the poets continued to sing:

> God made you the mirror of the Essence,
> A looking glass for the unique Essence;[46]

or:

> From "I was a treasure" your true nature has become clear:
> Your person is the mirror of the unqualified Light![47]

The Prophet is also seen as the seed and fruit of creation, or as the great tree—a reflection of ancient myths of the Cosmic Tree or the Tree of Life. Maulana Rumi interpreted someone's dream of a tree at the shore of the ocean as follows: "That endless ocean is the Greatness of God Most High, and that huge tree is the blessed existence of Muhammad and the branches of this tree are the ranks of the prophets and stations of the saints, and those big birds are their souls, and the different tunes they sing are the mysteries and secrets of their tongues."[48] Similar ideas—which were by far better known to the medieval Muslims than historical facts of the Prophet's life—are found, for instance, in Indo-Muslim literature.[49] In the sixteenth century Manjhan sings in his epic *Madhumālatī*, after mentioning the "Muhammadan light":

> Muhammad, having become the root of the [cosmic] tree,
> The whole universe is his branch.

God put a crown of nine *lākhs* [100,000s] on his head.
There is no one who can equal him.
He is the body and the whole world is his reflection.
He is the hidden creator whom everyone recognizes;
Muhammad, who is the manifestation of God, no one knows.
He who is visible, invisible and limitless,
The same has taken the form of Muhammad,
The name of the form remains Muhammad . . .[50]

This belief in the preexistence of Muhammad's essence, first elaborated by Sahl at-Tustari and Hallaj, praised in eloquent words by authors like ath-Thaʿlabi, and systematized into theory by Ibn ʿArabi, permeates later Sufism. As an Indian Naqshbandi of the late nineteenth century writes in one of his numerous treatises on "The Beloved,"

The seed of the essence of Muhammad was veiled and invisible in the ground of non-existence. When the sun of the Real Existent and Realized Beloved [i.e., God] radiated on it, and when that seed, which is "Mercy for the worlds," received the water of Mercy, it lifted its head from the earth of non-existence, and everything besides God, what is found between earth and the Throne, between East and West, lifted its head from the blessed womb of the Muhammadan Essence and found freshness and charm. Therefore God said, *Laulāka*, "But for your sake . . ."

If there were not Muhammad, nobody would be,
And the two worlds would not have existence.[51]

In Sufism after Ibn ʿArabi the preexistent essence of the Prophet, called *al-ḥaqīqa al-muḥammadiyya*, is considered to be the fountainhead of all prophetic activity. For this *ḥaqīqa muḥammadiyya*—a term often translated as "archetypal Muhammad"—manifests itself first in Adam, then in all the other prophets until it finds its full expression once more in the historical Muhammad, who thus becomes, as it were, the Alpha and Omega of creation. Muhammad the Prophet is the all-comprehensive and perfect manifestation of the primordial light, and with him the cycle of manifestations is completed, for he is the Seal of the Prophets. In the Arabic tradition, Ibn al-Farid (d. 1235) is among the first to express such thoughts, in his great *Tāʾiyya*:

And there was none of them [the former prophets] but had called his people
To the Truth by grace of Muhammad and because he was Muhammad's follower.[52]

These ideas are constantly repeated in later poetry. In the Persian tradition it was Jami who especially liked to sing, in the long introductory poems of his epics, about this miraculous development. According to his wording, the message of any prophet who ever lived was nothing but a fragment of Muhammad's comprehensive message:

His light appeared on Adam's forehead
So that the angels bowed their heads in prostration;
Noah, in the dangers of the flood,
Found help from him in his seamanship;
The scent of his grace reached Abraham,
And his rose bloomed from Nimrod's pyre.
Yusuf was for him, in the court of kindness
[Only] a slave, seventeen dirhams' worth.
His face lighted the fire of Moses,
And his lip taught Christ how to quicken the dead.[53]

Such lines help us understand why later Sufis usually strove for union with the *ḥaqīqa muḥammadiyya*, which was now considered the final station on the Path. On their way thither they ascended and finally surpassed the stages of all previous prophets. Thus the Sufi might feel at one moment that he had reached the station of Moses, at another time that of Abraham, or that he had reached the station of Noah and experienced the flood, and it might be that he or others would remain in one of these stations; for only a few might be blessed, perhaps, by union with the first principle of creation, that is the Archetypal Muhammad. We have reports by mystical leaders who tell of this ascending way toward the *ḥaqīqa muḥammadiyya*, and Sufi poetry, especially that written by the leaders of Sufi orders, abounds in references to progress in the stations.[54]

Yea, my growing in love was before Adam,
I was with the light of Ahmad in the heights,

sings Ibrahim ad-Dasuqi, the founder of a fraternity in Egypt during the thirteenth century.[55]

Under the influence of Ibn ʿArabi, who claimed to be the "heir to the totalizing nature of the Prophet," *aṭ-ṭabīʿa al-jamʿiyya*, and "heir to the Muhammadan Station," *al-maqām al-muḥammadī*, such poetry became increasingly popular. Ibn ʿArabi himself had inherited, at the age of thirty-three (in 1197–98), the *maqām muḥammadī* by a solemn investiture in the presence of the Supreme Company, *al-malʾa al-aʿlā*, and had become, as "seal of the saints," the sealing saint on the heart of Muhammad, *ʿalā qalb Muḥammad*.[56] This claim made him utter his ideas most daringly, but it is interesting to note that his younger contemporary Shams-i Tabrizi, the powerful inspirer of Maulana Rumi, remarked that although Ibn ʿArabi had stated, "Muhammad is our curtain-keeper," nonetheless "he did not [really] follow him"—an accusation that has been repeated to our day by many anti-Sufi Muslims.[57]

In Ibn ʿArabi's system Muhammad appears as the comprehensive figure, "nourished by the most holy, supreme flux of grace," *al-faiḍ al-aqdas al-aʿlā*. He is the Perfect Man, in whom the pleroma of the Divine attributes and names is reflected.[58] Hence arose the claim of those who reached union with the *ḥaqīqa muḥammadiyya* that they were endowed with the "totalizing" nature or distinguished by the epithet *al-jāmiʿ*, the Comprehensive One (as Mir Dard writes in his account of his ascent through the stages of the prophets).[59] In these theories, Muhammad assumes the position of the microcosm who represents, or reflects, in himself the macrocosm—he is indeed the mirror that God created to admire Himself. His heart, as Ibn ʿArabi's disciple Kashani remarks in his commentary on Sura 7:54, is equal to the Divine Throne: the Koranic word "Who was on the Throne" means "on the Throne of Muhammad's heart, by manifesting Himself completely with all His attributes to him."[60]

As the *insān kāmil*, the Perfect Man, Muhammad is as it were the suture between the Divine and the created world; he is, so to speak, the *barzakh*, the isthmus between the Necessary and contingent existence. This role of the Prophet as the intermediate principle is found, according to the school of Ibn ʿArabi, in the very words of the profession of faith, *Muḥammad rasūl Allāh*: Muhammad is the "manifested principle," *rasūl*, the messenger, is the "manifesting principle," and Allah is the "Principle in Itself." It is the element *rasūl* that relates the Principle in Itself to the manifested principle.[61] In this position the Prophet exhibits a twofold quality: contemplative and receptive, because he is the vessel for Divine inspiration, yet active in that he implements the Divine will in this world. He can be seen as the first principle of creation and is therefore equated, by some more philosophically inclined Sufis, with the Universal Intellect; sometimes, in poetical hymns, even the Universal Intellect is portrayed as an infant compared to him.[62] And as he is the first thing ever created, thus he is the last prophet to appear in the flesh. In this dual role he bears all the Divine Names in himself, whereas a normal human being is the locus of manifestation for only one. Thus the Koranic word in Sura 5:5, which was revealed during Muhammad's farewell pilgrimage, is interpreted as expressing this supreme rank of the Prophet: "Today I have completed your religion for you and completed My mercy, and it is My will that Islam be your religion." For Muhammad, the Seal of the Prophets, is the perfection of the prophetic message, and in him as the seal, all the perfections of his predecessors are united "as the sum of an arithmetic series represents all numbers. . . . Essentially they are one with him and share in the honours paid to him."[63]

The descriptions of the eternal Muhammad given by the mystics in prose and later in poetry are replete with grandiose hyperboles and radiate poetical beauty; they are a far cry from the sober statements of the Prophet, who saw himself only as "a human being to whom revelation has come." One fine example is found in the writings of ʿAbdul Qadir al-Gilani, the founder of the Qadiriyya, the Sufi order with the largest number of adherents, in the twelfth century (he died one year after Ibn ʿArabi was born):

> He has been glorified by all glorious qualities; he was granted all words. By his noble nature the props of the tent of the whole of existence stay firmly placed; he is the secret of the word of the book of the angel, the meaning of the letters "creation of the world and the heavens"; he is the pen of the Writer Who has written the growing of created things; he is the pupil in the eye of the world, the master who has smithed the seal of existence. He is the one that suckles at the teats of revelation, and carries the eternal mystery; he is the translator of the tongue of eternity. He carries the banner of honor and keeps the reins of praise; he is the central pearl in the necklace of prophethood and the gem in the diadem of messengers. He is the first according to the cause, and the last in existence. He was sent with the Greatest *nāmūs* to tear the veil of sorrow, to make the difficult easy, to push away the temptation of the hearts, to console the sadness of the spirit, to polish the mirror of the souls, to illuminate the darkness of the hearts, to make rich those who are poor in heart and to loosen the fetters of the souls.[64]

Muhammad thus becomes the only goal of creation, as illustrated by the *ḥadīth laulāka*; but even more, it is through him alone that the world assumes existence, and through him alone that Divine grace is mediated.

S. H. Nasr has pointed out that even such descriptions, which seem so alien to the historical picture of Muhammad, have developed perfectly logically from the veneration owed to the Prophet. Though Muhammad was reminded in the Koran to say, "I am only a human being like you," pious Muslims soon added, "True, but like the ruby among the stones."[65] Outwardly he resembled them, but inwardly he carried the Divine Light, whose rays became increasingly visible as time passed. S. H. Nasr is here in agreement with numerous Muslim mystics and poets who have argued in a similar vein. When Ghalib, writing in nineteenth-century Delhi, calls the Prophet the *imām*, that is, the long pearl in the Muslim prayer beads that hangs apart from the others and yet forms an integral part of the rosary,[66] he expresses the same feeling evidenced in comparing the Prophet to "the ruby

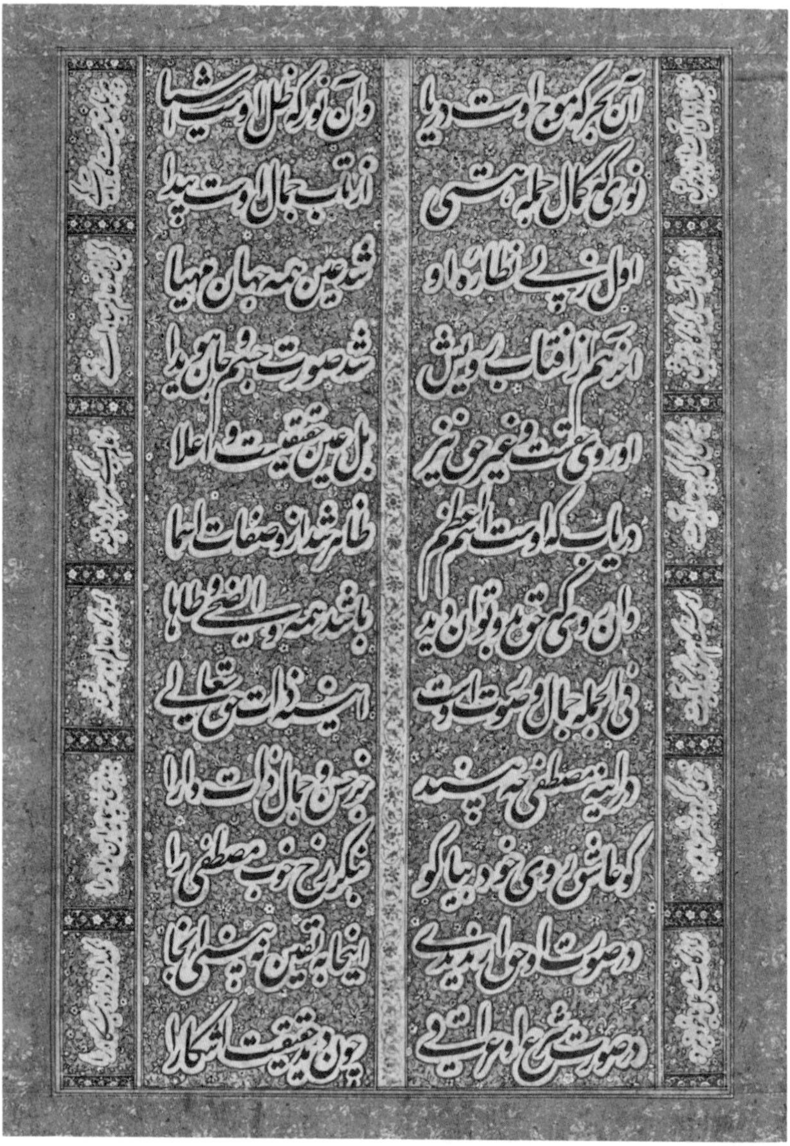

Poem in praise of the Prophet, "the light whose shadow the things are," by Fakhruddin ʿIraqi, Eastern Iran, ca. 1500 (Courtesy the Freer Gallery of Art, Washington)

among stones." To bring this comparison closer to the understanding of Western readers one should add that the ruby, according to oriental folklore, grows out of ordinary stones by patiently receiving the rays of the sun: the ruby is, as it were, sunlight transformed into stone. Thus the parallel with the Prophet as the human being who has been made transparent for the Divine Light becomes even more meaningful.

One should also not forget that Hallaj—as far as one knows, for the first time—expressed the idea of the twofold nature of the Prophet: as *sirāj*, as the lamp of prophethood (*nubuwwa*), he is pre-eternal; but his role as messenger (*risāla*) begins with his appearance on earth.[67]

In the theory of some mystics Muhammad appears sometimes as the *muṭāʿ*, "he who is obeyed." This epithet can easily be derived from the Koranic injunctions to obey him and from Sura 81:21. For Saʿdi he is *rasūlun muṭāʿun*, "the obeyed Prophet," and Jami calls him "the *muṭāʿ* [who is obeyed] for the people and the *muṭīʿ* [the obedient one] for God."[68]

In Ghazzali's esoteric work *Mishkāt al-anwār* (The Niche for Lights)—again an allusion to Muhammad's position according to the Light verse of the Koran—the *muṭāʿ* seems to be a kind of First Intellect, a being to whom the guidance of the world is entrusted—"a cosmic power upon whom the order and movement of the universe depends." The relation between God and the *muṭāʿ* is compared to that between the inaccessible essence of light and the visible sunlight.[69] Ghazzali's theories have puzzled the first interpreters of his work, as they seem to foreshadow an interpretation of Islam—the "gnostic" or "theosophical" interpretation—that he otherwise fought so relentlessly. However, in the context of the history of the veneration of the Prophet, his interpretation fits well with the one that became more and more common among the Sufis.

Muhammad, the prototype of the universe as well as of the individual, "the pupil in the eye of humanity," the Perfect Man who is necessary for God as the medium through which He can manifest Himself to be known and loved—all these ideas have been theologically elaborated after Ibn ʿArabi by his followers, among whom ʿAbdul Karim al-Jili in the late fourteenth century occupies an important place because of his theories about the Perfect Man. His ode to the Prophet contains the relevant theories in a nutshell:

> O Centre of the compass! O inmost ground of the truth!
> O pivot of necessity and contingency!
> O eye of the entire circle of existence! O point of the Koran and the Furqan!
> O perfect one, and perfecter of the most perfect, who has been beautified by the majesty of God the Merciful!

Thou art the Pole (*quṭb*) of the most wondrous things. The sphere of perfection in its solitude turns on thee.
Thou art transcendent, nay thou art immanent, nay thine is all that is known and unknown, everlasting and perishable.
Thine in reality is Being and not-being; nadir and zenith are thy two garments.
Thou art both the light and its opposite, nay but thou art only darkness to a gnostic that is dazed.[70]

This faith in Muhammad's role as the moving principle of the world forms the basis of most of the grand hymns in honor of the Prophet, as they were sung in Arabic and even more in Persian, Turkish, and Urdu. It is reflected also in the popular descriptions of Muhammad's birth and his heavenly journey. It sometimes seems as if the poets had preceded the theologians by applying to Muhammad ever more glorious names and epithets, and by praising him in wide-ranging hyperbole. The verse of Sanaʾi and ʿAttar, written long before Ibn ʿArabi's systematization of mystical "Muhammad-ology," proves that these ideas were in the air much earlier. After Ibn ʿArabi, whose teachings were generally accepted and propagated in the rapidly expanding Sufi orders, they percolated down to all levels of Sufism, and appear ever more outspokenly in hymns sung in the Prophet's honor from Morocco to India.[71]

To the later Sufi poets, the Prophet appears as the dawn that stands between the night of creaturely life and the day of Divine Light; it is he through whom one can experience this light, and who forms the beginning of the Divine Day. As a Naqshbandi Sufi of the eighteenth century in Sind says:

Wondrous is the reality of the friend
[i.e., the *ḥaqīqa muḥammadiyya*]:
One cannot call him Lord,
    but also not creature.
Similar to the dawn
    he unites night and day.[72]

One can interpret this role of the Prophet in different images: as the Seal of the Prophets, Muhammad is for this world what the stone is for the ring, for the stone bears the inscription with which the king seals his treasure chests. The numerous allusions to the heart as the seal that occur in Islamic literatures in the centuries after Ibn ʿArabi had written his work on prophetology, the *Fuṣūṣ al-ḥikam* (Bezels of Wisdom), may have been more or less inspired by this work, in whose title the symbolism of the seal is evident.

In the mystical interpretation of Muhammad's role, the Koranic allusions to him were constantly filled with new meaning, and their contents expressed in often very daring images—be it Sura 54:1, "The hour drew near, and the Moon was split," or Sura 93, "By the Morning light!" or Sura 17:1 with its allusion to the nightly journey, or the visionary Sura 53, "The Star." One short Koranic chapter, Sura 108, *Sūrat al-Kauthar*, has been a favorite with the Sufis, many of whom have held it to be the most beautiful expression of the fullness of grace that God bestowed upon His Prophet. The word *kauthar*, from the root *k-th-r*, "to be plentiful," has been interpreted as the name of a blessed fountain in Paradise; but it is at the same time the symbol of the comprehensive grace by which the Prophet was distinguished, whereas his enemy and slanderer is doomed to be *abtar*, "without issue." A typical example of a rather late interpretation of this sura is that written by a Naqshbandi mystic in Sind in the eighteenth century, ʿAbdur Rahim Girhori. His long poetical commentary on Sura 108, in Sindhi, is certainly influenced by the grandiose verse of Jami, who, like him, was a member of the Naqshbandiyya.[73] But he goes even farther than the master of Herat and makes God say, among other exalted words of praise for the Prophet:

> So many gifts gave I to none but you.
> You are the cup-bearer of the fountain: carry on now its distribution,
>   O brave one!
> The keys of power have I put into your hand, O friend;
> The sciences of heaven and earth are a gift for Ahmad.
> The philosophers' stone have I given you, the elixir of Adam,
>   O friend.
> To Jesus, a certain portion of grace was [given] from this elixir,
> With which the dead were quickened, the deaf became hearing;
> For the blind: seeing eyes; from the lepers fell their leprosy.
> Whatever is in the Torah is like a sip out of that ocean,
> The whole beauty of Joseph, a sign of that gift.
> A small quantity only of your love, O Ahmad, has reached Zulaikha;
> Paradise is part of that ocean, as though it were ice of the ocean.
> Hell is at your door supplicating like a beggar,
> Having without your permission no strength to burn the unbelievers.
> Paradise is your splendid manifestation, just a look of love;
> Your look of wrath, O pure one, is Hellfire.
> Heaven, earth, empyrean, God's Throne, humans, djinn, and angels
> Live, My beloved, always in dependence on you.
> Dearest, humanity became worthy because of your light,
> Thanks to your reflection, My darling, buds and flowers are
>   blossoming . . .[74]

It was of course possible that such lofty ideas about Muhammad's primordial rank and his central place in the history of the universe might degenerate into bizarre mythical images, particularly on the folk level, and the comfortable Persian expression *hama ūst*, "Everything is He," did lead ignorant bards to what one could call 'heretical" statements in their wish to praise Muhammad as intensely as possible. The more sober theologians and scholars, however, were always aware of this danger. Indeed, how could they not be, when an Urdu poet dared to sing:

> How could one know the rank of our Leader of the world?
> If you want to reach God, know Muhammad as God![75]

Even the most faithful followers of Ibn ʿArabi would probably have shuddered at such a remark, for "the Lord remains Lord, and the servant, servant."

It seems that mythological embellishments of the story of creation involving Muhammad were not unknown, especially in the Indian environment. Shaikh Chand, the medieval Bengali poet whose remarks about the Light of Muhammad we quoted earlier, describes the creation of the world from the body of the primordial Muhammad in very concrete terms reminiscent of Vedic mythology:

> The seven heavens were created from the seven parts of the body of
> Muhammad:
> The first heaven is in the palate, the second upon the forehead,
> The third is within the nostrils, the fourth at the base of the upper lip.
> The fifth, you know, is in the throat,
> The sixth within the chest,
> The seventh inside the navel.[76]

In Jili's classical system the angels were created from Muhammad's spiritual powers (Israfil from his heart, Azraʿil from his judgment, etc.).[77] But Shaikh Chand tells his listeners that they came out of the Prophet's primordial body:

> The *farista* [angel; Persian *firishta*] Israfil was created from the nose,
> And ʿAzra'il was from the ear,
> From the mouth came Zibril [Gabriel]
> From the eyes sprang Mika'il.
> With each and every *farista* came 70,000 more,
> From each and every hair of each *farista*'s body was born another
> *farista*,
> From 300 million bodily hairs came 300 million *farista*.
> Thus from *nūr Muḥammad* came creation.

And, as the author continues, on God's command this creation became the *murīd*, "disciple," of Muhammad.

In the light of the unique position of the Prophet it is not surprising that his name is used in innumerable prayers, and even in magical incantations, to secure success and help. A good example is a long Persian prayer, called *Munājāt -i kun fa yakūn* (Prayer of "Be, and It Becomes") in which not only the names of all prophets, companions, imams, and saints are mentioned but also a fortyfold invocation "By the honor of . . . Muhammad," usually in rhyming pairs or in alliterations; for instance:

> By the honor of Muhammad's character, *khū*, and Muhammad's tresses, *gēsū*,
> By the honor of Muhammad's heart, *dil*, and Muhammad's clay, *gil*,
> By the honor of Muhammad's beauty, *jamāl*, and Muhammad's perfection, *kamāl*,
> By the honor of Muhammad's taste, *dhauq*, and Muhammad's longing, *shauq*,
> By the honor of Muhammad's path, *ṭarīqat*, and Muhammad's law, *sharīʿat*.
> By the honor of Muhammad's crown, *tāj*, and Muhammad's heavenly journey, *miʿrāj*,
> By the honor of Muhammad's journey, *safar*, and Muhammad's victory, *ẓafar*,
> By the honor of Muhammad's intercession, *shafāʿat*, and Muhammad's braveness, *shajāʿat* . . .[78]

Another litany, said to "draw out ailments," uses similar formulas: after the profession of faith follows the formula

> There is no illness and no pain that has not a cure and a remedy—
> By the honor of Muhammad the Messenger of God.

Then follows the name of a Companion of the Prophet, then the same repetition of the initial formula, and so on until all Companions and all caliphs (or, in related litanies, all members of the Sufi orders from the Prophet to the leading medieval saints) are enumerated. The praise of Muhammad, however, is the focal point of all these litanies.[79] They too prove the unshakable faith of the pious in the power of the Prophet, and their trust in him, the first and the last in the chain of prophethood.

It is astonishing that despite this central position of the Prophet in the mystical tradition of Islam, and especially in popular, post–thirteenth-century Sufism, many outside critics have remained barely aware of the sublime role that he plays in the religious life of his followers. This becomes evident from the example of some Hindu interpreters of Muslim poetry in India. Although a number of Hindus were ardent followers of Muslim saints and even sang eulogies for the Prophet in Urdu and in Sindhi, it seems that many of them could not gauge the depth of the mystical veneration of the Prophet. A good example is Lilaram Watanmal, who in 1889 published the first comprehensive book about the Sindhi mystical poet Shah ʿAbdul Latif. He writes quite condescendingly:

> Shah Latif, too, has in his *Risālō*, in several places, impressed upon his hearer the necessity of believing in Mahommad as a prophet and something more. It is true that some of the verses in praise of the prophet, somewhat vulgar in language, are not our poet's. . . . But it cannot be doubted that there are several genuine verses in which our poet has expressed his full belief in the prophet. . . . The orthodox Mahommadans [*sic*] might well believe him as the chief prophet of God. But the Sufis cannot, consistently with their pantheistic doctrines, say that the prophet Mahommad is the only medium of salvation. . . . It may be that Shah Latif wanted to lead the minds of his followers slowly and gradually into higher Sufism by allowing them to believe first in their prophet, and then by degrees to ascend higher and higher.[80]

Watanmal, who, like all Hindu interpreters of Sindhi and Panjabi Sufi poetry, tries to explain Sufism as a more or less pantheistic, slightly Islamicized version of the Vedantic mysticism of Unity, might have known external Islam but was completely unaware of the central position of Muhammad as the intercessor and the "column of light," as the Perfect Man and the first and last of the prophets, as it had been expressed for so many centuries in multifarious images and symbols, and as it was indeed decisive for religious experience in wide circles in Islamdom.

However, one must keep in mind one important fact: even though Muhammad was elevated to luminous heights and reached a position comparable, in certain ways, to that of the Logos in Christian theology, yet even as the Perfect Man he remained *ʿabduhu*, God's servant and His creature—the most beloved of His creatures, to be sure. Even though some poets seem to transgress the proper limits in their encomia, the idea of an incarnation in the Christian sense was and is absolutely impossible in the Islamic tradition. Over the centuries Islamic orthodoxy has felt, understandably, uncomfortable with the growing mystical veneration of the Prophet, which seemed to many to be exaggerated and not in harmony with the essential spirit of Islam. They have rightly pointed out that the axis of Islam is not the person of the Prophet but rather the Word of God, as revealed through him and laid down in the Koran. Nevertheless, it seems that the overflowing love for the Prophet, the trust in him and the veneration of him, was a decisive factor in the formation of poetry and popular piety and offered the Muslims a human object to which they could devote their tender, admiring feelings. The human aspect of the Prophet, and the possibility of a person-to-person encounter with him, who seemed more accessible than the eternal Divine Essence, filled them with happiness. And it is probably a logical corollary of the "Gnostic" tendency of later Islamic mysticism, in which the loving encounter between man and a personal God who is at once Creator, Sustainer, and Judge was no longer deemed possible, that the pious imagination turned to the veneration of the Prophet, who with all his mystical grandeur still remained a person to whom his fellow creatures could turn in love, hope, and admiration, which they then tried to express in ever new, ever more colorful and ecstatic words.

EIGHT

THE CELEBRATION OF THE PROPHET'S BIRTHDAY

A Turkish dervish of the seventeenth century sings:

> The night in which the Messenger was born is
> Without doubt similar to the Night of Might,[1]

that is, to the night in which the Koran was revealed for the first time, which is called in Sura 97 "better than a thousand months." A century later, the Malikite mufti of Algiers, Ibn ʿAmmar, brought forth three scholarly proofs for this idea: (1) the birthday, *maulid*, has given the Prophet to the whole world, but the Night of Might, *lailat al-qadr*, was meant especially for him; (2) Muhammad's appearance was more important for the community, *umma*, than the "coming down of the angels" of which Sura 97 speaks, for Muhammad is superior to the angels; and (3) the *maulid* is a most important day for the entire universe, whereas the first revelation of the Koran is meant for the Muslims in particular.[2] These two statements clearly indicate the degree to which veneration of the Prophet had increased during the late Middle Ages, and how much it permeated the piety of the masses and the elite.

In general, the Prophet's birthday is called *maulid*, a word that also often denotes the festivities held on this day. An alternative term is *mīlād*, "birthday, anniversary," and the passive participle *maulūd*, from the root *w-l-d* that underlies all these terms, is also used. *Maulūd* (written in modern Turkish *mevlût* or *mevlûd*) appears, however, more frequently to denote poetry or literature written in honor of the Prophet's birth and even, more generally, of his life. (For instance: "We went to a *maulid* in his house and listened to a classical *maulūd*.")

To be sure, even in the earliest reports miraculous events are mentioned in connection with the night of Muhammad's birth. This was the night of 12 Rabiʿ al-awwal, the third lunar month, which was remembered also as the day of the Prophet's death.[3] Long after colorful celebrations of the Prophet's birthday had become popular in the Near East, the Indian Muslims still spent this night listening to earnest sermons and recitations of the Koran as well as in almsgiving; the day was called *bārah wafāt*, "the twelfth, [day of] death," and in some places a "general *ziyārat* [visit] of the dead" took place.[4]

In the late eighth century the house in Mecca in which Muhammad had been born was transformed into an oratory by the mother of the caliph Harun ar-Rashid, and pilgrims who came to Mecca to perform the *ḥajj* visited it in pious awe. It seems that the tendency to celebrate the memory of Muhammad's birthday on a larger and more festive scale emerged first in Egypt during the Fatimid era (969–1171). This is logical, for the Fatimids claimed to be the Prophet's descendants through his daughter Fatima. The Egyptian historian Maqrizi (d. 1442) describes one such celebration held in 1122, basing his account on Fatimid sources.[5] It was apparently an occasion in which mainly scholars and the religious establishment participated. They listened to sermons, and sweets, particularly honey, the Prophet's favorite, were distributed; the poor received alms.

However, this rather solemnly pious atmosphere changed before long. A lively description of early *maulid* festivities is given by the historian Ibn Khallikan in his account of Ibn Dihya, who had witnessed them in 1207 in Arbela, Ibn Khallikan's native city, in northern Iraq. Preparations for the *maulid* had begun during the first lunar month; wooden pavilions were erected and guest rooms for the numerous visitors from abroad prepared, and large quantities of sheep, goats, and cows were brought to be slaughtered for the guests. The princes of Arbela participated not only in the prayer meetings and the sermons but also in the *samāʿ*, the mystical concert arranged by the Sufis. There were processions with candles, and even "Chinese shadow-players."[6]

Illumination was later to become a typical aspect of many *maulid* celebrations. In Turkey, for example, the mosques are decorated with lights, and the day itself, called *mevlût kandīlī*, "the candle feast for the Prophet's birthday," is spent in fasting until sunset. It is evident that the Sufis played an important part in the elaboration of the *maulid* and contributed to its colorful character. But it is also understandable that orthodox theologians declared such celebrations to be *bidʿa*, an "innovation." The reformer Ibn Taimiyya (d. 1328) especially energetically attacked such lightheaded amusements, "which earlier Muslims did not consider right nor practiced."[7] But one of the early Arabic *maulid* works (which consists almost exclusively of *ḥadīth* concerning the night of the Prophet's birth) emerged from the pen of one of his disciples, Ibn Kathir.

Not only the Hanbalite Ibn Taimiyya, but the theologians of the Malikite school of law, which has its stronghold in North Africa, clearly spoke against the exaggerated festivities on 12 Rabiʿ al-awwal: on a day that is also the anniversary of the Prophet's death, neither music nor joy are permissible. The ecstatic mystical poetry often recited in connection with a *maulid* has remained a stumbling block for more sober Muslims to our day, as a Bengali scholar wrote a few years back, in his discussion of the *maulid* in his country: "The main theme of the *ghazal*s [which are sung after the *mīlād* proper] is to eulogize the Prophet in the most extravagant terms, often giving him an identical place with God. All the audience relish these songs enthusiastically without a murmur of dissent."[8]

Authorities of the fifteenth and sixteenth centuries, like the mystically minded polymath Suyuti (who composed a work defending the "good innovation" of the *maulid*)[9] and the traditionist Ibn Hajar al-Haithami, deemed it permissible that the Koran be recited and religious songs be sung, but they prohibited other musical entertainment and even more the use of lights and candles. Processions with candles and illuminations reminded them too much of the customs of their Christian neighbors and the celebration of Christmas or Candlemas (2 February)—which indeed may well have influenced the customs of the popular *maulid*, just as Christian critics of Islam would, in turn, sometimes see "parodies of Christ's life"[10] in the elaboration of the *maulid* stories as well as in some miracles told about Muhammad. Even some Muslim modernists tend to ascribe this development to "clearly jealous emulation of what the Christians say about Jesus the Christ."[11]

Despite all this criticism *maulid* celebrations became more and more common in Islamic lands, at least in the central and western areas.[12] In North Africa such celebrations are first mentioned as an innovation introduced by the Merinid ruler of Fez in 1291; ever since they have formed an important part of religious life in Morocco and the adjacent areas—all the more since several North African dynasties claim sharifian status, that is, descent from the Prophet. Thus religious and national emotions could be successfully blended in the *maulid* celebrations. As in Iraq, the Sufis in Morocco have participated actively in the festivities of the Prophet's birthday, which came to be considered in the hierarchy of festive days second only to the canonical feasts, that is, the *ʿId al-fiṭr* at the end of Ramadan, and the *ʿId al-aḍḥā*, the feast of sacrifices during the pilgrimage to Mecca. And just as a boy born during the fasting month of Ramadan can be called Ramadan (Persian and Turkish Ramazan), in North Africa—and probably elsewhere—children born on the *maulid* day may be named Maulud or (feminine) Mauludiyya, or similar forms. A recent article has shown that recitations of mystical poems and processions of dervish orders—like the Issawiyya and the Hamadsha—were at times integral parts of the *maulid* celebrations in North Africa; these performances often ended in a wild frenzy no longer compatible with the character of the celebrations.[13]

In Egypt, the tradition of *maulid* was continued from Fatimid days by all subsequent dynasties. The Mamluk rulers in the fourteenth and fifteenth centuries usually celebrated the feast (generally not on the twelfth but on the eleventh of the month) with great pomp in the courtyard of the citadel of Cairo.[14] There an enormous, beautifully decorated tent was pitched, and after recitations and readings from the Koran the sultan distributed purses and sweets to the religious dignitaries. Special letters of congratulation were sent out according to protocol.[15] The people outside the Mamluk military establishment had their own celebrations. One observer, a British orientalist, later published a lively account of a *maulid* in the Ezbekiyya Park in Cairo at the beginning of the nineteenth century, which certainly maintained many ancient features; the strophic poem in which the singers expressed their love for Muhammad reminded him somewhat of the love lyrics of the biblical Song of Songs.[16] Nowadays, recordings of famous *maulūd* songs are sold in stores, so that everyone can enjoy the special mood of the celebrations.

Throughout the Middle Ages the Prophet's birthday was lavishly celebrated in Mecca. In Kashmir—to mention a comparatively modern example from the Indian subcontinent—people liked to celebrate the first twelve days of Rabiʿal-awwal near the Hazratbal Mosque in Srinagar, where a hair of the Prophet is preserved. And from as early as the second half of the seventeenth century we have very colorful descriptions of the celebrations of the *maulid* under the Qutbshahi kings of Golconda.[17] In their capital, Hyderabad/Deccan, drums and bugles were played during the first twelve days of Rabiʿal-awwal, and *durūd* for the Prophet were repeated 101 times after the ritual prayers. A vast plain was transformed into a center of exhibitions, where merchants from all over India would sell their products, from toys to carpets and jewelry. The king (at that time ʿAbdallah Qutbshah) even inaugurated an exhibition of paintings, and in the evening, lectures on the life of the Prophet were delivered under a huge canopy. After that, one thousand pretty Telugu girls performed dances; acrobats showed off their tricks, and *ghazal*s were sung. The first day of the celebrations concluded with a luxurious dinner party; on the actual birthday an enormous amount of tasty food was distributed to all and sundry. On a simpler scale one could also, as is still done in India, cook some food, dedicate it to the Prophet's spirit, and then distribute it to the poor.[18]

In the latter days of the Ottoman Empire, in 1912, the 12 Rabiʿal-awwal was declared a public holiday, and it is celebrated as such today in Pakistan. We have, for example, a lively account (from the leading Pakistani newspaper) of the celebration of the Prophet's birthday on 29 December 1982: "another 'spectacular feature' of the day was the elaborately arranged Id-i milad procession in which thousands of participants participated to express their profound love with the Holy Prophet (peace be upon him). Cities and towns which had been tastefully decorated with flags, bunting, festoons and streamers wore a festive appearance, and an added attraction was the glittering illumination at night." A *Seerat* conference, dealing with the biography of the Prophet, was inaugurated by the president of Pakistan, and numerous *maḥfil*s (gatherings) took place, and "radio and television beamed out special programmes befitting the occasion. . . . The day began with a 31-gun salute in Rawalpindi and 21-gun salute in the provincial capitals. The national flag was hoisted over government and private buildings."[19]

Yet in the very same year a *fatwā* of the chairman of the Mecca-based *Rābiṭa*, an orthodox Muslim organization, declared the celebrations of the *maulid* to be an "evil innovation." This remark aroused sharp criticism from various corners of the Muslim world, from South Africa to Iran.[20]

During recent decades an increasing tendency has been observed throughout the Muslim world to use the *maulid* in the service of modernist ideas. In Pakistan, the whole month of Rabiʿal-awwal is devoted to remembrance of the Prophet and his ethical, political, and social role, and a similar attitude is found, more or less outspokenly, in other Islamic countries as well. Schools, the press, and broadcast media unite in their efforts to portray the Prophet in most impressive colors and to call the Muslims to strive to emulate his exemplary moral attitude.

It is therefore understandable that the touching popular, poetic stories about the miracles that accompanied his birth are no longer cited as they were in former days. In tune with many critical modernists, a Bengali scholar described a few years ago with utter dismay the celebrations of the *Fātiḥa dawāzdahum* (Fatiha of the twelfth), as the *mīlād* is called in Bengal, in which

> such fictitious stories are told as no rational man can believe. It is needless to say that in the narration of these stories decency is lamentably violated and the historicity of the Prophet's career is disgracefully disregarded. People are taught to believe that the Prophet presents himself in spirit in such parties, and this is why, when the mulla finishes his narration with the birth of the Prophet, the audience

> stands up from their seats to honor the spirit of the Prophet and hail him in chorus.[21]

In fact, in 1934 the minister of education in Egypt turned against the fanciful, useless stories with which the large part of popular *maulūd* poetry was filled, and tried, as had orthodox reformists from Ibn Taimiyya to the Wahhabis in Saudi Arabia, to purge these stories of all the accretions that seemed incompatible with a modern, scientific viewpoint and to reduce the veneration of the Prophet to a sound, sober level. But it was no less an authority than the famous blind literary critic Taha Husain, educated in France, who objected to such an intrusion upon the people's traditions. He wrote, among other arguments:

> It seems most fitting not to deprive people of ideas which do not contradict religion and do not spoil them in any part of their faith. What is the danger for the Muslims when one tells them the sweet and lovely stories of these *ḥadīth* and informs them that the communities of birds and beasts competed after the birth of the Prophet because all of them wanted to look after him, but were refused because it had been decreed that the Prophet should be nursed by the blessed Halima? And what is wrong for the Muslims when they hear that djinn, men, animals, and stars congratulated each other at the birth of the Prophet, and that the trees sprouted leaves at his birth, and that the gardens blossomed at his arrival, and that the sky came close to the earth, when his noble body touched the ground?[22]

It was precisely the miracles that were said to have happened on the occasion of the Prophet's birth that most delighted and uplifted the devout, and inspired poets and theologians to describe the birth of "the best of mankind" in ever new, ever more glowing images.

The earliest Arabic sources, basing their claims on Koranic epithets like *sirājun munīr,* "a shining lamp," tell that a light radiated from Amina's womb with the arrival of the newborn Prophet. Hassan ibn Thabit sings in his dirge for Muhammad that his mother Amina of blessed memory had born him in a happy hour in which there went forth

> a light which illuminated the whole world.[23]

It is not surprising that this spiritual light was soon given material reality in the accounts of the Prophet's birth, as can be seen first in Ibn Saʿd's historical work in the ninth century. Yunus Emre sings, like numerous poets in his succession in Turkey, Iran, and India:

> The world was all submersed in light
> In the night of Muhammad's birth.[24]

And Ibn al-Jauzi before him—without doubt a serious, critical theologian of Hanbalite persuasion and not a mystical poet—wrote in his *maulid* book, which is the first of this kind:

> When Muhammad was born, angels proclaimed it with high and low voices. Gabriel came with the good tidings, and the Throne trembled. The houris came out of their castles, and fragrance spread. Ridwan [the keeper of the gates of Paradise] was addressed: "Adorn the highest Paradise, remove the curtain from the palace, send a flock of birds from the birds of Eden to Amina's dwelling place that they may drop a pearl each from their beaks." And when Muhammad was born, Amina saw a light, which illuminated the palaces of Bostra. The angels surrounded her and spread out their wings. The rows of angels, singing praise, descended and filled hill and dale.[25]

An Andalusian scholar in the twelfth century, the Qadi Ibn ʿAtiyya, takes up this idea:

> The month of Rabiʿ precedes the [other] months
> And, by God! it has one night which is resplendent
> With luminous meteors between the horizons . . .[26]

Qadi ʿIyad, the great authority on the Prophet's biography, who was a devout North African Muslim, does not mention any miracle except the light in his brief description of Muhammad's birth. This is rather astonishing, for the narratives about the various wondrous events that happened during Muhammad's birth belong to the oldest layer of legends. It was said that a radiant light shone from the forehead of ʿAbdallah, Muhammad's father, and although several women tried to woo him away for the sake of this light, he married Amina, whom God had predestined to become the Prophet's mother. The light was carried in her womb.

In the night when the Prophet was begotten—thus Abu Nuʿaim's *Dalāʾil an-nubuwwa*—all the cattle of the Quraish talked among themselves to tell each other that the future leader of the community had been begotten. Amina was ordered to call the child Muhammad or Ahmad. She had an untroubled, easy pregnancy. But when the time came that she was to give birth, strange things happened:

> And while it became heavier and heavier for me and I was hearing an increasingly strong noise, lo, a white silken kerchief was spread between heaven and earth, and I heard a voice say: "Let him disappear from the views of men!" I saw men standing in the air, who held sil-

> ver ewers in their hands. The perspiration which dropped from me was like pearls and more fragrant than strong musk, and I exclaimed: "O that ʿAbdul Muttalib would come to me! Woe that ʿAbdul Muttalib is far from me!" Then I saw flocks of birds descending upon me and covering my lap; their beaks were of emerald and their wings of hyacinth. And God took away the veils from my eyes, and I saw the earth in the East and in the West. I saw three flags erected, one in the East, one in the West, and one on the roof of the Kaʿba. Labor set in, and it became difficult for me. . . . Thus I gave birth to Muhammad, and I turned to him to look at him, and lo, there he was lying in adoration, lifting his hands to heaven like one supplicating. Then I saw a cloud coming from the sky which covered him so that he became invisible to me, and I heard someone call: "Lead him around the earth in East and West, and lead him to the oceans that they may recognize him with his name and his stature and his qualities and that they may know that he will be called in the oceans *al-Māḥī* [the One Who Wipes Out] because he will wipe out all polytheism." Then the cloud disappeared quickly, and lo, there he was lying, wrapped in a white woolen garment, and beneath him there was a green cover from silk. He held three keys of white pearls in his hand, and someone exclaimed: "Look, Muhammad keeps in his hand the key of victory, the key of bloodshed, and the key of prophethood."[27]

Other reports tell that the newborn Prophet fell to the ground and, pressing his hands on the earth, looked up to the sky; this was interpreted as indicating his role as ruler of the whole earth.

No poet forgets to mention the light that "illuminated the world to the palaces of Bostra" in Syria. "A shining bow appeared like rainbow. This light which appeared was like television, for it brought nearby and showed clearly cities far away," is how a Swahili preacher explained this miracle in 1963.[28]

Significant signs were witnessed in the neighboring countries when the Prophet was born; it is said that the halls of the palaces of the Persian king were shattered, or that the Tigris and Euphrates flooded the capital, and later poets, especially in the Persianate tradition, have played in their encomia with the verbal connection between Kisra (Khosroes, the Persian emperor) and the Arabic word *kisr*, "breaking."[29]

The popular tradition according to which Amina was attended during her labor by Asiya and Mary, contains a hint at Muhammad's superiority over Moses and Jesus. Asiya is Pharaoh's believing wife who looked after the infant Moses, and Mary as Christ's virgin mother occupies along with her, and even more than she, a place of honor in Islamic piety.

It is also important to remember that Muhammad was born free from all bodily impurities. He was circumcised when he appeared from the womb; this legend is popularly taken as the basis for the circumcision of boys—a duty not mentioned in the Koran but known among Muslims as a *sunna* of the Prophet (it is therefore called *sünnet* among the Turks).

The first comprehensive book about the Prophet's birth, as far as one knows, was composed by the Andalusian author Ibn Diḥya, who had participated in the festive *maulid* in Arbela in 1207. Written in prose with a concluding poetical encomium, his work has the characteristic title *Kitāb at-tanwīr fi maulid as-sirāj al-munīr* (The Book of Illumination about the Birth of the Luminous Lamp), in which the light-mysticism associated with Muhammad is evident. Two Hanbalites, Ibn al-Jauzi and, a century and a half later, Ibn Kathir, devoted treatises to the *maulid*. Poetical works about this important event were also composed relatively early. It is noteworthy, however, that Busiri's *Burda* (late thirteenth century), the most famous of all Arabic eulogies, mentions the Prophet's birth only in passing, and does not give any special, detailed description of it. And one should keep in mind that Ahmad ad-Dardir's famous *maulid* begins with the praise of God "Who is free from 'begetting' and 'being begotten' [or, 'being born,' *maulūd*]."[30]

In the Turkish tradition, the best-known early *mevlût* was written by Süleyman Chelebi of Bursa around 1400. But more than a century earlier, Yunus Emre had already promised heavenly reward to those who recite *mevlût*, which shows—provided the verses are genuine—that *mevlût*s were popular among the Turks at a rather early stage. Süleyman Chelebi's poem is written in rhyming couplets, a literary form adopted from the Persian. Its rhythm is simple; the meter is the same as that used primarily in Persian mystical and didactic epics such as ʿAttar's *Manṭiq uṭ-ṭair* and Rumi's *Mathnawī*. The language is plain, almost childlike, and therefore the poem has not lost anything of its charm even today.[31] (But even this poem was considered an impious innovation by a stern Turkish theologian of the fifteenth century, Molla Fenari!) The *mevlûd-i sherif*, as it is called, is still being recited in Turkey, not only on the Prophet's birthday but also on the fortieth day after a bereavement, as a memorial service on a death anniversary, or in fulfillment of a vow, because it is credited with a very special blessing power. Similarly, Indian Muslims, especially women, used to celebrate *mīlād* parties at every great family event.

The celebration of a *mevlût* in a Turkish family is a festive affair, and as in other parts of the Islamic world one puts on fine clothes for such an occasion and then seeks what an East African poet describes in the beginning of his *maulūd* poem:

From the moment you set out toward the *maulid*,
You have gone out to experience the raptures of Paradise.[32]

Sometimes incense is burnt, and at the end of the recitation, which is interspersed with numerous recitations from the Koran as well as prayers, sweets are distributed. In North Africa one usually prepares *ʿaṣīda*, a kind of pudding made of hominy, butter, and honey, the same sweet that is given to the guests at a real childbirth.[33] In other areas the participants are offered cool sherbet and candies; in Turkey everyone used to take home a little paper bag filled with sweets.[34]

Süleyman Chelebi's *mevlût* was often imitated, so that there are about a hundred different versions of *mevlût* poetry in Turkish; but no other Turkish religious poem can compete with it for the favor of all classes of society. Its first part tells the story of Muhammad's birth as Amina experienced it. Full of amazement, she recounts (using the traditional imagery) what happened to her at the end of her pregnancy:

Amina Khatun, Muhammad's mother dear:
From this oyster came that lustrous pearl.
After she conceived from ʿAbdallah
Came the time of birth with days and weeks.
As Muhammad's birth was drawing near
Many signs appeared before he came!
In the month Rabiʿ al-awwal then
On the twelfth, the night of Monday, look,
When the best of humankind was born—
O what marvels did his mother see!
Spoke the mother of that friend: "I saw
A strange light; the sun was like its moth.[35]
Suddenly it flashed up from my house,
Filled with world with light up to the sky.
Heavens opened, vanquished was the dark,
And I saw three angels with three flags.
One was in the East, one in the West,
One stood upright on the Kaʿba's roof.
Rows of angels came from heaven, and
Circumambulated all my house;
Came the houris group on group; the light
From their faces made my house so bright!
And a cover was spread in mid-air,
Called 'brocade'—an angel laid it out.
When I saw so clearly these events

I became bewildered and confused.
Suddenly the walls were split apart
And three houris entered in my room.
Some have said that of these charming three
One was Asiya of moonlike face,
One was Lady Mary without doubt,
And the third a houri beautiful.
Then these moonfaced three drew gently near
And they greeted me with kindness here;
Then they sat around me, and they gave
The good tidings of Muhammad's birth;
Said to me: 'A son like this your son
Has not come since God has made this world,
And the Mighty One did never grant
Such a lovely son as will be yours.
You have found great happiness, O dear,
For from you that virtuous one is born!
He that comes is King of Knowledge high,
Is the mine of gnosis and *tauḥīd* [monotheism].
For the love of him the sky revolves,
Men and djinn are longing for his face.
This night is the night that he, so pure
Will suffuse the worlds with radiant light!
This night, earth becomes a Paradise,
This night God shows mercy to the world.
This night those with heart are filled with joy,
This night gives the lovers a new life.
Mercy for the worlds is Mustafa,
Sinners' intercessor: Mustafa!'
They described him in this style to me,
Stirred my longing for that blessed light."
Amina said: "When the time was ripe
That the Best of Mankind should appear,
I became so thirsty from that heat
That they gave me sherbet in a glass.
Drinking it, I was immersed in light
And could not discern myself from light.
Then a white swan came with soft great wings
And he touched my back with gentle strength.

As this verse is recited, every participant ever so gently touches his or her neighbor's back.

And the King of Faith was born that night:
Earth and heaven were submerged in light!"

Then begins the great Welcome, which all nature extended to the newborn Prophet, whose coming they had expected with such longing, a welcome to the Friend of God in whose intercession at Doomsday all can trust:

Welcome, O high prince, we welcome you!
Welcome, O mine of wisdom, we welcome you!
Welcome, O secret of the Book, we welcome you!
Welcome, O medicine for pain, we welcome you!
Welcome, O sunlight and moonlight of God!
Welcome, O you not separated from God!
Welcome, O nightingale of the Garden of Beauty!
Welcome, O friend of the Lord of Power!
Welcome, O refuge of your community!
Welcome, O helper of the poor and destitute!
Welcome, O eternal soul, we welcome you!
Welcome, O cupbearer of the lovers, we welcome you!
Welcome, O darling of the Beloved!
Welcome, O much beloved of the Lord!
Welcome, O Mercy for the worlds!
Welcome, O intercessor for the sinner!
Only for you were Time and Space created . . .

There follows an extended description of the Prophet's miracles, among which the heavenly journey occupies a central place. Importantly, every section ends with the verse

If you want to be rescued from Hellfire,
Utter the blessings over him with love and [longing] pain!

In Turkey, this *mevlût* (which, incidentally, has even been translated into Serbo-Croatian)[36] is concluded with a special prayer in which God is entreated to send the recompense for the recitation to Muhammad's Rauda in Medina; then follow prayers for the Prophet's family, for saints and scholars, and requests for the participants' happiness and long life, "so that they may enjoy participation in many, many more meetings of this kind"; then prayers for the caliph,[37] for soldiers, traders, and pilgrims, and for a peaceful death, and future life in Paradise.

The conviction that a *maulūd* has a blessing power is not peculiar to Turkish Muslims. Its *baraka* is acknowledged everywhere in the Muslim world. The East African Muslim is convinced, for example, that "when a person recites it there will be peace and blessing for a whole year, disasters and thieves will not come near, and you will not see the burning of his house."[38] From the Middle Ages onward it was believed that the recitation of the *maulūd* would grant the listeners not only worldly but also heavenly reward. As a Turkish verse says:

> If you want salvation from Hellfire,
> Come to the *mevlût* for God's messenger![39]

Yunus Emre, at a very early point in Turkish literary history, described the events at resurrection and during the Last Judgment:

> On Doomsday it will be called out:
> "He who has sung *mevlût*, shall come!"
> God gives a license made of light—
> He who has sung *mevlût*, shall come!
> He shall go fast to Paradise,
> He shall turn to the left and right—
> What grace the Lord has shown to him!
> He who has sung *mevlût*, shall come . . .[40]

One *maulid* that has been particularly popular in the African countries was written in the eighteenth century by al-Barzanji, a Malikite qadi of Medina.[41] Its original Arabic text was in prose, but later poets often transformed it into poetry; there are three poetical versions of it in Swahili. It is also widespread in India. On the African scene, an acrostic *qaṣīda* of 1,400 lines (28 × 10 × 5) by one al-Fayyazi also deserves mention; it is recited for *maulid* celebrations in Northern Nigeria.[42] Among the Arabs, the Hadramis seem to excel in *maulid* poetry; one anthologist and critic mentions more than twenty *qaṣīda*s, "each of which has a delightful Hadrami tune," that are used in *maulid* celebrations in southern Arabia, where the interaction between the singer, who recites the poem in *tarannum* (recitative) style, and the audience is very common.[43] One sees the same trend with many mystical *maulid* poems recited in *qawwāli* in India and Pakistan. In Egypt, a panegyric by the Sufi al-Munawi, from the seventeenth century, is recited with great affection during the *maulid* celebrations. A modern Egyptian writer, Ahmad ash-Sharabasi, even composed (in 1962) a play entitled *Maulid al-hudā* (The Birth of the Right Guidance).

In the Indian subcontinent, a *maulid* literature proper developed rather late and was written predominantly—at least as far as narrative poetry is concerned—in Persian. Popular *maulid*s in Bengali have a long tradition, but as can be understood from the remark of the Bengali scholar cited above, these seem to have been generally more fanciful than poems popular in other areas. Serious narrative *maulid*s in literary Bengali were composed only comparatively recently. However, in the Middle Ages there were some mystical accounts of the Prophet's birth in Bengali that placed the event within the all-embracing Indian religious scene by having Brahma, Vishnu, and others foretell the Prophet's coming.[44]

In some languages of the subcontinent, such as Sindhi, the so-called *maulūd* is a brief lyrical poem that is recited in a peculiar style. Its contents, however, are not restricted to the Prophet's birth but touch various aspects of his life.[45] The colorful legends connected with the *mīlād* are told, in Sindhi, in long, ballad-like poems, called *munāqibā*, a style that also serves to narrate the other miracles of the Prophet.[46] Panjabi poets might use the form of *Sīḥarfī*, or "Golden Alphabet," or write long *qaṣīda*s with fanciful titles like "The Most Beautiful Remembrance of the Birth of the Best of Mankind" to translate into simple Panjabi verse the loving greetings uttered by birds and plants to the newborn child.[47]

These poets loved to adorn their descriptions of the Prophet's birth with delightful embellishments from their own local environment—a practice no more astonishing than the depiction of Christmas in a Nordic winter landscape, to which we are accustomed in the West. Thus a poet from Gujarat around 1600 introduces into his *maulūd* a Brahmin who was present during the Prophet's birth and put his sacred thread around the newborn baby's neck.[48] Other poets have invented lullabies for the Prophet, like Faqir Muhammad Machhi in Sind, who tells in detail how God granted the Prophet before his birth the qualities of patience, wisdom, modesty, gratitude, intelligence, and love and after his birth ordered Gabriel to rock the cradle "lest my beloved cry."[49] God then taught the angel, or the poet, an Arabic lullaby; its refrain is an elaboration of a medieval verse:

> *qum qum yā ḥabībī kam tanām*
> *an-naumu ʿalāʾl-ʿāshiq ḥarām:*
> Get up, get up, my friend—how long will you sleep?
> Sleep is forbidden for the lover![50]

In the course of this certainly not exactly artistic but well-intended little poem all the things that cannot sleep from joy at the Prophet's birth are enumerated:

> The pond and the *kauthar* do not sleep—
> Get up, my beloved, how long will you sleep!
> The Creator of creation does not sleep . . .
> The Pen and the Tablet do not sleep . . .
> Heaven and Hell, they do not sleep . . .
> Sun and moon . . . Throne and Footstool . . .
> Days and nights . . . mountains and oceans . . .
> The right and the left, they do not sleep . . .

Sleep is forbidden for the lover:
Get up, my beloved, how long will you sleep?

In the course of the last century there has emerged a shift in the mystical and mythical orientation of the *maulid* celebrations, toward a more practical, timebound emphasis on Muhammad's political and social achievements, his moral behavior, and his intelligent way of organizing the communal life. This trend is quite in harmony with the more modern interpretation of the personality of the Prophet, and is reflected also in pious poetry. The early writings of Sir Sayyid Ahmad Khan, the leading Indo-Muslim modernist, aim at demythologizing the literature about the *maulid*, and following Sir Sayyid's example, his friend the reformist poet Hali clearly expressed this new spirit by citing the legend that the Persian palaces and the fire temples fell to ruin on the day of Muhammad's birth:

Extinguished the fire temple,
Crumbled down the idol temple,
Checkmated is dualism,
Vanished is the Trinity![51]

The birth of the Prophet means the victory of absolute monotheism over both Persian dualism and Christian trinitarianism, both being aspects of the victory over polytheism in general. The idea is of course not new, but in a country under Christian supremacy, as British India was during Hali's lifetime, these verses bore a very special meaning.

Still, despite all attempts at modernization, the old, tender, and colorful songs about the miracle of Muhammad's birth are still sung, and thanks to them, love for the Prophet is implanted in the children's hearts to become an integral part of their religious life.

NINE

THE PROPHET'S NIGHT JOURNEY AND ASCENSION

A folksong from the Indus Valley, composed in the eighteenth century, greets the Prophet dozens of times, taking up the welcome that once the angels and the blessed souls in Paradise accorded to him:

> Muhammad, you traveled to heavens high,
> The angels addressed you with "Welcome!"
> The inhabitants of the heavens too
> Said: "Welcome, a hundred times welcome!"[1]

The Prophet's mysterious night journey (*isrāʾ*) through the heavens has inspired a literature even more comprehensive than that about the miracles accompanying his birth.[2] Furthermore, from the viewpoint of both theologians and mystics, his ascension to heaven (*miʿrāj*) is much more important in the Divine *Heilsgeschichte* than the *maulid*.[3]

The nucleus out of which the story of the mysterious journey grew is the statement at the beginning of Sura 17: "Praised be He who traveled by night with His servant from the sacred mosque to the farthest sanctuary!" The "farthest sanctuary," or rather the "farthest mosque," *al-masjid al-aqṣā*, was interpreted as meaning Jerusalem:[4] hence the present name of the Al-Aqsa mosque in that city.

The earliest biography of the Prophet, the *Sīra* of Ibn Ishaq, tells the story thus: One night the angel Gabriel lifts the Prophet onto a heavenly mount called Buraq; Muhammad then travels with Gabriel, and on this night journey or *isrāʾ*, he is shown the marvels of heaven and earth en route to Jerusalem, where he meets with the former prophets and leads them in ritual prayer. Then, from the "farthest mosque" he begins his heavenly journey, first described as climbing a heavenly ladder, *miʿrāj*.[5] (Some commentators separate the two events—the night journey and the ascent to heaven—but even Ibn Ishaq combines both, and since he is regarded as the most reliable biographer of the Prophet, his account is generally the basis for further elaborations.) The ascent is described as followed in his *Sīra*:

> A trustworthy person has reported to me from Abu Saʿid that he had heard Muhammad tell: "After I had done the necessary in Jerusalem I was brought a ladder (*miʿrāj*), and I never saw a more beautiful one. It was the one upon which the dead turn their glances at the resurrection. My friend [Gabriel] made me climb until we reached one of the heavenly gates, which is called Gate of the Guard. There twelve hundred angels were acting as guardians.

Here, Ismaʿil asks Muhammad's name and inquires whether he is indeed a true messenger. After receiving a satisfactory answer, he allows Muhammad to pass through the heavens. In the lowest heaven the Prophet sees Adam, in front of whom the souls of mankind are paraded, and he is shown the punishments of the sinners, which correspond to the nature of their crimes. Those who have embezzled the money of orphans must swallow fire; usurers with terribly swollen bodies are chased by crocodiles into the fire and are trampled down; and so on, through many other, even more horrible punishments. Muhammad then visits the subsequent heavens and meets in them some of the prophets who preceded him. He sees Jesus in the fourth heaven and Abraham in the seventh. That Abraham is located in the highest possible sphere proves once more his very special position in the Islamic tradition both as the ancestor of the Arabs through Ismaʿil and as builder of the Kaʿba, and as the spiritual hero who smashed the idols. Finally the Prophet enters Paradise. In some redactions of the tale, he is offered on his way three cups, one with water, one with milk, and one with wine; he chooses the milk, which is interpreted as choosing the right "middle path." This brief interlude is a typical initiation rite.

According to one oft-repeated tradition, God then commands the Prophet to introduce fifty daily prayers in his community. While he descends to earth, Moses remonstrates with him, saying that his people will never be able to perform that many prayers and he should return to ask God that the number be reduced. After several repeated efforts God does finally reduce the number of required prayers to five. When Moses says that even this is too much, Muhammad refuses to ask for any lighter duty, so the number has remained at five for the Muslim ever since.[6] Thus the heavenly journey is shown to have a very practical purpose. But this purpose did not remain so central in later versions of the legend, which substitute other motives or supplement it with elaborations. In particular, the right of intercession by the Prophet is often seen as the chief result of his dialogue with the Lord.

According to Islamic tradition the *isrā'* and *mi'rāj* took place during the later Meccan period of Muhammad's life, not long before his Hegira to Medina. It is commemorated on 27 Rajab, the seventh lunar month. In some areas, for instance in Kashmir, the memory of the *mi'rāj* used to be celebrated for a whole week with recitations and illuminations. In Turkey, the night of the *mi'rāj* came to be treated parallel to the night of the Prophet's birth, as a *kandīl*, an illuminated night, in which the mosques are decorated with lamps. Children born on this auspicious day can be called, as I know at least from Indo-Pakistani practice, Miraj, Miraj Din, Miraj Muhammad, and the like.

No other aspect of the Prophet's life has interested orientalists and historians of religion more than the heavenly journey.[7] It appears to be a kind of *Berufungserlebnis*, or initiatory experience, and is therefore combined in some legends with the cleansing of Muhammad's heart. Scholars have even seen in the night journey parallels to the experiences of Siberian shamans; the seat of honor that Muhammad was accorded at the *Sidrat al-muntahā*, "the Lote Tree of the farthest limit" (Sura 53:14) in Paradise, has reminded historians of religion of the visions of shamans who reach the world-tree in their ecstatic flights. Influences from Iran have also been postulated, as they are found in the Middle Persian *Arda Viraf Nāmak*, and Indian parallels have been suggested as possible prototypes or at least as analogous religious phenomena. Needless to say, comparisons with Jewish and Christian apocalyptic visions have presented themselves as particularly appealing parallels.[8]

It is said that at Muhammad's return his bed was still warm and that the pitcher of water, which had tumbled over when he was carried away, had not yet leaked out completely.[9] Thus the heavenly journey became a model of the ecstatic state in which man can live in a single moment through years, nay, centuries and millennia; for the *nunc aeternum* with which the mystic's soul comes in touch during such an experience is beyond created, serial time. It is the *waqt*, the moment, or, as German medieval mystics would say, *das Nu*, that the Prophet experienced during his flight. In order to explain this experience of complete timelessness to doubting spirits present in every community, apologists like to use the old Indian tale of the man who, submerged in water, lives in a few instants through a whole lifetime—a story that has been used in India to exemplify the play of *maya*, illusion, and has been taken over into the Near Eastern and even European traditions.[10]

Islamic theologians have devoted much speculation to the heavenly journey, for it presents some difficulties to solve. First of all it had to be clarified whether Muhammad made this journey in the body or in the spirit. The remark of his wife 'Ai'sha that "his body was not missed" was countered by an increasing tendency to claim that the journey had indeed been a physical one. Certainly, the Muʿtazilite school considered the whole event a vision and admitted only of the possibility of a spiritual journey,[11] while the "orthodox," for example the leading Muslim commentator on the Koran, Tabari (early tenth century), were of the opinion that the Prophet's journey indeed took place in the body, for they were more literally inclined, and the Koran, as Tabari stresses, clearly states that God "traveled with His servant at night" and not "with His servant's spirit." And why would the Prophet have needed a mount like Buraq for a purely spiritual, visionary journey?[12] The modernists, again, have regarded the *miʿrāj* as a vision.[13] At least one scholar in the modern West has drawn a parallel to an ecstatic experience familiar to and accepted by Christians: he reminds us that Paul speaks in 2 Corinthians 12:1–10 of a seemingly similar event.

> I know a man . . . , whether in the body, or out of the body I know not, was caught up even to the third heaven . . . was caught up into Paradise, and heard unspeakable words, which it is not lawful for man to utter.

Perplexed though he was about the nature of his own experience, "with Paul this is the record of indubitably mystical experience, which was the occasion and ground of an unyielding assurance."[14]

Later literature, especially popular poetry, contains numerous tales that tell how terribly those were punished who denied Muhammad's bodily journey to heaven. For according to one widespread theory, which is particularly common among the Sufis, the Prophet's pure body could reach an immediate proximity to God that the normal believer, nay, even the greatest saint, can reach only in the spirit. The highest grace granted to a human being is thus that his spirit may attain the same purity as the Prophet's body: only then will he be able to perform a spiritual journey to draw closer to the Divine Presence. This point became an important argument in discussions whether the Prophet or the saint occupies a loftier place in the spiritual hierarchy: it is the heavenly journey in the body—a body that is "spirit embodied," as the Turkish poet Khaqani sings—that once and for all proves the unique position of the Prophet.

Another controversial question was whether Muhammad had really seen the Lord, and if so, whether with his eyes or with his heart. This problem was discussed particularly in connection with the interpretation of Sura 53, *An-Najm*, "The Star." This Sura describes in its first part a vision of the Prophet who "saw him on the highest horizon." One can take the "him" to refer to Gabriel, the bringer of the revelation, and thus understand the whole sura as an account of the Prophet's vision during a revelation; but as "Him" it has also been interpreted as pertaining to God.[15] That is the case when Sura 53, as later often happened, is interpreted as describing the heavenly journey. "Some said: He saw Gabriel at the highest horizon; others say he saw Allah with his heart and his inner view; still others say, he saw Him with his eyes; but all of them speak the truth for they only tell what they have heard."[16]

Those who regarded Sura 53 as an account of Muhammad's vision during the heavenly journey—and these were above all the mystics—point then to verse 17, "The eye did not rove." To them that means that even during the immediate vision of the Divine Essence, Muhammad did not turn away his eyes.

> I closed my eye tightly from both worlds—
> That is it that I learned from Mustafa:
> The mystery of *mā zāgha* [it did not swerve] and *mā ṭaghā* [it did not turn away]—
> Where but from him could I learn it?[17]

Thus says Rumi in words that are echoed time and again in later poetry. Nobody can imagine how close the Prophet was to the one he saw: *qāba qausain au adnā*, "two bows or closer" (Sura 53:9). This term has sometimes been explained as pertaining not to the length of two bows but rather to the fine juncture where the two halves of a bow are glued together; it is almost invisible and yet constitutes a distinct line of separation. So close did the Prophet come to his Lord.

It is a proof of Muhammad's superiority over all other prophets that in this extreme proximity "his eye neither swerved nor was turned away." Did not Moses faint when the Divine attributes were merely manifested to him through the Burning Bush? And he had heard only the Lord's voice and had been told "You will never behold Me!" (Sura 7:139), whereas Muhammad, without moving and turning away his eye, had experienced the vision of God.[18] "The lord of *qāba qausain*" has therefore been praised by poets in most daring hyperboles. Perhaps the most succinct description of the event was given by an Indo-Persian poet of the late fifteenth century, Jamali Kanboh, who sums up this mystery within a famous couplet:

> Moses went out of his mind by a single revelation of the Attributes—
> You see the Essence of the Essence, and still smile![19]

Not only the Sufis—as early as Hujwiri[20]—but also the orthodox theologians, including especially the Hanbalites, utilized the same argument from Sura 53 to prove Muhammad's superior position. They also used it to prove that the highest level of religious life is not mystical annihilation (as with Moses, who swooned) but rather the sober attitude of the Prophet, who experienced God's presence in full consciousness.[21]

According to one tradition, Muhammad claimed to have seen his Lord "in the most beautiful shape"[22] or, in a later version, as a beautiful unbearded youth wearing his cap awry[23]—a *ḥadīth* that the majority of Muslims of course refuted vehemently, though it gave certain groups of Sufis a justification for their admiration of "unbearded" youths.

Other interpreters, particularly among the later mystics, see in the heavenly journey the true consecration of the Prophet, because they relate the word *istawā*, "he stood upright," in Sura 53:6 not to the one whom Muhammad saw but rather to the Prophet himself. Likewise the phrase "he came closer and descended" (53:8) was taken to mean Muhammad, who after the initiation came down again to his beloved community to look after them. This interpretation fits well with later descriptions of the ideal religious path as exemplified by the Prophet: he is ready to take upon himself the descent into the world after experiencing the Divine Presence in order to preach what he has learned there. Animated and sanctified by his inexplicable, face-to-face dialogue with God, he will try to change the conditions of the world (even though, as some traditions have it, he also suffered under the burden of this duty).[24] Muslim theologians and Western historians of religion would agree that in this interpretation of the *miʿrāj* the basic difference between the mystical and prophetic types of religion is indeed well expressed; a difference so succinctly summed up by Muhammad Iqbal in the beginning of the fifth chapter of his *Lectures on the Reconstruction of Religious Thought in Islam*, where he quotes the saying of the Indian Sufi ʿAbdul Quddus Gangohi: "Muhammad of Arabia ascended to the highest heaven and returned. I swear by God, had I been in his place, I would not have come back."[25] These words point unambiguously to the different attitudes of mystic and prophet toward the experience of the Divine, and its consequences for one's relation to the world and its inhabitants. But even a number of Muslim mystics, such as Ibn al-Farid, interpreted the night journey as "the third stage of Oneness in which the mystic returns from the 'intoxication of union' to 'the sobriety of union,' "[26] which exactly corresponds to the "prophetic" way back, as Iqbal explains it, in the succession of earlier thinkers.

Furthermore, Islamic modernists (and again particularly Iqbal), when discussing the heavenly journey, have pointed out that Muhammad was able to speak to God in a true I-and-Thou relationship. This seemed to Iqbal a very important corrective of the widespread doctrine of the Unity of Being: the legend of the heavenly journey confirms that God is not a mute, remote *prima causa* but indeed a personal power who can be addressed, and thus proves that there is the possibility of a fruitful person-to-person dialogue between Creator and creature, a dialogue in prayer, out of which true religious activity can grow.

Connected with this person-to-person encounter is another aspect of the heavenly journey that has been frequently discussed: the interpretation of the word *ʿabduhu* at the beginning of Sura 17. It is stated there that God had traveled by night with *ʿabduhu*, "His servant." This led many exegetes to conclude that because it is used in the Koran to designate the Prophet during his supreme religious experience, *ʿabduhu* must indeed be the highest possible and most honorific attribute to be given to a human being. This is all the more logical as the same word *ʿabduhu* is used in Sura 53:10, to mean either the act of revelation or the Divine address to the Prophet at the culmination of his heavenly journey. A remarkably large literature developed out of this concept of *ʿabduhu*; it was discussed in the eleventh century in the *Risāla* of the mystical writer Qushairi,[27] which remained one of the most widely read manuals of Sufism for centuries, and it has been given a central place in this century in Muhammad Iqbal's anthropology and prophetology (see chapter 12 below). At the same time, the emphasis on *ʿabduhu* served to remind Muslims always to remember that Muhammad remained a created being even during his highest mystical experience, however much God had glorified him and exalted him among all creatures.

But the mystics in the tradition of Ibn ʿArabi have often repeated the idea that there cannot be a real *miʿrāj* in the spatial sense, for God is omnipresent. "God spoke: 'How could My servant travel to Me? I am always with him!' "[28] This truly mystical interpretation of the *miʿrāj* has found its most poignant expression in a quatrain by the much maligned Persian Sufi Sarmad, who was executed for heresy in Delhi in 1661.

> The mullah says that Ahmad went to heaven—
> Sarmad says that heaven descended into Ahmad![29]

At least as important as the elaborate discussion about and various interpretations of the heavenly journey by theologians and mystical teachers is the role the *miʿrāj* plays in Islamic art and poetry. The poets, especially in the Persian and Persianate areas, have depicted this mysterious event through increasingly fantastic and grandiose images, using all their imagination to vie with one another in fanciful descriptions of the Prophet's journey through the spheres. Most of the great epic poems in Persian include, after the praise of God and a eulogy for the Prophet, long descriptions of the heavenly journey, in which every conceivable rhetorical device is used to give the reader at least a faint idea of this unique event. The story was embellished with ever more charming details, such as the growing of the rose from Muhammad's perspiration that fell to earth during his nocturnal flight. And the poets tried to express the paradox that the Sun of Existence had risen heavenwards *at night*.[30]

In the regional languages of Indo-Pakistan, for instance in Panjabi, long *sīḥarfīs*, "Golden Alphabets," are devoted to the mystery of the *miʿrāj* and also to the punishment of those who deny that miracle.[31] Among the Persian mystics ʿAttar is particularly expressive when depicting the heavenly journey in novel images. The introduction of his *Ilāhīnāma* (available to nonspecialists in John A. Boyle's English translation) gives a good idea of the boundless flood of colors that he used to depict the Prophet's journey through the spheres. When reading his and related poems one has to keep in mind that an important motif of the early tradition is gradually disappearing, that is, the ladder; the whole journey is now made on Buraq.

Helmut Ritter's edition of the Persian text of the *Ilāhīnāma* presents a version of the introduction that is simpler than the one used by Boyle, but it contains important elements of mystical prophetology; it does not mention the reduction of fifty ritual prayers to five, but rather combines the heavenly journey with Muhammad's role as the intercessor for his community, a development that seems to have set in rather early. Here is what ʿAttar sings:

At night came Gabriel, and filled with joy
He called: "Wake up, you leader of the world!
Get up, leave this dark place and travel now
To the eternal kingdom of the Lord!
Direct your foot to 'Where there is no place'
And knock there at the sanctuary's door.
The world is all excited for your sake,
The Cherubs are tonight your lowly slaves,
And messengers and prophets stand in rows
To see your beauty in this blessed night.
The gates of Paradise and skies are open—
To look at you, fills many hearts with joy!
You ask from Him tonight what you intend,
For without doubt you will behold the Lord!"
Buraq was now brought near, as lightning swift—
God had created him from His pure light,
From head to toe enlivened by God's light—
And from the wind he learned swiftness and speed.
The Prophet mounted him in time and space;
He left this place for "Where there is no place."
There rose a tumult in the greatest Throne:
"Here comes the first, the full moon of the worlds!"
The angels stood with trays to scatter coins
For him, whom they all loved with heart and soul.
He saw the prophets on his road in line
To tell him of the mysteries divine . . .[32]

Beginning with Adam, the Prophet is now introduced by all messengers of God into the mysteries of God's beauty and majesty, for every prophet experiences the Divine Essence in a different way; Muhammad alone is granted knowledge of It in Its fullness.

When Jesus saw him, lofty and sublime,
He made him then unique in Poverty.
Then, when he felt the nearness of the Friend,
He went to see the presence of the Friend.
When Ahmad ran beyond the Sidra-tree,
To find the essence of the Highest Friend,
His faithful guide, this mighty Gabriel,
Whose one wing covers all from sky to earth,
Stayed there behind; but Mustafa went on,
Soon drawing closer to the Royal Hall.
The prince turned now to Gabriel and asked:
"Why do you stay behind? Come with me now!"
He answered: "O, my King of mysteries,
I cannot farther go, cannot proceed!
You, ruler of the world, must go ahead—
My way ends here, and more is not allowed:
Should I proceed a hair's breadth in my flight,
My wings would burn in God's consuming light!
But you must go toward the Friend Supreme,
For it befits to you to be so close!"
Thus went the lord and left him there behind,
Cut off his heart from ev'rything but God.
He went so fast that when he looked again,
The mighty Gabriel looked like a wren.
Proceeding farther he left this behind
And looked into the veils of the Unseen.
He saw no place, direction, reason, thought,
No Throne nor floor and not the dusty earth:
He saw the Non-Place without soul and eye—
He, in bewilderment, was hidden there.
When he perceived the end in the beginning,
He heard a call, a message from the Friend.
A call came from the Essence of the All:
"Leave soul and body, transitory one!
You, O My goal and purpose, enter now
And see My Essence face to face, My friend!"
In awe, he lost his speech and lost himself—

Muhammad did not know Muhammad here,
Saw not himself—he saw the Soul of Souls,
The Face of Him who made the universe!

The poet goes on to depict in more detail the Prophet's state of total bewilderment and depersonalization; but then God once more graces Muhammad with His address and finally tells him:

"You are My goal and purpose in creation
And what you wish, request it, seeing eye!"
Muhammad said: "Omniscient without How,
You inward secret, outward mystery—
You know my innermost and dearest wish:
I ask you now for my community!
Sinful is my community, but, sure,
They are aware of You, Your boundless grace.
They know the ocean of Your love and grace—
How would it be if You forgave them all?"
Once more he was addressed by God Most High:
"I have forgiven altogether, friend:
You need not worry for your people, for
My boundless grace is greater than their sins."

And after the intercession for the Muslim community has thus been accepted, the Lord initiates the Prophet, whom He addresses as "unique among the creatures" and "seeing eye of all" into three times thirty thousand mysteries.[33] ʿAttar then speaks of the real mystery of the heavenly journey and finally ends with a prayer addressed to him who was thus distinguished among the prophets, that is, to the Prophet of Islam, in whom he trusts and whom he loves.

In ʿAttar's description the role of Gabriel is of special importance. A *ḥadīth* of which the mystics were very fond alludes to the archangel's situation: he has to stay back at the *Sidrat al-muntahā*, "the Lote Tree of the farthest limit" (Sura 53:14),[34] "like a nightingale separated from his rose" (so the Turkish poet Ghanizade in his *Miʿrājiyya*).[35] Whatever Gabriel's greatness, Muhammad's was of a special order. According to legend, the Prophet had once requested to see the archangel, who usually appeared as a handsome friend, in his true form;[36] the reality was so awe-inspiring and terrible that Muhammad fainted. Still, even this mighty angel, whose one wing fills the space between heaven and earth, has no access to the Divine Presence; as Yunus Emre sings in unison with all great mystics,

For lovers even Gabriel is a veil.[37]

In the famous *ḥadīth* connected with this mystery the Prophet said, *Lī maʿa Allāh waqt . . .* , "I have a time with God to which even Gabriel, who is pure spirit, is not admitted."[38] This remark is interpreted as pertaining to the mystery of the heavenly journey, in which the Prophet was taken out of serial, created time and touched the Eternal Now of God. The term *waqt*, "time," then, became a central concept in Sufi life: the Sufi is called to give himself over completely to this Divine moment, to be *ibnu'l-waqt*, "son of the moment," that is, to live in the moment of Divine inspiration. Even more, the *ḥadīth* about *waqt* also relates to the experience of prayer. After his return from heaven, the Prophet used to call his Ethiopian muezzin Bilal, "O Bilal, quicken us with the call to prayer!"[39] whenever he longed to return into the Divine presence and leave time and space. For it is in prayer that man can feel this immediate relation with God. Ritual prayer is, therefore, as the Prophet once said, a heavenly journey. Maulana Rumi formulated this secret of prayer in a famous reply to a question posed by one of his disciples:

> Formal prayer has an end, but the prayer of the soul is unlimited. It is the drowning and unconsciousness of the soul so that all these forms remain without. At that time there is no room even for Gabriel who is pure spirit.[40]

Drawing on the same tradition, Rumi in his *Mathnawī* used Gabriel as the symbol of intellect, which can lead man all the way to the door of the Beloved, but is not admitted within to experience loving union: intellect has to stop at the threshold of love, for, like Gabriel, it has to fear lest the consuming Divine light burn its wings.[41]

Numerous embellishments accrued to the basic story of the *miʿrāj*, especially in Sufi circles. A delightful legend from Balochistan goes even farther than the tradition just mentioned and accords the great medieval Sufi ʿAbdul Qadir Gilani a place superior to Gabriel. It is said that when Muhammad wanted to alight from his heavenly mount Buraq to enter the secret chamber of God's presence, Gabriel had already withdrawn. But ʿAbdul Qadir stepped forth: he, the future founder of the most widespread mystical fraternity in the Islamic world, offered the Prophet his neck that he might step on it to alight without discomfort. Out of gratitude, Muhammad granted the future saint a very special rank: when he would appear on earth some five centuries later his foot would be "on the neck of every saint."[42] Thus ʿAbdul Qadir's famous claim to precedence, "My foot is on the neck of every saint," which was heard by all saints of his age, is charmingly connected with his presence at a crucial point of Muhammad's heavenly journey. The Mevlevi tradition does not lag behind in inventiveness. According to the *Manāqib al-ʿārifīn*, the Prophet saw a wonderful effigy (*timthāl*) at the Divine Throne; it was the portrait of Jalaluddin Rumi.[43] And it is not at all surprising that in some Shia traditions, ʿAli ibn Abi Talib accompanies the Prophet into the Divine Presence.

The *miʿrāj* never ceased fascinating the poets, even the nonmystical ones. Nizami, ʿAttar's senior compatriot, offered in his romantic epics some most artistic descriptions of the heavenly journey, and in the course of time every detail, the colors of the sky, the garments of the angels that surrounded the Prophet and flew before him, the luminous clouds and the reactions of the seven planets, were elaborated with ever-increasing love and imaginative power. Jami's great epics contain a whole set of such poems, represented perhaps most beautifully in *Yūsuf and Zulaikhā*, where he sings of the blessed night in which wolf and lamb, sheep and lion, lie peacefully together and Gabriel, swifter than a green peacock, brings Muhammad the lovely Buraq. Jami (following Nizami)[44] loves to recount the reactions of the different spheres and planets that the Prophet traverses; he describes the fourth sphere, for instance, as bringing the Prophet a ewer of water with which to wash his feet, while Mercury and Venus join in serving him, and melancholy Saturn is consoled by the lovely sight of the Sun of Existence.[45]

Later poets all over the Islamic world, especially in the Persianate tradition, elaborated on the examples set by Nizami, ʿAttar, and Jami, and whether one reads Sayyid Bulaqi or Nusrati in seventeenth-century Bijapur,[46] or, to mention a particularly fine example, their contemporary in Turkey, Ghanizade, one always meets with surprising, fanciful descriptions. Thus the idea that the Prophet's sandals touched the Divine Throne and that "the dust of his road was the crown for the Throne" is repeated over and again.[47]

Ghanizade's *Miʿrājiyye* from seventeenth-century Turkey seems to me an outstanding example of this art, surpassing most other descriptions of the heavenly journey in baroque images.[48] The poet describes the blessed night in which "the darkness was black sable," and then sings of the innumerable miracles of the Prophet until he admonishes himself to come at last to the theme proper of his poem, the heavenly journey. Here, it is especially the description of Buraq, a quadruped larger than a donkey but smaller than a horse, that is very attractive. The poets have always loved to describe this creature, which was created from light, had a woman's head and a peacock's tail, and swiftly carried the Prophet through the galaxies of angels, all of whom greeted him full of admiration.

> The heavenly messenger came to the holy Prophet in that night,
> He brought a Buraq, fast like lightning and sky-traversing,

It was a strange mount, trotting speedily, running about now on earth and now on the heavenly Throne.
In the earthly realm a hastening gazelle, in the heavens a swiftly flying phoenix.
Its body, roses; its hair, hyacinth; imperial its tail, that delightful tail;
Its ear a lily's petal; its reddish eye a shimmering narcissus . . .

While the Prophet flies through the spheres, everything in the cosmos is happy to serve him:

Mercury wrote the order of that prince on the tablet of the sky:
For him the night was letters; the stars, blotting sand; and the moon's forehead the imperial handsign (*ṭughrā*) . . .

Then Gabriel must remain behind near the Lote tree, and Buraq itself is exchanged for a mysterious vehicle called *rafraf* (cf. Sura 55:76, where it is said to mean a kind of heavenly cushion),[49] and finally even the *rafraf* (here perhaps a green cloud) remains behind "like a leaf, separated from the fresh fruit in the fall." Now, Muhammad moves on alone into the Divine Presence, experiencing what the mystics in the Plotinian tradition used to call "the flight of the one to the One."

Buraq looms large in the whole process and becomes so prominent in these poems that the central object of the earlier versions, the heavenly ladder or *miʿrāj*, seems completely forgotten, even though it continues to lend its name to the whole experience.[50]

Not only the poets loved the scene of this heavenly journey that gave them the opportunity to display all their rhetorical skills to glorify the Prophet. The miniaturists of Iran and the countries under its cultural influence also devoted their most beautiful painting to the *miʿrāj*. The superbly illustrated Uyghur manuscript of the *Miʿrājnāma* from the Timurid court in Herat, now preserved in Paris, belongs among the first examples of this genre, which began to develop in the late fourteenth century.[51] This *Miʿrājnāma* (available in a fine facsimile edition) gives a lively account of all the stages and stations that the Prophet passed on his journey. In most other cases, only his passage through the starry skies is painted and, as the Sindhi folksong says:

Gabriel before him afoot,
the bridegroom riding on horseback.[52]

One sees the Prophet, his face veiled, surrounded by multicolored clouds, flying on Buraq through the night sky; in modern times he is sometimes symbolized by a graceful white cloud or a rose on Buraq's back. Angels in precious garments surround him, carry incense before him, and accompany him, as befits a prince, in pomp and circumstance to the gate of the Divine Presence. Anyone who has seen Sultan Muhammad's painting of the heavenly journey, in the Nizami manuscript now in the British Library, knows that poets and painters were equally inspired by the Prophet's ecstatic experience to create deeply religious masterpieces.[53]

The Prophet's heavenly journey was a favorite subject of popular poetry too, for folk poets enjoy telling stories about miraculous events in which the Prophet's glory can be described in highly colorful terms.[54] Typical of this genre is a poem by Yunus Emre, composed around 1300 in Anatolia (close parallels can be found in the folk poetry of Indo-Pakistani Muslims as well):

> God sent out Gabriel and said:
> "My Muhammad shall come!" He said.
> "Take the Buraq, draw it to him—
> My Muhammad shall mount!" He said.
>
> "He shall go to Medina first,
> In front of him shall angels fly,
> Open the gates of Paradise—
> Enter, my Muhammad!" He said.
>
> "My Muhammad shall come, shall come,
> He shall see and look at My Throne
> Shall pluck the rose of Paradise—
> My Muhammad, smell them!" He said.
>
> "I shall bring near the farthest things,
> I shall fulfill his every wish,
> And all the angels in green robes—
> My Muhammad shall see!" He said.[55]

Such poems correspond to the simple paintings of the *miʿrāj* found in Indian or Turkish manuscripts but even more to those that nowadays adorn freight and tanker trucks in Afghanistan and Pakistan: one can find on them a more or less elegant Buraq in full bridal attire, sometimes even with the bride's nosering, the hooves gracefully crossed, all painted with great care and love. One can be sure that this sacred creature will protect the vehicle, leading it along rugged Pakistani roads, as it once had carried swiftly and carefully the beloved Prophet through the galaxies.

As the image of Buraq has become an amulet or talisman for simple truck drivers in the mountainous areas of Pakistan, or for visitors to the major shrines of saints in the Indian subcontinent, so too was the heavenly journey of the Prophet understood from early centuries onward as a paradigm for the spiritual experience of the mystics. Since the ninth century the Sufis have

Buraq, painted on the back of a Pakistani tanker truck

been wont to describe their own ecstatic transports as a journey through the heavens, because—as we saw earlier—they experience in the spirit what the Prophet had experienced in the body. Bayezid Bistami, the lonely mystic of northern Iran, whose visionary account of his flight through heavenly realms belongs to the earliest "paradoxes of the Sufis," was apparently the first to utilize this symbolism.[56] As Shams-i Tabrizi said: "To follow Muhammad is, that he went to the *miʿrāj*, and you go behind him."[57] From Avicenna and Suhrawardi the *shaikh al-ishrāq* to Ibn ʿArabi, mystical visions, which led the seeker's soul into the Presence of the Divine, were described in the terminology of the *miʿrāj*.[58] Remembering—at least subconsciously—that the *miʿrāj* is a kind of initiation experience, the Bektashis in Turkey until recently used that term as the name of the day on which a new member of the order "took his share," that is, was initiated into the order, and would felicitate him with the words *Miracın kutlu olsun!* "May your *miʿrāj* be blessed!"[59]

In high mystical poetry, then, Buraq sometimes becomes an equivalent of Love, the Divine Love that, as Rumi repeatedly sings, can bring man in the twinkling of an eye into the Divine Presence while intellect lags far behind in the dust like a lame donkey.[60] It is quite possible that the Persian word *nardabān*, "ladder," which occurs so frequently in the mystical verse of Sana'i and, following him, Rumi, was intended to be an allusion to the heavenly *miʿrāj* that the Prophet ascended, for it is generally used to describe the mystic's journey to "the roof of the Beloved." And Rumi calls *samāʿ*, the mystical dance, "a ladder that leads higher than the seventh sphere," for in *samāʿ*, the mystic can reach the unitive experience, the "time with God."[61]

While enjoying the mystical and poetical renderings of the *miʿrāj* one has to keep in mind that the story of Muhammad's heavenly journey has also exerted a considerable influence on other cultures. When looking at the miniatures in the Uyghur *Miʿrājnāma* manuscript in Paris, so many of whose images are devoted to the Prophet's visions of Heaven and even more of Hell, one cannot help feeling that one has here to do with illustrations of Dante's *Divine Comedy*. Indeed, several decades ago Miguel Asín Palaćios discovered possible Islamic influences from the *miʿrāj* stories on Dante's visions.[62] These first studies caused quite a sensation in Europe, and somewhat later, Enrico Cerulli was able to prove that Arabic books about the heavenly ladder, *Kitāb al-miʿrāj*, and the Prophet's ascension were not unknown in the Mediterranean world during the Middle Ages; in fact, they were apparently well enough known to influence some of Dante's descriptions of the Otherworld.[63] How ironic that the hero of the true *miʿrāj*, the Prophet Muhammad, should have been placed by Dante among the schismatics in the lowest part of Hell!

In the history of Islamic literatures the motif of the journey through Heaven and Hell was also used outside the mystical tradition. One immediately thinks, for example, of satirical works like Abu'l-ʿAla' al-Maʿarri's (d. 1057) *Risālat al-ghufrān*, which can be classified as a very witty parody of a journey through the otherworldly realms.[64] In this work the author displays a breathtaking knowledge, especially of philology, but also other kinds of scholarship, and the whole is studded with innumerable ingenious puns, apt comparisons, and delightfully malicious observations. This complicated but highly enjoyable masterpiece from the eleventh century found a rather dull echo in an Arabic poem published in 1931, Jamil Sidqi az-Zahawi's "Rebellion in Hell," which takes up the satirical approach of Maʿarri to explain in the end the whole experience as a bad dream, caused by indigestion.[65] A year later, Muhammad Iqbal published in Lahore his Persian *Jāvīdnāma* (The Book of Eternity), in which the motif of the journey through the heavens receives a modern philosophical content.

Guided by Maulana Rumi, whom he invokes in the beginning and who, as it were, assumes the role of Gabriel in the classical *miʿrāj*, and of Virgil in the *Divine Comedy*, the poet discusses political, social, and religious problems with prominent inhabitants of the different spheres. In the end, he stands all alone in the Divine Presence, which is "growing without diminishing."[66]

Of course, an orthodox Muslim who is aware of modern technical achievements may look at the heavenly journey from a different angle. In 1978 at the University of Peshawar I heard a noted theologian draw the conclusion that man's landing on the moon was a stringent proof for the reality of the Prophet's heavenly journey.[67]

TEN

POETRY IN HONOR OF THE PROPHET

Sana'i (d. 1131), the first great Persian exponent of the genre, explains very aptly why *naʿt*, poetry in honor of the Prophet, has never lost its broad appeal across all Islamic cultures:

> To speak any word but your name
> Is error, is error;
> To sing any artistic praise but for you
> Is shame, is shame![1]

And an Urdu poet of the early nineteenth century exclaims:

> Friend, before all of us is the journey into nonexistence—
> But when one has words of the *naʿt*, then one has provisions for the road![2]

Such lines express a feeling that has been shared by most poets and authors who have undertaken to praise the Prophet in verse. But at the same time all of them have been convinced that it is next to impossible to do justice to his greatness, or to describe his beauty and mildness in appropriate words. Yet

> How should not men, angels, and djinn praise him
> Since God Most High Himself has praised him?

This question was posed not by a Muslim but by a Hindu poet, Shivprasad Dohi, who claimed that his soul was "a moth around the candle of meeting with Mustafa."[3]

It is in fact exactly this formulation, that "God Himself has praised him," that has caused serious difficulties for poets and collectors of *naʿtiyya* poetry. One notable example is Yusuf an-Nabhani, a pious lawyer from

Beirut who spent a lifetime collecting devotional works about the Prophet; he published the entire corpus of Arabic eulogies for the Prophet in a four-volume work and himself composed thousands of verses in praise of Muhammad. He begins his massive anthology with a chapter in which he states the traditional disclaimer that "the poets are incapable of praising Muhammad as it behooves and as it is necessary," because it is impossible to record the greatness of Muhammad's rank with panegyrics.[4] He records the same sentiments in one of his own poems:

> They say to me: "Did you not praise Muhammad,
> The Prophet of the God of everything created,
> The most worshipable among men?"
> I said to them: "What shall I say in his praise
> Since his Creator has praised him and has not left anything to say?"[5]

In other words, the very fact that Muhammad is mentioned in the Koran with words of praise and that God Himself utters blessings upon him renders human beings incapable of praising him as he deserves to be. As the Spanish author Lisanuddin ibn al-Khatib asks:

> The verses of the Holy Book have praised you—so how
> Could the poem of my eulogy possibly praise your greatness?[6]

Similarly Busiri says in a fine pun in his *Hamziyya*, is not the true miracle, *muʿjiza*, of the Prophet that tongues are incapable, *ʿijz*, of describing him?[7] Is not his praise like an unfathomable ocean without a shore, which the divers cannot measure out?[8]

And yet even though theologians and poets are well aware of this dilemma, they have returned time and again to eulogies of the Prophet, praising him in tender, colorful, or grandiloquent images, for "the heart longs to mention his noble name and his qualities" and thus to establish a spiritual relation with him, "because it belongs to the nature of the lover to mention the beloved constantly." These are the words of the editor of a comprehensive collection of *naʿt*s in Sindhi, who says in another place:

> The Prophet's distinctive role in the history of man's spiritual revolution is generally accepted. With the revolutionary theory of monotheism he has laid the foundation stone for the unity of humanity and the intellectual elevation of men. Instead of "form" he has quickened "spirit"; he has liberated thought and made it world-embracing; instead of conjectures and fanciful ideas he has illuminated the way of action and experience; and has made the use of hearing and seeing, of knowledge and intellect, a common feature; has brought the glad tidings of [man's capacity] to make sun and moon, nay, heaven and

> earth, subservient; and has inspired mankind to understand and grasp the primordial Reality by studying creation and psychological facts. To praise and eulogize such an august leader and benefactor of mankind as well as his companions and lovers is happiness for everyone endowed with sound nature.[9]

At about the same time that this Pakistani scholar from Hyderabad/Sind compiled the Sindhi eulogies for the Prophet, an Indian Muslim, professor of Persian literature in the Osmania University, Hyderabad/Deccan, wrote a long article about the central role of *naʿtiyya* poetry in Muslim life. According to him, praise of the Prophet goes much farther than simply expressing veneration for the Prophet; rather, it excels by its "character-building power"[10] and stimulates a "longing for the Perfect Man":

> The Prophet's character, as determined in the *naʿt* poetry, presents to the world an ideal example of submission to and harmony with God's Will.
>
> The most part of *naʿtia* poetry is related to the moral and spiritual values which are directly concerned with the training of the individual and the collective self of man.
>
> The chaos and the unrest brought about by the Second World War has naturally created an urge for a new world order. This is apparently reflected in the efforts which are being made on a large scale for co-existence. The *naʿt* is a branch of literature which plays an important part in building up the type of character aiming at breaking the racial, geographical and class barriers.[11]

The feelings that these scholars expressed in modern terminology were well known to Muslims in every part of the Islamic world during the Middle Ages and were popularized through the *maddāḥūn ar-rasūl*, the singers of eulogies, who formed, for centuries, regular guilds in the Arab countries and were called to perform at every important festivity.[12] The legends that surrounded Muhammad and the descriptions with which the Sufis had glorified him were all integrated in the poetical praise of the Seal of the Prophets and Beloved of God, to praise whom appropriately one selected the choicest expressions and most artistic forms.

THE ARABIC TRADITION

The first praise poems for the Prophet were written during his lifetime. Hassan ibn Thabit served him as a poet in Medina. His duty was in a certain sense that of a journalist who poetically noted down the important events that happened in the young Islamic community. He was there to denigrate the Prophet's enemies and to extol the brave deeds of the Muslims. His poems are therefore an important source for the earliest history of Islam. At the same time they contain many rudiments that came to be elaborated in later theology and poetry, such as the dogmatic statement:

> I witness with God's permission that Muhammad
> Is the messenger who is higher than heaven.[13]

Even though Hassan's poetry still contains allusions to wine and love as they were commonplace in pre-Islamic poetry, "his eulogies of the Prophet, which extol his spiritual virtues and his religious mission, and enumerate the graces bestowed on him by God, breathe a true Islamic spirit."[14] Hassan states:

> We know that there is no Lord but God,
> And that the Book of God is the best guide.[15]

We have mentioned earlier Hassan's repeated allusions to the light that radiated from the Prophet, to his miraculous birth and his hoped-for intercession. It is therefore not surprising that in later times every major poet who excelled in praise poetry for the Prophet was called the Hassan of his country. As a Persian poet modestly says:

> How could I, in all this confusion, perform
> [The role of] Hassan in laud and praise?[16]

Other poets besides Hassan were part of the Prophet's entourage, and their verse likewise contains some source material for the first period of Islam. Among them are Kaʿb ibn Malik and ʿAbdallah ibn Rawaha;[17] their names, however, are barely mentioned in the later, non-Arabic tradition. But even in non-Arabic tradition one work is repeatedly mentioned, which indeed belongs to the great masterpieces of early Arabic poetry: a *qaṣīda* by Kaʿb ibn Zuhair, who had slandered the Prophet and then, moved by fear, recited that long poem in his presence. It begins with the words *Bānat Suʿād*, "Suad went away . . . ."[18] The poet describes in the traditional style of the pre-Islamic *qaṣīda* the separation from his beloved, and the pains and fatigue caused by his journeying through the desert (a journey that allows him to praise his lightfooted, powerful camel), and then in a daring transition switches over from the description of a burning hot noon in the desert to the picture of the poor widow who lifts her arms in distress because the news of her son's, that is, Kaʿb's, death has just reached her. His she-camel's swift movement is

Like the movement of the hands of a bereaved elderly woman,
Who stands and [whose cries] are answered by others who have lost their children [as well],
As those that announce death, bring her the news of her first-born son's death;
She tears her breast with her hands while her bodice
Is ripped from her bones and torn to tatters.
The slanderers spread [calumny] at her side
And say: "Verily, Son of Abu Salma, you are about to be killed!"
And every friend in whom I had put hope said:
"I cannot spend time with you, for I am busy [with other things]!"
So I said: "Go away—may you have no fathers!"
For whatever the Merciful decrees has come to pass.
Everyone born by a woman—even though his life last long—
Will be carried one day on a curved [bier].
I have been told that the Prophet of God has threatened me—
But forgiveness is hoped for from God's Messenger . . .

Then the poet turns to the Prophet, apologizing for his mistakes, and asking forgiveness. Muhammad was so impressed by this poem that he cast his own mantle, the *burda*, on Kaʿb's shoulders, thus granting him forgiveness.

Even though some critics doubt the historicity of this event,[19] Kaʿb's ode—called the *Burda*—soon gained a very special place in Arabic poetry and not only became the model of all later poems in praise of the Prophet but assumed a sanctity of its own. To our day it has been commented upon, enlarged, and imitated, and in the remote Indus Valley the popular poets who specialize in extolling the Prophet derive their appellation, *bhān*, in a fanciful etymology from the words *Bānat Suʿād*.[20] And the *burda-i yamānī*, the Prophet's cloak of striped Yemenite material, has become in Persian poetical parlance, primarily in Jami's verse, a symbol of the veil that the Prophet is asked to lift from his sun-like face to bless the loving faithful with the view of his countenance.[21]

When the Prophet died, numerous short dirges were composed for him, some of them by the first caliphs. But the multifaceted and elaborate description of his qualities and virtues was developed during the first centuries in prose rather than in poetry. We have already mentioned that this sonorous rhyming prose, in which the beauty and strength of the Arabic language reveals itself most expressively and which almost defies translation due to its density, contains numerous works about the *shamāʾil* and *dalāʾil an-nubuwwa*, the signs pointing to the Prophet's unique qualities and attributes. At the turn of the first millennium A.D. Thaʿlabi was able to collect a long line of rhyming designations of the Prophet that one should use when mentioning him, for instance, in the introductory sentences of learned works or belles lettres. In his collections one finds statements like these:

> He brought his community from darkness to light, and afforded shadow for them when the sun was burning bright; Muhammad, God's messenger and closest friend, his prime choice among his creatures, the best one ever created by God and His proof on His earth; he, guiding to His truth and alerting to His wisdom and calling to His guidance; he, whose birth was blessed and whose arrival was fortunate; radiant is his morning light and glowing his lamp at night; he, whose wars are victorious and whose sermons are glorious, . . .[22]

The genre of poetical panegyrics for the Prophet emerged, as far as one can see, in the early eleventh century, and expressions like those collected by Thaʿlabi percolated into poetry.

As the mystics were mainly responsible for the development of the veneration of the Prophet into an elaborate literary genre, it was also a member of a mystical fraternity who composed the poem that to our day is regarded as the uniquely comprehensive, and hence most valued, expression of the praise of the Prophet. Its author, Muhammad al-Busiri (d. 1298), was a writer from Abu Sir in Egypt who had given allegiance to the Shadhili master Abu'l-ʿAbbas al-Mursi. He composed, besides some lighter verse, several eloquent hymns in honor of the Prophet.[23] The most beautiful, poetical, and expressive ode among them is probably the *Hamziyya*, a poem rhyming in *ā'*, which contains inter alia a long description of the Prophet's best-known miracles. Yet it was not the superb *Hamziyya* that made Busiri's name immortal, but rather his poem rhyming in *m*, which soon became famous as *Al-Burda* (in Turkish usually *Al-Bur'a*). According to legend the poet had suffered a stroke, and in his misery he turned to the Prophet and wrote a poem in his honor. Faith in the Prophet's healing power was and is still strong,[24] and indeed Muhammad appeared to Busiri in a dream and cast his mantle over him as he had done during his lifetime with Kaʿb ibn Zuhair after listening to his ode *Bānat Suʿād*. And as Kaʿb was granted forgiveness of his trespasses, Busiri was healed by the touch of the Prophet's mantle and could again move about the next morning.

The correct title of this second *Burda* is *Al-kawākib ad-durriya fī madḥ khair al-bariyya*, "Glittering Planets in the Praise of the Best of Mankind." Numerous legends are connected with the auspicious qualities of the poem. It was soon praised for its blessing and healing power, which worked not only for its author but also for those who recited or copied it. One might put it on one's eye to be cured from pain and inflammation; specific verses were supposed to avert poverty or pestilence, or ward off enemies and enviers.

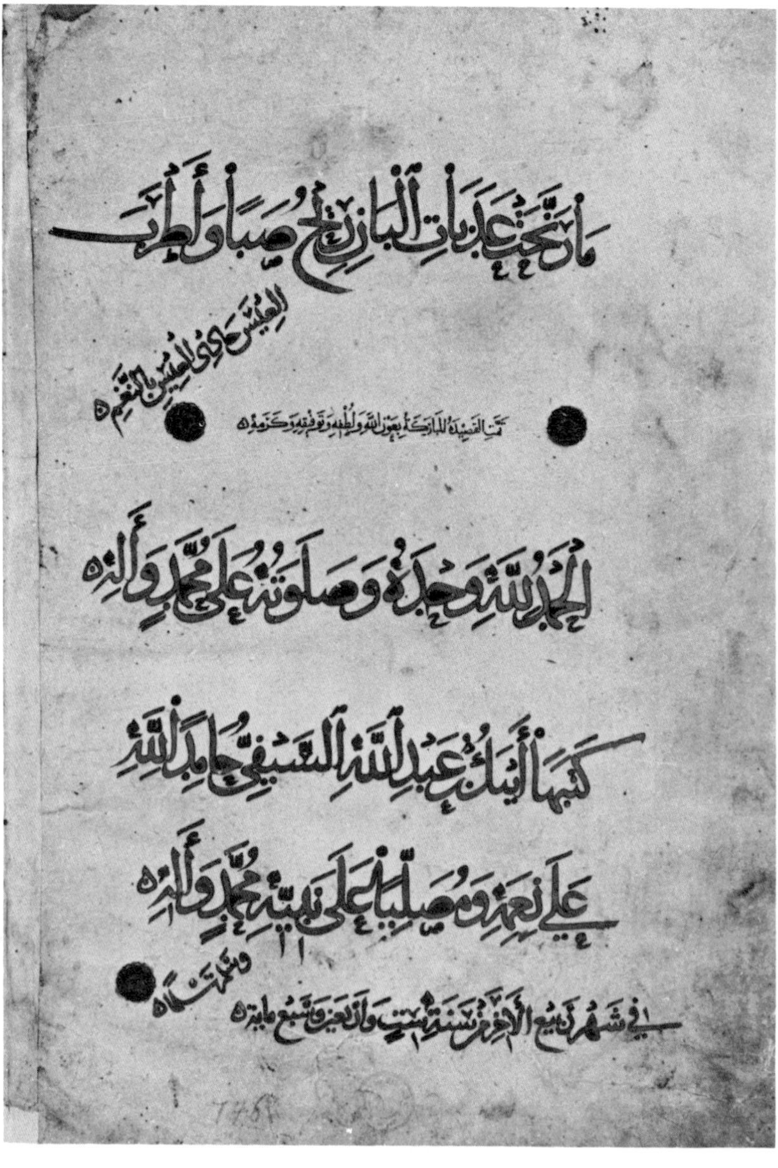

End of a manuscript of Busiri's Burda,
by Aibek ibn ʿAbdallah as-Saifi, Egypt, 1346
(Courtesy Österreichische Nationalbibliothek, Vienna)

Lines 23 and 24, if recited at dawn, convey peace to a broken heart.[25] For this reason the *Burda* is often used in amulets or written on the walls of religious and private buildings.[26] Precious copies of the poem were produced in the course of the centuries for leading statesmen or theologians, especially in Mamluk Egypt, where the ode originated.[27] The poets in the Arabic-speaking countries, and later also in India, expanded the *Burda* by inserting their own verses between the original lines, thus creating long strophic poems; this method is called *tashṭīr*, "splitting." The favorite variation was to place three of one's own lines before one verse of the *Burda* and thus to obtain a *takhmīs*, a poem with five-line stanzas, a technique often used for other famous religious poems as well. More than eighty such *takhmīs* of the *Burda* are known from Egypt alone. The Arabic-writing poets of southern India too vied with those whose mother tongue was Arabic in preparing new versions of the auspicious poem. Very soon the *Burda* was translated into other Islamic languages.[28] In the Persian tradition the most skillful poetical rendering was composed in the second half of the fifteenth century by Jami, who himself is famous for his *naʿtiyya* poetry. Turkish and Urdu translations followed; Panjabi[29] and Pashto in the Indian subcontinent have also their own versions, and Swahili in East Africa does not lack some renditions of the poem.[30] There is a Malayan version of the *Burda* dating from the sixteenth century,[31] and a more recent translation into Shilha-Berber. Typical of the belief in the blessing and talismanic power of the *Burda* is the touching little prayer poem that one of the Swahili translators added to his work:

> Lord, help my wife!
> Let the disasters of this life avoid her
> And tomorrow, in the other life,
> May she enter Paradise without reckoning or blame![32]

In the non-Arabic countries people liked to write, and later to print, copies of the *Burda* in the Arabic original accompanied by one or two translations, so that the blessing power of the original text is fully transmitted while at the same time the foreign reader can enjoy the highly complicated text in a lyrical rendering in his own language. Interlinear versions of the *Burda* are easily available in the bookshops in Lahore, Delhi, and elsewhere; a beautifully calligraphed edition with interlinear Persian and Urdu verse renderings was recently published in Hyderabad/Deccan. In the Deccan the recitation of parts of the *Burda*, interspersed with numerous readings from the Koran and eulogies for the Prophet, is still celebrated in a festive atmosphere,[33] and the Sufis have very special rules for its proper recitation.[34]

But not only the Muslims have reverted to the *Burda* time and again.

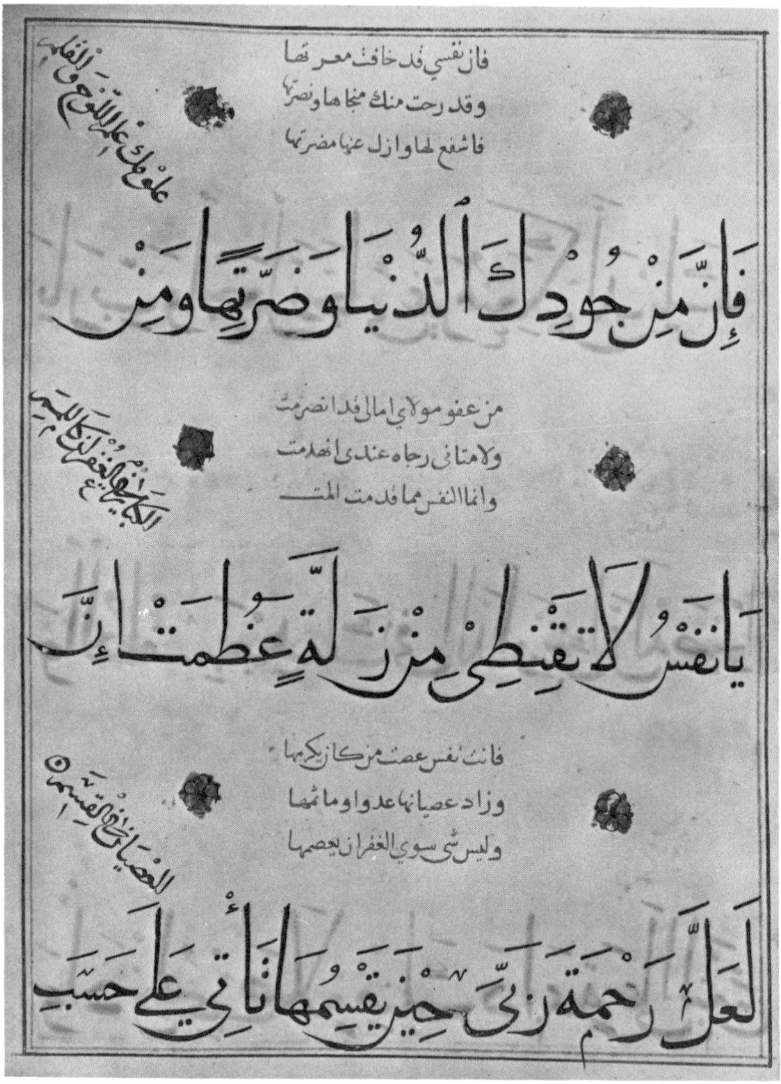

فان نفسي قد خافت معرتها
وقد رجت منك منجاها ونصرتها
فاشفع لها وازل عنها مضرتها

علومك علم اللوح والقلم

فإن من جودك الدنيا وضرتها ومن

من عفو مولاي امالي قد انصرمت
ولا اتاني رجاه عندي انهدمت
وانما النفس مما قدمت المت

الكبائر في الغفران كاللمم

يا نفس لا تقنطي من زلة عظمت إن

فانت نفس عصت من كان يكرمها
وزاد عصيانها عدوا وماثمها
وليس شي سوى الغفران يعصمها

العصيان في القسم

لعل رحمة ربي حين يقسمها تأتي على حسب

*Page from an enlargement (*takhmīs*) of Busiri's* Burda*,*
Egypt, fifteenth century
(Courtesy Staatsbibliothek Preussischer Kulturbesitz, Berlin)

European scholars too became interested in the poem at a very early stage of oriental studies. The poem was printed first in 1761 in Leiden in the Netherlands, and is thus one of the earliest literary Arabic texts published in the West. After Rosenzweig-Schwannau's poetical rendering of 1824, a young German orientalist, C. A. Ralfs, edited the work along with a Turkish and a Persian poetical version and translated it into fine but very heavy German prose; unfortunately he died prematurely from consumption, and his work was seen through the press by others. The great French orientalist Sylvestre de Sacy translated Busiri's poem for Garcin de Tassy's *Exposition de la foi musulmane* (1822). Still frequently cited is the translation by the French scholar René Basset, who despite his aversion to "mystical" poetry gives a useful commentary that explains many of the allusions in which the *Burda* abounds. The British scholar J. W. Redhouse published his version in a privately printed book;[35] the most handy and reliable modern translation for an English-speaking audience is that by Arthur Jeffery in his *Reader on Islam*.[36]

The *Burda* is indeed a true compendium of medieval prophetology, and although its highly elaborate verses sound somewhat sober and not so enticing when translated into Western languages, yet each of them contains certain articles of faith and statements about the Prophet that were central to the medieval Muslim world view. That is why the poem became so immensely popular.

The poet begins his *qaṣīda* in traditional classical style with a complaint about his separation from his friends:

> Have you, remembering the neighbors in Dhu Sallam,
> Mixed with blood the tears which flow from the eyeball?

Then, in line 35, he turns to the Prophet, from whom he expects spiritual help and whom he extols in the following 150 lines:

> Muhammad, the lord of the two worlds and of men and djinn,
> Of the two communities, the Arabs and the non-Arabs,
> Our Prophet, who commands and prohibits—and not a single one
> Is more truthful than he in saying No or Yes;
> And he is the beloved for whose intercession one hopes
> In every horror and in hazardous undertaking.
> He has called [us] to God, and those who cling to him
> Are grasping a rope that cannot be severed.
> He surpassed the prophets in bodily form and character,
> And they came not close to him in knowledge nor in kindness . . .

Busiri sees the Prophet as the spiritual guide of the community and intercessor at Doomsday, the performer of miracles and the Seal of the

Prophets. Only a very brief remark concerning his miraculous birth is made, but other miracles—such as the prostration of the trees—receive extensive attention.

> Answering his call, the trees came, prostrating themselves,
> Marching toward him on one leg without foot,
> As if they were drawing a line for the delightful writing
> That their branches wrote in the middle of the road,[37]
> Like the cloud that was trailing wherever he went,
> Protecting him from the furnace-like heat at noon . . .

The Prophet's heavenly journey is described in well-chosen images:

> At night you traveled from one sanctuary to the other
> As the full moon in the gloomiest of darkness,
> And you rose until you reached a way-station,
> Namely "Two bows' length"—that had never been reached
> or aimed at.
> And for that all the messengers gave you preference,
> And [also] the prophets; a preference [as befits] a lord who is served,
> from his servants,
> And you traversed the seven spheres, passing through them
> In a triumphal procession in which you carried the banner . . .

The Prophet is, as Busiri sings in an oft-imitated verse,

> Like a flower in tenderness and like the full moon in glory,
> Like the ocean in generosity and like time in grand intentions.

But at the same time this tender and generous Prophet is also a hero in warfare, and his military achievements are elaborated in gruesome detail:

> He did not cease to meet them in every battlefield
> Until they resembled, by dint of their lances, meat on a butcher's
> block . . .
> He led an ocean of an army on floating steeds
> That threw up clashing waves of heroes,
> Each of them entrusted to God and expecting heavenly reward,
> Assailing, and completely devoted to the extirpation of infidelity.

Again, like many poets before and after him, Busiri too refers to the fact that he himself, by virtue of his name Muhammad, has a very special relation to the Prophet, who is bound to protect his namesake. However, he is also careful to warn his coreligionists that all the praise that he bestows upon the Prophet so lavishly should not be confused with the veneration of Christ by the Christians, for they have considered Jesus to be the Son of

God. Muhammad, even though distinguished by every possible virtue and excelling in every conceivable noble quality, is a created being:

> Leave aside what the Christians claim about their prophet,
> But award to him whatever you want in terms of praise,
> and stand by it,
> And ascribe to his person whatever you want in terms of nobility
> And ascribe to his power every greatness you want,
> For the excellence of the Messenger of God has no limit
> So that anyone who speaks with his mouth could express it
> [completely].

Thus, Busiri's *Burda* comprises all those ideas that the medieval Muslim loved and accepted, and has therefore contributed substantially to the formation of the ideal picture of the Prophet in Arabic, and, as a result, also in non-Arabic Islamic poetry.

By the middle of the thirteenth century one finds quite a few writers in Arabic countries whose odes show the direction that religious poetry in large part was to take in the subsequent centuries, that is, an increasing artificiality that almost suffocates the real concern of the poets. These poets competed with each other as it were in complicated representations of the Prophet's qualities; their style was often overburdened with farfetched rhetorical devices and affected puns. One can of course interpret such poetry as a "poetical offering" in which the poets applied all their skills to the production of something really worthy of the Prophet. Some of them composed verses in which each line began with the rhyming letter of the poem, others wrote odes in exclusively undotted letters, and some included every single figure of speech as enumerated by Arabic rhetoricians—in this last category Safiuddin al-Hilli (d. 1349) is probably the most famous.[38] A good example of the tendency to artificiality is a eulogy by as-Sarsari, who was killed when the Mongols under Hulagu sacked Baghdad in 1258. It is so "artistic" that each of its lines contains all the letters of the alphabet! Like his predecessors and successors, Sarsari also placed the Light of Muhammad at the center of his verse. He opens one poem, for instance, with a widely used rhetorical device, *tajāhul al-ʿārif*, "feigned ignorance," and asks:

> Is it your face or the morning light that dawns?
> Or the full moon in its perfection, that annihilates darkness?
> Or the sun in its exaltation during a cloudless day?[39]

Some of the eulogies for the Prophet composed by al-Witri (d. 1264) became particularly popular in later times.[40] In India they were elaborated into strophic forms and used for various rhetorical games.[41]

It seems that the poets of Morocco, or rather of the entire Spanish–North African area, were especially fertile in producing poetic eulogies and prayers for the Prophet. Some of these soon became classics in their own right, among them the blessing formulas invented by Ibn Mashish and somewhat later Jazuli's *Dalā'il al-khairāt*; these poets excelled in elated, worshipful poems and show some special features of *naʿtiyya* poetry, such as the praise of Muhammad's sandals (see chapter 2 above). One often finds long chains of anaphora, addressing the Prophet: "O lord . . . O lord! . . . O lord!" or "Mercy . . . mercy . . . mercy!"

> O messenger of the one God! I am a stranger—
> Succor me, O refuge of the strangers!
> O messenger of the one God, a poor man am I,
> Help me, O helper of the poor!
> O messenger of the one God, I am ill and weak—
> Heal me, for you are sought for healing.
> O messenger of the one God, if you do not help me
> To whom could I look to be my recourse?[42]

Thus writes an Arabic poet of the fifteenth century in his *Sunrises in Laudatory Poems for the Prophet*, touching a chord well known in popular poetry from all Islamic countries, as in the laments of village bards in the Panjab or Sind. In this later Arabic poetry, skillful plays on words, in which the author enjoys using all possible derivations from and cross-relations between the Arabic roots, alternate with unadorned, simple exclamations in which he asks for forgiveness of sins and are often supplemented by endless descriptions of the Prophet's qualities and his miracles.

Famous pre-Islamic poems such as Imru'l-Qais's *Qifā nabki* (Let's Stay and Weep, You Two Friends . . .) were "split" and filled with new verses to be transformed into strophic odes extolling the Prophet.[43] Yusuf an-Nabhani has offered in his anthology of *naʿtiyya* poetry examples of this style along with numerous specimens of his own art, among which one should mention *naʿtiyya* verse in all the sixteen meters of Arabic poetry, with the technical name of each meter (e.g. "light," "long") cunningly worked into the appropriate text.[44]

The classical form of the laudatory ode has remained alive in Arabic. Ahmad Shauqi, poet laureate of Egypt in the early twentieth century, produced an impressive religious poem in his *qaṣīda* "In the Style of the *Burda*," *Fī nahj al-burda*, and he also imitated Busiri's *Hamziyya* and wrote some poems on the *maulid*. But popular forms, even in *naʿtiyya* poetry, likewise became increasingly common in the Arabic countries. Many of these poems could be sung and were easy to memorize; all styles of nonclassical verse were used, and the language assumed forms in which the classical rules of grammar were only partly observed. The strophic form of the *muwashshaḥ*, not exclusively in classical style, especially gained in popularity, so that even a leading Sufi author such as the learned ʿAbdul Ghani an-Nabulusi (late seventeenth and early eighteenth centuries) might choose to use it for his songs in honor of the Prophet.[45]

It is interesting to note that the traditional form of the Arabic *qaṣīda* was preserved not only in the Arabic lands themselves but also in Muslim India. Both in northern India and in the Deccan one finds poets and theologians who continued to write in the same style as the medieval Arabic poets had done, for Arabic was, after all, the commonly used language of theology.[46] Not in vain was the polyhistor Azad Bilgrami (d. 1786 in Aurangabad) called for his artistic Arabic *naʿt* poetry "the Hassan al-Hind." Somewhat before him, the great reformist theologian of Delhi, Shah Waliullah, wrote Arabic verses in traditional imagery about the same miracles of the Prophet that he also discussed in a rather more sober fashion in his scholarly works. In southern India not only were the *Burda* and similar famous poems strophically enlarged by numerous insertions,[47] but mystically-minded poets introduced the classical Arabic tradition into their own linguistic environment: Tamil, for instance, boasts a remarkable Islamic literature, among which Omar Pulavar's *Sīra Purānam* (ca. 1700), a long biographical poem about the Prophet's life, is especially worthy of mention.[48]

THE POETS' LONGING FOR MEDINA

The Egyptian mystical poet Ibn al-Farid (d. 1235), who had dwelled for many years in the Hijaz, sang of his longing for the holy cities of Islam:

> When the anguish of pain settles on my soul, the aroma
> Of fresh herbs of the Hijaz is my balm . . .[49]

He seems to have been among the first to express his love and longing for the Prophet's native land in artistic verse, but in the various types of eulogies for the Prophet, the topic became predominant in poetry after the thirteenth century.

It is especially the longing for Medina, the last resting place of the Prophet, that has animated poets even down to our day. Tor Andrae has rightly pointed out that the idea that a visit to the Prophet's tomb would guarantee his intercession "moves in an area which is essentially completely alien to orthodox Islam";[50] hence the Wahhabi aversion to such visits, which was anticipated by Ibn Tamiyya.[51] The Egyptian scholar ʿAli Safi Husain thinks that the motif was first introduced into literature by the Egyptian poet and traditionist Ibn Daqiq al-ʿId (d. 1302),[52] but it may well go back to earlier times.

Poets were able to elaborate the motif of the visit to Medina by applying to it the classical Arabic form of the *qaṣīda* and its erotic introduction, the *tashbīb*. The traditional description of the journey to the dwelling place of the distant beloved could be transformed into that of a journey to the tomb of the beloved Prophet; to the traveling poet's longing heart the thorns in the Arabian desert could seem to turn into silk and brocade, caressing his feet.[53] This topic, the description of the arduous journey to the beloved's home, was taken over into folk poetry as well. In Shah ʿAbdul Latif's *Sur Khanbath*, the camel (that is, man's restless, restive soul) is driven to the beloved Prophet, who "is sweeter than honey and more fragrant than musk," and the radiant moon is asked to kiss his feet to express the traveler's loving thoughts.[54] Poets who could not undertake the journey to the Hijaz themselves (or at least describe it according to their imagination in ever new imagery) might ask the morning breeze to convey their greetings to the Prophet and tell him of their love—again a motif taken from profane love poetry, and found frequently in *ghazal*s in the non-Arabic countries. Out of it, the *salām*, "Greeting," developed into a distinctive genre of religious poetry.[55]

Though Egyptian poets of the fourteenth and fifteenth centuries were especially fond of describing the country they longed to see because the Prophet was dwelling there, the same topic is even more in evidence in countries of the African and Persianate world. The farther the poet lives from Medina, the more eloquent he waxes in singing of his yearning for the Rauda, the "garden" of the Prophet. A description of a visit to Medina by a modern, highly sophisticated Turkish lady, Emel Esin, in her fine book *Mecca the Blessed, Medinah the Radiant*, proves that this longing for the Prophet's presence is still very much part of the living faith.[56] Indeed pilgrims from India and Pakistan who have just returned from the *ḥajj* to Mecca will tell of their visit at the Rauda in ecstatic words and often dissolve in tears when recalling the blessed moment when they were standing at the gate of the Prophet's last resting place.

A handbook by the fifteenth-century Egyptian scholar as-Suyuti informs the pilgrim how to behave when offering greetings to the Prophet in Medina:

> When he enters the Prophet's mosque it is preferable that he shall offer a prayer of two prostrations in the "Garden" [*rauḍa*, the pillared space west of the tomb]. Then he shall approach the Noble Tomb in the direction of its *qibla* and stand in front of it four cubits from the head of the Tomb, in such a way that the lamp is above his head and the nail in the wall of the noble enclosure is facing the lamp (it is a

> silver nail driven into red marble); and he who is facing the nail is confronting the face of the Prophet.
>
> Let him stand gazing down at the lower part of the Tomb-enclosure opposite to him, his eyes abased, in the station of awe, lowliness, and reverence. Then let him say, "Peace to Thee, Thou Joy of God's creation! Peace to Thee, Thou beloved of God! Peace to Thee, Thou lord of the divine messengers! Peace to Thee, Thou seal of the prophets! Peace to Thee, Thou leader of the Festal Band! Peace to Thee, Thou bearer of glad tidings! Peace to Thee, Thou warner! Peace to Thee and to the Pure Ones, people of Thy house! Peace to Thee and to Thy pure wives, mothers of the faithful! Peace to Thee and to all the Companions! Peace to Thee and to all the Prophets and Apostles and to all the righteous worshippers of God![57]

Those who for some reason were unable to visit the holy cities never ceased to sing about them. Yunus Emre (ca. 1300) expresses his longing for the sacred places by imagining vividly how he would feel if only he were there:

> If my Lord would kindly grant it,
> I would go there, weeping, weeping,
> And Muhammad in Medina
> I would see there, weeping, weeping . . .[58]

Some 150 years later, Jami in Herat praised Medina in a long *naʿt* where the name of the Prophet's city forms the *radīf*, or recurrent rhyme. For example:

> It is we who, like the tulip in the desert of Medina,
> Bear in our heart the scar of longing for Medina.
> Passionate longing for Paradise may disappear from the wise man's head, but
> It is not possible that the passionate longing for Medina should leave him. . . .
> The Tuba tree that has lifted its head on the apex of the Throne
> Is [only] a branch from the garden-adorning palm tree of Medina.
> When you eat dates, kiss their kernels, for
> The kernels of the dates of Medina are the beads of the angels' rosary![59]

After Jami describes how the dust of Medina has been transformed into water thanks to the Prophet's presence, so that the Universal Intellect now dives in the ocean of Medina, he turns once more to his favorite pun on the letter *m*: does not the very name Medina contain, after the "Prophet's letter," *m*, at its very center the word *dīn*, "religion"?

More than elsewhere, poets in the Indian subcontinent implored the help of the "Prince of Medina":

> Prince of Medina, listen to my calling—
> The journey is under your protection.
> You lead the travelers to the other shore.
>
> Lord of Medina, listen to my calling,
> My hopes are directed to you,
> I do not think of any other helper.
>
> Bridegroom of Medina, listen to my calling!
> Come again, Muhammad, the sinner hopes in you![60]

These are verses from Shah ʿAbdul Latif's great Sindhi *Risālō* of the early eighteenth century. His compatriot ʿAbdur Raʾuf Bhatti, who wrote at about the same time, devoted dozens of poems to the beloved Prophet and expressed his hope to draw closer to him, in little lilting songs:

> In the luminous Medina—could I be there, always there!
> Could I say with all the pilgrims blessings for the intercessor—
>   In the luminous Medina . . .
> Could I pray close to the Kaʿba, bowing down, my humble prayers!
>   In the luminous Medina . . .
> Could I tell some little matter of my heart to him, our leader!
>   In the luminous Medina . . .
> Could I, the repulsive sinner, could I speak the pure profession!
>   In the luminous Medina—could I be there, always there![61]

Even the former Hindu prime minister of Hyderabad/Deccan, Sir Kishan Prasad Shad (d. 1943), poetically expressed his love of the Prince of Medina and his longing for the Rauda, in eloquent Urdu verse.[62] Poets like him want "to leave their native country and leave their garden like a disturbed nightingale"[63] and ask God "to lift the veil of separation" between them and the beloved Prophet, for:

> Don't seek in both worlds any place for the poor—
> The Gate of Muhammad is there for the poor;
> The zephyr that passes by Ahmad's abode—
> It raises and brings healing dust for the poor . . .
> This rebel is naked, no shelter, no veil—
> The kindness of Ahmad: a cloak for the poor![64]

کافر ہوں کہ مومن ہوں خدا جانے میں کیا ہوں
پر بندہ ہوں ان کا جو ہیں سلطانِ مدینہ

Urdu verse of the Hindu prime minister of Hyderabad, Sir Kishan Prasad Shad, in honor of Muhammad, the "Prince of Medina"

Another modern Hindu poet, Kaifi, adopts a traditional image comparing the heart to the compass needle (called in Urdu "compass-bird") and implores God to make that bird fly toward Yathrib, where the visitor will recite the *Surāt an-Nūr* (Sura 24), because there he experiences the Divine Light.[65]

> For the believer, how should the visit to the Prophet's tomb not be a heavenly journey?
> The dust of this Rauda, replete with light, is the highest Paradise![66]

Long before, Jami had written that the sky, envious of the dust in which the Prophet is laid to rest, exclaims: "Oh, that I were dust!" (Sura 78:41).[67] And only a few years ago the Egyptian progressive poet al-Faituri wrote in his "Diary of a Pilgrim to the House of God" verses that take up the ages-old imagery of light, for in Medina the Radiant the "lights of Taha al-Mustafa" shine forth from the dust.[68]

> Over the Prophet's bones every speck of dust
> Is a pillar of light
> Standing from the dome of his tomb
> To the dome of the skies,
> And the awe that makes our foreheads bow
> Draws a horizon, and ever higher horizons,
> From hands and from lips—
> The road "In the name of God."[69]

In Medina the poet—here, an Indian Muslim—may find everything he has ever dreamt of:

On the tongues of the nightingales of this Rauda are words of wisdom,
More beautifully colored than all flowers are the flowers of Medina![70]

Even the destruction of the Prophet's tomb by the Wahhabis in the early nineteenth century was only a passing phase in the long history of devotion to the holy site. The Wahhabis considered such visits and the cult of tombs as something that contradicted Koranic injunctions and admonitions in early *ḥadīth* against tomb-worship. And yet very soon visitors again thronged to the sacred place where they felt protected from all danger, and were certain that their prayers would be heard:

Lord of Medina, you friend of the poor—
You will not turn me back empty-handed!

One finds the wish to visit the Prophet's tomb—along with the recitation of blessings upon him—in simple songs with which Tunisian workmen accompany their chores,[71] and there are whole collections of poems about Medina and the Prophet's presence there published in India and Pakistan. Even Iqbal's last collection of poems, the *Armaghān-i Ḥijāz* (Gift of the Hijaz), derives its title from this very tradition. And recently a young Indian Muslim from the Deccan, Sayyid Ghiyath Matin, has described in a dramatic Urdu poem his vision of the tomb of the Prophet, his ancestor:[72] the Prophet's hand appeared from the velvet curtains and was placed on his head so that he was able to "kiss the radiant feet of the Prophet with his eyes."[73] Would it not be wonderful, he asks, if this vision became reality? For it is only this hope that keeps him alive, constantly waiting for the blessed moment of meeting the Prophet. This poem is perfectly in tune with traditional Sufi stories according to which the Prophet can indeed address a visitor from his grave (for he is said by some to be alive in his tomb): for instance, the fourteenth-century saint of Ucch, Makhdum Jahaniyan, whose claim to *sayyid* status some Arabs doubted, was thus greeted by his ancestor, who answered his *salām* in the Rauda with the words: "And peace upon you, my son!"[74]

The motif of longing for the Prophet's tomb permeates pious verse from everywhere in the Islamic world, and only rarely will a poet admit that he is so close to the Prophet that he need not travel abroad:

Do not ask me, friend: "Where is Muhammad?"
Hidden in my heart, there is Muhammad!
Is there need to wander to Medina?
Here and there—apparent is Muhammad.
In my heart and eyes resides for ever
From the day of Covenant, Muhammad . . .[75]

NAʿTIYYA POETRY IN THE PERSIANATE AND POPULAR TRADITION

The special charm of Arabic eulogies for the Prophet consists in their linguistic perfection, which as a rule cannot be conveyed in any translation, for no language can successfully imitate the complicated web of allusions that Arabic can convey to the delighted listener. The reader without Arabic will probably gain access more easily to the multicolored, mystically heightened world of poetry that is encountered in Persian, Turkish, and Urdu *naʿtiyya* verse. The imagery in these three languages is almost identical, and the favorite images of the urban and court poets of Iran have percolated into the literature of the regional languages of Muslim India as well. A line from Mir ʿAli Shir Qaniʿ (18th century, Sind),

> The water in the canal of the *Dīwān* runs from the fountainhead
> of *naʿt*,[76]

captures precisely the central importance of the eulogy for the Prophet in the compositions of Persianate poets: it is this very topic that gives their works life and luster.

Apparently it was with Sana'i of Ghazna in Eastern Afghanistan that the tradition of Persian *naʿtiyya* poetry proper began, around 1100. Sana'i had renounced his former activities as a court panegyrist and shifted his interest to religious, more specifically, ascetic poetry to become the founder of the ascetic-mystical *mathnawī* tradition in the Persian tongue. But at the same time he appears as the first and, in certain respects, greatest panegyrist of the Prophet. The superb rhetorical technique he had acquired in singing the praise of worldly rulers was now applied, even more skillfully, to the praise of the Prophet; and as he had hoped for handsome rewards in cash or kind from princes and grandees, he now hoped for much more important spiritual rewards from God's messenger, the intercessor at Doomsday and embodiment of all physical and spiritual beauty.

We owe to Sana'i one of the most impressive odes in honor of the Prophet in the Persian language, a poem which at the same time sets the stage for the whole of subsequent literature in this field. This is his poetical commentary on Sura 93, *Waʾḍ-ḍuḥā*, "By the Morning Light."[77] This sura had already been interpreted as pertaining to the Light of Muhammad and remains to this day a pivotal part of mystical prophetology. Sana'i recited this poem extemporaneously during a meeting of learned scholars, and its very first lines immediately capture the listener's attention:

> The manuscript of *jabr* [predestination] and *qadar* [free will]
> Is contained in the form of his face and his hair;

This one becomes known from "By the Night" (Sura 92), and that one from "By the Morning Light" (Sura 93).
Infidelity and faith, in darkness and purity respectively
Have no other kingdom but Mustafa's cheek and tresses.
If his hair and his face did not bring to the desert Divine wrath (*qahr*) and Divine kindness (*luṭf*)
Infidelity would remain without provision, and faith helpless.

That means that in the Prophet the two complementary attributes of God, His beauty, *jamāl*, and majesty, *jalāl*, are manifested—attributes whose interplay keeps the whole universe in motion. Later poets, from Nizami to Iqbal, took over Sana'i's technique of juxtaposing the Prophet's beautiful and majestic attributes: combining Moses' sternness and Jesus' mildness in a higher unity, he is able to awaken fear in the hearts of his enemies and love in the souls of his friends.[78] Sana'i then continues his poem, now addressing the Prophet himself:

The radiance of your face is what one calls "morning";
The shade of your two tresses is where you say "evening."

This comparison of the radiant dawn with the luminous countenance of Muhammad, with which the light of faith is also connected, and the connection of Sura 92, "By the Night!" with the dark tresses of the Prophet and, in a different line of thought, with the blackness of infidelity, became a standard formula in Persianate poetry. Gesudaraz, the saint of Gulbarga in the Deccan, in the early fifteenth century, expressed it like this:

Good morning!—that is your sun-illuminating face!
Good evening!—that is your night-showing tress![79]

ʿAshiq Pasha in medieval Turkey used this comparison,[80] as did the great poets of Iran; and the last Moghul ruler of India, Bahadur Shah Zafar, wrote in one of his Urdu *naʿts*:

"By the night!"—that is the praise of your musk-like tresses;
"By the sun!"—that is the oath by your luminous cheek![81]

This tradition remains alive even in recent *naʿt* poetry in Indo-Pakistan.

Just as Sana'i's great *mathnawī*, the *Ḥadīqat al-ḥaqīqa* (The Orchard of Truth), became the model of all later mystico-didactic Persian poetry, so too his hymns in honor of the Prophet offer the basic ideas that were elaborated in all following mystical eulogies. Besides his extensive and often surprising interpretation of Sura 93, Sana'i's huge *Dīwān* contains numerous other *naʿts*. Based on a *ḥadīth*,[82] they describe the Prophet who attracts everyone to loving service:

In heaven he has friends like Michael and Gabriel,
On earth he has servants like ʿUmar and Siddiq,[83]

that is, the first two caliphs, Abu Bakr as-Siddiq and ʿUmar ibn al-Khattab. These caliphs are invited in Sana'i's poems to sing the appropriate praise of the Prophet, as they are mentioned in many later *naʿt* poems by Sunni poets as his most loyal friends and supporters. This line of thought goes from Rumi's and Jami's imaginative verse to the folk poetry of the Pathans[84] and Sindhis, and even in the verse of Dakhni Urdu poets, who were living in a predominantly Shia environment, the first caliphs are mentioned often in connection with the introductory *naʿt*s of epic poems, though sometimes a special position is allotted to ʿAli.[85]

Sana'i's poetical imagination shows but scant regard for historical fact, and he applies the whole vocabulary of mystical and mythical thought to his poems of praise. Is it not the Prophet for whom everything was created and whose name is the power that miraculously works through all things?

I asked the wind: "Why do you serve Solomon?"
It said: "Because Ahmad's name is engraved on his seal!"[86]

Only by the blessing power of Muhammad's name is Solomon able to subdue djinn, wind, oceans, and animals, for it was a sign of Muhammad's greatness that God took an oath by his name in the Koran[87]—the name of him who was the reason for the existence of the whole universe, the Sun of Everything Created.

In his *Ḥadīqat al-ḥaqīqa*, Sana'i devotes the entire third chapter to the question why Muhammad is preferable to all other prophets, and proves his greatness in various novel ways:

In order to extol you, there came from the realm of time
Friday, the White Nights, the Night of Might, the Great Feast, and
the *shab-i barāt*,
And out of space came, with bent statures,
Mecca, Yathrib [Medina], [the cave of] Hira, and the Haram.[88]

Friday is the day on which the communal prayer is held in Islam; the White Nights are the nights before and after the full moon; the Night of Might is the night in which the Koran was revealed for the first time, usually celebrated on 27 Ramadan (Sura 97); the Great Feast is the feast of sacrifice during the pilgrimage to Mecca; and the *shab-i barāt* is the night of the full moon in the month of Shaʿban, in which Muhammad victoriously entered Mecca and in which, as traditional belief has it, the fates for the coming year are destined in heaven. All these events are depicted here as having appeared only for the Prophet's sake. So also do the sacred cities, Mecca and Medina, the cave on Mount Hira where Muhammad received the first revelations, and the sanctuary of the Kaʿba exist only because of Muhammad. Faithful to the mystical tradition, Sanaʾi acknowledges the Prophet's preexistence:

> Ahmad's external form comes from Adam, but in essence
> Adam became manifest from Ahmad![89]

For even the first human being and first prophet is nothing but a reflection of the primordial Light of Muhammad.

Sanaʾi's background in courtly panegyrics allows him to apply the daring puns and rhetorical wordplay he once had used to praise worldly figures to the exaltation of the Prophet instead.

> Those who say No (*lā*) to him, become turned over like [the crooked letter] *lā*,
> But blessed by bounty (*niʿma*) is he who has said Yes! (*naʿam*) to him.[90]

More importantly, Sanaʾi emphasizes Muhammad's decisive role for the definition of faith and infidelity:

> If God had not called you "Mercy for the worlds"—
> Who in the whole world would see the difference between the Eternal (*ṣamad*) and an idol (*ṣanam*)?[91]

A century and a half later Busiri expressed almost the same idea in his *Ḥāʾiyya*:

> If there were not the Prophet Muhammad and his knowledge,
> One would not know what to accept as good and what to blame![92]

For Muhammad defines the borderline between those who acknowledge the Eternal Lord and those who venerate transient false deities; he is the Prophet who brings the conclusive Divine law, and:

> As long as the breeze of your name does not rise over the garden of religion,
> The branch of religion does not grow, and the root of the *sunna* does not sprout.[93]

It is he who determines the limits within which the Muslims must stay and marks the borders of Islam as a historical religion. This idea surfaces time and again in later poetry and mystical treatises, particularly among the "sober" mystical thinkers.

Another aspect that was to become central in the development of *naʿtiyya* poetry in Persian during the next centuries was Sanaʾi's tendency to contrast the Prophet and the revelation brought by him with the teachings of philosophy. The philosophers—those who pursued Greek philosophical thought—had always been the target of orthodox Muslims, and it is in this vein of thought that Sana'i says:

> "Mercy for the worlds" came as your physician, and from him came healing (*shifā'*)—
> Why do you seek it from this or that rebel?
> For the salvation (*najāt*) and healing (*shifā'*), that the follower of the Prophetic *sunna* has sought
> Are not contained in [Avicenna's two books] *An-Najāt* and *Ash-Shifā*.[94]

Avicenna (Ibn Sina), who had been active in Eastern Iran exactly one century before Sana'i and whose philosophical and, even more, medical works were well known and widely read not only in Islamic lands but in medieval Christian Europe, appears in one branch of Sufism as the exemplar of the loveless, intellectualist philosopher (although his philosophy contains some mystical elements as well).[95] One reason for this image may be that the great medieval theologian Ghazzali had vehemently criticized Avicenna's system in his *Tahāfut al-falāsifa*, and his compatriot Sana'i transplanted this criticism a few decades later into poetry. Then, a century after Sana'i, the Sufi Majduddin Baghdadi was informed by the Prophet in a dream that Avicenna had tried to reach the Divine Truth without his, Muhammad's, mediation, whereupon he had pushed him away so that he fell into Hellfire.[96] This view remained prevalent in mystically-tinged orthodox circles, for it highlighted the incompatibility of the Divine *sharī'a* as proclaimed by Muhammad with the attempts of the philosophers to reach the truth on a different, more rationalistic, path. Sana'i's verdict was taken up after some decades by his successor in the realm of mystical verse, Fariduddin 'Attar, whose poetical work is a treasury of mystical prophetology. In the long introduction to his *Muṣībatnāma* 'Attar writes:

> Indeed, two hundred worlds of the First Intellect (*'aql-i kull*)
> Disappear before the majesty of the [Koranic] order [to the Prophet] "Say!" (*qul*)
> Not a single person is farther away from the Hashimite *sharī'a* than a philosopher.
> *Sharī'a* is to follow the Prophet's order, to throw dust on the head of philosophy![97]

Another two generations later, Maulana Rumi combines this idea with his favorite miracle story:

> The philosopher who denies "the sighing palm trunk" (*ḥannāna*)
> Is unaware of the inner meaning of the saints![98]

He expresses Sana'i's and ʿAttar's feelings about the philosophers in even stronger terms when addressing the Prophet:

> O you royal rider of the order "Say!"—O you, in the presence of whose intellect the Universal Soul
> Is like an infant who out of childish ignorance chews his sleeve![99]

In our own century it was Muhammad Iqbal who took up in his verse once again the old dichotomy between Love, as manifested in Muhammad, and intellect, whose prototype, Ibn Sina, is doomed to failure.[100]

ʿAttar's poetry incorporates many of Sana'i's thoughts and images. At times he gives them an even deeper meaning and adds some novel elements. Some of the best known apocryphal *ḥadīth* concerning the names Muhammad and Ahmad (such as the one that says "I am Ahmad without *m*," that is, *Aḥad*, "One") may in fact have originated in the visions of this great Persian mystic. One should also remember that the Prophet appears as the highest mystical guide in the forty stages of the seeker's spiritual development as ʿAttar describes them poetically in the forty chapters of his *Muṣībatnāma*; it is Muhammad who shows the wayfarer the path toward the "ocean of his soul" where he will finally find his Lord, whom he has sought in vain in heaven and earth. The introductions to all of ʿAttar's epic poems contain very colorful descriptions of the Prophet and his heavenly journey (see chapter 9 above), and the Light of Muhammad plays an even greater role in his verse than in that of Sana'i. Indeed, ʿAttar states that

> Whatever is the radiance of both worlds,
> Is the reflection of his, Muhammad's, heart.[101]

ʿAttar also takes up the doctrine of the pillar of light that bowed down before God in pre-eternity. This concept, first mentioned by Sahl at-Tustari in the late ninth century, appears—as we saw—in the introductory passages of ʿAttar's *Manṭiq uṭ-ṭair*: Muhammad's light, a luminous pillar, performs the full cycle of a ritual prayer in the presence of God, before the world and its inhabitants are created out of it.

> From his light are Throne and Footstool,
> Cherubim as well as spiritual powers, and the holy ones.
> This world and the next are dependent upon him,
> And the world is cheerful through the light of his essence.[102]

ʿAttar sees the Prophet at the end of the long chain of previous prophets and observes that he, who cannot read the alphabet, is yet reading from the

Tablet of the Lord. For as *ummī*, "illiterate," Muhammad is "silent in himself but speaking through the Lord."[103] Even the First Intellect is only part of the reflection of the Prophet's soul, and

> Paradise is one sip from his glass;
> The two worlds are from the two *m*'s of his name.[104]

'Attar's prophetology is as deep as it is poetical, and certainly deserves an extended analysis, as would the prophetology of other medieval Persian poets. For although the basic forms of praise are everywhere and always similar, the elaborations and the shifts of emphasis around this or that peculiar aspect of the Prophet result in a surprisingly multicolored picture.

In the succession of Sana'i and 'Attar, Maulana Jalaluddin Rumi's work is also replete with allusions to the Prophet, the "caravan leader Mustafa," and his verse presents the scholar with even more difficulties than does 'Attar's, for his prophetology seems almost inseparably connected with the name of his mystical beloved, Shamsuddin of Tabriz, the "Sun of Religion," who was for him the true interpreter of the mysteries of the Prophet,[105] because he, as Maulana implies, was united with the pre-eternal, archetypal principle of Muhammad, the *ḥaqīqa muḥammadiyya*:

> Say, who is the confidant of Ahmad the Messenger in this world?
> Shams-i Tabriz, who is "one of the greatest" (Sura 74:38).[106]

For:

> When you recite "By the Morning Light!" see the Sun![107]

This also means that Shams "breathes together with Mustafa in love,"[108] for the true essence of the Prophet is love, that primordial Love, for whose sake God addressed Muhammad as *Laulāka*, "But for your sake. . . ."[109]

Single verses inserted in Rumi's *ghazal*s contain highly poetical descriptions of some of the Prophet's wonderful qualities, of his light and his glory:

> The dervishes find their happiness from "Mercy for the worlds,"
> Their frocks are radiant like the moon, their shawls fragrant like
> roses![110]

Muhammad's Hegira from Mecca to Medina becomes for Rumi the model of the mystic's journey, for it is by leaving one's home and traveling constantly that one's soul becomes purified.[111] He also often mentions "Muhammad's wine,"[112] that permissible wine which inspires mankind and can be found at the gate of Tabriz.[113] For Muhammad is not only the cupbearer but rather the very goblet that contains the wine of Divine Love[114]—a fine allusion to his quality as the *ummī* receptacle of the Divine word (see chapter 4 above). And he is the great elixir that can transform man's copper-like, base nature into pure gold.[115] Like ʿAttar, Rumi alludes to the "Ahmad without *m*," and in an ode in mixed Arabic and Persian, abundant in Koranic allusions, he calls the breeze of Najd to convey his greetings to the beloved Prophet.[116] Rumi's great *Mathnawī*, the didactic poem of some 26,000 lines, is a veritable treasure-trove of stories about the Prophet, who is praised (with extensive anaphora) in his role as Seal of Prophets and the one who opens the seal.[117] Rumi weaves numerous well-known *ḥadīth* into his poetry and elaborates them into long and sometimes quite surprising stories. His warm trust in the Prophet, whose religion "is firmly rooted even after 650 years have passed,"[118] becomes as evident from his verse as the role that Muhammad plays as the spiritual leader of the road to a better world.

The numerous instances in Aflaki's *Manāqib al-ʿārifīn* that refer to Rumi's and Shams' deep love for the Prophet deserve systematic treatment. Like Shams, Rumi stressed that no one can reach God unless he comes first to Muhammad, for the Prophet is the way through which the faithful can reach God:

> When the form of Mustafa became annihilated,
> The world took the "God is greatest!"[119]

"Know that Muhammad is the guide. Until a man first comes to Muhammad he cannot reach Us": that is what Rumi learned by Divine inspiration, for all gifts are showered upon the Prophet first and then distributed from him to other people.[120] "So it is realized that Muhammad was the foundation. . . . Everything that exists, honor and humility, authority and high degree, all are of his dispensation and his shadow, for all have become manifest from him."[121]

But Rumi also acknowledges the difficulties of the Prophetic office, and devotes a talk to why the Prophet once sighed, "Would that the Lord of Muhammad had not created Muhammad!" For, as Rumi defends this strange-sounding dictum, "being a prophet in comparison with that absolute union is all burden and torment and suffering."[122] In another talk he comes back to this tale:

> He [God] occupied Muhammad first wholly with Himself; thereafter He commanded him, "Call the people, counsel them and reform them!" Muhammad wept and lamented, saying: "Ah, my Lord, what sin have I committed? Why drivest Thou me from Thy presence? I have no desire for me!" But God consoled him: "Even in the midst of that occupation you shall be with Me. In whatever matter you are engaged, you will be in very union with Me."[123]

Here, the secret of the "second sobriety" of the Prophetic way is beautifully alluded to.

Everyone who has ever listened to the *naʿt-i sharīf* that is sung, in a melodious tune, at the beginning of the mystical dance of the Mevlevi dervishes, will feel how deeply Rumi loved the Prophet, whom he addresses:

> *Yā ḥabīb Allāh rasūl Allāh ki yaktā tūʾī* . . .
> O God's beloved, O messenger of God—unique are you!
> You, chosen by the Lord of Majesty—so pure are you!

He goes on to call him "light of the eyes of the prophets," he who places his foot on the nine green spheres during his *miʿrāj*, and then he appeals to his mercy:

> O Messenger of God, you know how incapable your community is—
> You are the guide of those weak ones without head and foot!

But the Prophet is also

> Cypress of the garden of prophethood, springtime of gnosis,
> Rosebud of the meadow of the Divine law and lofty nightingale.

And in the end Shams-i Tabrizi is invoked, who "knows the *naʿt* of the Prophet by heart," for he is the one whom this highest lord has chosen and elected.[124]

One of Rumi's contemporaries in the thirteenth century is Fakhruddin ʿIraqi, who spent twenty-five years of his life in Multan in the southern Panjab at the threshold of the Suhrawardi saint Bahaʾuddin Zakariya Multani. He was inspired to write *naʿtiyya* poetry during his stay in Medina, and described in pompous words

> The Mercy for the worlds, the messenger of God,
> He, at whose gate the heavenly beings say: "At your service, God
> revealed what He revealed!" (Sura 53:10) . . .
> Since in pre-eternity the style of addressing him was dictated as "By
> the Morning Light!" (Sura 93:1)
> The fixed time came that the ceremonial drumming (*nauba*) of
> "Praised be He who traveled at night with His servant" (Sura 17:1)
> was exercised.[125]

ʿIraqi means with this clever wordplay that because the Divine oath "By the Morning Light!" referred to Muhammad from the very moment that that light was created, the official drums and pipes of Sura 17:1 (the verse that alludes to his night journey) are played for him during his life on earth.

Again, like other poets, he points to the contrast of daylight and night as manifested in the Prophet, who stands between the Divine day and the darkness of the world of matter, who is the Sun of Existence and yet "travels at night."

ʿIraqi's eulogies are typical examples of the Persian style, which abounds in puns and sophisticated notions. This refined style had reached its first culmination among the nonmystical poets of Iran, in the work of Khaqani. This twelfth-century poet from Caucasia was extremely learned and endowed with an almost unbelievable skill in the use of rhetorical devices, and has extolled the Prophet in grandiose hymns. For him, the Prophet was "religion personified."[126] His veneration of the Prophet earned him the surname Hassan al-ʿajam, "the Hassan of the non-Arabs," and his descriptions of his pilgrimage and visit to Medina are indeed among the most rapturous but also most difficult Persian *qaṣīda*s ever written. Khaqani invented numerous new meaningful combinations of terms, among them the comparison between Muhammad and the Kaʿba, and between the Prophet's black mole and the black stone of the Kaʿba, which every Muslim aspires to kiss during the pilgrimage to Mecca. From his time onward this combination appears as one of the favorite topics of Persianate poets. Maulana Qasim Kahi, in sixteenth-century India, sings, for example:

> Ahmad, that is the Kaʿba toward which we all strive,
> The black stone is certainly his black mole.[127]

Among the poets in the Islamic Middle Ages who were not exclusively panegyrists or mystics, Saʿdi (d. 1292) has always been a favorite of Persian readers because of his elegant, clear, and limpid language. Although the number of his *naʿtiyya* poems is comparatively small, Persian literature owes to him one of its most frequently recited poems, which is especially well-loved in India. It is found in the introductory part of his *mathnawī* entitled *Būstān* (The Garden), and praises the Prophet in plain but graceful words in the very simple, easily remembered *mutaqārib* meter. Here the Prophet appears as

> *nasīmun qasīmun jasīmun wasīm*,
> well-shaped, graceful, elegant, of noble appearance,

words which, as we have seen, also influenced Islamic nomenclature. In the first half of the same stanza Saʿdi addresses the Prophet as

> *shafīʿun muṭāʿun rasūlun karīm*,
> Intercessor, one who is obeyed, a noble messenger.[128]

Muṭāʿ, "he who is obeyed" (Sura, 81:21), is a perfectly natural appellation for Muhammad when one recalls the verses in the Koran that order the faithful to "obey God and obey His messenger." But about 150 years before Saʿdi this very term had been used by Ghazzali in his mystical treatise *Mishkāt al-anwār*, where it seems to designate, as we saw earlier, a mysterious power that is usually identified with the archetypal Muhammad. Saʿdi's use of the term proves that the word *muṭāʿ* as an epithet of the Prophet must have been very common, whatever its additional implications were, and it occurs quite regularly in the *naʿtiyya* poetry of other writers, such as Jami.

Another poet who adopted the term was Amir Khusrau. Although he is considered primarily a court poet, his close relationship with the great mystical teacher of northern India, Nizamuddin Auliya of Delhi, had acquainted him with the language of Sufism, and in the introductory passages of his epic poems he uses many grand and refined epithets for the Prophet Muhammad (see chapter 6 above). He states in the beginning of his *Majnūn Lailā*, for instance, that Muhammad is

> The king of the kingdoms of messengerdom,
> The *ṭughrā* of the page of Majesty.[129]

According to the imaginative Amir Khusrau, the moon in the sky gives witness of Muhammad's greatness: it becomes first a semicircular *nūn*, ن, and then a circular *mīm*, م, in honor of the Prophet, thus forming the Persian word *nam*, "dew," which proves that the moon is nothing but "a drop of dew from Muhammad's ocean"; and the angels' wings serve to sweep the road that leads to his sanctuary.[130] Amir Khusrau also plays with the Divine word "I am Ahmad without *m*," a theme repeated during his lifetime and in the following centuries throughout the eastern realm of Islam. Again, he sees the round *m* as the Seal of Prophethood[131] and claims that one who puts this sacred *m* around his neck like a collar will walk in full faith like the ringdove.[132] "The dove's necklace" in Arabo-Persian imagery means an extremely close relation to something, which cannot be dissolved or severed (just as the band of feathers around the dove's neck is part of the bird's plumage).

But Amir Khusrau does not reach the heights of ecstasy that his model in epic poetry, Nizami, had attained; for Nizami was one of the greatest panegyrists of the Prophet among the nonmystical writers of Iran and may have invented the combination of "creation," *āfrīnish*, of the Prophet, with "praise," *āfrīn*, that later became very popular in Persian *naʿtiyya*.[133]

Probably the most prolific writer in the field of *naʿtiyya* poetry is Jami, poet and hagiographer of the fifteenth century, who delved deeply into the mysteries of the *ḥaqīqa muḥammadiyya* and combined immense technical skill with deep religious feeling. We have already quoted him several times for his novel and poignant definitions. His *naʿtiyya* poetry, highly admired by Iqbal,[134] comprises majestic *qaṣīda*s, tender *ghazal*s, and long introductory chapters in his seven great epic poems. In one of them, he produces a sequence of no fewer than five *naʿt*, not to mention his vivid verbal depictions of the Prophet's heavenly journey. But another of his poems is especially worthy of detailed attention here.[135] It is a *tarjīʿband*, a strophic poem consisting of twelve *ghazal*s each of which has the word Muhammad as *radīf*—almost certainly inspired by Saʿdi's much simpler *qaṣīda* with the same rhyme:

> The moon does not reach the beauty of Muhammad,
> The cypress does not possess the harmoniously shaped stature of Muhammad . . .[136]

The *band*, that is, the repeated verse that connects the *ghazal*s, in Jami's poem is the Arabic couplet

> My speech cannot seek to attain the laudatory description of his perfection—
> O my God, bless the Prophet and his family!

The first part of the poem begins with the rhetorical question

> What is the spring of water? The dust of the feet of Muhammad!
> And the "firm rope"? The noose of devotion to Muhammad!

Then follows the traditional statement:

> The limits of his praise—who knows them except God?
> Who am I, that I should dare to extol Muhammad?

In the second *ghazal* Jami turns to the primordial greatness of the Prophet:

> Whatever was noted down on the page of existence,
> Is only a selection from the book of Muhammad.

Later, the poet employs the imagery of chess:

> Don't call him king (*shāh*), for everyone who is not checkmated by Muhammad
> In this arena [or, chessboard], walks crooked like the queen [in chess].

But he soon returns to the cosmic glory of the Prophet and begins the fourth *ghazal*:

> The sky, having become curved because of its prostration before Muhammad,
> Is only a water bubble from the oceans of Muhammad's generosity.

Likewise, as he states in the seventh *ghazal*,

> The moon is a reflection of Muhammad's beauty,
> Musk is a little whiff from Muhammad's mole and tresses.
> In the garden of "Stay upright!" no walking cypress
> Has set foot, [which would be] comparable to the harmonious stature of Muhammad!

Because Jami believes that "there is no undue exaggeration of the loftiness of Muhammad," he can close his long encomium with the statement:

> The chain of beings has no other source
> Than Muhammad's musk-flavored tresses!

As in the Arabic tradition, in Persian too an increasingly complicated, stilted language developed in which Muhammad was praised and implored. Eulogies composed by some later poets became almost incomprehensible because they had appropriated the whole technical terminology of theosophical mysticism as developed in the succession of Ibn ʿArabi. This abstract terminology, not easily understood even in theological treatises, makes some Persian hymns seem like veritable enigmas. A good example is a poem by ʿUrfi from the late sixteenth century, in which the poet—who had migrated from Shiraz to the Moghul court in India; he is still celebrated as one of the leading panegyrists in Persian—strives to explain that because preexistence (the primordial light that was created before anything else) and temporal existence are mysteriously united in Muhammad, the Prophet is absolutely unique. The idea itself was not at all unknown to earlier writers, for Jami had expressed it in some of his *naʿt*s, but ʿUrfi utilizes the vocabulary of classical Arabic poetry to explain this mystery and introduces the traditional feminine names of Salma and Laila into his imagery.[137] Thus he writes, inter alia:

> The day that they reckoned who among the impossible could be equal to you,
> They wrote "nonexistence" as the date of birth for anyone like you.
> Until they wrote your existence to be the confluence of contingency and necessity,
> The object for a common epithet could not be determined.
> Destiny placed two litters on one camel:
> One for the Salma of your being created in time, the other for the Laila of your preexistence . . .

And the reader who has struggled his way through forty-eight lines of this kind marvels at the last verse of the ode, in which ʿUrfi claims:

I praise you through sincerity, not with the help of learning—
How could I bring forth the gazelle of the Kaʿba from an idol-temple?

ʿUrfi's poetry was highly admired in Moghul India and also, for a time shortly after his death, in Ottoman Turkey, where it inspired similarly complicated verse. His contemporary Naziri followed him in the use of the full theological vocabulary in his *naʿtiyya* poetry, which culminates in a very long *qaṣīda* that can be considered a mystical commentary on the profession of faith. Naziri's description of the Prophet, developed out of Koranic verses and *ḥadīth*, is of great poetical beauty and translates a central theme of prophetology into powerful verse, that is, the perfect harmony of Muhammad's internal and external qualities and actions, of his modesty and strength, his "poverty" and majesty:

Against the stubborn he flung the idea "There is no prophet after me";
For his dear friends, the word "I am only a human being" was sent down . . .[138]

Impressive as Naziri's *naʿts* are, it was a poem by another Indo-Persian poet that was much more appreciated by the masses: a rather simple, beautiful song by Qudsi Mashhadi, still a favorite of the *qawwāl*s of the Indian subcontinent.[139] Taking up again formulations first used by Jami, Qudsi addresses the beloved Prophet:

Marḥabā sayyid-i makkī-yi madīni'l-ʿarabī . . .
Welcome, O Meccan, Medinan, Arab lord—
May my heart and soul be sacrificed for you—what wonderful surnames you have!
Open the eye of mercy, cast a glance at me,
O you with the epithets Quraishi, Hashimi, and Muttalibi . . .

This emphasis on the Arabic attributes of the Prophet is typical of many Persian and, especially, Indo-Muslim poets, because a large segment of Muslims in India have long tended to highlight the Arabic element in their Islamic heritage. They have always remained aware that Arabia is the real homeland of their religion and culture and that their fathers—as Shah Waliullah of Delhi expressed it in the eighteenth century—"have fallen in exile" in India.[140] The same tendency to stress the Arabic heritage of the Prophet is palpable, perhaps even more than in high literature, in the popular poetry of the Indian Muslims, where it resounds everywhere. In one of the first poems in honor of the Prophet written in Sindhi, by Shah Mian ʿInat around 1700, the "friend, Quraishi, Arab" is repeatedly addressed:

Be with us, Arab!
Help us, Medinan prince![141]

As for Qudsi, he continues his *naʿt* with the traditional surnames and figures of speech and calls himself, toward the end, a dog at the Prophet's threshold. But even this designation sounds to him too daring:

I related myself to the dog, but am very distressed
Because to relate oneself to the dog of your street is unmannerly.

The claim to be the dog at the Prophet's door or rather to be lower than such a lucky dog occurs quite often in Persian poetry, especially in the work of the successors of Jami, for Jami is noted for his frequent use of the comparison with dogs and even claims to be the lowliest slave of the Prophet's dog. The term is used in popular poetry as often as in urban verse, and a Panjabi devotee of the Prophet sings:

I am the dog of the Prophet's family
And faithfully keep watch at their door.[142]

These remarks in which the poets pretend to be the dog at the Prophet's threshold may have grown out of the idea that even the unclean dog—which is not allowed into the house and whose presence spoils ritual prayer—can be purified by seeking the presence of noble human beings. The Muslims knew from the legend of the Seven Sleepers (Sura 18:17–21) that the dog that remained with the seven youths in the cave for 309 years became honored for its faithfulness; the poets may thus have intended in their self-identification with the dog not only an expression of modesty but also the implicit hope that they might be purified by constantly sitting at the Prophet's doorstep.

Qudsi closes his poem with a mixed Arabic-Persian request to the Prophet who is, as in traditional verse, both the beloved, *ḥabīb*, and the physician, *ṭabīb*, of his heart.

The *naʿt* in later Indo-Persian and early Urdu poetry shows, as far as one can discern, two major lines of development. One is the ever-increasing use of esoteric concepts in which the entirety of medieval theosophy was condensed in complicated terms and exotic images, as for instance in this quatrain devoted to the Prophet in the eighteenth century:

O you whose light is the *basmala* of the Koran of manifestation:
Your body is all light, and your cheek is the sura "The Light."
Here you are the leader of your people, there their intercessor,
O you locus of manifestation of the [Divine] names "Guiding" and "Forgiving"![143]

This development is equally visible in Ottoman Turkish literature, which was largely inspired by Persian models, and long poems with high-soaring titles were composed both in Turkey[144] and in India—as for instance a "Eulogy for the Star of the Sphere 'He approached and descended' [Sura 53:8] and the Constellation in the Zodiacal House, 'And he was two bows' length or closer' [Sura 53:9], in the Presence of Whose Radiance the Sun and the Moon of Every Morning and Evening are Smaller than [the diminutive star] Suha," composed by a mystical poet of South India in the nineteenth century.[145] By means of such poems the mystical concepts connected with the Prophet were carried into wider circles, for even though the masses were not conversant with Persian, high-sounding poetry impressed them considerably and filled them with awe and fervor and the awareness of being in the presence of something extremely grand and mysterious.

On the other hand, however—this is the other line of development—the expression of love for the Prophet waxed ever stronger in Persian and even more in Urdu poetry. This was perhaps due to the influence of poetry in the regional languages, which especially emphasized the tender, warm, and soft aspects of the relationship of the faithful with the Prophet. In the canonical collections of *ḥadīth* one finds the Prophet's word, "Nobody is a believer until I have become dearer (*aḥabb*) to him than his father, his son, and all human beings."[146] The relation of the faithful to the Prophet was indeed, as another *ḥadīth* mentioned, like that of children to a father, a most revered, loved, and therefore exemplary elder in the family.[147] But poets later came to use a stronger term for the love due to Muhammad: *ʿishq*, which can have a slightly erotic overtone of passionate longing. Numerous books were written in which the Prophet's devotees called themselves *ʿāshiq*, "lover" (or, better in keeping with Western usage, "infatuated," or "in [spiritual] love"), such as the *Miʿrāj al-ʿāshiqīn* (The Heavenly Ladder for the Lovers)[148] or *Qūt al-ʿāshiqīn* (Food for the Lovers), a Sindhi book of the early eighteenth century that contains legends about the Prophet by which his lovers' faith and devotion are nourished.

> From the day of the primordial Covenant I have been the confused
> lover of Muhammad . . .
> God will ask me on the Day of Resurrection: "Whose lover are you?"
> Then I'll say: "That of Muhammad, of Muhammad, of
> Muhammad!"[149]

Thus sang the Urdu poet Shefta in the nineteenth century; slightly earlier, the Rohilla prince Mahabbat Khan pursued the theme in a more romantic vein:

Muhammad Mustafa is the color of the rose of Love,
And his curls are the spring of the hyacinths of Love.
Certainly, he, he alone is the most radiant sun of Love,
And through him are illuminated the luminous stars of Love.[150]

Such verses, written by a man whose mother tongue was not Urdu but Pashto, are quite close to the popular poetry written in Pashto and other idioms, with their emphasis on Love. A little sidelight: in a Pashto poem written by a Hindu, Sukya, the author tells how the daughter of the Prophet's grimmest enemy, Abu Jahl, immediately fell in love with Muhammad when he addressed her![151]

A delightful combination of popular and high style in *naʿtiyya* poetry was created by Muhsin Kakorawi (d. 1905), who is regarded as the leading master of *naʿtiyya* in premodern Urdu. He begins his most famous *naʿt* in plain Hindi terms:

From Benares flies the cloud toward Mathura,
And the wind put the pitcher with Ganges water on the lightning's
shoulder.

After taking up in the *tashbīb*, the erotic introduction of his poem, the traditional imagery of the rainy season (in which lovers complain of separation and long for union) and of the tales about Krishna and his dalliance with his lovesick girlfriends, the gopis, the author suddenly turns to praise of the sun-like Prophet and changes his language into sophisticated Urdu with a heavy admixture of Arabic and Persian expressions.[152]

When studying the development of the *naʿt* in Indo-Pakistan one must also remember that in this area the tradition of religious music was very much alive. Therefore most of the poems in honor of the Prophet are singable, that is, they have a strong rhythmical quality and comparatively simple rhymes, which are often repeated like a litany. Many of them use alliteration in the refrain, in which the letter *m*, the first letter of Muhammad, seems to play a particularly important role.

Miṭṭhā Mīr Muḥammad, madad māṛṛ kar,
Sweet prince Muhammad, give help and support![153]

sings a Sindhi poet; and the *miṭṭhā Muḥammad*, the "sweet Muhammad," is often connected, as well, with the appellations *Makkī* and *Madīnī* and related terms.

Certain favorite expressions are repeated in many of these poems, such as allusions to Faran, the area near Mecca, or the description of the Prophet as *durr-i yatīm* or *yatīma*, "the unique pearl" (*yatīm*, "orphan," refers of course to Muhammad's orphan childhood). To be sure, this combination appears as early as in Sana'i's verse,[154] and Jami, the constant source of inspiration for later poets, was fond of it,[155] but the singers in the Indian subcontinent seem to delight even more in its constant use. One may say that, in general, *naʿtiyya* poetry in Urdu as it has developed in the last four centuries is less burdened with theological subtleties and highflown terminology than Persian poems of this type from the same period.

Jan Knappert's remark that "Swahili pious literature breathes a spirit of great love and devotion to the Prophet, of dedicated obedience to God's own most loved creature" holds true for popular poetry in practically all Islamic languages; for, as Knappert continues, "all love which a Muslim has to give is concentrated upon God's shining representative."[156] Therefore the recitation of eulogies for the Prophet is usually connected with the great events of personal life. In Sind and in Kashmir, and certainly in many other areas, *naʿts* are recited or sung at weddings, at the celebration of a birth, at circumcision, and so on, and Indo-Pakistani Muslim ladies enjoy special gatherings in which poetry praising the Prophet is recited.

The verses of many *sīḥarfīs*, "Golden Alphabets," in the languages of the subcontinent begin with Koranic quotations or *ḥadīth* that allude to Muhammad's unique position. The letter *m* may remind the poet of *mā zāgha*, "the sight did not rove" (Sura 53:17); *q* sometimes evokes *qalbī lā yanām*, the *ḥadīth* "my heart does not sleep," but more frequently *qāba qausain*, "two bows' distance" (Sura 53:9); *b* may recall the *ḥadīth qudsī* "[I am Ahmad] *bilā mīm*, without *m*, *Aḥad*, One."

A different type of Golden Alphabet is found in the Arabic tradition. One example, a *mukhammas* by ʿUthman Mirghani, called *An-nūr al-barrāq fī madḥ an-nabī al-miṣdāq* (The Brilliant Light in the Praise of the Truthful Prophet), is a strophic poem rhyming at every fifth line in a letter according to the sequence of the *abjad* alphabet.[157]

The Indian *bārahmāsa* poems, which deal with the peculiarities of the twelve months of the year as seen by a loving woman, are a genre used all over the subcontinent.[158] Each poem describes through the mouth of a lovesick girl her different feelings during her bridegroom's or husband's absence. In the Muslim context the girl often becomes the human soul who pines for the beloved Muhammad. In such cases, the *bārahmāsa* follows the sequence not of the Indian but of the Islamic months, and the bridal soul reaches proximity to God in Mecca and the presence of the Prophet in his Rauda in Medina in the last month of the lunar year, Dhu'l-hijja, the month of the pilgrimage. Here there develops a mood somewhat comparable to the "bridal mysticism" of the Judaeo-Christian tradition, basically alien to the Muslim approach to the Prophet but apparently assimilated from Hindu motifs such as Radha's longing for Krishna and the entire terminology of that literature. That is why in this genre of poetry, which is common in Sindhi and Panjabi, the poet addresses himself to imaginary girlfriends as though he himself were a bride, and the Prophet assumes the qualities of the longed-for bridegroom:

> Hail! Hail bridegroom, Muhammad the Arab!
> Have mercy, O most merciful one![159]

The "bridegroom of Medina" is so much a standard topos of Sindhi devotional poetry (dating at least from the day of ʿAbdur Raʾuf Bhatti in the early eighteenth century) that the poet can even maintain that during the heavenly journey,

> Gabriel went in front, afoot, the bridegroom riding his horse.[160]

This imagery seems, however, to be restricted to the poetry of the Indian Muslims, and there again mainly to the plains of the Indus Valley and the Panjab, where the mystical poets also like to compare their souls to the heroines of Sindhi folk tales, such as Sassui or Sohni, both of whom sacrificed themselves in search of the beloved—who in this case symbolizes the faraway Prophet.

Sometimes verses in the popular languages point to inexplicable mystical secrets. This is especially apt to happen when they are composed in the environment of an important local religious center, which has likely accumulated its own traditional lore. In Gulbarga, where the great Chishti saint Gesudaraz lies buried, one sings during celebrations of the anniversary of his death a very old Hindi song in which it is said:

> Put in water, some salt—
> When it dissolves, what shall it be called?
> Likewise Mustafa melted his self into God.
> When the self is dissolved, whom could one call God?[161]

Such an image is certainly not easily compatible with the orthodox interpretation of the role of the Prophet, but the verse is obviously a favorite among local believers.

Everywhere the poets have hoped to see the beloved Prophet in their dreams, to be blessed by him as Busiri had been. A few decades after Busiri's time, Yunus Emre in Anatolia recorded his own good fortune:

> In an inspired dream tonight
> I saw Muhammad.
> In the clean mirror of the heart
> I saw Muhammad.

The angels stood in rows and rows,
They donned green garments, beautiful
And they exclaimed: "Muhammad!"—Thus
I saw Muhammad.

Muhammad gave a bowl to me,
Intoxicated was I then—
The Lord bestowed such grace on me:
I saw Muhammad.

I, like a drop sunk in the seas,
Found healing for my suffering;
Today I was so greatly blessed—
I saw Muhammad![162]

Other folk poets describe how proud and happy they are that they belong to the community that has been elected by God and upon whom His mercy has descended:

In Muhammad's community I put on the trousers of faith
And came, strutting like a peacock.[163]

Thus sang Eshrefoghlu Rumi in Turkey in the fifteenth century; three centuries later one of his compatriots, Sazayi, wrote, in more sophisticated lines:

You are that sun of truth before whom the whole world is nothing but
  a speck of dust,
Your existence is the motive for time and space, O messenger of God!
Those who drink the goblet of your love, don't care for Khidr's water
  of life—
For your love is eternal life, O messenger of God![164]

And Egyptian folksingers in our day say with similar intentions but in less artistic style:

All [passionate] love is prohibited,
    But for the Prophet it is permitted,
And the drinking of wine is prohibited,
    But permitted is [drinking from] the Prophet's saliva.[165]

For the popular bards, love of the Prophet is the heart of their faith. Even more, it is the center of life, not only of human life but of the life of everything created, for stones and trees, animals and walls, have proclaimed his glory. That is why a Sindhi poet can sing:

The lotus sees the sun in longing dream,
The moth's enamored by the candle's beam,
The nightingale repeats the rose's theme,
And full of love you hear the partridge scream—
But all of them, they love that glorious prince![166]

Popular poets as well as the masters of high, classical literature know that just as the Prophet is the meaning and end of creation, he also will be the one to guide them to eternal life. For he is the caravan leader "who first stepped forth from the concealment of non-being, and led the entire caravan of creation out onto the plane of being," as Najmuddin Razi Daya says.[167] And on this "plane of being," he is the mystical guide who—as at the end of ʿAttar's *Muṣībatnāma*—guides the seeker into "the ocean of his own soul" where he will find the Lord.

When Maulana Rumi proudly states that

Our caravan leader is the pride of the world, Mustafa,[168]

he is in tune with the poets in the Indus Valley and in Anatolia, who praise the great caravan leader who guides them safely on their way to the central sanctuary in Mecca, which is the reflection of the heavenly Kaʿba.[169] And if the poets happen to live in the valleys of the great rivers, or close to the ocean, they praise him as the pilot who steers the fragile boat of life through the deep waters, between sandbanks and whirlpools, to the faraway shore of peace, as Shah ʿAbdul Latif in Sind describes it in *Sur Sarīrag*.[170] So also the Bengali folk poet uses images taken from the life of fishermen and sailors, who know that they depend upon the experience and wisdom of the pilot to find their way to the other shore:

I shall never find again
A compassionate friend like you.
You showed yourself—
Now do not leave, O Prophet of the faith.
You are the friend of God,
Helmsman to the far shore of truth—
Without you we would
Never again see that world on the other shore.

ELEVEN

THE "MUHAMMADAN PATH" AND THE NEW INTERPRETATION OF THE PROPHET'S LIFE

As much as the Muslims in general refuse to be called Muhammadans, the expression *ṭarīqa muḥammadiyya*, "Muhammadan Path," was used by quite a few premodern mystical groups who wanted to express, with this designation, their faithful adherence to the *sunna* of the Prophet to the exclusion of later usages that had been adopted into the mystical way of life. The term *ṭarīqa muḥammadiyya* was used in this fashion in eighteenth-century India by some mystical leaders, and the members of this *ṭarīqa* were to play an important political role in the subcontinent during the first half of the nineteenth century.[1] At the same time, several North African mystical fraternities used the same term to emphasize the exemplary role of the Prophet in their religious life. Recently, a related movement of the "Muhammadiyya" has become prominent among Indonesian Muslims.[2]

One of the precursors of the Indian *ṭarīqa muḥammadiyya* was, in a certain sense, the reformer Ahmad Sirhindi, called by his admirers the *mujaddid-i alf-i thānī*, "the renovator of the second millennium," for he appeared on the scene shortly after A.H. 1000 (A.D. 1591–92).[3] Ahmad Sirhindi was a member of the Naqshbandi order, which had developed in Central Asia and played an important role in Central Asian politics during the fifteenth century; almost all the scholars and poets connected with the Timurid court of Herat were associated with the Naqshbandiyya, among them the poet Jami and the powerful minister Mir ʿAli Shir Nawaʾi. At the same time, politics in Bukhara and adjacent areas were largely under the influence of the Naqshbandi master ʿUbaidullah Ahrar, a man of great charisma and political acumen, to whom Jami dedicated one of his major didactic epics, the *Tuḥfat al-aḥrār*. The Naqshbandiyya reached India via Afghanistan in the late sixteenth century; the major figure in this development was Khwaja Baqi-billah, a friend of many intellectuals in Akbar's days. Ahmad Sirhindi joined the order and soon began to preach against the tendencies of the emperor Akbar, which seemed to many to blur the borders between Islam and "infidelity." He would not accept any religious way as valid with the exception of Islam. His concept was that of a mystically tinged Islam which yet retained its pristine purity without any admixture of pagan, that is in his case, Hindu, elements. In this definition of Islam, the person of the Prophet was central, for it was he who defined the borderline between Islam and infidelity—an idea expressed by ever so many poets in their highflown *naʿts*. The first half of the profession of faith, which acknowledges the Oneness and Uniqueness of God, could be accepted by Hindus and members of other religious traditions, but the second half, which gives Muhammad his unique position as the messenger of God, defines Islam as a distinct and distinctive religious system.[4]

Ahmad Sirhindi, like many other Naqshbandi leaders, certainly had political ambitions, and this political role of his, which proved important for the development of Indo-Muslim self-consciousness, has been highlighted during our own century by the defenders of the Two Nations theory: that the Muslims of India form a closed community, sharply distinguished from the Hindu majority. Ahmad's mystical speculations and his remarks about his own mystical role have attracted comparatively little interest. Yet his sayings about his role in the divinely ordered plan of world history were so daring in his era that the emperor Jahangir, Akbar's son, had him imprisoned for some time "until the heat of his temperament and confusion of his brain were somewhat quenched," as Jahangir himself tells in his memoirs, horrified and perhaps also somewhat amused by Ahmad's claims as found in his letters, "that album of absurdities."[5]

As far as I can see, the formula *Anā Aḥmad bilā mīm*, "I am Ahmad without *m*, *Aḥad*," a favorite of most poets and mystics in the eastern lands of Islam, was not used by the Naqshbandis because they were afraid that it might lead to pantheism and did not define the unique position of Islam sufficiently. But even Sirhindi could not avoid puns on the names of Muhammad, as they had been widely popular from at least the days of ʿAttar. Thus he claimed that Muhammad during his lifetime had two individuations, which are manifested in the two ringlets of the two *m*'s of his name (*mḥmd*). One is the human, bodily one, the other is the angelic, spiritual one. In the course of the first millennium of Islamic history, said Sirhindi, the first *m* of Muhammad's name slowly disappeared and was replaced by the letter *alif*, *a*, which is the cipher of Divine Unity and Unicity. Thus, Muhammad (*mḥmd*) became Ahmad (*aḥmd*). (The reader will have no difficulty seeing here a subtle allusion to Ahmad Sirhindi's own name.) The reformer then developed the theory that a "normal believer" (which perhaps means someone who is closest to the ideal of the normative Muslim as the perfect follower of the Prophetic *sunna*) is called to reconstitute the original manifestation of Muhammad. That means that the believer would make apparent in the world not only the spiritual but also the political and social aspects of the Prophet's teaching, and thus give Islam new luster. Then the "perfections of Prophethood" would reappear in their fullness and perfect glory.

Ahmad Sirhindi considered himself and three of his descendants to be *qayyūm*, that is, in his terminology, the highest spiritual power, which keeps intact the course of the world.[6] It is a strange coincidence that the fourth and last *qayyūm*, Pir Muhammad Zubair, died in 1740, not long after the conquest and pillage of Delhi by Nadir Shah in 1739—an event that indeed marked the beginning of the end of the once mighty Moghul empire. The empire had been slowly breaking to pieces since the death in 1707 of Aurangzeb, the last powerful emperor, aged nearly ninety. Internal and external wars and tensions shook its very foundations, and the sack of Delhi in 1739 was merely an outward sign of the end of Moghul supremacy over the larger part of India. But it was in this very time of disintegration that a group of Muslim theologians recalled the significance of the role of the Prophet as the "beautiful model"; and during the same period, three great mystical thinkers in Delhi, all of them affiliated to the Naqshbandiyya (though also to other Sufi orders) appeared as leaders of the new "Muhammadan" theology that intended to give the desperate Muslims a new impetus and lead them back to the Golden Age of the Prophet and his first four successors.[7]

The most famous of these leaders is Shah Waliullah, whose political role in northwestern India was remarkable. He saw himself as called by the Prophet and invested as his "vicegerent in blaming," *muʿātaba*, and the thirteen visions in which the Prophet appeared to him allow us interesting insights into the formation of his religious identity. Thus, Shah Waliullah realized that he was called to guide a small fraction of the Prophet's people, the *umma marḥūma*, "those upon whom God has shown mercy." Beside Shah Waliullah stood his friend and senior colleague, Mazhar Janjanan the *sunnītrāsh*, "Sunnicizer," a Naqshbandi famed for his absolute, unflinching imitation of the Prophet's *sunna*. Not only did Mazhar lead an exemplary mystical life, but he was also a good poet in both Persian and Urdu, even distinguished as one of the "four pillars of Urdu poetry." The third figure in this group was Khwaja Mir Dard, known primarily as the only truly superior mystical poet in Urdu, a language that had become increasingly refined and served as a vehicle of poetry in Delhi and Lucknow from the early eighteenth century onward. However Dard was also a speculative theologian who was instrumental in the formation of the *ṭarīqa muḥammadiyya*. His father, Nasir Muhammad ʿAndalib, friend and devotee of the fourth *qayyūm*, had been blessed by a vision in which Imam Hasan showed him the fundamentals of the *ṭarīqa muḥammadiyya*. (Incidentally, Hasan ibn ʿAli, the Prophet's elder grandson, was also an important source of inspiration to the Shadhiliyya, which like the Naqshbandiyya is a "sober" order.) Probably Imam Hasan was chosen as a model by the non-Shiite and even anti-Shiite Sufi orders instead of Husain because the latter's veneration among the Shia had assumed dimensions that the Sunnites, despite their high respect for the Prophet's family, could not tolerate.

ʿAndalib initiated his son Mir Dard, who was at the time of his father's vision (ca. 1734) about thirteen years old, into the Muhammadan Path; other members followed. This *ṭarīqa* is basically nothing but a mystically heightened fundamentalism in which the unification of the seeker with the principle of the *ḥaqīqa muḥammadiyya* constitutes the goal of the Path. One can say that the old Sufi tripartition of the Path, *sharīʿa–ṭarīqa–ḥaqīqa*, was expressed by Dard and his disciples in the idea that the faithful observance of the Muhammadan *sharīʿa* in the Muhammadan *ṭarīqa* finally leads to unification with the *ḥaqīqa muḥammadiyya*, in which the wayfarer is endowed with the pleroma of the Ninety-nine Names and becomes the Perfect Man (even though Mir Dard does not use this term in his writings). For "Humanity consists of Muhammadanism."[8]

Mir Dard composed numerous Persian works meant to serve exclusively the cause of spreading the Muhammadan Path, for he believed that only this path would save the population of Delhi, which was suffering from incessant raids, attacks, famines, and political instability in the decades following Nadir Shah's invasion. In the *ṭarīqa muḥammadiyya* as elaborated by Mir Dard, his father ʿAndalib appears for all practical purposes as the representative of the Prophet, whose corporeal descendant he was (being a *sayyid*), but with whom he had also reached perfect mystical union in *fanā fi'r-rasūl*, "annihilation in the Prophet." The reports that Dard gives about his own investiture as the vicegerent of the Prophet and his ascent through the stages of various prophets until he reached the *ḥaqīqa muḥammadiyya* are psychologically highly interesting and attempt to express in long-winded, swinging Persian prose the same ideas that other mystical poets had sung in ecstatic verses.[9]

However, Dard, who never left his hometown, Delhi, and who also—contrary to Naqshbandi ideals—loved and sponsored music, was not interested in politics, and one never finds in his work any derogatory remarks about the large Shia component in the country. Mazhar Janjanan, on the other hand, was violently anti-Shia and was even killed, at a great age, after ridiculing a Shiite Muharram procession. It was in the circles around Mazhar and Shah Waliullah that the political importance of the Prophet was emphasized. With an argumentation typical of modern Islamic polemics Mazhar, for example, wrote about the relations between the two major branches of Islam:

> According to the agreement of both sides [Sunnites and Shiites] our Prophet is the mercy for the inhabitants of the world and the worthiest of prophets; his nation is also the best of nations, and his religion abolishes all religions. . . . Thus it is necessary that his law be more powerful than the other laws and that his nation be more numerous in relation to other nations. . . . It is absolutely clear that the largest part of the Muslims are Sunnites; no other group has the multitude and strength that this group possesses, and all the saints and most of the scholars, nay rather most of the rulers and princes of Islamic countries, with whom the strengthening of the firm religion is connected, have been in the past and still are at present members of this [the Sunni] faction.[10]

That means that according to Mazhar's conviction the greatness of the Prophet can be proved by the number of the members of his community: the greater number of believers is therefore proof for the truth of a religion. This proof of the truthfulness of the Prophet, which is derived from the success of his teaching and his political activities, was known in earlier times as well, but it seems that the tendency to interpret the Prophetic office as a sociopolitical factor began to attract more scholars during the eighteenth century. Shah Waliullah too claims that the truth and sincerity of a prophet's claim can be examined by looking at the political and social results of his preaching, for

> God gave him intelligence by which he could find the proper means to institute a healthy society, [means] such as good breeding, domestic economy, social intercourse, civic economy, and the management of the community.[11]

It is interesting to notice that more than 150 years later Muhammad Iqbal, the great modernist interpreter of Islam, expressed a similar opinion, only with the difference that instead of complicated Persian phrases he uses philosophical English:

> Another way of judging the value of a prophet's religious experience, therefore, would be to examine the type of manhood he has created, and the cultural world that has sprung out of the spirit of his message.[12]

This shows that—as Iqbal states somewhere else, correctly—the modern approach to Islam indeed begins with Shah Waliullah: scholars are no longer interested in the miracles of the Prophet but rather in his role as nation-builder and model for social conduct.

This viewpoint, of necessity, confronts the Muslims constantly with the ideal of the Prophet and the reality of their own political disintegration, and thus creates a permanent tension between the elusive ideal and the sad political reality. The Golden Age of the Prophet and the first four caliphs remains the yardstick by which the Muslims measure their present situation. In a time like eighteenth-century India, when the Muslim rule virtually collapsed, and foreign imperialists such as the British and the French encroached upon the subcontinent, the *person* of the Prophet became increasingly central in the Muslim community. Even though Muhammad's role as intercessor at Doomsday was mentioned time and again, and his help implored by the poets, the reformers understandably emphasized the practical aspects of his message. This emphasis was needed, for the Muslims had to cope in various ways with resurgent non-Muslim communities such as the Mahrattas and the Sikhs, but more importantly they had to learn how to adjust their lives to the rule of the British, who extended their power successfully in practically every realm of life. In this respect it is worth mentioning that Shah Waliullah, who so energetically called upon the Pathans (Rohillas and Ahmad Shah Durrani) for help against the Mahrattas and Sikhs, never speaks of the British—who during his lifetime, in 1757, gained their first, decisive victory at Plassey in Bengal and whose influence increased day by day.

Convinced that he was the Prophet's "vicegerent in blaming,"[13] Shah Waliullah scolded with hard words all those who neglected their duties and the God-given commandments, indulging in vices of sorts; those who performed pilgrimage to the shrines of saints instead of praying exclusively to the one and unique God; and those who did not even oppose the construction of wineshops and brothels on their lands if they were able to make some money from such dirty business. In holy wrath the reformer also attacked those who studied philosophy instead of concentrating upon the Word of God and the traditions of the Prophet: are these people not meaner than dogs, he asks, these misguided "scholars" who lick the dry bones of two-thousand-year-old Greek philosophy?[14] One thinks immediately here of the verses of Sana'i, ʿAttar, Rumi, and other early Sufi poets who stated, time and again, that no one is farther away from the *sharīʿa* brought by the Hashimite Prophet than a philosopher.

It is somewhat difficult to describe Shah Waliullah's own system of thought in detail. His numerous works are written in a complicated, idiosyncratic Arabic or Persian style, and it is not always easy to discover the exact meaning of his sentences (even though his grandson, Shah Ismaʿil Shahid, composed a special book to explicate his grandfather's terminology). Like many other Indian Muslims, Shah Waliullah highlights the Arabic aspect of the Prophet, and the "Hashimi, Quraishi, Makki, Madini" Prophet of whom Qudsi had sung a century before him is the focal point of his meditations, just as he was to be later the pivot of Iqbal's prophetology. The Arabic character of Islam in its pristine purity and simplicity is clearly contrasted by Waliullah with the confusing plethora of the Indian religious tradition. In this context the Indian Muslims are given a very special place in the world: among the Hindu "idol-worshipers" they are called to bear witness to the Divine Unity.

According to Shah Waliullah, every prophet bears in himself the different grades of perfection: the perfection of proximity that is reached by the performance of supererogatory works of piety, *qurb an-nawāfil* (this comprises the station of the saints); of proximity to God that is attained by the punctual fulfillment of religious duties, *qurb al-farā'iḍ* (this is the station of the prophets); and of proximity to the angelic world, *malakūt*. The Prophet of Islam has a very special relation to the angelic plane from which events on earth are guided and arranged, for his heart is a mirror of the Sphere of Holiness, *ḥaẓīrat al-quds*. This is that sphere in which the events from the highest level of the heavenly realms are reflected. The soul of Muhammad is compared to a polished stone, *ḥajar baḥt*—an idea found much earlier in Ibn ʿArabi's philosophy.[15] Only such a perfectly polished heart was able to receive and reflect all divine illumination and inspiration. After God had entrusted to the Prophet the rule over the world and the care of his community, it was necessary that his soul, the polished stone, should participate in the great actions of the Highest Assembly, *al-mal'a al- aʿlā*, and be endowed with knowledge of past and future events. Thus this prophetic soul reflected the stories of generations past and knew of things that were important for the welfare of the community; likewise the Prophet was granted knowledge of the events that will come to pass at Doomsday. So Shah Waliullah explained the Prophet's knowledge of events past and future, a knowledge that cannot be understood and explained by reference to natural causes.

One of Shah Waliullah's passages seems quite mysterious: he sees Muhammad develop in three circles that wax, like crescent moons, into a full moon until the full completion, that is, his position as Seal of the Prophets, is achieved. In another passage the Prophet appears to him as someone who is distinguished by complete inner harmony and supported by the Sphere of Holiness. However, even more important is his active role in creating a successful community. Again, in a different connection, Muhammad appears in the traditional Islamic way, as the Seal of Prophethood, who was sent to humankind and djinn, who is going to intercede for the sinners of his community, and who admonishes the faithful to busy their tongues without interruption in reciting his virtues.

Iqbal, who praised Shah Waliullah as the first Muslim who felt the need for a new spirit in Islam, took up in his own works the latter's remark that every Prophet has educated one special people, who then could be used as the nucleus for building an all-embracing law. It seems that this idea goes back to a quotation from Shah Waliullah's comprehensive Arabic work *Ḥujjat Allāh al-bāligha*, and it is interesting to note that the eighteenth-century reformer voices the opinion that the nature of the prophetic message is related to the character of the people to whom the respective prophet is sent:

> Prophethood is something like refining and polishing something to make it as beautiful as possible, whether this thing be a lamp or a lump of clay. . . . The innate character of a nation is comparable to the material, be it a lamp or clay.[16]

This explains why the prophets preach on different levels. Their messages, which were addressed to one people after another, became increasingly refined until the message became all-comprehensive in Muhammad. Only he comprises all aspects of the revelation; the messengers that worked before him had to gear their words toward the specific race to whom they were sent, or had to adapt it to more or less elevated levels of consciousness.

Shah Waliullah sometimes surprises his readers with amazingly modern-sounding remarks, particularly when he tries to explain the miracles of the Prophet. Thus the Splitting of the Moon, as we saw earlier, appears to him as perfectly intelligible in the light of natural causes. He even explains the details of Muhammad's heavenly journey in a novel way: all the human perfections of the Prophet were manifested in his pure body, while his "animal perfections" were materialized in the shape of Buraq. And yet this same scholar who attempted to rationalize miracles like the Splitting of the Moon, which people loved so dearly, also praised the signs and miracles performed by the Prophet in a long, traditional poem that takes up exactly the same imagery that had been used by hundreds of pious poets in the Persianate world.

One problem that was always stressed in the later Naqshbandiyya, and which therefore plays an important role in the theology of the *ṭarīqa muḥammadiyya*, is the difference between the two types of proximity man can attain, that is, the *qurb an-nawāfil* and *qurb al-farā'iḍ*. The first term, "proximity reached by supererogatory works," is derived from a well-known extra-Koranic Divine Word, the so-called *ḥadīth an-nawāfil*, in which the Lord says: "My servant does not cease to come closer to me by means of supererogatory works, and when he approaches me a span, I approach him a cubit, and if he comes walking I come running, and then I love him until I become his eye by which he sees, his ear by which he hears, and his hand by which he grasps." This *ḥadīth qudsī* was interpreted by the mystics as pointing to a transformation of man, who by constant service reaches divine proximity and is lost in God. This is at the same time the final point on the "way of intoxication" for those who are so completely carried away that they lose themselves in God and do not want to return to this world.[17] The "proximity achieved by the performance of religious duties," on the other hand, is regarded as the way of the prophets, who experience the Divine Unity as a result of punctual fulfillment of all religious duties. This idea is based on another *ḥadīth qudsī*, which is elaborated by Razi Daya, a typical representative of "sober" Sufism: "God says: 'There is naught that brings men so nigh unto Me as performing that which I have made incumbent upon them.'" For according to this medieval Sufi leader, "each commandment of the Law is a key to one of the locks of the supreme talisman."[18] Those who pursue this path will return into the world sober and inspired to work there for the realization of the kingdom of God. This was, for the Naqshbandis, the highest possible station, and it fits perfectly with the interpretation of Muhammad's return from the *miʿrāj* in order to guide his community. These two types of possible response to the experience of proximity to God show with perfect clarity the difference between what historians of religion (since Nathan Söderblom) have called the "prophetic" and "mystic" types of experience.

One of the three mystical theologians of Delhi, Mir Dard, devoted many chapters in his Persian works to this very problem. Being a *sayyid* on both sides of his family and hence closely related to the Prophet, he felt that by following the example of his noble ancestor earnestly and by performing unceasingly the duties laid down in the *sharīʿa* he could further enhance his relation to Muhammad. At last he reached a stage where he experienced himself as the true successor of the Prophet charged with calling mankind to the true "Muhammadan" faith:

> He [God] spoke to me: ". . . O Vicegerent of God and Sign (*āya*) of God! Verily I have witnessed your state of servanthood; now witness My Divinity, for you are My servant and he whom I have accepted and whom My Prophet has accepted. . . ."

And after Dard has acknowledged that he is "the descendant of Your beloved and part of Your nightingale [ʿAndalib]," God addresses him: "I have called you to the final sum total and the Muhammadan sum total; whoever obeys you obeys God and the Prophet."[19]

Thus, around 1750–60 not only did Shah Waliullah consider himself to be the "vicegerent of the Prophet in blaming," but Mir Dard experienced his own investiture as the Prophet's vicegerent in all his aspects. This may be one reason for the fact that neither of the two mystics, who lived not very far from each other in Delhi, ever mentions the other's name in his works (though Waliullah's sons studied Urdu poetry with Dard).

One may surmise that the new importance given to the historical or at least semihistorical Muhammad in India during the eighteenth century can be largely explained from the political situation: the suffering community needed a strong, radiant model for their survival. One can also sense in this movement a nostalgia, a longing for the Golden Age. Did not the Prophet create the "best of all nations," one that was called to be the bearer of the final Divine law? And yet this nation, despite its former glory and power, had now nothing to counteract the incursions of the Sikhs, Hindus, and Europeans in their area except, at best, their pride in their past. Such nostalgia has been an important ingredient of the veneration of the Prophet up to the present, for the ideal of the Muslims has remained the time when Muhammad led them from victory to victory. The only way open to the beleaguered Muslims in India was, they felt, to go back to him in the hope that in this way the community might prosper again.

Even so, their situation deteriorated almost from year to year. After 1806, the last Moghul rulers were more or less puppets in the hands of the British East India Company. But the *ṭarīqa muḥammadiyya* was alive under the surface. Some thirty-five years after Mir Dard's death in 1785, the name of the *ṭarīqa muḥammadiyya* served to designate a political movement that was theologically supported by the descendants of Shah Waliullah. The leader of this movement, Sayyid Ahmad of Rai Bareilly, tried, along with his followers, to drive the Sikhs out of the northwestern areas of the subcontinent, which were inhabited by a Muslim majority.[20] As in early Islam, the personality of the Prophet was regarded by the freedom fighters as the axis around which the true believers gather, and the remembrance of his life inspired them to believe in the final victory of Islam over all its enemies. Even when Sayyid Ahmad and his theological adviser, Shah Waliullah's grandson Ismaʿil, were killed by the Sikho in 1831, and the community apparently then dissolved, the enthusiasm of the remaining fighters remained unshaken; on the contrary, for decades afterwards they fought for their ideals, now no longer against the Sikhs but rather against the British, still hoping to reinstate a truly Islamic rule in India.

A political movement centered upon the Prophet was not, however, peculiar to India. At almost the same time that Indo-Muslim fighters rose up in the name of the Prophet, similar fraternities appeared in North Africa and the central Islamic lands. Both the Sanusiyya and the Tijaniyya are mystical fraternities that from their inception have placed the figure of the Prophet in the center of their religious life; on the basis of his role as leader of the victorious armies, they began to fight the French and Italian colonial powers "in the name of God and His Prophet."

In the Sanusiyya the identification of the mystic with the Prophet, upon whose essence he must concentrate, is the pivot of piety. In yet another order, the Mirghaniyya, which began to blossom at about the same time in Mecca and then expanded into Egypt and the Sudan, constant remembrance of the Prophet and unflinching love for him are, even more than in other orders, the true badge of identity, as one can see from the litanies and invocations used by the members of these religious groups to the present day.

Constance E. Padwick mentions the basic experience of the leaders of these movements. It is said of Ahmad at-Tijani:

> Among the graces with which God honoured him was the waking vision of the Prophet, continuously and ever, so that it was never absent from him for the twinkling of an eye. And (another grace was) his questioning of the Prophet on everything and asking his counsel in small things and great, and undergoing training at his hands.[21]

Similarly, the founder of the Sanusiyya (and the Mirghaniyya) was in constant contact with the beloved Prophet:

> This order is founded on the absorption of the inner life of its founder in the spectacle of the Very Self of the Prophet, with the building up of his outer life on the following of him in word and deed, and the occupation of his tongue with the calling down of blessing upon him and his perseverance in this during the greater part of his solitary and his public devotions, till the magnifying of the Prophet dominated his heart and was mingled with his inmost being, so that he was moved at the very mention of him. And the vision of the Prophet's essential being reigned in his heart so that no created being other than the Prophet had any weight with him.[22]

As we saw (p. 100), the Tijaniyya recommends the prayer called *Al-Fātiḥiyya* more than any other prayer to its followers. The Sanusiyya prefers the so-called *ʿAẓīmiyya* prayer:

> My God, I ask Thee by that light of the Face of the great God which filled the bases of the Great Throne, and by which uprose the worlds of the Great God, to call down blessing on our Lord Muhammad, the great in rank, and on the family of the Prophet of the great God.[23]

In the Mirghaniyya, which has produced a vast literature of prayer poetry and blessings for the Prophet, the faithful may pray:

> O God, by the rank of Thy Prophet, by Thy love to him and his love to Thee I ask . . . : Double, O Lord, my love to him; adorn my hearing with the earrings of the joy of his speech![24]

The nineteenth century, when such prayers were popular in both East and West among the faithful, was a time of increasing political tension for the entire Islamic world. It thus may come as somewhat of a surprise that even during this period some Indian Muslims could devote their time to seemingly hairsplitting problems concerning the role of the Prophet, but so it was. The theologian Fazl-i Haqq Khairabadi, who was later banished to the Andaman Islands for his active participation in the unsuccessful military revolt against the British in 1857, had a dispute with the leader of the *ṭarīqa muḥammadiyya*, Ismaʿil Shahid. The problem at stake was whether God could create another Muhammad in case the necessity to do so should emerge. Fazl-i Haqq held that God could by no means create another Muhammad, whereas Ismaʿil Shahid believed that He could do so but would not do it. Mirza Ghalib, who soon afterwards composed his grandiose *naʿt* of 101 verses, was asked his opinion, and to the disappointment of his friend Fazl-i Haqq he sided with Ismaʿil, though couching his thought in carefully chosen Persian verses:

> Wherever a tumult of a world arises,
> There "Mercy for the worlds" is also found.[25]

That means that should God create other worlds with intelligent creatures, He would not deprive them of prophetic guidance. A century later Iqbal took up this idea in his *Jāvīdnāma*; for the problem, which was really insignificant in the early nineteenth century, had gained importance with the progress of science—for instance, with the astronomers' discoveries of more and larger galaxies, the structure of which seemed to allow the possible existence of organic life of some kind or the other elsewhere. What would happen to these extraterrestrial beings? Would they not also need spiritual guidance by prophets? But if so, how to combine Ghalib's answer with the central dogma of Islam, that of the finality of Prophethood? Iqbal, wisely enough, averted further discussion of this delicate point through a skillful turn of his poem; we learn from his correspondence with Sayyid Sulaiman Nadwi that Ghalib's verse had caused him some anxiety.[26]

But during the nineteenth century it was comparatively rare that such ideas occupied Muslim thinkers. The Muslims in India and somewhat later in Egypt had completely different and more pressing problems. Their

British colonial overlords had introduced them—at least a few of them—to books written by European orientalists about their beloved Prophet, and with amazed horror they studied the biographies of Muhammad by William Muir and Aloys Sprenger. It is therefore quite natural that a new theological approach should have emerged from the first clash with the European "critical" approach to the Prophet's life. This new theology was, understandably, largely apologetic, and centered mainly upon the person of the Prophet.

The great reformer of Indian Islam, Sir Sayyid Ahmad Khan, was one of the first, if not the first, to construct his modernist theology with regard to the Prophet, whom he deeply loved.[27] To be sure, Muslim orthodoxy attacked him vehemently for his cooperation with the British and also because he, a layman without the traditional theological education in a *madrasa*, had arrogated to himself the right to modernize the outlook of the Muslims. In his early youth Sayyid Ahmad—in this period an extremely *sunna*-conscious Muslim—had composed a kind of "reformed *maulid*," a work in which he intended to rid the figure of the Prophet of later legends and mythical accretions. His ideal was, like that of the Naqshbandiyya, that the true Muslim should realize in his life the *akhlāq-i muḥammadī*, the noble qualities of the Prophet, and imitate him in every respect in the sphere of ethics. Like Shah Waliullah before him, Sayyid Ahmad recognized that the enormous mass of commentaries, scholia, and supercommentaries on the Koran constituted a great danger to the Muslims, for these commentaries seemed to obscure rather than illuminate the simple, clear message of the Holy Book. He therefore lamented that God's commandments, "which that innocent, honest, simpleminded prophet of sweet character" had brought to the ignorant, illiterate desert dwellers in such plain, clear, and simple words had now been changed by unnecessary additions of empty distinctions, refined metaphysical propositions, and logical improvements in such a way that it was impossible to recognize their original purity and simplicity.[28] Fifty years later Iqbal was to complain in similar words: "I am sure that, if the Holy Prophet would appear once more and teach Islam in this country, then the people of this country would not be able to understand the Islamic truth due to the existing conditions and modes of behavior."[29]

Sir Sayyid constantly pondered how to make the Prophet once more a living reality for his community and to prove his greatness to the world—that greatness which contrasted so dramatically with the present situation of Muslims vis-à-vis the Western powers. He therefore composed numerous articles and speeches on this topic,[30] and his *Essays on the Life of Mohammed* also contain quite a number of quotations from Western authors who had uttered positive statements about Muhammad's greatness.[31] Such quotations became an important part of apologetic literature. The favorite author of all Islamic modernists in India has been Thomas Carlyle, whose admiring remarks about Muhammad in his book *On Heroes and Hero Worship* have been repeated so often by Muslims that his critical words about the Prophet are completely overlooked or negated.[32] Washington Irving was also cited with approval.[33] Unfortunately none of the reformers could read German to see Goethe's positive evaluation of the Prophetic spirit as expressed in "Mahomet's Gesang" and the *West-Östlicher Divan* (one of Carlyle's sources of inspiration), and it was another fifty years before Iqbal remedied this regrettable omission. It also seems that the reformers—even in areas under French colonial rule or at least cultural influence—were not aware of the books written in French during and following the period of the Enlightenment, in which several authors (beginning with Boulainvilliers) had approached the life of the Prophet in a rather admiring way.

Shah Waliullah had made the first shy attempts at demythologizing one legend or the other; Sir Sayyid followed him in this respect and quoted him extensively even though his own early work contains a special section on the "thousands and thousands of miracles of the Prophet."[34] He did not, for instance, deem it necessary to believe that during the battle of Badr angels had supported the Prophet; he preferred to think that Divine grace alone was at work, and that God did not really burden the angels (whatever they are!) with accomplishing the task.[35] Sir Sayyid also believed that prophethood is an innate human quality; here, his part-time collaborator Maulana Shibli followed him closely: prophethood is "the last and most perfect stage in the development of natural, inborn qualities; it is a 'spiritual faculty,' i.e., the *quwwat-i qudsiyya*, 'faculty of sanctity,' or *malika-i nubuwwat*, 'habitus of prophethood.' "[36]

As for the verbal inspiration of the Koran, Sir Sayyid took a stance almost more orthodox than even Shah Waliullah, refusing to accept the possibility that only the meaning of the Koran was inspired to the Prophet, who then expressed it in human language. For him, every word is Divinely inspired, hence so powerful. Muhammad is to his mind "the uniquely qualified guide for giving *tauḥīd* (the Oneness of God) adequate expression in practical life."[37] And this same man, who was harshly attacked for his modernism, also composed a touching prayer that is as ardent as any prayer uttered by a mystic in the centuries before him:

> O my God, give me a burning breast!
> O my God, bestow on me weeping eyes!
> O my God, keep me utterly intoxicated with the love of Ahmad!

O my God, the one who is ill of love for him—he is forgiven.
O my God, give me the pain of the passionate love of Mustafa and
give me then the balm of communion with him.
O my God, make me the dust of Medina,
fasten my boat to its *ghāt* [landing place]!
O my God, free me from the negligence of time
into the place of al-Mustafa, the lord of the Universe.
Grant me to rest in faith in his city
in a grave in al-Baqiʿ [Medina's graveyard]. . . .
My soul is laid out on your footsteps, O Ahmad;
This station it has asked for from God.[38]

One of Sir Sayyid's collaborators in his educational journal *Tahdhīb al-akhlāq* (The Polishing of Morals) was Chiragh Ali from Hyderabad/Deccan. In critical radicalism he by far surpassed Sir Sayyid and rejected the majority of traditional *ḥadīth*, claiming that the traditions formed "a chaotic sea."[39] He accepted Muhammad's authority only insofar as religious—in the widest sense of the word—problems were at stake: "That, in which he supports them in their religion, we have to accept, but when he expresses his own opinion, he too was only a human being." In other words, the Prophet possessed a kind of infallibility as long as he spoke as it were *ex cathedra*, that is, when he taught religious matters—but not when speaking of affairs of this world. He should therefore not be regarded as a teacher of agriculture or medicine. This conviction, as we saw, can be found in classical Islam as well, for instance in Baqillani's theology, but Chiragh Ali's criticism of *ḥadīth* surpassed by far the hitherto valid standards (and was almost as radical as, if not more so than, Goldziher's critique, published in Germany in his *Muhammedanische Studien* a few years after Chiragh Ali's death; the two men were never acquainted). This overcritical attitude of Chiragh Ali's may well have been one reason for the deeply felt aversion of the *Ahl-i ḥadīth* in India to Sir Sayyid and his modernist ideas.

But neither Sir Sayyid nor any of his numerous friends who tried to interpret Prophetic tradition in a modern way and to show that Islam is absolutely compatible with progress was able to offer as impressive a picture of the Prophet and the culture he inaugurated as was Syed Ameer Ali. His book *The Life and Teachings of Muhammad, or The Spirit of Islam*, published shortly before Sir Sayyid's death, became the model of a completely new genre of literature in Islamic lands: books, as Wilfred Cantwell Smith puts it, "which show the Muslims a Prophet of whom they may well be proud."[40] In them the Prophet is depicted as the embodiment of all good qualities that a human being can imagine. It is not, however, so much the external aspects of Muhammad's life—the way he tied his turban, or which fruits he was fond of—that form the main topic of these books, but rather his spiritual attitude, his *Weltanschauung*, and his morals. The Prophet's modesty and humility are duly emphasized, as is his loving care for all those who are part of his community. His patience and perseverance under duress and difficult conditions serve as a model for the Muslims. Thus Muhammad appears no longer as the Perfect Man on the mystical plane but as the most perfect human being ever born on earth.[41] To Syed Ameer Ali and all those who followed him Muhammad is the truly modern man; they were convinced that once Muslims understood this they would also understand that Islam is not only compatible with progress but rather *is* progress in itself.

The modernists were interested primarily in educational problems, much more than in scholastic hairsplitting and theological niceties. They therefore asked themselves why children should learn all those charming but unnecessary legends about the Prophet, or memorize poems about his mystical qualities. Would it not be much more useful to give them a rational image of the founder of their religion, first, so that they might be prepared to fight against the Western scholars with their derogatory interpretation of the Prophet—and second, so that they might also redirect their own lives according to the practical model given once for all by the Prophet?

Much as Protestant theology of the late nineteenth and early twentieth centuries gravitated to an interest in the *Leben-Jesu-Forschung* at the expense of devotion to the mythical Christ, in the Islamic world the so-called *sīrat* movement set in, resulting in a flood of new, more or less scholarly, biographies of the Prophet. (Interestingly, Muhammad ʿAbduh, the Egyptian reformer of the late nineteenth century, had a copy of David Friedrich Strauss's *Life of Jesus* in his library; it would be worthwhile to follow the influence of this book on Muslim biographical literature.)[42] The *sīrat* movement began in India in the first half of the present century. The bookshops of the subcontinent were soon filled with an immense variety of biographies, ranging from the important scholarly evaluation of the Prophet's life, *Sīrat an-nabī*, written in Urdu by Maulana Shibli Nuʿmani (completed by his disciple Sayyid Sulaiman Nadwi),[43] to innumerable popular treatises and tracts about "Our Beloved Prophet" or "The Dear Life of the Sweet Prophet." The new interest in the historical Muhammad was so intense that in 1911 a Hindu schoolmaster in Sind, Lalchand Jagtiani, published a Sindhi work about the life of the Prophet because he felt embarrassed that his Muslim pupils did not know anything about the historical roots of their religion and the biography of the Prophet, but rather clung to the purely legendary tales preserved in popular poems.[44] It was three more years before the first Sindhi biography written by a Muslim appeared in Hyderabad/Sind, and the modern reader cannot but admire the unbiased attitude of the Hindu biographer, who relied on both European and Persian sources.[45] Numerous other works in Urdu, Panjabi, Sindhi, and other languages followed in both poetry and prose, one of the latest vernacular products being a Sindhi *Mathnawī Muḥammadī* (1958), a long poem about the Prophet's life by Hafiz 'Abdullah Bismil of Thikur. A single look at the publishing lists of Shaikh Mohd. Ashraf in Lahore and, more recently, of Ferozsons in the same city suffices to give an impression of the various works on Muhammad, the number of which has lately again been growing. Yet even in the 1960s my questions about the age of some mausoleums in an East Bengali village were answered by the innocent statement of the village elder: "Very, very old, Mem, many thousand years old, like our Holy Prophet." Despite the *sīrat* movement, historical awareness was (and still is) largely lacking among the Indian Muslims.

Nevertheless, the attempt to teach historical facts has changed the Muslims' outlook on the Prophet's miracles to some extent. As early as 1906 Shaikh Qidwai (Kidwai), speaking about the miracles wrought by Muhammad, stated that his greatest miracle was not, as the masses tended to believe, the Splitting of the Moon, the Sighing Palm Trunk, or the Speaking Sheep but rather the social, spiritual, moral, and religious transformation of Arabia. This attitude was to form the focal point of Muslim apologetic literature in the following decades. Was not Muhammad's true miracle, as Sir Sayyid had put it, that he turned "marauding Bedouins" into civilized human beings? Or, seen from another viewpoint, that he, a human being, could reach such unsurpassable perfection?

The Prophet's character and his personal achievements became central to Muslim modernist theology.[46] His exemplary qualities are sometimes colorfully depicted in anecdotal style, sometimes simply enumerated. As formerly in poetry, the Prophet now appears in prose as the model of everything positive and beautiful; he is the paragon of kindness, generosity, politeness, friendliness, purity, and patience; his love of children, so charmingly described in many popular poems, is highlighted, for, as Sarwar writes,

> What was the keynote of his life? It was nothing but love of God, love of mankind . . . love of children; love of the gentler sex; love of friends, love of foe.[47]

Wilfred Cantwell Smith has called such descriptions manifestations of the "ideals of bourgeoisie,"[48] and it may be true that, as he claims, many modern Muslims find it easier to revere Muhammad as a person than to ponder dogmatic statements or mystical speculations, not to mention complicated theological reasoning, about his nature:

> Those who are too modern, too intelligent, or too busy, to adhere to the *sunna* or even the Qur'an; too lax to devote themselves to God, or to socialism; can derive great emotional and religious satisfaction from their "love of the Prophet."[49]

The literature about Muhammad grew steadily, and more books were written about his life in the fifty years between Sir Sayyid's death and the end of World War II than in all previous centuries. Mystical or devotional books, however, which had formed the larger part of religious literature in the Middle Ages and premodern times, were (and still are) no longer so prominent. The new interest in the energetic, politically active and socially responsible Prophet found expression even in poetry. Thus an Urdu poet of the beginning of this century, Safi Lakhnawi, describes the Prophet in new terms derived from Sir Sayyid's reformist theology:

> He, who has caused to bend the heads of the headstrong Arabs,
> He, who has transformed animals into human beings,
> He, who has brought the teaching of fraternity
> And treated [human beings] with equality,
> The reformer of capitalism,
> The protector of those who are marked by labor . . .[50]

Such language prefigures the idea of Muhammad as the "imam of socialism," which has been put forth more than once in our age.

The new interest in the person of the Prophet was of course not restricted to India, for other Muslim countries were faced with similar problems. Among the Arab countries it was particularly in Egypt that reformist theologians such as Muhammad ʿAbduh strove to reach a new understanding of the Koran and of the role of the Prophet. The results of their studies were in many respects the same as those achieved by their Indian colleagues, and generally it seems that the "task of dishing up the biography [of Muhammad] to suit the taste of the Christian West upset some Islamicists beyond measure"—or so W. H. Temple Gairdner remarked in an unusually biting article about an international gathering of Muslims at the Woking Mosque in London that sought to show "the ideal Muhammad during the celebrations of his birthday in 1917."[51]

It is remarkable that the image of Muhammad in the thought of Jamaluddin Afghani—who mercilessly condemned Sir Sayyid's "naturalism"—was in many respects similar to that of his Indian contemporary. Yet he too shifted emphasis, realizing (as Albert Hourani puts it) that "the center of attention is no longer Islam as a religion: it is rather Islam as a civilisation,"[52] and that the *umma* had been "great as long as it followed the teaching of the Prophet."[53] Muhammad ʿAbduh took up these ideas and—

again like Sir Sayyid and his followers—claimed that "Muhammad was sent not only to preach a way of individual salvation but to found a virtuous society."[54]

This very issue of Muhammad's role as the founder of a community also formed the center of the intense discussion about the caliphate (*khilāfat*) that arose after Ataturk had abolished that office in March 1924. In this discussion ʿAli ʿAbdur Raziq held that "Muhammad created a community, but not of the type we normally call a 'state'; it was a community which had no essential relationship with one government rather than another or one nation rather than another."[55] However, his theological adversary, Shaikh Bakhit, stressed the necessity of the implementation of the *sharīʿa* and hence an "Islamic Government," for "to execute the law was an essential part of his [Muhammad's] mission; but this implies that he had political power, and that from the start the Islamic community was a political community."[56] This problem, never completely resolved, still looms large wherever a truly "Islamic" state is envisaged.

However aside from in-depth discussion of Muhammad's role in the formation of his community, major biographical works about his life appeared in the Arabic-speaking world only from the mid-1930s onward. They tried to do justice to the person of the Prophet by applying to his biography the tools of modern historical research.

Modern Western critics have nevertheless sensed a lack of historical concreteness in the image of the perfect Prophet, who is the "beautiful model" of all virtues. Rotraut Wielandt, for example, claims that the image of the Prophet as it appears in Muhammad ʿAbduh's theology "radiates a strange, colorless light."[57] The Prophet embodies and does everything good, noble, lofty, and wise, and in the light of this absolute perfection all those contours that could give real life to his person seem to fade away. That is, despite ʿAbduh's attempt to offer a picture of the historical Muhammad, there yet remains (as Arthur Jeffery correctly states) a clear-cut separation between the Muhammad of history and the Muhammad of faith, between "the historical preacher and the mystical figure of the Prophet which lives in the faith."[58]

ʿAbduh's spiritual successor, Muhammad Rashid Rida, wrote a *Khulāṣat as-sīra al-muḥammadiyya*, a quintessence of the Prophet's biography in rhymed prose, in which, however, as little "modern" approach is visible as in at-Tahtawi's *Nihāyat al-iʿjāz fi sīra sākin al-Ḥijāz* (The Outmost Marvel in the Biography of the Dweller of the Hijaz; published 1868–74), one of the earliest books in the Egyptian *sīra*-movement (if one can speak of such a movement at all). But in the first half of the twentieth century poets too took up the praise of the Prophet in a more or less modernized style. The poet laureate of Egypt, Ahmad Shauqi, wrote *naʿtiyya* poetry "in the style of the *Burda*" (*fī nahj al-burda*). His contemporary Mahmud Sami al-Barudi composed a biography of the Prophet in verse, based on Ibn Hisham's *Sīra*; published in 1909, it is not of great poetical or historical value, and certainly does not make very exciting reading. Much later, Ahmad Muharram took up a similar task in his historical poem *Dīwān majd al-Islām au al-Iliyād al-islāmiyya*.[59] Ahmad Amin, the indefatigable Egyptian apologist for Islam, wrote numerous articles between 1937 and 1950 in which he portrayed Muhammad not only as a social reformer but also as a perfect Sufi, so that he appears as the exemplar of humanity par excellence:[60] this is simply a logical development of the Koranic *uswa ḥasana*.

In the Arabic-speaking countries one of the most important steps toward a new evaluation of the Prophet as a historical personality was Muhammad Husain Haikal's work *Ḥayāt Muḥammad*, which appeared in 1935 with a foreword by Mustafa al-Maraghi, then rector of al-Azhar. In his *Geschichte der arabischen Literatur* Carl Brockelmann writes that Haikal "succeeded in bringing the person of his hero close to his readers in the human sphere and yet preserved his religious position."[61] Like some Indian reformers before him, Haikal also tried to explain in a somewhat rationalistic way those miracles of the Prophet that seemed to contradict the modern scientific world view. The harmonization of reason and revelation is the pivot of his work; his most interesting venture in this respect is his interpretation of the heavenly journey in psychological terms, in an effort to give this miracle a meaning that could be easily accepted by a modern mind. But with all his modernist attitude, Haikal too shows the Prophet as the great leader of his people, as a man "who had a power which can uplift humanity to the heights of the spirit, where life consists of fraternity and love, and an ambition to know everything that exists in the world." Muhammad remains, as is natural, the only guide on the road toward spiritual, scientific, and religious progress. Haikal's book certainly responded to a deeply felt longing among Egyptian readers: in three months, the first ten thousand copies had been sold, and al-Azhar honored the author, whose work saw numerous editions and was soon translated into Chinese, Turkish, Persian, and Urdu.

Of course, Haikal's modern analysis of legends and miracles was not found acceptable in more orthodox circles. Shortly after his book was published a refutation appeared from the pen of an orthodox Wahhabi critic, in which the reality of all the Prophetic miracles was maintained. The author likewise points out, with some right, that Haikal had done full justice to Muhammad the leader of the army and Muhammad the politician but not to Muhammad the Prophet.[62] He touches here on a problem common to a large number of modern biographies of the Prophet: that their authors often overlook the genuinely religious quality of the Prophet, which does not fit with the tightly rationalistic image until recently in favor, in which interest in "true" detail seems to supersede that in the special charisma of the biographical subject himself. Improved historical accuracy is certainly a laudable goal; but the secret of the great founders of religions lies beyond the analytical approach of "pure" scholarship.

A few years after Haikal's study, another very important work appeared in Egypt, ʿAbbas Mahmud al-ʿAqqad's *ʿAbqariyyat Muḥammad* (The Genius of Muhammad; published in 1942).[63] In this book, ʿAqqad explains the ingenious achievements of the Prophet, whose *ʿiṣma* is defined as "being free of moral defects."

> He entered a world that had lost its faith, and hence had lost the secret of internal peace and external order, a world that was waiting for the liberating voice of Islam. Muhammad was the exemplar of virtues, virtues both of the preacher and of the soldier; he had the eloquence, convincing power, and intensity of the preacher, and the courage, gallantry, and success of the warrior. Superb in his talents and his character he ruled his time as he dominated later times. No event that has since taken place has been the same as it would have been without Muhammad. History before him and after him is completely different.[64]

Muhammad appears here as the axis of history—an idea that is, as it were, a secularized expression of the same feeling that the mystics had revealed in their superb hymns through poetical images.

It is worth mentioning in this context that the great literary critic of modern Arabic, Taha Husain, produced in 1933 a kind of historical novel, *ʿAlā hāmish as-sīra* (At the Margin of the *Sīra*), in which he elaborated most fancifully on traditional topics of the early life of the Prophet; this he continued, somewhat later, with a second volume, *Rāʿī al-ghanam* (The Shepherd), which tells of Muhammad's life up to the time of his marriage with Khadija; a third volume appeared in 1943. Brockelmann—probably correctly—suspects that the author, trained in France, used Ernest Renan's romanticizing *Vie de Jésus* as his model.[65]

Modernist biographies and mystically heightened pictures of the Prophet (as in the work of S. H. Nasr) are equally common today. But there are also other images of him, for the light in which he is seen varies with the vantage point of each author.[66] Labib ar-Riyashi, for instance, published in 1934 a book entitled *As-sūbarmān al-ʿālamī al-awwal* (The First Universal Superman); by contrast, the founder of the Baath party, Michel Aflaq, sees in the Prophet "the summary of the Arab spirit."[67] This latter characterization is interesting, for it reminds us of the emphasis on the Arabic element that was so common among the earlier Muslims in India. But Aflaq certainly intended a purely political statement. Quite a few scholars of our age have striven hard to prove the truly socialist character of the teachings of Islam, and the Egyptian prime minister Gamal ʿAbd an-Nasir (Nasser) called the Prophet in 1964 "the imam of socialism." Ten years earlier, Fathi Ridwan, minister in Nasser's first cabinet, had praised Muhammad as "the greatest revolutionary," *ath-thāʾir al-aʿẓam*, and at about the same time Mahmud Shalabi had written for Nasser his book *Ishtirākiyya Muḥammad* (Muhammad's Socialism). Also during Nasser's tenure the noted novelist ʿAbdur Rahman ash-Sharqawi published his outright leftist work *Muḥammad rasūl al-ḥurriyya* (Muhammad, the Messenger of Freedom), in which he shows the Prophet as "a kind of Marx before Marx."[68] Such ideas can easily be derived from some earlier works concerning the Prophet.

In India, F. K. Durrani, who wrote for some time under Iqbal's influence, depicted the Prophet in 1931 as the founder of the new era, the great leader who had proclaimed freedom from imperialism and the destruction of slavery. Part of this new evaluation of the Prophet in modern terms is "his monistic morality," which does not permit any oppression of the body as does Christianity, with its division between the spiritual and the worldly. Another element with a definite modern appeal is his constant struggle against poverty.[69] Even M. Hamidullah, whose biography of the Prophet is probably the best introduction to the life of the Prophet as seen by a devout modern Muslim scholar, has devoted an article to the problem of Lenin's perception of the Prophet, in which he quotes some positive remarks by the Russian leader.[70]

One should not forget the considerable amount of new material for the study of the Prophet's life, or eulogies of him, that were published in Turkey after 1950, when the trend toward Islam could again be professed openly and publicly, and the Ministry of Religious Affairs in Ankara began to print numerous educational books and treatises. One also encountered during that time publications by pious individuals, and I still remember the stir when one author published, in 1958, a book entitled *Hazrat-i Muhammad Türk'mi idi?*—Was the Noble Muhammad a Turk?[71] One should not ridicule this attempt but understand that the author desired to show that his beloved Prophet was also a member of his beloved Turkish people, and thus combined every possible good and lofty quality in the world.

It was in light of such modernist interpretations that an Indian scholar of Persian could praise *naʿtiyya* poetry as a "character building force" and consider poetry in honor of the Prophet as "a branch of literature which plays an important part in building up the type of character [aimed] at breaking the racial, geographical and class barriers."[72]

There have even been some attempts to dramatize Muhammad's life. In 1936 the noted Egyptian author Taufiq al-Hakim composed a drama designed to counteract Voltaire's pernicious description of the Prophet in his drama *Mahomet, ou le fanatisme*; in this modern drama, the author mainly relies on Ibn Ishaq's *Sīra* for the dialogues, which gives the drama great power.[73] Yet, although published in print, Taufiq al-Hakim's play was never staged.[74] Aversion to dramatic portrayal of the Prophet is still very strong (and may even be increasing among Muslims in some areas), as was evident from the public's reaction to a motion picture about him a few years back, even though the film did not show the Prophet's face and had been cleared by the authorities.

Every modern writer sees in the beloved Prophet the ideal realization of those qualities that he himself considers highest and most needed in the world—and the multicolored image of the Prophet which thus emerges draws on the most divergent strands of the centuries-old tradition and translates the praise of the "best of mankind" into modern idiom. An excellent survey of the different trends in interpreting his role in the modern Muslim world can be seen in the protocol of the International Seerat Conference, held in Karachi in 1976. Its subjects range from the "mystical light of Muhammad" to "the relevance of his thought for business management." Whatever happens in terms of reform and development in the Islamic world will inevitably be related to the "beautiful model" of the venerated and beloved Prophet.

TWELVE

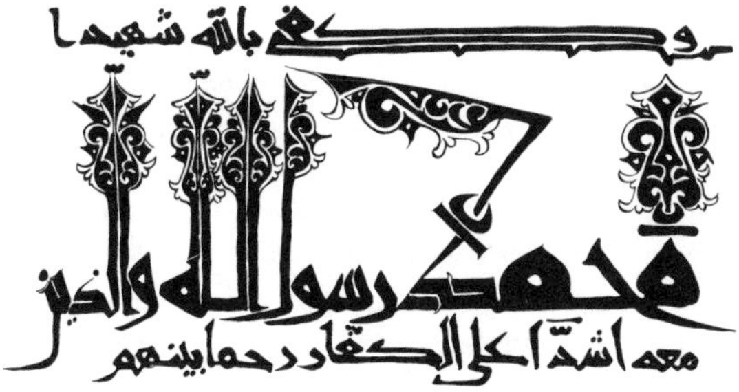

THE PROPHET MUHAMMAD IN MUHAMMAD IQBAL'S WORK

All the different aspects of the veneration of the Prophet seem to converge in the work of Muhammad Iqbal, the Indo-Muslim philosopher-poet who for the first time expressed the idea of an independent Muslim state in the northwest of the Indian subcontinent and who is therefore acclaimed as the "spiritual father" of Pakistan. That nation came into existence nine years after his death (21 April 1938), on 14 August 1947.

Iqbal's work is a fascinating web of diverse strands that range from Islamic fundamentalism to the most recent scientific theories of the West, from mystical flights into the Divine presence to rational analyses of spiritual phenomena. This multifariousness is evident in his major English prose work, *The Reconstruction of Religious Thought in Islam* (which almost certainly owes its title to Ghazzali's *Iḥyāʾ ʿulūm ad-dīn*, The Revivification of the Sciences of Religion) and in some English articles; but it is also, and indeed predominantly, expressed in Urdu and Persian verse. Old images, with which Muslim readers have been familiar for centuries, are taken up in this poetry and given new content. The Prophet of Islam appears in Iqbal's work as in that of thousands of earlier poets and thinkers as the central figure of Muslim spiritual life, a figure who reveals himself in constantly changing facets and whose description by Iqbal culminates in the daring remark in the *Jāvīdnāma* (which tells of the poet's own *miʿrāj*):

> You can deny God, but you cannot deny the Prophet![1]

After completing his studies in philosophy and law at Cambridge, Iqbal spent about six months in Germany in 1907; there he turned into an enthusiastic admirer of Goethe, whose work constitutes for him the highest manifestation of creative poetry. It is therefore understandable that he felt a particular attraction to the figure of Faust, the ever-striving man in search of self-realization, and to the *West-Östlicher Divan*. In 1923 he composed the *Payām-i Mashriq* (The Message of the East) as a Persian reply to the *West-Östlicher Divan*, and he points out in his foreword that Goethe had shown interest in things Islamic from his early days. Goethe's poem "Mahomets Gesang," written when the young author was planning a drama about the Prophet of Islam in 1772, inspired Iqbal to such a degree that he offered his readers a Persian version in the *Payām-i Mashriq*, which he himself characterizes in a footnote:

> It is an extremely free translation of Goethe's famous "Mahomets Gesang." In this poem, which was written long, long before the *West-Östlicher Divan*, the German poet has shown the Islamic idea of life extremely beautifully. Originally it was part of an Islamic drama which he intended [to write] but could not complete. The intention of this translation is nothing but to show Goethe's viewpoint.[2]

Iqbal begins his translation with the lines

> Look at the stream of water, how it runs, intoxicated,
> Like a galaxy in the middle of the meadows!

and he finishes the rather long poem with a matching couplet:

> O wonderful! The ocean without shore—how it runs, intoxicated,
> Unique in itself, alien to everything else, it runs!

This image of the river as a metaphor for prophetic activity is indeed quite close to Islamic mystical thought. The medieval Shiite theologian al-Kulini even quotes a saying attributed to ʿAli ibn Abi Talib, the first imam of the Shia: "Who is the great river? The messenger of God and the knowledge that has been granted to him."[3] And when Iqbal, nine years after the *Payām-i Mashriq*, describes his own heavenly journey in the *Jāvīdnāma* he is given the heavenly name Zindarud, "Living Stream." This name clearly points to his relation to the Prophet, whom he ardently strove to follow in all walks of life, and whose dynamic message he wanted to renew in the world.

Iqbal's praise of the Prophet is often traditional. In an early Urdu poem, which he excluded from publication and which is therefore presented only in a collection published long after his death, he even uses an allusion to the traditional *ḥadīth qudsī* "I am Ahmad without *m*, *Aḥad*, One," claiming that the "veil of the *m* is lifted for the lover's sight," that is, that the lover sees God through the Prophet.[4] Later he carefully avoided this *ḥadīth* because it seems to lead to pantheistic consequences, which he, in his mature years, thoroughly disliked.

With hundreds of poets throughout the history of Islam Iqbal also sings:

> The dust of Madina and Najaf is collyrium for my eyes![5]

Therefore, as he states, the glittering and seductive charms of European knowledge cannot confuse him or make his eyes deviate from the right direction.

It is remarkable how clearly Iqbal's love for and trust in the Prophet is manifest in his private correspondence with friends, in which he generally touched upon numerous matters of personal and scholarly interest. His friends tell that he often shed tears when the Prophet was mentioned, "[at] the name of whom—a shivering of excitement fills every strand of my soul when I think of that elevated name!—at the name of him who has brought mankind the final message of freedom and equality," as he wrote in an article in 1909.[6] The *sīrat* movement, which strove to impart a deeper knowledge of the Prophet's biography and of the historical person of the Prophet in general, had all his sympathies. During 1929 he received its then leader in his home in Lahore, and in the same year he mentioned in one of his letters with great satisfaction that the Prophet's birthday had been recently celebrated in southern India in a festive style, saying that "to connect the Islamic nations of India, the most holy person of our venerated Prophet can constitute the greatest and most effective power."[7]

Even though he wrote in truly classical style only the aforementioned *naʿt* that was excluded from publication, Iqbal's poetry contains numerous verses in honor of the Prophet. One of the most obvious themes of his verse is absolute trust in the Prophet, expressions of which permeate his work from beginning to end.

> Your love is greater for rebels—
> In forgiving sins it is like a mother's love.[8]

Thus he wrote around 1936 to express a feeling that, as we have seen, was central in Islamic piety. It is, however, remarkable that Iqbal speaks rather rarely of Muhammad's role as the *shafīʿ*, the intercessor at Doomsday, for it was this role of the Prophet that both classical urban and, more especially, folk poets had emphasized in their prayer poems. To be sure, in the *Asrār-i khudī* (The Secrets of the Self), which he published in 1915 in Persian, and which is the first manifestation of his new dynamic philosophy of the Self, he does say:

> We trust in him at the Day of Judgment,
> And in this world too he is our protection.[9]

But the remark is rarely, if ever, repeated, probably because Iqbal's concept of death, resurrection, and Last Judgment during his later years was fundamentally different from the traditional eschatology of theologians and popular preachers. For him, the Prophet was much more a support in this life: at the end of his second Persian *mathnawī*, *Rumūz-i bēkhudī* (The Mysteries of Selflessness), composed in 1917 to convey his ideas about the role of the perfected individual in an ideal Islamic state, he asks the Prophet, typically, to grant him the strength for activity.[10]

Still, his faith in the supernatural powers of the Prophet was apparently as strong as that of millions of faithful before him. While he was staying in Bhopal in 1936, afflicted with serious illness, he saw in a dream the reformer Sir Sayyid Ahmad Khan, the grandfather of his host, Sir Ross Masood.[11] Sir Sayyid advised him to turn to the Prophet and ask him to heal him. Iqbal immediately composed a rather long poem; in it he first describes the sad political situation of the Muslims and then implores the Prophet's help for his illness.[12] Evidently he was influenced by Busiri's *Burda* and the belief in its healing power, as he mentions this poem also in other connections.[13]

One year earlier he had written to a *sayyid*: "Interior medicine for me is only that I recite blessings (*durūd*) for your ancestor [the Prophet]."[14] But like the poets of earlier centuries he too felt at times that he was not even worthy to pronounce Muhammad's sacred name:

> I recited the blessing for the Prophet—
> From shame my body became like water.
> Love said: "O you who are submitted to others—
> As long as you have not received color and scent from Muhammad,
> Do not sully his name with your blessings!"[15]

Muhammad was for Iqbal, as he had been for the theologians and mystics before him, the visible aspect of God's activity. God cannot be seen with human eyes, as the Koran states (Sura 7:139), but the Prophet is visible and palpable:

> O Messenger of God, with God I speak through veils, with you openly—
> He is my hidden one, you are my evident one![16]

Therefore Iqbal turns to Muhammad both to implore him for help and to praise him, as is particularly evident in his last verses, which were posthumously published as *Armaghān-i Ḥijāz* (The Gift of the Hijaz).[17]

The Muslim knows that he can experience God's presence best when he recites the Koran, for then God's own words become audible to him. Likewise generations of pious Muslims have felt that the study of themes from the Prophet's life, of *ḥadīth* or of juridical topics based on his words, grants them a certain proximity to the Prophet. Iqbal felt the same way when he worked on subjects connected with Islamic history and Islamic jurisprudence, as he did mainly toward the end of his life:

> The differentiation of juridical problems and the argumentation of Islamic jurisconsults, in which the love of the Seal of Prophethood is hidden—the study of all these things gives me endless spiritual joy![18]

Thus he wrote in 1936. And how much greater was his joy when he saw something that belonged to the Prophet! The experience of visiting Qandahar, where a cloak of the Prophet, *khirqa-i sharīf*, is preserved, during his sojourn in Afghanistan in the fall of 1932 led him to compose a fine Persian hymn—just as in former times the sight of the Prophet's sandals or even of their picture had inspired numerous poets to glowing verse. In his poem about the *khirqa-i sharīf* Iqbal compares his heart to Gabriel, who has seen the Prophet in the flesh; he also tells how he began to dance, to sing, and to recite poetry in the presence of the sacred relic:

> That coat of the "*barzakh* which the two cannot
> transgress" (Sura 55:20)
> I saw it in the light of the *ḥadīth* "I have two coats."
> To see him, is our heavenly night journey,
> His religion and his ritual are the commentary of the universe,
> On his forehead the destiny of all things is written.[19]

The interpretation of Muhammad as the *barzakh*, the borderline between the two worlds, had been applied to the Prophet much earlier: in Jami's verse, he stands between the ocean of pre-eternity and that of contingency; that is, he forms the meeting point between the Divine and the human spheres.[20] The "two coats" are Poverty and the Holy War; the tradition that Muhammad saw the "coat of poverty" during his *miʿrāj* lies in the background of the second and third lines of Iqbal's encomium.

It is natural that Iqbal ardently aspired to visit the Prophet's Rauda in Medina, together with fulfilling the duty of pilgrimage to Mecca, and he mentions this hope repeatedly in his letters and poems.[21] As early as 1908 he wrote praises of Yathrib (Medina), where "the prince of *laulāka*" rests and which therefore constitutes the veritable center of the life of the human race. During the Balkan War he dreamed of dying in Medina, the hope of many pious souls who long to be buried close to the beloved Prophet.[22] It was for this reason that his posthumous collection of poetry was called *Armaghān-i Ḥijāz* (The Gift of the Hijaz), for the older the poet grew, the stronger waxed his longing to visit the last resting place of the Prophet. He felt sure that such a journey would result in immense spiritual benefits.[23] Had he not spoken in one of his early poems of the *shifā'khāna-i Ḥijāz*, "the healing place of Hijaz," where the weary soul would find new hope?[24]

Once, on his return from a Round Table Conference in London, Iqbal stopped in Jerusalem to attend a Muslim conference. At this point he contemplated a journey to Medina but then considered it bad manners to combine a pilgrimage with a journey undertaken for political reasons.[25] It was in those days that he composed the great Urdu hymn to the Prophet, which closes with the line:

> You are the Well-preserved Tablet, and you are the Pen![26]

In the hymn, he takes over the style of earlier mystical poets and even seeks to surpass their praise by applying the most high-flown comparisons to the Prophet.

Like many writers, especially in the mystical and poetical tradition, Iqbal preferred to call the Prophet by the name Mustafa, "The Chosen One." Muhammad Mustafa was for him the source of everything good and useful in human life, and like the reformist poets of the nineteenth century he too saw one cause of the present miserable situation of the Muslims in the sad fact that they had been alienated from "the Prophet's beauty." They should know that his path is the only path that should and must be chosen![27] This thought permeates the quatrains in Iqbal's last poetical work; but he had already expressed it decades earlier in one of his great Urdu poems, *Jawāb-i Shikwā* (The Answer to the Complaint). In this poem of 1912 God addresses the Muslims, to whose *Shikwā* (Complaint) he gives a long, powerful answer that ends with the command:

> Be faithful to Muhammad, then We too belong to you,
> Not only this world but Tablet and Pen belong to you![28]

A few years after writing these lines, Iqbal continued this thought in his *Asrār-i khudī*. There he teaches no longer, as the majority of Sufi poets before him had done, the submersion of the human self in the ocean of the Divine Essence, where it would disappear like a raindrop, but rather the strengthening of the human personality (or individuality), which grows in increasing proximity to God, finally to reach a person-to-person encounter with Him, the Greatest Self. The human self, however, can be strengthened only by love, and this love is inseparably connected with Muhammad. Therefore, Iqbal turns to the Prophet:

> A beloved is hidden in your heart . . .
> In the Muslim's heart, there is Muhammad's home,
> All our glory is from Muhammad's name.[29]

This same blessing power of the name of Muhammad, which as we have seen is a traditional topic of Islamic literature, had been mentioned in the end of the *Jawāb-i Shikwā*, when Iqbal hears God's command:

Make high everything low with the strength of love,
Illuminate the world by Muhammad's name![30]

In the enthusiastic description of the Prophet in the third chapter of the *Asrār-i khudī*, Iqbal goes even farther:

Eternity is less than a moment of his time,
Eternity receives increase from his essence.
He slept on a mat of rushes,
But the crown of Khosroes was under his people's feet.[31]

In these lines Iqbal, following many *naʿt* poets and in particular, it seems, Naziri, juxtaposes poverty and power, a contrast that serves him again and again in characterizing the Prophet's comprehensive character. We find it in verse written twenty years later:

Poverty and kingdom are Mustafa's inspirations;
They are the manifestations of Mustafa's essence.[32]

This is an allusion to one of the favorite *ḥadīth* in the Sufi tradition: "Poverty is my pride."[33] This poverty is not, however, destitution, or even less the neediness of the beggar; it is rather the state of someone who completely rests in God, the Eternally Rich (*al-ghanī*), and therefore does not need secondary causes any more. In this twofold quality as "poor" and "powerful" the Prophet becomes the locus of manifestation of God's beauty, *jamāl*, and His majesty, *jalāl*, those two complementary Divine attributes whose interplay alone can maintain the flow of created life.[34] And the combination of these two aspects makes Muhammad the ideal prophet who (as is implied in this description) surpasses both the mildness of Jesus and the lawbound sternness of Moses, thus providing the exemplar of most perfect humanity.

In the hour of battle, iron melted before the radiance of his sword;
In the hour of prayer tears dropped from his eyes like raindrops.[35]

This comprehensive greatness of the Prophet inspired Iqbal's poetry throughout his life. In his last years he returned to old mystical imagery to express this mystery of the Prophet's personality:

He is the meaning of Gabriel and the Koran;
He is the watchman of the wisdom of God;
His wisdom is higher than reason . . .[36]

Iqbal's more practical views on prophetology—which, however, still preserve a strongly mystical flavor—are laid before the reader most clearly in the *Rumūz-i bēkhudī*, the poem in which he discusses his social and political ideals. Here, Muhammad is compared, in the classical metaphor of light, to the lamp in the darkness of creation, a lamp that already existed when Adam was still "between water and clay."[37]

Iqbal's purely mystical interpretation of the essence of the Prophet has been expressed most impressively in the *Jāvīdnāma*. Here, in an ingenious turn, the poet puts a hymn in honor of the Prophet in the mouth of the martyr-mystic al-Hallaj, who, more than a thousand years before him, had composed the first grand description of the primordial Prophet, the source of light and of wisdom. In the poem Iqbal takes up once more the classical idea that *ʿabduhu*, "His servant," is the highest possible rank man can strive to reach, for during his heavenly journey the Prophet was given this same epithet (Sura 17:1). Moreover, Sura 53:10, which as we saw earlier is often interpreted as pertaining to the *miʿrāj*, states that "God revealed to His servant what He revealed." In the Sphere of Jupiter in the *Jāvīdnāma* Hallaj is asked about the mysteries of the Prophet and answers in a long poem:

> "His servant" is higher than your understanding,
> Since he is both man and essence.
> His essence is neither Arabic nor Persian,
> He is a man, and yet previous to Adam.
> "His servant" is the painter of destinations,
> In him lies the repair of ruins.
> "His servant" is both soul-giving and soul-taking;
> "His servant" is both glass and hard stone.
> "Servant" is something, and "His servant" is something else—
> We all are waiting; he is the awaited one.
> "His servant" is without beginning, without end,
> "His servant"—where for him is morning and evening?
> Nobody is acquainted with the secrets of "His servant"—
> "His servant" is nothing but the secret of "but God."[38]

The last line here once more takes up the idea that the Prophet, as God's most perfect servant, is the manifestation of God's activity, and the only way through which one can find the secret of the profession of faith: "There is no deity save God."

In Iqbal's thought this role of Muhammad as "His servant" is of special importance, for his ideal man, the *mard-i mōmin*, is quite different from Nietzsche's Superman, with whom he has sometimes been confounded. The latter appears "when God is dead," but the *mard-i mōmin*, emulating the Prophet's example, is the most perfect servant of God and can reach the greatest possible approximation to God by assuming that role. This is basically the concept of the "sober" mystical orders of *qurb al-farāʾiḍ*, "proximity to God brought about by sincerely following the Prophet's example" and doing one's duty in this world.

For Iqbal, the Prophet is much more than a luminous mystical figure who mediates the true faith to "this handful of dust," man; he is even more than the "servant of God" who stands beyond time and space and yet never becomes deified. He is also the leader of his community, the "beautiful model" not only for personal but also for political and social conduct, he "who opens the door of this world with the key of religion."[39]

One should read such verses—they occur frequently, for instance, in the *Asrār-i khudī* and even more in the *Rumūz-i bēkhudī*—in light of the correspondence that Iqbal conducted much later, in 1933, with Sayyid Sulaiman Nadwi. He had asked his scholarly friend about the problem of *ijtihād-i nabawī*, that is, the capacity and power of the Prophet to decide independently juridical and other problems that are not discussed in the Koran. Sayyid Sulaiman Nadwi replied that "the prophetic intelligence is higher than normal human intelligence" and that the prophet is guided in all his decisions on the absolutely right path.[40] It is in fact this very capacity that made him the divinely guided leader of the community.

This political and social role of the Prophet becomes at times more central to Iqbal than his mystical aspects; and here he stands in the succession of the modernists. He speaks up most daringly in his poem *Nubuwwat* (Prophethood), written late in his life, when he asserts that though he cannot discuss the essence of *nubuwwat* as do theologians and mystics,

> That kind of prophethood is hashish for the Muslim
> In which there is not the message of power and energy![41]

The poet-philosopher never tired of comparing the prophet who works in this world to the mystic who, as he says in the *Jāvīdnāma*, is seduced by Satan to devote himself entirely to a retired life of asceticism and to claim that only by such an otherworldly occupation can he reach his goal.[42] At the beginning of the fifth lecture in his *Reconstruction of Religious Thought in Islam* Iqbal has stated this problem with unusual clarity while interpreting the experience of the *mi'rāj*:

> "Muhammad of Arabia ascended the highest heaven and returned. I swear by God that if I had reached that point, I should have never returned." These are the words of a great Muslim saint, 'Abdul Quddus of Gangoh. In the whole range of Sufi literature it will probably be difficult to find words which, in a single sentence, disclose such an acute perception of the psychological difference between the prophetic and the mystic types of consciousness. The mystic does not

> wish to return from the repose of "unitarian experience," and even when he does return, as he must, his return does not mean much for mankind at large. The prophet's return is creative. He returns to insert himself into the sweep of time with a view to control the forces of history, and thereby to create a fresh world of ideals. For the mystic the repose of "unitary experience" is something final; for the prophet it is the awakening, within him, of world-shaking psychological forces, calculated to completely transform the human world. The desire to see his religious experience transformed into a living world-force is supreme in the prophet. Thus his return amounts to a kind of pragmatic test of the value of his religious experience.[43]

Certainly, such a unitive experience during the *miʿrāj* can be attained only by those with "high ambition" (*himmat*). Yet for them, it is only a moment away:

> For high ambition, it is just one step to the highest Throne![44]

For Iqbal, as for the other Indo-Muslim reformist theologians, the way in which the Prophet of Islam was depicted in European books was utterly repellent. Among the biographies available to him he selected for a special attack that of Aloys Sprenger, the Austrian orientalist who had worked for years in India and was, on the whole, more sympathetic to Islam and especially to the Islamic revival in India than most other Europeans. But Sprenger had claimed that the Prophet had been a psychopath, and this remark spurred Iqbal to a biting reply in one of his essays in *The Reconstruction of Religious Thought in Islam*:

> Well, if a psychopath has the power to give a fresh direction to the course of human history, it is a point of the highest psychological interest to search his original experience which has turned slaves into leaders of men and has inspired the conduct and shaped the career of whole races of mankind. Judging from the various types of activity that emanated from the movement initiated by the Prophet of Islam, his spiritual tension and the kind of behaviour which issued from it, cannot be regarded as a response to a mere fantasy inside the brain. It is impossible to understand it except as a response to an objective situation generative of new enthusiasms, new organisations, new starting-points. If we look at the matter from the standpoint of anthropology it appears that a psychopath is an important factor in the economy of humanity's social organization.[45]

Iqbal rightly saw that the true peculiarity of the prophetic message consisted in its power to free a people from traditional world views, to lead them from *Volksreligion* to *Weltreligion*, and "to oppose, with energetic consistency, those tenets in the Arabian philosophy of life" (as Goldziher wrote) that were entrenched in the old structures of family and clan.[46] By destroying them the Prophet could form a spiritual community that was no longer based upon blood, race, or nation. The philosopher-poet expressed this idea in a fascinating chapter of the *Jāvīdnāma* in which he makes the reader listen to the complaint of Abu Jahl, one of the bitterest adversaries of the Prophet among the Meccan aristocracy.[47] This representative of pre-Islamic ideals of conduct curses the revolutionary activities of Muhammad, which run counter to all that was accepted by Bedouin and Meccan society:

> We are utterly heartsick because of Muhammad!
> His teaching has put out the lights of the Kaʿba!
> His religion abolishes the distinctions of race and blood—
> Though himself from Quraish, he disowns the superiority of the Arabs.
> In his religion the high and low are one,
> He ate out of the same dish with his slave!

And after enumerating a number of other "crimes" of the Prophet, the old Meccan chieftain concludes his long poetical sermon with a curse upon Muhammad. Iqbal is certainly right in highlighting the supernational aspects of the Prophet; but he himself, like many other poets of Muslim India, also emphasizes the "Arabic" character of the Prophet and the Arabic roots of Islam.

On the whole, the negative portrayal of Abu Jahl fits well with Iqbal's general attitude. Like most modernists, he stresses the antiracist, "democratic" teachings of Islam, particularly when contrasting them with the Hindu caste system. As early as 1910 he had interpreted the meaning of Muhammad's Hegira from Mecca to Medina in a new, political sense. Mystics such as Maulana Rumi had long used the same event as a paradigm for man's pilgrimage from this world to the spiritual realms. But Iqbal notes in his diary the interesting remark:

> Islam appeared as a protest against idolatry. And what is patriotism but a subtle form of idolatry; a deification of a material object? . . . What was to be demolished by Islam could not be made the very principle of its structure as a political community. The fact that the Prophet prospered and died in a place not his birth place is perhaps a mystic hint to the same effect.[48]

The choice of the Hegira as the beginning of the Muslim calendar was for Iqbal deeply meaningful: had the Meccans immediately accepted Muhammad's message the course of history would have been different; by severing the bonds of family and clan the Prophet wanted to give an example to future generations. That is why Iqbal wrote (at about the same time that he jotted down similar thoughts in English prose as *Stray Reflections*) an Urdu poem, *Waṭaniyyat* (Patriotism), in which he states:

> To leave one's native country is the *sunna* of the beloved of God![49]

The growing nationalist tensions that he had witnessed as a student in England and Germany from 1905 to 1908, and that became such a dangerous factor in Near Eastern politics after the First World War, had incited Iqbal rather early on to develop an attitude that is incompatible with narrow political nationalism:

> Native country (*waṭan*) is something different in the right teachings of the Prophet,
> And native country is something different in the words of the politicians.[50]

He therefore never ceased repeating that Islam is opposed to racism; indeed, "the greatest miracle which the Prophet performed was the formation of a (spiritually united) nation."[51] One may see in this remark an echo of Sir Sayyid's statement that the greatest miracle of Islam was the formation of a true community of believers out of gangs of "marauding Bedouins." The entire argument of the *Rumūz-i bēkhudī* is based upon the nation-building power of the Prophet, and two decades after publishing that didactic poem Iqbal still was moved to repeat his point:

> The Prophet was able to perform the miracle of restoration by his word *Qum*, "Rise!"
> By awakening the call "God is greater [than anything else]" in the heart of a nation.[52]

This conviction made him believe that humanity could begin a completely new life if they would only turn back to the simple, plain, and practical message of the Prophet. To adhere to the same revelations brought by a God-sent messenger will create the greatest possible feeling of solidarity in a group of individuals, a feeling that will then spur the emerging group to unexpected heights of activity. Iqbal's argument here reminds one somewhat of the teachings of the medieval North African philosopher of history, Ibn Khaldun, for whom the concept of *ʿaṣabiyya*, "esprit de corps, solidarity," formed the pivot of his philosophy; he too believed that this esprit de corps is strongest in a group motivated by religious fervor.[53]

According to Iqbal, Muhammad has not only provided an example for the way such a supernational community of the faithful can and should be built; he is at the same time the symbol of the unshakable unity of that community. As early as in the *Asrār-i khudī* the poet states, in his great encomium on the Prophet:

> We are like a rose with many petals but with one perfume:
> He is the soul of the society, and he is one.[54]

The Prophet "is the heart in this handful of dust" of which mankind consists.[55] That is, he is the life-giving power that transforms humanity into a living organism. Therefore all manifestations of singular, politically based nationalist movements are for Iqbal nothing but new idols, nationalism being a modern brand of Baal-worship. The ideal Muslim nation, however, will not succumb to the temptation of Baal and the idols, as described in the *Jāvīdnāma* (in the Sphere of Venus), but will be kept alive by its heart, the Prophet.

From this vantage point Iqbal directed his hard criticism against various nationalist movements in the Middle East, among them Iran under Reza Shah Pahlavi and Turkey under Mustafa Kemal Ataturk (much though he had praised Ataturk after his victory over the Greeks in 1922).[56] In the 1920s and early 1930s, Afghanistan seemed to him the only country in which the teachings of the Prophet were preserved in purity; that is why this country is specially mentioned in "Iblis's Advice to his Political Children" in *Żarb-i Kalīm*, a poem in which Iqbal addresses the Spirit of Muhammad to inquire where his Muslims have gone, and where the camel driver, who leads the caravan with his song, has gone.[57]

The *Jāvīdnāma* contains in the Sphere of Mercury a long discussion about the concept of nationhood as conceived by the Prophet; and at the very end of his life Iqbal wrote, in a more prosaic style:

> It is a peculiar greatness of the Holy Prophet that the self-invented distinctions and superiority complexes of the nations of the world are destroyed and there comes into being a community which can be styled *ummatan muslimatan laka* ["as a Muslim community for thee," Sura 2:122], and to whose thought the Divine dictate *shuhadā' ʿalā'n-nās* ["witnesses for the people," Sura 22:78] justly applies.[58]

The ideal community, *millat*, of which Iqbal dreamed should become the realization of all-embracing *tauḥīd*, the confession of Divine Unity that the Prophet had preached in his lifetime, and this community would follow the Prophet, who had shaped and realized by his example the ideals of universal freedom, equality, and fraternity. Therefore Iqbal said in the *Rumūz-i bēkhudī*:

From Prophethood is our foundation in the world
From Prophethood has our religion its ritual,
From Prophethood are hundreds of thousands of us one,
Part from part cannot be separated.
From Prophethood we all have the same melody,
The same breath, the same aim.[59]

The most important factor that can contribute to the formation of these ideals is glowing love for the Prophet, which would enable both the individual and the community to live in harmony, according to the exigencies of Divine love. Indeed, Iqbal maintains that dynamic love, the center of his poetical theology, is "all Mustafa"; analytical intellect can be equated with the archenemy of the Prophet, Abu Lahab.[60] (The tendency of medieval Sufis to contrast Muhammad, the embodiment of love, to the philosophers, immediately comes to mind.)

Iqbal also develops another important idea: as Muhammad was the leader and the completion of a long line of God-sent messengers, so too should the nation created by him be the leader of nations and the final, hence most perfect, exemplar of a community based exclusively upon God.

He is the Seal of the Prophets, we that of the nations![61]

And as the Prophet was sent *raḥmatan lil-ʿālamīn*, "as Mercy for the worlds," the Muslims who belong to him should also be a manifestation of mercy for the people of the world. Iqbal went even farther in his analogy between the Prophet and the community. That God addressed the Prophet with the word *Laulāka* implies that every believer who strives to emulate the Prophet's example participates in this word as well.[62] The world has been created for his sake and he has to act in it; and if this holds true of the Muslim individual it also holds true for the ideal community of the faithful, which, in succession to the Prophet, is expected to rule the world supreme. This leading role necessarily includes power: here too the individual Muslim as well as the community should realize in themselves the Prophet's power, as much as they seek his poverty, which rests in God's absolute richness. But Iqbal was certainly aware of the dangers that would oppose the realization of this Prophetic ideal, and he knew well that his dream of a return to the Golden Age of the first four caliphs could not really materialize; for he saw clearly that the Islamic peoples of his day were all too eager to forget the Prophet's "poverty" and confuse "power" with mundane advantages.

Iqbal's interpretation of the Prophet in the mystical, religious, and political realms is generally similar to that of earlier mystical poets on the one hand, of modernist reformers on the other. But his ingenious way of combining these two major aspects of the tradition almost without a seam makes his work fascinating. Besides, the poet-philosopher also had specific contributions to offer to the field of prophetology, primarily in his interpretation of the doctrine of the finality of Muhammad's prophetship. Because the Koran states (Sura 5:5) that "Today We have perfected for you your religion," it had always been accepted that the revelation was indeed finished with Muhammad, the Seal of the Prophets. Iqbal himself expressed this conviction poetically in the *Rumūz-i bēkhudī*:

> Now God has completed for us the Divine law,
> And has completed prophethood for our Prophet.
> Now the office of cupbearer is given to us:
> He gave us the last goblet He had.[63]

But what does the finality of prophethood mean for Iqbal? Would not a new prophet be required to translate the message of the Koran into the language of our time? Iqbal's reply to this rhetorical question is very thought-provoking:

> The Prophet of Islam seems to stand between the ancient and the modern world. In so far as the source of his revelation is concerned he belongs to the ancient world; in so far as the spirit of his revelation is concerned he belongs to the modern world. In him life discovers other sources of knowledge, suitable to its new direction. The birth of Islam . . . is the birth of inductive intellect. In Islam prophecy reaches its perfection in discovering the need of its own abolition. This involves the keen perception that life cannot for ever be kept in leading strings; that in order to achieve full self-consciousness man must finally be thrown back on his own resources.[64]

The Koran has opened for mankind the endless field of scientific knowledge and methods because it teaches the importance of exact observation of natural and psychological phenomena; the admonition to observe God's signs "in the horizons and in themselves" (Sura 41:53) appears as the beginning of true scholarly research. Likewise the Prophet is, for Iqbal, the first critical observer of psychic phenomena, as he concludes from a *ḥadīth* that tells of Muhammad's interest in observing a mentally deranged Jewish boy. It was this thirst for knowledge that led the Prophet to encourage studies and research.[65] This interpretation of the Prophet's attitude is offered at the very beginning of the *Reconstruction of Religious Thought in Islam*:

> The search for rational foundations in Islam may be regarded to have begun with the Prophet himself. His constant prayer was: "God grant me knowledge of the ultimate nature of things!"[66]

In poetical language, Iqbal had expressed this same conviction some years earlier in the dedicatory poem of the *Payām-i Mashriq*:

> Even though he had seen the Essence of the Essence without veil,
> Yet the words "O God, increase me in knowledge!" came from his lips.[67]

This verse was written to kindle the interest of Amanullah, then king of Afghanistan, in scholarly research and scientific activities. Iqbal's response to the problem of education is all the more remarkable when one remembers the traditional attitude of many mullahs in most Islamic lands, who were absolutely opposed to "worldly" knowledge and saw nothing but satanic insinuations in acquaintance with Western scientific methods. Iqbal however, following the earlier modernists, sought to prove that science had been brought to Europe during the Middle Ages by Muslim philosophers, physicians, and astronomers; in Europe it was developed to its present standards; and since it is a legitimate heirloom of the Muslims, it should be taken up again without hesitation for the benefit of the community.

The finality of Muhammad's prophetic office meant for Iqbal at the same time the opening of new ways in scientific research and a scientific world view. For this reason one of Iqbal's more radical interpreters, ʿInayatullah Mashriqi, the founder of the militant Islamic faction of the Khaksar in the Northwestern Frontier, went so far as to declare that modern scientists are the true successors of the Prophet.[68] Somewhat later another interpreter of Iqbal's thought, Ghulam Parvez, claimed that only the door of *nubuwwa*, the "personal" aspect of Muhammad's work, was closed, whereas the *risāla*, the "ideology," was left to the Muslims to act upon and elaborate.[69] Thus Iqbal's unusual interpretation of the finality of Prophethood led to unexpected conclusions in certain progressive circles. Some leftists in India have drawn even more far-reaching conclusions from the paragraph quoted above, which has been misunderstood as condoning a purely scientific approach to life without the necessity of any prophetic guidance—which meant, for such authors, the introduction of a plain Marxist scientific world view.[70] Iqbal would have been horrified by such an atheistic interpretation of his words, for he had defined his viewpoint concerning the finality of Muhammad's message in another passage very lucidly:

> No spiritual surrender [is possible] to any human being after Muhammad, who emancipated his followers by giving them a law which is realizable as arising from the very core of human conscience. The-

> ologically the doctrine is that the socio-political organisation called Islam is perfect and eternal. No revelation, the denial of which entails heresy, is possible after Muhammad.

These words are directed against the modernist movement of the Qadianis, which had emerged in the late nineteenth century in the Panjab and whose founder, Mirza Ghulam Ahmad, had uttered certain remarks that could be interpreted as arrogation of prophetic or, perhaps, messianic claims. Iqbal fought against this movement with all his strength, for he believed that the acceptance of the finality of Muhammad's message

> is really the factor which accurately draws the line of demarcation between Muslims and non-Muslims and enables one to decide whether a certain individual or group is part of the community or not. . . . According to our belief Islam as a religion was revealed by God, but the existence of Islam as a society depends entirely on the personality of the Holy Prophet.[71]

This is probably the most categorical definition of the political role of the Prophet in Iqbal's work. Iqbal's aversion to the Qadianis and the Ahmadiyya (as the more liberal group is called, which split off in 1914) is also expressed in a poem in which he voices his anger about those who refute the concept of "holy war" and instead discuss useless problems connected with the Messiah and the Mahdi. For he was deeply committed to the unquestioning trust that

> For us, Mustafa is enough![72]

One should add here, out of fairness, that the chapter entitled "Muhammad, the Excellent Exemplar" in the book *Islam* by Sir Zafrulla Khan, a prominent jurist and member of the Ahmadiyya, is written with such heartfelt devotion that it would be difficult to see why it should be unacceptable to an orthodox Muslim. Iqbal, however, would have been happy to know that the Ahmadiyya was declared a non-Muslim religion in 1975.

When one recognizes the central position that the Prophet occupies in Iqbal's thought and poetry, many of his metaphors, images, and symbols appear in a new light. Thus the word "love" in his verse often denotes love of the Prophet or love inspired by him because he is the true embodiment of Divine Love, as Iqbal sings in the succession of Rumi and other mystics: the great ode "The Mosque of Cordoba," like numerous other verses in the collection of his most mature Urdu poems, *Bāl-i Jibrīl*, repeatedly equates "Love" with "Mustafa."[73]

Likewise, Iqbal's constant allusions to Arabia, to the Najd and Hijaz, gain their real value in the light of his deep veneration of the "Arabian friend," as he loved to call the Prophet, following the example of many Indian poets before him. A key to Iqbal's way of thinking in this context is the final verse of his *Tarāna-i millī*, the "National Song," composed in the early years of this century:

> The caravan leader for us is the prince of Hijaz,
> By his name our soul acquires peace!

This line is followed by the revealing words:

> Iqbal's song is as it were the sound of the caravan bell![74]

These words, which gave his first Urdu book its title, *Bāng-i Darā* (The Call of the Caravan Bell), especially reveal the poet's close relation with the Prophet: acting as the bell on Muhammad's camel's leg, he guides with his sound the erring Muslims back to the central sanctuary of Mecca, and calls them to return, under his guidance, on the Prophet's way, leaving behind them the glittering streets of European life as well as the fragrant rose gardens of Persian mystical dreams.

Iqbal's work comprises theological and political, mystical and sociological interpretations of the Prophet. But toward the end of his life he turned once more to the Prophet as the faithful, loving, and consoling friend and sang in simple words, almost like one of the folk poets of his native Panjab, of his longing for the last resting place of the Prophet:

> Just like a bird who, in the desert night,
> Spreads out his wings when thinking of his nest.[75]

And in an unforgettable image Iqbal sums up what millions and millions of pious Muslims have felt over the centuries and still feel about the Prophet:

> Love of the Prophet runs like blood in the veins of his community.[76]

APPENDIX
THE NOBLE NAMES OF THE PROPHET

Muḥammad (Suras 3:144, 33:40, 47:2, 48:29)
Aḥmad (Sura 61:6)
Ḥāmid, Praising
Maḥmūd, Praised
Qāsim, Divider (it should rather be *Abū'l-Qāsim*, Father of al-Qasim, which is the normal *kunya* of the Prophet)
ʿĀqib, Following, the Last
Fātiḥ, Opener, Conqueror
Shāhid, Witness (Sura 33:45)
Ḥāshir, Who Gathers People (at Doomsday)
Rashīd, Well Guided (Sura 11:78)
Mashhūd, Witnessed
Bashīr, Bringer of Good Tidings (Sura 7:88)
Nadhīr, Warner (Sura 33:45 and often)
Dāʿī, Caller (Sura 33:46)
Shāfī, Healer
Hādī, He Who Guides Right (Sura 13:7)
Mahdī, He Who Is Well Guided
Māḥī, He Who Wipes Out (Infidelity)
Munjī, He Who Saves, Delivers
Nājī, Safe
Rasūl, Messenger (frequently in the Koran)
Nabī, Prophet (frequently in the Koran)
Ummī, Unlettered (Sura 21:107)
Tihāmī, From the Tihama
Hāshimī, From the Family of Hashim
Abṭaḥī, Belonging to al-Baṭḥa (the area around Mecca)
ʿAzīz, Noble, Dear (Sura 9:128). Also a Divine Name
Ḥarīṣ ʿalaikum, Full of Concern for You (Sura 9:128)
Raʾūf, Mild (Sura 9:128). Also a Divine Name
Raḥīm, Merciful (Sura 9:128). Also a Divine Name
Ṭāhā (Sura 20:1)

Mujtabā, Elect
Ṭāsīn (Sura 27:1)
Murtaḍā, Content
Ḥā-mīm (beginning of Suras 40–46)
Muṣṭafā, Chosen
Yā-sīn (Sura 36:1)
Aulā', Worthier, Most Worthy (Sura 33:6)
Muzammil, Wrapped (Sura 74:1)
Walī, Friend. Also a Divine Name
Mudaththir, Covered (Sura 73:1)
Matīn, Firm
Muṣaddiq, Who Declares for True (Sura 2:101)
Ṭayyib, Good
Nāṣir, Helper. Also a Divine Name
Manṣūr, Helped (by God), Victorious
Miṣbāḥ, Lamp (Sura 24:35)
Amīr, Prince, Commander
Ḥijāzī, From the Hijaz
Tarāzī (?)
Quraishī, From the Clan Quraish
Muḍarī, From the Tribe Mudar
Nabī at-tauba, The Prophet of Repentance
Ḥāfiẓ, Preserver. Also a Divine Name
Kāmil, Perfect
Ṣādiq, Sincere (Sura 19:54, used for Isma'il)
Amīn, Trustworthy (Suras 26:107, 81:21)
'Abdallāh, God's Servant
Kalīm Allāh, He to Whom God Has Talked (usually epithet of Moses)
Ḥabīb Allāh, God's Beloved Friend
Najī Allāh, God's Intimate Friend (usually epithet of Moses)
Ṣafī Allāh, God's Sincere Friend (usually epithet of Adam)
Khātam al-anbiyā', Seal of the Prophets (Sura 33:40)
Ḥasīb, Respected. Also a Divine Name
Mujīb, Complying, Replying. Also a Divine Name
Shakūr, Most Grateful. Also a Divine Name
Muqtaṣid, Adopting a Middle Course (Sura 35:32)
Rasūl ar-raḥma, The Messenger of Mercy
Qawī, Strong. Also a Divine Name
Ḥafī, Well-Informed (Sura 7:187)
Ma'mūn, Trusted
Ma'lūm, Well-Known
Ḥaqq, Truth (Sura 3:86). Also a Divine Name

Mubīn, Clear, Evident (Sura 15:89)
*Muṭī*ʿ, Obedient
Awwal, First. Also a Divine Name
Ākhir, Last. Also a Divine Name
Ẓāhir, Outward, External. Also a Divine Name
Bāṭin, Internal, Inner. Also a Divine Name
Yatīm, Orphan (Sura 93:6)
Karīm, Generous (Sura 81:19). Also a Divine Name
Ḥakīm, Wise, Judicious. Also a Divine Name
Sayyid, Lord (Sura 3:39)
Sirāj, Lamp (Sura 33:46)
Munīr, Radiant (Sura 33:46)
Muḥarram, Forbidden, Immune
Mukarram, Honored, Venerated
Mubashshir, Bringer of Good News (Sura 33:45)
Mudhakkir, Who Makes Remember, Preacher
Muṭahhar, Purified
Qarīb, Near. Also a Divine Name
Khalīl, Good Friend (usually epithet of Abraham)
Madʿū, Who Is Called
Jawwād, Generous, Magnanimous
Khātim, Seal (Sura 33:40)
ʿĀdil, Just
Shahīr, Well-Known
Shahīd, Witnessing, Martyr. Also a Divine Name
Rasūl al-malāḥim, The Messenger of the Battles of the Last Days

One of the most frequently mentioned names is not found in this particular list: *ʿAbduhu*, His (i.e., God's) Servant, which appears in Suras 17:1 and 53:10 and is common as a proper name (Muḥammad ʿAbduh). Likewise, *Muṭāʿ*, Obeyed (Sura 81:21) is missing.

Source: The list is taken from the author's copy of the Koran (Lahore: Taj Company), which contains 17 × 6 = 102 names, among them twice *Rasūl ar-raḥmat*, plus *nabī ar-raḥmat*, while the Prophet's *kunya* Abu'l-Qasim is not mentioned.

ABBREVIATIONS

ARW	*Archiv für Religionswissenschaft*
BEA	*Bulletin des études arabes*
BIFAO	*Bulletin de l'Institut Français d'Archéologie Orientale*
BSOAS	*Bulletin of the School of Oriental and African Studies*
EI	*Encyclopaedia of Islam*, 2nd ed. (unless stated otherwise)
GMS	Gibb Memorial Series
IBLA	*Institut des Belles Lettres Arabes*
IC	*Islamic Culture*
JRAS	*Journal of the Royal Asiatic Society*
MW	*The Moslem* (later *Muslim*) *World*
RHR	*Revue de l'histoire des religions*
RMM	*Revue du monde musulman*
SEER	*Slavonic and East European Review*
SI	*Studia Islamica*
WI	*Die Welt des Islams*
WZKM	*Wiener Zeitschrift für die Kunde des Morgenlandes*
ZDMG	*Zeitschrift der deutschen Morgenländischen Gesellschaft*

NOTES

INTRODUCTION

1. The Metropolitan Museum of Art, New York, no. 40.164.2a.

2. Jeffery, "Ibn al-ʿArabi's *Shajarat al-kawn*," p. 2 (Lahore ed.).

3. On this topic see especially Haas, *Das Bild Muhammads*; Chew, *The Crescent and the Rose*; Kritzek, *Peter the Venerable and Islam*; Saunders, "Mohammed in Europe"; and Daniel, *Islam and the West.* The very useful dissertation by Hamadeh, "Muhammad the Prophet: A Selected Bibliography," which contains 1,548 titles, deals with the interaction of Islam and the West, pp. 23–27, 43–59.

4. W. C. Smith, *Modern Islam in India*, pp. 69–70. This feeling is very typical of Muslims' attitude toward the Prophet and is reflected even in popular stories. Paret, *Die legendäre Maghāzī-Literatur*, p. 178, writes: "Mag der Muslim im Notfall seinen Glauben verleugnen, so wird er sich doch nie dazu bereit finden, eine Schmähung gegen Muhammad auszusprechen und sich von ihm loszusagen, selbst wenn ihm im Weigerungsfalle der Tod droht." (In case of emergency, the Muslim might deny his faith, but he would never be willing to utter a word of slander against Muhammad or to renounce him, even though he were facing death in case of refusal to do so.)

5. *Dawn Overseas* (Karachi), November 1978. The closing hemistich of our extract is frequently quoted in India, as by Mufti ʿAbdul ʿAziz Dihlawi in the early nineteenth century (see *Muslim Digest*, Jan.–Feb. 1982, p. 54). Sir Sayyid Ahmad Khan alluded to it in his "Credo," *Maqālāt-i Sir Sayyid*, 13:52; see also Troll, *Sayyid Ahmad Khan*, p. 324. It also occurs in popular songs in the regional languages of Pakistan; see Baloch, *Ṭih Akharyūñ*, 2:304–7.

6. Boulainvilliers, *La vie de Mahomet* (first published 1730), is called by Arthur Jeffery, "The Quest for the Historical Muhammad," p. 392, "a bombastic laudation of Muhammad in the interest of belittling Christianity." On the other hand, Voltaire uses the figure of the Prophet in his *Mahomet, ou le Fanatisme* not so much as a caricature of Islam but rather as a polemical device aimed at the Catholic church and its clergy.

7. This feeling still prevails among Muslims. When I mentioned in my class at the Ilâhiyat Fakültesi (Faculty of Islamic Theology) in Ankara that several Christian sects and groups do not believe in the immaculate conception or virgin birth, one of my students angrily exclaimed, "But then we are better Christians than you!" The respect shown to Hazrat ʿIsa (Jesus) by Muslims is integral to their

faith. This is reflected even in German Romantic literature; Novalis, the author of *Heinrich von Ofterdingen*, has the imprisoned Saracen woman Zulima complain that she does not understand why the Christians fight against the Muslims, who "have always honored the grave of Jesus, whom we too revere as a prophet."

8. Muir, *The Life of Mohamet*, appeared in four volumes from 1858 to 1861. He also edited (in 1887), for missionary purposes, *The Apology of al-Kindi*, the anti-Muslim *Risāla* of the ninth-century Arab Christian writer al-Kindi.

9. Rodinson, "A Critical Survey of Modern Studies on Muhammad."

10. It happens frequently that young Pakistani children write charming little poems in English or Urdu in honor of the Prophet, and children's songs in his honor are a regular feature of the Sindhi children's magazine *Gul Phul* (issued in Hyderabad/Sind).

11. Royster, "The Study of Muhammad."

CHAPTER ONE

1. An attempt to understand Muhammad's personality on the basis of the Koran alone is Foster, "An Autobiography of Muhammad." A similar attempt in the Arab world, which, of course, does not ascribe the Koranic words to the Prophet, but to divine revelation, is Darwazah, *Sīrat ar-Rasūl*.

2. Jeffery, "The Sīra," in *Reader on Islam*, pp. 283–338; Ibn Ishaq, *Sīrat rasūl Allāh: Das Leben Muhammads*; Guillaume, *The Life of Muhammad*; Horovitz, "The Earliest Biographies of the Prophet"; Levi della Vida, "Sīra."

3. An interesting Turkish narrative, interspersed with Turkish and Arabic verses and illustrated with numerous miniatures, is Darir, *Sīrat-i nabī*, originally written in 1388. This *Sīrat-i nabī*, or *Siyar an-nabi*, consisted of six volumes in a special, illustrated edition prepared for the art-loving Ottoman sultan Murad III. Volumes 1, 2, and 6 are in the Topkapu (H 1221–1223), volume 3 is in the New York Public Library (Spencer Collection no. 157), volume 4 is in the Chester Beatty Library (Minorsky, *Catalogue of the Turkish Manuscripts and Miniatures*, T no. 419), and the fifth volume seems lost. Four pages from this manuscript, with glorious miniatures depicting the Prophet performing various miracles, were auctioned in Paris on 23 March 1984. The scribe was Mustafa bin Vali; the paintings were executed in the atelier of Lutfi ʿAbdullah and completed in 1595.

4. The Turkish poet Necip Fazīl Kīsakürek presented in his book *Es-selâm* sixty-three (not very good) poems, each corresponding to a year of the Prophet's life. Written in jail, the poetry was completed in 1972. Interestingly, a modern Persian elaboration of the *sīra*, Rahnema's *Payambar: The Messenger*, was written while the author was in exile. It seems that in pressured circumstances the Muslim author feels particularly close to the Prophet, and probably takes Muhammad's steadfastness in tribulations as a model. The same feeling—the Prophet as helper for those in need, or suffering in prison—is expressed, on a lower level, in the song of the Indian motion picture *Moghul-i aʿẓam*, where Anarkali, imprisoned by Akbar for her alleged love affair with Prince Salim, sings: *Bēkas pe karam kijiyē*, "O Prophet of Medina! Have mercy on the helpless! My world is in ruins, and you alone can save it!" (information supplied by Ali S. Asani).

5. Jeffery, "The Quest for the Historical Mohammad," gives a good survey of various approaches to the Prophet's biography: historical, critical, psychological, apologetic, mystical, etc.

6. Hamidullah, "La date de naissance du Prophète Muhammad."

7. Abu Nuʿaim, *Dalāʾil an-nubuwwa*, p. 100. The elephant "who performed prostration" as well as the *abābīl* birds of Sura 105 occur frequently in popular poetry as the first miracle to portend Muhammad's future role in Mecca, and in the world.

8. About her, see the romanticized account by Bint ash-Shaṭiʾ, *Āmina bint Wahb.*

9. Ibn Ishaq, *Sīra*, 1:104; see Meier, *Abū Saʿīd-i Abū l-H̱ayr*, p. 46, n. 32.

10. Rumi, *Mathnawī*, vol. 4, line 976.

11. See Abu Nuʿaim, *Dalāʾil an-nubuwwa*, pp. 120–21, n. 2.

12. Watt, *Muhammad, Prophet and Statesman*, p. 1, where the meeting with Bahiraʾ is told in extenso.

13. Abu Nuʿaim, *Dalāʾil an-nubuwwa*, pp. 125–31, with variants; Baihaqi, *Dalāʾil an-nubuwwa*, pp. 32–88.

14. *Bbārānā gītā*, p. 10.

15. Jurji, "Khadīja, Mohammad's First Wife"; Karahan, "Un nouveau *mathnawī* de la littérature turque-ottomane"; Littmann, *Mohammad im Volksepos*. A modern Arabic book in praise of Khadija is ʿAlayili, *Mathaluhunna al-aʿlā*.

16. Kĭsakürek, *Es-selâm*, p. 41.

17. Rumi, *Mathnawī*, vol. 5, lines 3535 ff.

18. Bukhari, *Ṣaḥīḥ*, "Badʾ al-waḥy," 1: no. 2.

19. Lüling, *Die Wiederentdeckung des Propheten Muhammad.*

20. Lehmann and Pedersen, "Der Beweis für die Auferstehung im Koran."

21. "The Sufi clings to the Prophet like Abu Bakr," says Rumi, *Dīwān*, no. 2275.

22. Ibn Ishaq, *Sīra*, 1:341 ff.; Hamidullah, *The First Written Constitution in the World.*

23. Rumi, *Mathnawī*, vol. 6, line 3197, concludes from this Koranic statement (as did many other Sufis) that

> To see him is to see the Creator;
> To serve him is to serve God,
> [You] see the day [when you] look through this window.

24. Thus Jami, "Salamān u Absāl," in *Haft Aurang*, p. 454; his *naʿtiyya* poetry contains numerous allusions to this event. But even as early as the twelfth century, Nizami speaks in his verse of the "teeth and stones"; see "Khusrau u Shīrīn," in *Kulliyāt-i Khamsa*, p. 128.

25. For a new interpretation of Muhammad's oft-discussed attitude toward the Jews see Barakat Ahmad, *Muhammad and the Jews.*

26. The topic of Muhammad's patience in adversities is alluded to in the title of one of his biographies, *The Book of "Who Perseveres Will Overcome"*; see Nicholson, "An Unknown Biography of Muhammad Entitled *Kitābu man ṣabara ẓafira.*"

27. The problem whether *al-ʿālamīn*, "the worlds" or "the inhabitants of the

worlds," originally meant "all of humanity" has been discussed time and again. A good survey of the earlier studies is Buhl, "Fasste Muhammad seine Verkündigung als eine universelle . . . Religion auf?"

28. The first major book in the long line of studies on this topic was Geiger's *Was hat Mohammed aus dem Judentum aufgenommen?* (Bonn, 1833).

29. Fück, "Die Originalität des arabischen Propheten," p. 145.

30. The "farewell sermon" is translated in Jeffery, *Reader on Islam*, pp. 306–8.

31. Bedil Rohriwaro, *Dīwān*, p. 348, gives the chronogram for his death, the year 11 of the Hegira, as *hū*, "He" (h = 5, w = 6, h + w = 11): "he [the Prophet] became united with HE [God]."

32. Fück, "Muhammad—Persönlichkeit und Religionsstiftung," p. 175.

33. Padwick, *Muslim Devotions*, p. 137, from Muhammad Hasanain Makhluf, *Dalīl al-ḥajj*.

34. About the Prophet's daughters see Bint ash-Shati', *Banāt an-nabī*; she has also devoted a book to the Prophet's wives, *Nisā' an-nabī*.

35. According to the Shia theologian Muhammad Baqir Majlisi in his *Jalā' al-ʿuyūn*, Fatima was conceived when the Prophet returned from his heavenly journey, and therefore carried a fragrance of Paradise; see McAuliffe, "Chosen of all Women," p. 26. An excellent survey is the article "Fāṭima" in *EI*, 2nd ed., 3: 841–50. One should compare the biting sarcasm of Lammens's book *Fatima et les filles de Mahomet* with the interpretation given of her role by a devout Shia modernist such as ʿAli Schariʿati, *Fatima ist Fatima*. For her role in popular piety see also Ayoub, *Redemptive Suffering in Islam*.

36. Ibn Ishaq, *Sīra*, 4:305–6.

37. Families with the surname Siddiqi (or Siddiqui) claim descent from him.

38. ʿUmar was the father of Hafsa, one of the Prophet's wives; hence the frequent combination of the name of ʿUmar with the *kunya* (agnomen) Abu Hafs. Families with the surname Faruqi claim descent from him.

39. Most recently by Lazarus-Yafeh, in *Some Religious Aspects of Islam*, pp. 1–16.

40. The *fātiḥa* is recited at a great number of occasions. "To have *fātiḥa*" means in common parlance, at least in the non-Arab countries, to have a religious gathering, either in memory of deceased persons or for purposes of blessing.

41. Schuon, *Islam and the Perennial Philosophy*, p. 100, explains the different loyalties of the "proto-Sunnite" and "proto-Shiite" attitudes with the following interesting comparison: "The spiritual ancestors of the Shiites were those companions who could not live without the presence of the Prophet" (hence their love for his descendants); the Sunnites "were those who could not accept any substitute whatever for this presence and who, thus, had no choice but to live by his memory and in his *sunna*."

42. Ayoub, *Redemptive Suffering in Islam*; a good survey of the later development appears in Chelkowski, *Taʿziya: Ritual and Drama in Iran*.

43. Hallaj, "Riwāyāt," quoted in Baqli, *Sharḥ-i shaṭḥiyāt*, para. 639.

44. For this high regard for the descendants of the Prophet as expressed by Mir Dard, a *sayyid* himself, see Schimmel, *Pain and Grace*, p. 38: they "were elected

before all people and possessed the special grace which God had bestowed upon their ancestor Muhammad." Braune, *Die Futūḥ al-Ġaib des ʿAbd ul-Qādir*, p. 12; Meier, *Abū Saʿīd-i Abū l-Ḫayr*, p. 67, speaks of the veneration in which the Sufi master Abu Saʿid (d. 1049) held the descendants of the Prophet and how he supported those who were impoverished. Islamic history is full of such examples. See Mrs. Meer Hasan Ali, *Observations on the Musulmauns*, 1:6: "Syads . . . are the first to be considered, when the rich have determined on dispensary gifts in charity. The syads, however, are under peculiar restrictions, as regards the nature of those gifts which they are permitted to accept." One has also to think of the political role played by the *sayyid* or *sharīf* families as founders of dynasties (as in Morocco and Libya), or more recently in party politics in some Islamic states.

45. Rumi, *Dīwān*, no. 169.

46. Furuzanfar, *Aḥādīth-i Mathnawī*, no. 48; Rumi, *Mathnawī*, vol. 6, lines 888 ff.

47. Sana'i, *Dīwān*, p. 363.

48. Examples from modern Arabic writing: ʿAqqad, *Dāʿī as-samā'*; Ibrahim, *Bilāl ibn Rabāḥ*; Sahhar, *Bilāl mu'adhdhin ar-rasūl*.

49. Iqbal, *Bāng-i Darā*, pp. 78, 272.

50. For him see Cameron, *Abū Dharr al-Ghifārī*.

51. Abu Nuʿaim, *Dalā'il an-nubuwwa*, pp. 213–19, devotes a lengthy chapter to his strange career. Paret, *Die legendäre Maghāzī-Literatur*, pp. 189–90, speaks of the important role of Salman in the cycles of legends that developed around the Prophet and highlights his relation to ʿAli and his family. Later poets, up to Iqbal, like to contrast the poverty of Salman and the glory of Sulaiman (the biblical Solomon, grammatically, a diminutive of Salman): the poor Persian and the mighty prophet-king represent the complementary aspects of Islam.

52. See Donaldson, "Salmān the Persian"; Horovitz, "Salmān al-Fārisī"; Huart, "Selmân de Fârs"; Massignon, "Les origines de la méditation Shiite sur Salmân et Fâtima" and "Salmân-i Pâk et les prémices spirituelles de l'Islam iranien."

53. In Turkish barber shops, one might find, in former days, a plate with the verse:

> Every morning our shop opens with the *basmala*;
> Hazret-i Salman-i Pak is our *pir* and our master.

In some Turkish dervish orders, the expression *selman etmek*, "to make someone Salman," meant to send him out to beg and learn humility. Gölpĭnarlĭ, *Tasavvuftan dilimize geçen deyimler*, pp. 288–89.

54. Furuzanfar, *Aḥādīth-i Mathnawī*, no. 195. Uwais has been praised by poets especially in the folk tradition. See, for example, the verses of Yunus Emre (d. 1321, Anatolia), *Divan*, p. 572, no. CCXLVI:

> The dearest friend of the Beloved of God:
> In the lands of Yemen—Uwais al-Qarani.
> He does not lie; he does not eat forbidden food,
> In the lands of Yemen—Uwais al-Qarani.

In the morning he gets up and takes his way,
He recites in *dhikr* God's thousand and one names;
With the word *Allāhu Akbar* he drives the camels
In the lands of Yemen—Uwais al-Qarani. . . .

55. The "ten who were promised Paradise" are, according to the most common tradition, Abu Bakr, ʿUmar, ʿUthman, ʿAli, Talha, Zubair, ʿAbdur Rahman ibn ʿAuf, Saʿd ibn Abi Waqqas, Saʿid ibn Zaid, and Abu ʿUbaida ibn Jarrah. In calligraphy the names of God and the Prophet are added so as to form a decorative octagon; an example of this device may be found on the dust cover of Martin Lings's *Mohammad*. Pious Sufis were often blessed with the company of ten particularly dear friends and thus followed even in this respect the Prophet's example. See Meier, *Abū Saʿīd-i Abū l-Ḫayr*, pp. 364–66.

CHAPTER TWO

1. Aflaki, *Manāqib al-ʿārifīn*, p. 666, chap. 4, para. 67.
2. Cf. Schuon's interpretation of the Muslim ideal (*Islam and the Perennial Philosophy*, p. 96): "Love of God is not the point of departure; it is a grace which God may bestow upon him who fears Him." For "if you wish God to love you, you must love His messenger by following his *sunna.*"
3. W. C. Smith, *The Faith of Other Men*, pp. 60–62, discusses this aspect of Islamic prophetology.
4. Söderblom, *The Living God*, p. 224.
5. See Andrae, *Die person Muhammads*, p. 182. Aflaki, *Manāqib al-ʿārifīn*, p. 242, chap. 3, para. 152, quotes Rumi: "To follow the messenger of God, belongs to the duties of the *ahl-i maʿnā* [those who have reached the interior meaning of life]."
6. Goldziher, "Chatm al-Buchârî." See Schimmel, "Sufismus und Heiligenverehrung," p. 275, for medieval Egypt: according to Ibn Taghribirdi, *Annals, Entitled An-nujūm az-zāhira*, 6:376, Sultan Muʾayyad Shaikh had learned this custom in 1417 in Jerusalem and then introduced it in Cairo.
7. Badaoni, *Muntakhab at-tawārīkh*, 3:154 (trans. p. 215).
8. Sprenger, *Catalogue of the Arabic, Persian and Hindustany Manuscripts*, 1:xiii.
9. A good example is ʿAbdul Haqq Muhaddith Dihlawi (d. 1642), who collected, among other works, forty *ḥadīth* concerning the good or bad proprieties of the days of the week (*Al-aʿmāl al-maʾthūra fīʾl-ayyām al-mashhūra*, Urdu trans., Delhi, 1891). See Brockelmann, GAL 2:416, S2:603. People collected "Forty *ḥadīth* about arrow shooting" (thus Al-Qarrab), about writing (Mustaqimzade), about prayers, or whatever appeared most important to them. For the topic in general see Karahan, *Islam-Türk edebiyatînda Kîrk hadis*, and his article "Aperçu général sur les 'quarante *ḥadīth*.'"
10. In the Persian tradition, Jami's *Arbaʿīn* in their Arabic text with his Persian verse translations were often copied by the masters of calligraphy. For two exqui-

site examples see Arberry et al., *Catalogue of the Persian Manuscripts*, no. 172, by Sultan-ʿAli Mashhadi in 1495; and no. 227, by Shah-Mahmud Nishaburi in 1557.

11. See Goldziher, *Muslim Studies*, 2:164–80, about *ṭalab al-ḥadīth*, "search for *ḥadīth*." However, Ibn al-Jauzi (*Talbīs Iblīs*, p. 113) attacks even those scholars who travel searching for *ḥadīth* in order to show off, while neglecting more essential duties; they are considered to be misguided by Satan.

12. Hamidullah, *Ṣaḥīfa Hammām ibn Munabbih*. There are numerous traditions according to which ʿUmar ibn al-Khattab, the second caliph, was strictly against the reporting of *ḥadīth* and even had people flogged for divulging words—or alleged words—of the Prophet, for he was afraid that the Prophet's example might supersede the clear words of the Koran, or that ignorant listeners might forget the distinction between the two categories of words, Divine and Prophetic.

13. The Sufis sometimes objected to collecting *ḥadīth* and stressed the importance of following the Prophet's example by one's actions rather than by "blackening books" by writing down the traditions. A well-known example is that of the illiterate Persian mystic Kharaqani; see Jami, *Nafaḥāt al-uns*, p. 299.

14. Mez, *Die Renaissance des Islam*, p. 183; see also Goldziher, *Muslim Studies*, 2:366–68, about women in *ḥadīth* studies.

15. Andrae, *Die person Muhammads*, pp. 182–83.

16. Rahman, *Islam*; the whole of his third chapter deals with these problems in a masterly way.

17. See *Handwörterbuch des Islam* (*Shorter Encyclopedia of Islam*), s.v. "sunna" for definitions.

18. Schuon, *Islam and the Perennial Philosophy*, p. 29.

19. Nasr, *Ideals and Realities of Islam*, pp. 80 ff.

20. Troll, *Sayyid Ahmad Khan*, p. 45.

21. For excerpts from his writing see Aziz Ahmad and von Grunebaum, *Muslim Self-Statement in India and Pakistan*, p. 52.

22. Aziz Ahmad, *Islamic Modernism in India and Pakistan*, gives a good survey of the different trends. For Pakistan see also Baljon, *Modern Muslim Koran Interpretation*, esp. pp. 18–19, 73; for Egypt, Juynboll, *The Authenticity of Tradition Literature*.

23. Andrae, *Die person Muhammads*, p. 192, after Qadi ʿIyad, *Shifāʾ*, 2:14.

24. Thus Rumi in Aflaki, *Manāqib al-ʿārifīn*, p. 196, chap. 3, para. 105.

25. Furuzanfar, *Aḥādīth-i Mathnawī*, no. 228.

26. Typical for the *sunna*-bound attitude is the quotation at the beginning of Ibn al-Jauzi's *Talbīs Iblīs*, which refers to the saying of the leading Sufi master of Baghdad in the formative period, Junaid: "All the roads are closed for people, with the exception of him that picks out the works of the holy Prophet and follows his *sunna* and keeps always to his path, for to him all ways of good actions are open."

27. Ghazzali, *Iḥyāʾ ʿulūm ad-dīn*, 2:300–344, trans. by Zolondek as *Book XX of Ghazzali's Iḥyāʾ ʿulūm ad-dīn*.

28. Aflaki, *Manāqib al-ʿārifīn*, p. 219, chap. 3, para. 128.

29. Meier, *Abū Saʿīd-i Abūʾl Ḫayr*, pp. 364–65, shows how the great mystic

Abu Saʿid arranged his whole life according to the Prophet's example: the Sufis were even keener to form their lives according to the pattern of his life than Muslims in general.

30. Schuon, *Islam and the Perennial Philosophy*, p. 29.

31. Furuzanfar, *Aḥādīth-i Mathnawī*, no. 12.

32. Padwick, *Muslim Devotions*, p. 140.

33. Thus M. Khaqani, *Ḥilya*, p. 33; according to Tirmidhi, *Shamāʾil*, with commentary of Bajuri, pp. 11, 65, 66, it was either twenty or fourteen white hairs. Cf. also Burton, *Sindh, and the Races That Inhabit the Valley of the Indus*, p. 135, where he tells that schoolboys in Sind about 1850 learned that the Prophet had exactly 104,472 hairs on his body.

34. Makhdum Muhammad Hashim was a Naqshbandi mystic in the city of Thatta, Sind; see Brockelmann, *GAL* S2: 612–21. A complete enumeration of his works appears in Ibrahim Tattawi, *Takmilat Maqālāt ash-shuʿarā*, pp. 43 ff.

35. A very comprehensive, though rather late (seventeenth-century) Indo-Persian source is ʿAbdul Haqq Muhaddith Dihlawi's *Madārij an-nubuwwa.*

36. It forms the basis of a lecture by the Swiss Professor Goergens in 1878: *Mohammad, ein Charakterbild. Auf Grund der Darstellung Termidī's.* The manuscript of Tirmidhi's *Shamāʾil* was given to the author by Aloys Sprenger. A good English translation by Hidayet Hosain was published in the journal *Islamic Culture,* 1933 and 1934.

37. Andrae, *Die person Muhammads*, p. 60. The edition of the *Shifāʾ* used by Andrae was not available to the present writer.

38. Khafaji, *Nasīm ar-riyāḍ* (commentary on the *Shifāʾ*), 1:4.

39. Yusuf an-Nabhani has summed up Qastallani's work as *Al-anwār al-muḥammadiyya*. Among his numerous other compilations of sayings, verse, and theological works in honor of the Prophet, one may mention *Al-faḍāʾil al-muḥammadiyya* (Beirut, 1900) and the anthology in four volumes, *Jawāhir al-biḥār fī faḍl an-nabī al-mukhtār* (Beirut, 1909).

40. Zolondek, *Book XX*, pp. 74–76, from Tirmidhi's *Shamāʾil* (with commentary of Bajuri, pp. 29–35). Unfortunately the translator consistently renders the "full moon," *badr*, as "the moon in the night of Badr."

41. Abu Nuʿaim, *Dalāʾil an-nubuwwa*, p. 38.

42. Rumi, *Dīwān*, no. 1348. Cf. ʿAttar, *Muṣībatnāma*, p. 28.

43. Enevoldsen, *O Måne!* no. 188. This saying may be based on verses like that of Jami, "Salamān u Absāl," in *Haft Aurang*, p. 452:

> The rose which is the perspiration of his face,
> Is only a dew drop from his rose garden.

A lovely rose poem is also found in Sindhi (Baloch, *Maulūd*, p. 151, no. 3), with the refrain:

> All flowers opened and turned into a rosebed
> When the Prophet entered the garden.

The poet goes on to state that the Prophet and the rose were equal in beauty and fragrance.

44. Abu Nuʿaim, *Dalāʾil an-nubuwwa*, p. 380.

45. Saghir Nizami, in Siddiqi and Asi, *Armaghān-i naʿt*, p. 216.

46. Horten, *Die religiöse Vorstellungswelt des Volkes*, p. 38, with an exact description.

47. Dagh, in Siddiqi and Asi, *Armaghān-i naʿt*, p. 102.

48. Furuzanfar, *Aḥādīth-i Mathnawī*, no. 49.

49. Furuzanfar, *Aḥādīth-i Mathnawī*, no. 106.

50. The idea that the Muslims worshiped golden effigies of Muhammad remained alive in European literary tradition; even in the works of the German romantics such as Novalis, the *goldnen Mahomsbilder* occur now and then.

51. The Prophet was often represented in Islamic miniatures during the Middle Ages, even with his face unveiled. A typical example is Rashiduddin's *Jāmiʿ at-tawārīkh*, especially the Edinburgh manuscript, which illustrates all events of his life; see Rice, *The Illustrations to the "World History" of Rashīd al-Dīn*. Miniatures are often found in the Turkish tradition; see the examples in Esin, *Mecca the Blessed, Medinah the Radiant*. But the publication of these representations was recently criticized by a number of Pakistanis, and a growing aversion to them is also felt in Egypt, not to mention, of course, in Saudi Arabia, where any representation of persons is out of the question.

52. M. Khaqani, *Ḥilya*, p. 13.

53. S. B. Bukhari, *Jawāhir al-auliyā*, pp. 225–27.

54. S. B. Bukhari, *Jawāhir al-auliyā*, p. 229.

55. Mustaqimzade, *Tuḥfa-i khaṭṭāṭīn*, p. 606, speaks at length of the blessings involved in writing the *ḥilya*.

56. Inal, *Son Hattatlar*, p. 802.

57. In Urdu, an equivalent of the poetical *ḥilya* is the *sarāpā*, "[description] from head to foot"; a famous example is Luṭf's *Sarāpā sarwar al-anbiyā*, of the mid-nineteenth century.

58. M. Khaqani, *Ḥilya*, p. 12.

59. M. Khaqani, *Ḥilya*, p. 22.

60. M. Khaqani, *Ḥilya*, p. 23. Cf. also Jami, whose encomia evidently form the model for Khaqani (as for many other post–fifteenth-century Persian and Turkish poets); he says in "Salamān u Absāl," in *Haft Aurang*, p. 454:

> The "Night of Might" is a thread from your hair,
> The sent-down inspiration is the speech of your mouth . . .
> *Qāba qausain* [two bows' length] is evident from your eyebrows,
> The form of *Ḥā-mīm* is the bending of your tress . . .

61. Darmesteter, *Chants populaires des Afghans*, no. 110, lines 8–10.

62. Cachia, "The Prophet's Shirt," with texts and translations.

63. Baloch, *Munāqibā*, p. 37.

64. Margoliouth, "Relics of the Prophet Mohammad," mentions some more relics, and gives also the prices that were offered for some of them. Goldziher, *Muslim Studies*, 2:322–32, mentions that India was a particularly good market for such relics.

65. Iqbal, *Musāfir*, pp. 64–71.

66. Tirmidhi, *Shamāʾil*, with commentary of Bajuri, pp. 93–99, devotes a

whole chapter to the sandals. See also St. Elie, "Le culte rendu par les Musulmans aux sandales de Mahomet," which is mainly a translation of a small treatise by the indefatigable Yusuf an-Nabhani; a footnote mentions that there are also Turkish works on the *bashmaq-i sharīf* (printed in Kazan).

67. Jami, "Lailā u Majnūn," in *Haft Aurang*, p. 756; cf. S. B. Bukhari, *Jawāhir al-auliyā*, pp. 233 ff. But already Nizami in his "Khusrau u Shīrīn," *Kulliyāt-i Khamsa*, p. 128, had addressed the Prophet: "Your sandals are the crown for the Throne's seat." Khaqani then sings in his *Ḥilya*, p. 11: "The Divine Throne gained honor from kissing his sandals."

68. Jami, "Tarjīʿband," *Dīwān*, p. 95; see also his "Silsilat adh-dhahab," in *Haft Aurang*, p. 11.

69. Jami, *Dīwān*, no. 48, p. 74.

70. Jami, "Silsilat adh-dhahab," in *Haft Aurang*, p. 10, and "Yūsuf u Zulaikhā," ibid., p. 587. The sandals are mentioned also by Aflaki, *Manāqib al-ʿārifīn*, p. 364, chap. 3, para. 269. It is believed that the Abbasid caliph Mahdi received as a gift a pair of sandals attributed to the Prophet, and paid the person who brought it handsomely even though he did not believe in their authenticity. Horten, *Die religiöse Vorstellungswelt des Volkes*, p. 149.

71. Nabhani, *Al-majmūʿa an-nabhāniyya*, 2:398.

72. Maqqari, *Fatḥ al-mutaʿāl fī madḥ an-niʿāl*, with numerous drawings. A different use of the term "shoe of the Prophet" is apparently current in East Africa. See Knappert, *Swahili Religious Poetry*, 1:40: "Shoe of the Prophet" is a "formidable talisman which lends its wearer good luck. . . . One writes on the soles the profession of faith and the Arabic phrase *tawajjah ḥaithu shiʾta faʾinnaka manṣūr*, 'Turn wherever you want, you are victorious (or, "supported by God").' " Classical Islam would have refused to sanction such a custom: how can one step on Arabic letters, especially when they contain the name of God and His prophet, as is the case in the *shahāda*?

73. Nabhani, *Al-majmūʿa an-nabhāniyya*, 3:386–416.

74. Goldziher, *Muslim Studies*, 2:397.

75. Memon, *Ibn Taimiyya's Struggle against Popular Religion*, p. 362 n. 301. The book contains many other examples of the veneration of relics to which Ibn Taimiyya objected.

76. S. B. Bukhari, *Jawāhir al-auliyā*, p. 222.

77. Nath, *Monuments of Delhi*, p. 39.

78. Badaoni, *Muntakhab at-tawārīkh*, 2:310 (trans. 2:320).

79. Tapish, *Gulzār-i naʿt*, fol. 7b.

80. Tapish, *Gulzār-i naʿt*, fol. 8b.

81. M. Khaqani, *Ḥilya*, p. 44, compares the Prophet's beard to the Night of Might (Sura 97) and the sura "By the Night!" (92:1).

82. Abu Nuʿaim, *Dalāʾil an-nubuwwa*, pp. 381–82.

83. For "hairs of the Prophet" in Turkey see Kriss and Kriss-Heinrich, *Volksglaube im Bereich des Islam*, 1:330–31; in Bursa the hair is shown and paraded during the *lailat al-qadr*, the Night of Might, on 27 Ramadan. Goldziher, *Muslim Studies*, 2:329–31, quotes from ʿAbdul Ghani an-Nabulusi (d. 1728) that the latter

had met an Indian who claimed that these hairs grow and increase on their own. See also Zwemer, "Hairs of the Prophet."

84. ʿAndalib, *Nāla-i ʿAndalīb*, 1:446 ff.

85. Juynboll, "Dyeing the Hair and Beard."

86. Nabhani, *Al-majmūʿa an-nabhāniyya*, 1:204–87.

87. Andrae, *Die person Muhammads*, p. 192 (for Malik ibn Anas *read* Anas ibn Malik). Abu Nuʿaim, *Dalāʾil an-nubuwwa*, pp. 375–76, tells how the Prophet, invited to a meal, enjoyed eating the lamb's forelegs; after eating two he asked for another one, whereupon his host remarked: "But a sheep has only two forelegs!" The Prophet rebuked him: "If you had kept quiet, then you would have given me what I had asked for!"—that is, probably, another piece might have mysteriously appeared in the pot.

88. Troll, "Sayyid Ahmad Khan and Islamic Jurisprudence," p. 2.

89. Aflaki, *Manāqib al-ʿārifīn*, p. 628, chap. 4, para. 22. This story was so well known that Iqbal alluded to it in the *Asrār-i khudī*, lines 422–24.

90. Ibn Qayyim al-Jauziyya, *Aṭ-ṭibb an-nabawī*, p. 223.

91. Furuzanfar, *Aḥādīth-i Mathnawī*, no. 134; Ibn Qayyim al-Jauziyya, *Aṭ-ṭibb an-nabawī*, p. 12.

92. There are *ḥadīth* about *taḥnīk*, rubbing a child's gums with saliva. The story that ʿAli's eye was cured in this way is mentioned by Ibn Hisham and has since been repeated frequently, as in the legendary *maghāzī* tales.

93. Healing miracles are found in Abu Nuʿaim, *Dalāʾil an-nubuwwa*, pp. 390 ff.; medical explanations of the Prophet's sayings and actions appear in Ibn Qayyim al-Jauziyya, *Aṭ-ṭibb an-nabawī*.

94. Rumi, *Dīwān*, no. 1335.

95. M. Khaqani, *Ḥilya*, pp. 17, 22. *Khaṭṭ*, "down on the cheeks," means primarily "line, script," hence the pun with the "text of the revelation." For further puns on the double meaning of *khaṭṭ*, as they were commonplace in mystical and profane poetry, see Schimmel, *Calligraphy and Islamic Culture*, esp. pp. 128–34.

96. Abu Nuʿaim, *Dalāʾil an-nubuwwa*, p. 139: *khulquhuʾl-Qurʾān*.

97. Andrae, *Die person Muhammads*, p. 261, according to Qadi ʿIyāḍ, *Shifāʾ*, 1:9.

98. Furuzanfar, *Aḥādīth-i Mathnawī*, no. 157.

99. Zolondek, *Book XX*, pp. 28–30; cf. Sellheim, "Das Lächeln des Propheten."

100. Tirmidhi, *Shamāʾil*, with commentary by Bajuri, p. 193; trans. H. Hosain, *Islamic Culture* 8:288–89; retold in Zafrulla Khan, *Islam*, pp. 69–70, and often.

101. Furuzanfar, *Aḥādīth-i Mathnawī*, no. 680.

102. Tirmidhi, *Shamāʾil*, with commentary by Bajuri, p. 176; Andrae, *Die person Muhammads*, pp. 200–201.

103. Furuzanfar, *Aḥādīth-i Mathnawī*, no. 20.

104. Furuzanfar, *Aḥādīth-i Mathnawī*, no. 338. For similar traditions see Goldziher, "Influences chrétiennes dans la littérature religieuse de l'Islam."

105. Rumi even calls him "lord of *ʿabasa* [he frowned]," *Mathnawī*, vol. 4, line 282.

106. Andrae, *Die person Muhammads*, p. 201, citing Tirmidhi, *Shamā'il*, with commentary of Bajuri, pp. 275–77.

107. Rumi, *Mathnawī*, vol. 5, lines 64 ff. See Furuzanfar, *Aḥādīth-i Mathnawī*, no. 449. Andrae, *Die person Muhammads*, pp. 216–18, 374, has pointed out how Sufi ideals have colored this picture of the Prophet. His mildness and his caring for people is also well attested in the legendary *maghāzī* tales; see Paret, *Die legendäre Maghāzī-Literatur*, p. 177.

108. Tirmidhi, *Shamā'il*, with commentary of Bajuri, pp. 289–91.

109. For the elaboration of such themes see Jami, "Silsilat adh-dhahab," in *Haft Aurang*, p. 9, and other instances in his epics.

110. Furuzanfar, *Aḥādīth-i Mathnawī*, no. 89.

111. The tradition is not part of the classical collections of *ḥadīth*.

112. Furuzanfar, *Aḥādīth-i Mathnawī*, no. 320.

113. Andrae, *Die person Muhammads*, p. 217.

114. Aflaki, *Manāqib al-ʿārifīn*, p. 407, chap. 3, para. 344: Rumi admonishes his daughter Malika Khatun with this *ḥadīth*, which he transforms into a little poem.

115. Furuzanfar, *Aḥādīth-i Mathnawī*, no. 54.

116. Furuzanfar, *Aḥādīth-i Mathnawī*, no. 3.

117. Thus Baloch, *Munāqibā*, p. 343.

118. Yunus Emre, *Divan*, p. 569, no. CCXLIII; this expression was apparently well known at least in Turkey, for it is used still in our day by Kĭsakürek, *Es-selâm*, p. 111, no. 51.

119. Abu Nuʿaim, *Dalā'il an-nubuwwa*, p. 485. Folk poetry often uses the theme of Gabriel announcing to the Prophet the death of his little grandsons, even though their actual demise was not to occur until some thirty or, in Husain's case, almost fifty years after the Prophet's own death. For examples see also Paret, *Die legendäre Maghāzī-Literatur*, p. 210. The theme of course plays a central role in the Shia tradition; see Ayoub, *Redemptive Suffering in Islam*. In a ladies' mourning session, *majlis*, that I attended last Muharram (October 1983) in Lahore, the preaching woman dwelt extensively on this legend.

120. Furuzanfar, *Aḥādīth-i Mathnawī*, no. 15.

121. Aflaki, *Manāqib al-ʿārifīn*, p. 478, chap. 3, para. 453, with the closing remark "Show love, and be it to a cat," *taʿashshaqū wa lau bi'l-hirra*.

122. Darmesteter, *Chants populaires des Afghans*, p. 104, no. 42.

123. Quoted as motto in Graham, *Divine Word and Prophetic Word*; cf. also the Turkish saying *kedi sevenin imanĭ gürdür*, "Who loves cats has a strong faith." For more examples see Schimmel, *Die orientalische Katze*.

124. Dailami, *Sīrat Ibn al-Khafīf*, introduction, p. 20; Aflaki, *Manāqib al-ʿārifīn*, p. 8, chap. 2, para. 1.

125. Altogether 1,210 *ḥadīth* go back to her, but only about 300 of them have been incorporated into the *Ṣaḥīḥān*.

126. Furuzanfar, *Aḥādīth-i Mathnawī*, no. 118.

127. Furuzanfar, *Aḥādīth-i Mathnawī*, no. 47.

128. This *ḥadīth* is found frequently; its most complete form is reported in Muslim, *Ṣaḥīḥ*, "bāb ar-raḍāʿ," no. 59.

129. Andrae, *Die person Muhammads*, p. 205.

130. Nasr, *Ideals and Realities of Islam*, p. 76.

131. Andrae, *Die person Muhammads*, p. 220, after al-Hakim at-Tirmidhi, *Nawādir al-uṣūl*, p. 201.

132. Furuzanfar, *Aḥādīth-i Mathnawī*, no. 480.

133. See, for example, Furuzanfar, *Aḥādīth-i Mathnawī*, the *ḥadīth* stating *shāwirūhunna wa khālifūhunna*, "Ask their opinion and then act contrary to it," which is very often quoted. A collection of Koranic injunctions and Prophetic sayings about women was published by Nawwab Siddiq Hasan Khan, the prince consort of the ruling princess of Bhopal; see Siddiq Hasan, *Ḥusn al-uswa bimā thubita min Allāh wa rasūlihi fī'n-niswa*.

134. Furuzanfar, *Aḥādīth-i Mathnawī*, no. 182. Ibn ʿArabi devoted the whole last chapter of his *Fuṣūṣ al-ḥikam* to this *ḥadīth* and its esoteric meaning; see for the translation Austin, *The Bezels of Wisdom*.

135. Nasr, *Ideals and Realities of Islam*, p. 77.

136. Nasr, *Ideals and Realities of Islam*, p. 74.

137. Furuzanfar, *Aḥādīth-i Mathnawī*, no. 34.

138. Söderblom, *The Living God*, p. 298: "Without No there will be no proper Yes. For then all that denies and destroys, degrades and delays what is right and good would be allowed to remain unattacked and unabolished. That is why a No is necessary in the moral warfare of the individual, in the evolution of religion and in the history of the race."

139. Padwick, *Muslim Devotions*, p. 85.

140. Razi, *The Path of God's Bondsmen*, p. 320, explains this *ḥadīth* as follows: " 'Temptation comes to my heart and I seek forgiveness of God seventy times a day' means that 'through intercourse with men, the conveying of the message, and the practice of social relationships, each moment a new existence is born within me and comes in front of the true sun like a cloud. By seeking forgiveness I negate that existence seventy times a day.' "

141. Furuzanfar, *Aḥādīth-i Mathnawī*, no. 597.

142. Padwick, *Muslim Devotions*, p. 40.

143. Fück, "Die Originalität des arabischen Propheten," p. 152.

144. Andrae, *Die person Muhammads*, p. 212.

CHAPTER THREE

1. For this topic see Andrae, *Die person Muhammads*, chap. 3: "Die Unfehlbarkeit des Propheten." See also Horten, *Die religiöse Gedankenwelt der gebildeten Muslime*, pp. 109–10.

2. See Bell, "Muhammad and Previous Messengers," about the role of the stories of the prophets in the Koran; and Jeffery, "Muhammad among the Prophets," in *Reader on Islam*, pp. 333–36.

3. Gätje, *Koran und Koranexegese*, p. 78, citing Zamakhshari, *Tafsīr* ad Sura 22:52, which deals with the prophets preceding Muhammad. See also Horten, *Die religiöse Gedankenwelt der gebildeten Muslime*, p. 111.

4. Bell, *Love Theories in Later Hanbalite Islam*, p. 161.

5. See Schimmel, *As Through a Veil*, p. 39.

6. The *Sanūsiyya* is translated in Horten, *Muhammedanische Glaubenslehren*, pp. 45–53, and Hartmann, *Die Religion des Islam*, pp. 43–50.

7. See Bravmann, "The Origin of the Principle of *ʿiṣmah*."

8. Jeffery, "Was Muhammad a Prophet from His Infancy?" deals critically with the material.

9. Abu Nuʿaim, *Dalāʾil an-nubuwwa*, pp. 143–47. It is remarkable that he extends the concepts of *ʿiṣma*, to which he devotes a long chapter (pp. 143–70), also to Muhammad's being protected from the evil intentions of his fellow creatures and of animals.

10. Gätje, *Koran und Koranexegese*, citing Zamakhshari's *Tafsīr* ad Sura 93: 6–8.

11. Padwick, *Muslim Devotions*, p. 192.

12. Ibn Hazm, *Al-faṣl fīʾl-milal . . . waʾn-niḥal*, 4:29; see also Andrae, *Die person Muhammads*, p. 134.

13. Andrae, *Die person Muhammads*, pp. 138–39, citing Tabari, *Tafsīr* ad Sura 48:1. Interesting is the attack launched in *Muslim Digest*, March–April 1982, p. 3, against a new translation of the Koran in which the translator had written "so that God might forgive thee all that is past of sins and all that is yet to come"—"and in this manner," says the outraged reviewer, "contradicts the firm belief of Muslims that EVERY PROPHET OF ALLAH IS MAʿSOOM [innocent]."

14. Andrae, *Die person Muhammads*, p. 149, based on Qadi ʿIyad, *Shifāʾ*, 2:115.

15. See *EI*, s.v. Bāḳillānī; McCarthy, *Al-Bāqillānī . . . : Miracle and Magic*.

16. Andrae, *Die person Muhammads*, pp. 149–50.

17. Andrae, *Die person Muhammads*, p. 169, based on ʿAbdul Qadir al-Gilani, *Futūḥ al-ghaib*, p. 18; see chapter 2 n. 140 above.

18. Furuzanfar, *Aḥādīth-i Mathnawī*, no. 459. Rumi, who loves this *ḥadīth*, says in the *Dīwān*, no. 82:

> From *aslama shaiṭānī* your lower self (*nafs*) will become dominical (*rabbānī*).

19. Aflaki, *Manāqib al-ʿārifīn*, p. 169, chap. 4, para. 8.

20. Aflaki, *Manāqib al-ʿārifīn*, p. 600, chap. 3, para. 592.

21. Andrae, *Die person Muhammads*, p. 245, citing Qadi ʿIyad, *Shifāʾ*, 1:102. Rumi, *Mathnawī*, 3: line 451, explains this as pertaining to the Prophet's night journey: his journey was into the height, Jonah's into the depth, but the proximity of God is beyond reckoning. The same idea is also elaborated in *Fīhi mā fīhi* (trans. Arberry, *Discourses of Rumi*, p. 114). See Furuzanfar, *Aḥādīth-i Mathnawī*, no. 298. But cf. Graham, *Divine Word and Prophetic Word*, p. 167, where a Divine saying (no. 44) admonishes man in general: "My servant must not say that he is better than Yunus ibn Matta."

22. Andrae, *Die person Muhammads*, p. 246. See also Razi, *The Path of God's Bondsmen*, p. 153.

23. Razi, *The Path of God's Bondsmen*, p. 155.

24. Razi, *The Path of God's Bondsmen*, p. 168.

25. Bell, *Love Theories in Later Hanbalite Islam*, p. 176.

26. ʿUrfi, *Kulliyāt*, p. 100 (*qaṣīda*); p. 469 (*mathnawī*).
27. Khaqani, *Dīwān*, p. 99: *qaṣīda ḥirz al-ḥijāz*.
28. Rumi, *Dīwān*, no. 1700.
29. ʿIraqi, *Kulliyāt*, p. 74.
30. Jami, "Lailā u Majnūn," in *Haft Aurang*, p. 754. That becomes a commonplace in later Persian poetry; see Naziri, *Dīwān*, p. 472, *qaṣīda* no. 32.
31. Padwick, *Muslim Devotions*, p. 170.
32. ʿAlam Muzaffarnagari, in Siddiqi and Asi, *Armaghān-i naʿt*, p. 170.
33. Amir Mina'i, in Siddiqi and Asi, *Armaghān-i naʿt*, p. 104.
34. Ismaʿil Meeruthi (Mirathi), in Siddiqi and Asi, *Armaghān-i naʿt*, p. 108.
35. Robson, "Does the Bible Speak of Mohammad?" calls this idea "crooked thinking." A good survey of these traditions appears in ʿAbdul Haqq Muhaddith Dihlawi, *Madārij an-nubuwwa*, pp. 111–26. A number of books on this subject have been published, mainly by Indian Muslims, such as Vidyarti and Ali, *Muhammad in Parsi, Hindoo and Buddhist Scriptures*; Jairazbhoy, *Muhammad: A Mercy to All the Nations*, discusses the topic in an appendix.
36. Andrae, *Die person Muhammads*, pp. 266–68.
37. Wagner, *Abū Nuwās*, p. 132. Cf. also Anwari, *Dīwān*, p. 190.
38. A typical instance from early sixteenth-century Egypt is told by Ibn Iyas; it happened on 26 Ramadan 918 (November A.D. 1512).
39. Hamadeh, *Muhammad*, no. 1452, mentions the work of Alvare of Cordova, *Iudiculus luminosus*, written in ninth-century Spain "to justify the wave of martyrdom which took place in Muslim Spain." Alvare "calls upon the Church to venerate the people who sacrificed themselves as martyrs when they insulted Muhammad."
40. See W. C. Smith, *Modern Islam in India*, p. 69; Ikramullah, *From Purdah to Parliament*, p. 46.
41. *Iqbālnāma* 1:189; see Schimmel, *Gabriel's Wing*, p. 170.

CHAPTER FOUR

1. For the early development of this tradition see Horovitz, "Zur Muhammadlegende" (The Growth of the Mohammad Legend); Mez, "Die Wunder Muhammads"; Jeffery, "The Miracles of the Prophet" (based on Ibn Saʿd), in *Reader on Islam*, pp. 309–30.
2. Razi, *The Path of God's Bondsmen*, p. 160.
3. For the early period see Antes, *Das Prophetenwunder in der frühen Ǎsʿarīya*; for the later nineteenth century see Troll, "The Fundamental Nature of Prophethood and Miracle"; and the interesting discussion by Sir Sayyid Ahmad Khan, "*Kiyā muʿjiza dalīl-i nubuwwat hai?* Is the Miracle Proof for Prophethood?" in Ahmad Khan, *Maqālāt-i Sir Sayyid*, 13:92–103.
4. For this event see Birkeland, *The Opening of Muhammad's Breast*; Guillaume, *The Life of Muhammad*, p. 72. An interesting variant of the story was told in medieval Bengal, where it was said that the young Muhammad, "while tending goats with other boys, hit an intransigent goat with a stick. Allah, disapproving of such anger in the Prophet, sent Jibril to rip open Muhammad's body," and then his

heart was cleansed from all lowly tendencies. Roy, *Islamic Syncretistic Tradition*, p. 101.

5. Baihaqi, *Dalā'il an-nubuwwa*, 1:12.

6. Abu Nu'aim, *Dalā'il an-nubuwwa*, from which this account is taken, has different versions (p. 117): the opening of the breast may have happened in Muhammad's fourth year, or in the tenth. He also mentions the weighing; both events are signs for the beginning of Muhammad's prophetic office (pp. 175–76).

7. Abu Nu'aim, *Dalā'il an-nubuwwa*, pp. 233–36. The various commentaries on Sura 54:1 give a survey of possible interpretations.

8. Andrae, *Die person Muhammads*, p. 107, citing Qadi 'Iyad, *Shifā*, 1:239.

9. Friedmann, "Qiṣṣat Shakarwātī Farmāḍ." Işīk, "Shocking Writings," pp. 34–35, and his South African editors repeat the story of the Indian king, although with a different name, but they add that Neil Armstrong saw on the moon a straight line estimated at some 240 km in length, which clearly proves that the moon was split in historical time.

10. In the Jagdish and Kamala Mittal Museum, Hyderabad/Deccan, published in Schimmel, *Und Muhammad ist Sein Prophet*, plate IV.

11. Sana'i, *Dīwān*, p. 377.

12. Baljon, *A Mystical Interpretation of Prophetic Tales*, p. 60.

13. Rumi, *Dīwān*, no. 48.

14. Rumi, *Dīwān*, no. 463. Cf. Naziri, *Dīwān*, p. 498:

How did the Splitting of the Moon happen, you know?
Out of longing for his [the Prophet's] face,
The moon, when tearing her shirt, split her breast!

15. Jami, "Yūsuf u Zulaikhā," in *Haft Aurang*, p. 585.

16. Rumi, *Dīwān*, no. 1989.

17. The German translation *heidnischer Prophet*, the "heathen Prophet," which was lately used for *ummī*, sounds absurd and conveys a wrong meaning.

18. On this problem see Zwemer, "The 'Illiterate' Prophet," with an enumeration of orientalists (p. 352) who, up to 1921, had voiced their opinions, pro and con, of the illiteracy of the Prophet. A fine story concerning the Prophet's "illiteracy" is found in the legendary *maghāzī* tales: Paret, *Die legendäre Maghāzī-Literatur*, p. 175 n. *a*, quotes from the story of Muqaffa': "When a letter came to the Prophet and there was nobody to read it, he used to put his index finger on the writing, and then it spoke to him." Interestingly, the vizier Rashiduddin at the Ilkhanid court of Tabriz composed a treatise about the virtue of the Prophet's illiteracy (*Tauḍīḥāt* no. 13; Paris Ms. no. 2324, ff. 137a–138a)—perhaps, as Josef van Ess speculates (*Der Wesir und seine Gelehrten*, p. 15), in order to flatter his king, Öljäitu, who himself was illiterate.

19. Rumi, *Dīwān*, no. 1135.

20. Hallaj, *Kitāb aṭ-ṭawāsīn*, "Ṭāsīn al-azal wa'l-iltibās."

21. Nizami, "Makhzan al-asrār," in *Kulliyāt-i Khamsa*, p. 16.

22. Jami, "Silsilat adh-dhahab," in *Haft Aurang*, pp. 8–9.

23. Rumi, *Mathnawī*, vol. 1, line 529; cf. also Jami, "Yūsuf u Zulaikhā," in *Haft Aurang*, p. 583, and M. Khaqani, *Ḥilya*, p. 9.

24. Arberry, *Discourses of Rumi*, p. 151.

25. Sa'di, *Būstān*, p. 5. The poem was imitated by many other poets in the Persian tradition.

26. Ikram, *Armaghān-i Pāk*, p. 174.

27. Naziri, *Dīwān*, p. 11, *ghazal* no. 15. The formulation is somewhat reminiscent of the—more modest—claim of the Salimiyya, according to which "Muhammad knew the text of the Koran by heart before he was called to be a prophet" (Hallaj, *Kitāb aṭ-ṭawāsīn*, commentary p. 159).

28. Aslah, *Tadhkirat-i shu'arā-i Kashmīr*, suppl., 1:135: Bulbul Kashmiri.

29. Jami, "Silsilat adh-dhahab," in *Haft Aurang*, p. 9, and "Yūsuf u Zulaikhā," *Haft Aurang*, p. 585.

30. Jami, *Dīwān*, p. 147, *ghazal* no. 37.

31. Andrae, *Die person Muhammads*, p. 86.

32. Darmesteter, *Chants populaires des Afghans*, no. 41, "L'oiseau du Prophète"; similarly in Baloch, *Mu'jizā*, p. 209, with the difference that the bird is from silver, gold, and ambergris; in another Sindhi poem (*Mu'jizā*, p. 212), a bird of pearl comes to life.

33. Abu Nu'aim, *Dalā'il an-nubuwwa*, pp. 383–85, *istisqā'*; water miracles, pp. 345–53.

34. Köprülüzade, *Eski Şairlerimiz*, pp. 201–2. This poem is not found in Fuzuli's *Divan*, ed. Gölpĭnarlĭ, but there one of the last *ghazal*s ends with the line (p. 310):

Don't say, Fuzuli, that it is difficult to reach the hoped-for goal—
Is it not sufficient to keep the hem of the law of Ahmad the Elect?

35. Abu Nu'aim, *Dalā'il an-nubuwwa*, pp. 353–68, deals with food miracles.

36. Baihaqi, *Dalā'il an-nubuwwa*, 1:196.

37. Abu Nu'aim, *Dalā'il an-nubuwwa*, p. 155.

38. A green lizard greeted the Prophet with *As-salām 'alaika yā nabī Muḥammad, yā rasūl Allāh!* Therefore the green lizard is called in Swahili *mjusi muumini*, "the Muslim lizard." Knappert, *Swahili Islamic Poetry*, 1:35.

39. Abu Nu'aim, *Dalā'il an-nubuwwa*, pp. 331–37, "The greeting of the trees"; pp. 318–20, the talking wolf; p. 321, the lizard; pp. 324–31, the prostration of sheep, camels, etc., where the famous story occurs: When the Meccans saw that a camel prostrated itself before the Prophet they thought it would be better if they too would do so, but the Prophet remarked: "If it were allowed that anyone prostrate himself before another human being, I would say that wives should prostrate themselves before their husbands"—a tradition repeated by Ghazzali, and still well known, particularly in Muslim India.

40. Rumi, *Mathnawī*, vol. 1, lines 2154 ff.

41. Jami, "Silsilat adh-dhahab," in *Haft Aurang*, p. 9.

42. Abu Nu'aim, *Dalā'il an-nubuwwa*, p. 370.

43. See Andrae, *Die person Muhammads*, p. 48; it is also often mentioned in the legendary *maghāzī* tales.

44. Braune, *Die Futūḥ al-ġaib*, p. 14, citing Shattanaufi, *Bahjat al-asrār*, p. 26.

45. Baloch, *Mu'jizā*, introduction p. 6. For this reason one finds a great number of popular books on the Prophet's miracles in all Islamic languages. Among the

most recent, one may mention Mehmet Öten's Turkish work *Peygamberimizin mucizeleri*, and Tayyib Hashmi's Urdu publication *Muʿjizāt-i sarwar-i kāʾināt*, which bears on the title page the sentence "If you wish the kindness and love of His Highness [the Prophet], then read this book!"

46. Nabhani, *Al-majmūʿa an-nabhāniyya*, pp. 477–79.

47. Abu Nuʿaim, *Dalāʾil an-nubuwwa*, pp. 340–45.

48. Rumi, *Dīwān*, nos. 1649, 427; *Mathnawī*, vol. 1, lines 2115 ff.

49. Abu Nuʿaim, *Dalāʾil an-nubuwwa*, p. 320. A Hadrami poem (Snouck Hurgronje, "Zur Dichtkunst der Bâ ʿAṭwah in Hadhramaut," p. 107) ends:

> Our final word is: Utter blessing upon [the Prophet] to whom the gazelle spoke,
> Muhammad, the model of Shafiʿi as well as of Abu Hanifa!

Even Damiri mentions this story in his zoological encyclopedia, *Kitāb al-ḥayawān*, 2:126–27. In Swahili too an epic poem has been composed about the speaking gazelle; see Dammann, *Dichtung in der Lamu-Mundart des Suaheli*, p. 285. The story was well known in Bengal; see Roy, *Islamic Syncretistic Tradition*, p. 102.

50. Thus Darmesteter, *Chants populaires des Afghans*, no. 40. Cf. also Serjeant, *Prose and Poetry from Hadramaut*, p. 70, text no. 11.

51. Baloch, *Muʿjizā*, pp. 130 ff.

52. Baloch, *Muʿjizā*, p. 146.

53. Abu Nuʿaim, *Dalāʾil an-nubuwwa*, p. 154.

54. Rumi, *Mathnawī*, vol. 3, lines 3110 ff.

55. The finest examples are found in Jami, as in the third *naʿt* in "Tuḥfat al-aḥrār," *Haft Aurang*, pp. 379–80; "Salamān u Absāl," ibid., p. 453; "Yūsuf u Zulaikhā," ibid., p. 583; and a long *qaṣīda* in *Dīwān*, pp. 82–84, in which the poet enumerates all the Prophet's miracles. The *qaṣīda* begins in classical style with the description of the poet's journey to Medina and then tells of the sighing palm trunk and the advancing trees, of the poisoned sheep and the witness of the wolf, of the prostration of the lion and the appearance of the spider and the dove to protect the cave where the Prophet and Abu Bakr were hiding; food miracles, water miracles, and the like are not lacking either, and Jami also tells that the Prophet did not cast a shade. He closes with the lines:

> Due to all the happy things [mentioned in it] the eulogy for him grants the soul steadfastness;
> This is the pure water of life; be the tongues wetted with it!

56. Baloch, *Muʿjizā*, p. 176.

57. This is clearly expressed by Bodley, *The Messenger*, p. 4: "The nomads with whom I lived on the desert did not speak of Mohammed as someone remote and mystic, as Christians do of Jesus . . . [they] spoke of the founder of their faith as someone they knew." And this experience, he says, induced him to write a book about the life of the Prophet.

58. Goldziher, "The Appearance of the Prophet in Dreams," gives many examples of dreams in which theological and political issues were settled through the Prophet's interference. The instances cited in history and literature are much too numerous to be quoted here, but we may mention some notable examples. One of

the earliest works on dreams of the Prophet is Ibn Abi'd-Dunya's *Kitāb al-manām*; see Kienberg, "The Book of Dreams by Ibn Abī'd-Dunyā," introduction and text, where numerous examples are given. S. A. Krenkow, "The Tārīkh Baghdād," Appendix: "The Appearance of the Prophet in Dreams," pp. 77–79. The Prophet might appear to a poet in his dream because he had composed a particularly touching threnody, *marthiya*, on the events of Kerbela (see Azad, *Khizāna-yi ʿāmira*, p. 22), and Shah Waliullah of Delhi devoted a special treatise to *ḥadīth* taught by the Prophet to a dreaming scholar: *Ad-durr ath-thamīn fī mubashsharāt an-nabī al-amīn*. A dream of special interest is told about the Kubrawi mystic ʿAlaʾuddaula as-Simnani, who "ate" the Prophet, which is interpreted as meaning that he incorporated into himself the *sunna* of the Prophet; his feeling that his feet were heavy after this kind of "communion" is an indication of his being straight and without deviation on the Prophet's path. Cordt, *Die Sitzungen des ʿAlāʾ ad-dawla as-Simnānī*, p. 126. Numerous instances of guiding dreams of the Prophet in the circles of the founders of the theological school of Deoband in the last decades of the nineteenth century are attested in Metcalf, *Muslim Revival in British India*, pp. 43 (Shah Waliullah), 79, 80, 175, 177 ff., 272; someone's identity as a *sayyid* was ascertained by such a dream, p. 247. The medieval Persian panegyrist Anwari—certainly not a paragon of piety—mentions such dreams several times in his verse (*Dīwān*, pp. 342, 345), and the Ilkhanid vizier Rashiduddin was introduced in a dream to the Prophet by Abu Bakr, ʿUmar, and ʿUthman to discuss the problem of his *ummiyya*, "illiteracy," with him (Van Ess, *Der Wesir und seine Gelehrten*, pp. 19–20). Even in our day such appearances are quite common; in December 1982 a Turkish woman told me that the Prophet had appeared to her mother and persuaded her that she, the daughter, might marry a German non-Muslim (who later converted to Islam).

59. Dailami, *Sīrat Abī ʿAbdillāh Ibn al-Khafīf*, chap. 2, para. 6, a story often retold, as in ʿAttar, *Tadhkirat al-auliyāʾ*, 2:127. For the same legend applied to Abu Saʿid (d. 1049) see Meier, *Abū Saʿīd-i Abūʾl Ḫayr*, p. 69.

60. Aflaki, *Manāqib al-ʿārifīn*, p. 326, chap. 3, para. 252.

61. Aflaki, *Manāqib al-ʿārifīn*, p. 334, chap. 3, para. 260.

62. Aflaki, *Manāqib al-ʿārifīn*, p. 767, chap. 6, para. 19.

63. Jami, *Nafaḥāt al-uns*, p. 373, a dream by Shadhili.

64. Meier, *Abū Saʿīd-i Abūʾl Ḫayr*, p. 257, and similarly Andrae, *Die person Muhammads*, p. 377.

65. S. B. Bukhari, *Jawāhir al-auliyā*, p. 310.

66. Hamadhani, *Maqāmāt*, no. 10, in Rotter, *Vernunft ist nichts als Narretei*, pp. 61–62.

67. Razi, *The Path of God's Bondsmen*, pp. 292–93.

68. Padwick, *Muslim Devotions*, pp. 149–50. The idea that the Prophet's fragrance is felt even in a dream appearance seems to have been rather common, for Ibn al-Farid says in one of his odes:

> The perfume of musk is wafted abroad whenever my name is mentioned,
> Since thou didst summon me to kiss thy mouth.

Arberry, *Aspects of Islamic Civilization*, p. 66, and Nicholson, *Studies in Islamic Mysticism*, p. 174.

69. Mustaqimzade, *Tuḥfa-i khaṭṭāṭīn*, p. 105. Similarly, a Turkish author of the sixteenth century, Thana'i, was induced by a dream of Fariduddin ʿAttar to write a book *Shawāhid an-nubuwwa*, "Testimonies for the Prophethood," because, as ʿAttar suggested, this was the "subject which would eventually secure him a place in Paradise." Thana'i dedicated his work to Sultan Suleyman the Magnificent. Minorsky, *Catalogue of the Turkish Manuscripts*, p. 15, no. T 410.

CHAPTER FIVE

1. See Jairazbhoy (published in 1937 with an introduction by the Aga Khan); review by Arthur Jeffery, *MW* 28 (1938): 180–86. The book by Q. M. S. S. Mansoorpuri, *Rahmatun lilʿalamin: Mercy for the Worlds*, was not accessible to me although there are two translations, one (in three volumes) by A. J. Siddiqui, with introduction by S. S. Nadvi (1978), and one with the title *Muhammad, Mercy for the Universe*, translated by A. Rauf (1979).
2. Razi, *The Path of God's Bondsmen*, p. 325.
3. Abu Nuʿaim, *Dalāʾil an-nubuwwa*, chap. 1.
4. Jami, *Dīwān*, p. 67, no. 43; cf. his "Yūsuf u Zulaikhā," in *Haft Aurang*, p. 587.
5. See Schimmel, "Der Regen als Symbol in der Religionsgeschichte."
6. Nwyia, *Exégèse coranique et langage mystique*, pp. 326 ff.
7. In Siddiqi and Asi, *Armaghān-i naʿt*, pp. 71, 74.
8. Rumi, *Dīwān*, no. 2443.
9. ʿAbdul Latif, *Shāh jō Risālō*, "Sur Sārang," cantos 7, 10, 29, 30, 33, 34, *wāʾy*.
10. For the whole problem see Andrae, *Die person Muhammads*, pp. 234–44; Huitema, *De voorspraak (shafāʿa) in den Islam*.
11. Hassan ibn Thabit, *Dīwān*, no. 130, verse 9.
12. Andrae, *Die person Muhammads*, pp. 236–38. A very old collection of *ḥadīth*, Asad ibn Musa's *Kitāb az-zuhd*, pp. 73–76, contains this tradition in slightly different wording. See also Leszynski, *Mohammedanische Traditionen über das Jüngste Gericht*.
13. The *nafsī nafsī* of all prophets and, contrasting with it, Muhammad's *ummatī ummatī* is a favorite topic of folk poetry. See Baloch, *Ṭih akharyūñ*, 1:37.
14. Furuzanfar, *Aḥādīth-i Mathnawī*, no. 225.
15. Aflaki, *Manāqib al-ʿārifīn*, p. 285, chap. 3, para. 197.
16. Andrae, *Die person Muhammads*, after al-Hakim at-Tirmidhi, *Nawādir al-uṣūl*, p. 294.
17. Padwick, *Muslim Devotions*, p. 41.
18. From *Dalāʾil al-khairāt wa shawāriq al-anwār fī dhikr aṣ-ṣalāt ʿalā an-nabī al-mukhtār*, trans. in Padwick, *Muslim Devotions*, p. 42.
19. Graham, *Divine Word and Prophetic Word*, Saying no. 59; Andrae, *Die person Muhammads*, p. 243.
20. Furuzanfar, *Aḥādīth-i Mathnawī*, no. 331. "There is no prophet from among the children of Adam up to Muhammad who is not under Muhammad's banner."

21. Goethe, *West-Östlicher Divan*, Noten und Abhandlungen.

22. Padwick, *Muslim Devotions*, p. 44; cf. Aflaki, *Manāqib al-ʿārifīn*, p. 202, chap. 3, para. 111.

23. Ibn Daqiq al-ʿId, quoted in A. S. Husain, *Al-adab aṣ-ṣūfī*, p. 235.

24. Furuzanfar, *Aḥādīth-i Mathnawī*, no. 79.

25. Siddiqi and Asi, *Armaghān-i naʿt*, p. 229.

26. *Muslim Digest*, January–February 1981, pp. 55–80.

27. Thus Menghi Faqir Shar (d. 1895) in his Sindhi *Sīḥarfī*, in Baloch, *Ṭih akharyūñ*, 1:150.

28. Jami, "Salamān u Absāl," in *Haft Aurang*, p. 451.

29. Abun-Nasr, *The Tijaniyya*, p. 43.

30. Nabhani, *Al-majmūʿa an-nabhāniyya*, 1:457.

31. Nabhani, *Al-majmūʿa an-nabhāniyya*, 1:437.

32. ʿAbdul Latif, *Risālō*. "Sur Kalyāṇ," canto 1:2.

33. Mir, *Kulliyāt*, p. 354.

34. Buddruss, *Khowar-Texte*, p. 72. For Pashto see Enevoldsen, *O Måne!* no. 197: "God is my Lord, the Koran my Pir [mystical guide], the Messenger of God will intercede for me." Likewise Nasir-i Khusrau, the great Ismaili missionary of the eleventh century, expresses in one of his Persian poems the "hope that by the grace of God I may be one of the lowest members of the community (*umma*) of Muhammad." *Dīwān ashʿār-i Ḥakīm Nāṣir-i Khusrau*, p. 151.

35. Zajączkowski, "Poezje strofniczne . . . sultan Qanṣūh Gavrī," p. 4.

36. Brunel, *Le monachisme errant dans l'Islam*, p. 150.

37. Yunus Emre, *Divan*, p. 557, no. CCXXV.

38. *Tuḥfa-i Raḥīm Yār Khān*, pp. 13–17.

39. Baloch, *Madāḥūñ ain munājātūñ*, pp. 121–32.

40. Baloch, *Madāḥūñ ain munājātūñ*, p. 313.

41. Siddiqi and Asi, *Armaghān-i naʿt*, p. 140.

42. Yunus Emre, *Divan*, p. 560, no. CCXXX.

43. Yunus Emre, *Divan*, p. 559, no. CCXXIX. Is not Muhammad's role as intercessor indicative of his proximity to God? Najm Razi expresses the mystery of the Prophet's exclamation "My community!" in a strange but fascinating image: "Muhammad . . . has immolated, mothlike, the entirety of his being in the candle of the glory of the unity of the Essence, and sacrificed all of his Muhammadan being to the fiery tongue of love that leaps forth from that candle. He cries out instinctively 'My people! My people!' and the tongue of the candle has become his tongue." Razi, *The Path of God's Bondsmen*, p. 177.

44. Knappert, *Swahili Islamic Poetry*, 1:37.

45. Qaniʿ, *Maqālāt ash-shuʿarā*, p. 468.

46. Darmesteter, *Chants populaires des Afghans*, p. 88, no. 32; cf. also no. 31. Rumi said, much earlier (*Dīwān*, no. 1245):

Whoever has seized one edge of Mustafa's cloak—
I bring him from the depth of Hell to the gardens of Paradise.

47. Naziri, *Dīwān*, p. 472, *qaṣīda* no. 32; cf. p. 491, *qaṣīda* no. 36.

48. In *Kulliyāt-i naʿt-i Maulwī Muḥammad Muḥsin*, pp. 95–123.

49. Naziri, *Dīwān*, p. 450, *qaṣīda* no. 24.

50. S. B. Bukhari, *Jawāhir al-auliyā*, p. 229.

51. Thus in a touching verse in a Sindhi *Sīḥarfī* by Gul Muhammad, in Baloch, *Ṭih akharyūñ*, 1:45, under the letter *y*:

. . . save also mother, father, sisters, brothers, nephews,
bring all of them on the day of Resurrection to Paradise!

52. Arberry, *Discourses of Rumi*, p. 79.

53. Robson, "Blessings on the Prophet," dwells upon this development and quotes forty *ḥadīth* pertaining to the blessings upon the Prophet, taken from Ibshihi's *Mustaṭraf*.

54. Ghazzali, *Iḥyāʾ ʿulūm ad-dīn*, 1:278–79. See also Andrae, *Die person Muhammads*, pp. 276 ff., and Graham, *Divine Word and Prophetic Word*, pp. 176–77, Saying no. 52.

55. Ghazzali, *Iḥyāʾ ʿulūm ad-dīn*, 1:278–80.

56. Sindhi, *Inbāʾ al-anbāʾ*, p. 13, according to Nasaʾi and Ibn Maja. The Prophet admonished the companions to utter the formula of blessing upon him on Friday "because it is brought before me." They asked: "O Messenger of God, how that, when you are already decayed?" He said: "God has prohibited the earth to eat the prophets' bodies." Another tradition claims that "Who says the blessings upon me in my grave, I hear him." See Andrae, *Die person Muhammads*, pp. 285–87. According to some traditions the bodies of the prophets stay in their tombs as fresh as the day that they were buried; Suyuti, the great polymath of Egypt in the late fifteenth century, who was often blessed with the vision of the Prophet, went so far as to declare that even in dire need "the eating of the dead body of a prophet is not permitted" (*lā yajūzu liʾl-muḍṭarr aklu maitati nabiyyin*), for he is still alive (quoted in Sindhi, *Inbāʾ al-anbāʾ*, p. 15).

57. Andrae, *Die person Muhammads*, p. 279.

58. Andrae, *Die person Muhammads*, p. 280, from Qadi ʿIyad, *Shifā*, 2:56.

59. That Muhammad during his night journey met all the previous prophets in Jerusalem is explained by assuming that their bodies are still in their graves but their spirits have been personified (Sindhi, *Inbāʾ al-anbāʾ*, p. 32), but according to another tradition (ibid., p. 35) the bodies of the prophets do not stay in the tomb more than forty days.

60. Ibn Hazm, *Al-faṣl fīʾl-milal . . . waʾn-niḥal*, 1:88–89.

61. Horten, *Die religiöse Gedankenwelt der gebildeten Muslime*, p. 107.

62. Waliullah, *Tafhīmāt*, 1:15.

63. Rumi, *Dīwān*, no. 301: "I bring the blessings on you, so that proximity may grow."

64. Baloch, *Ṭih akharyūñ*, 1:28 (Sahibdina).

65. Siddiqi and Asi, *Armaghān-i naʿt*, p. 109.

66. Makhdum Muhammad Hashim, *Dharīʿat al-wuṣūl ilā janāb ar-rasūl* is a very good collection of *durūd* as used in eighteenth-century Sind.

67. Jeffery, "Litany of Blessings on the Prophet," in *Reader on Islam*, pp. 530–36. Cf. Minorsky, *Catalogue of Turkish Manuscripts*, p. 96, about a manuscript of the *Dalāʾil al-khairāt* (T 459): "An English translation of it was published for private circulation: 'Guide to Happiness; a manual of prayer.' Translated from the

Arabic of al-Jazuli by the Rev. J. B. Pearson. With the life of al-Jazuli, and directions for using the book, from the Arabic by A. G. Ellis. 1907, 76 pages."

68. Padwick, *Muslim Devotions*, p. 146.

69. *EI*, 2:527–28, s.v. Djazuli.

70. Padwick, *Muslim Devotions*, p. 257.

71. Padwick, *Muslim Devotions*, p. 154.

72. Padwick, *Muslim Devotions*, p. 154.

73. Mirghani, *An-nūr al-barrāq*, p. 44; cf. pp. 60 ff.

74. Padwick, *Muslim Devotions*, p. 155.

75. Ghawwasi, *Saiful Mulūk wa Badīʿul Jamāl*, p. 179.

76. Kriss and Kriss-Heinrich, *Volksglaube im Bereich des Islam*, 2:13, after Lane, *Manners and Customs of the Modern Egyptians*, 2:52.

77. A good example is Burney, *Mishkaat us-salawaat: A Bouquet of Blessings*.

78. Gramlich, *Die Gaben der Erkenntnisse des ʿUmar as-Suhrawardī*, pp. 260–61; the Arabic text appears at the margin of Ghazzali's *Iḥyāʾ ʿulūm ad-dīn*.

79. Aflaki, *Manāqib al-ʿārifīn*, p. 412, chap. 3, para. 354.

80. Mahmud, *Al-fikr aṣ-ṣūfī fīʾs-Sūdān*, p. 65.

81. Andrae, *Die person Muhammads*, p. 388.

82. Gilsenan, *Saint and Sufi in Modern Egypt*, p. 14, see also p. 19.

83. Abun-Nasr, *The Tijaniyya*, pp. 51–52, text of the prayer p. 182, Appendix I.

84. Abun-Nasr, *The Tijaniyya*, pp. 52–53, text of prayer p. 187, Appendix I.

85. Abun-Nasr, *The Tijaniyya*, p. 31.

86. Abun-Nasr, *The Tijaniyya*, p. 180.

87. Littmann, *Mohammad im Volksepos* (the first line of the poem is not translated quite correctly there).

88. Kahle, *Der Leuchtturm von Alexandrien*, German text p. 50, Arabic p. 14.

89. Zajaçzkowski, *Poezje stroficzne ʿAšïq-paša*, p. 8.

90. Baloch, *Ṭih akharyūñ*, 2:222 (Thanaʾullah Thana).

91. Baloch, *Munāqibā*, p. 235.

92. Baloch, *Ṭih akharyūñ*, 1:55 (Gul Muhammad, 1861).

93. Yunus Emre, *Divan*, p. 524, no. CLXXV.

94. ʿAli ibn Abi Talib is connected in a mysterious way with the bees, and is sometimes even called "amīr of the bees" because he was the commander of a swarm of believing bees; a number of unbelievers, seeing such a miracle, embraced Islam. Paret, *Die legendäre Maghāzī-Literatur*, pp. 195–96.

95. Baloch, *Munāqibā*, pp. 196–98. One also remembers here the line in another Sindhi *Sīḥarfī* (Baloch, *Ṭih akharyūñ*, 1:51), by Gul Muhammad (1869), that the remembrance, *dhikr*, of the Prophet is "much sweeter than butter, honey, and sugar."

CHAPTER SIX

1. For the whole subject see Andrae, *Die person Muhammads*, pp. 272–74, and Fischer, "Vergöttlichung und Tabuisierung der Namen Muhammads." Badaoni tells in *Muntakhab at-tawārīkh*, 2:314 (trans. 2:324), that the emperor Akbar, after

introducing the *dīn-i ilāhī*, forbade people to use names like Muhammad, Ahmad, and other names related to the Prophet. That seems to be exaggerated, but it shows that these names were considered to express a proximity to the Prophet.

2. Yunus Emre, *Divan*, p. 562, no. CCXXXIII; cf. also no. CCXXIV.

3. Hassan ibn Thabit, *Dīwān*, no. 152; Abu Nuʿaim, *Dalāʾil an-nubuwwa*, p. 11.

4. Grimme, "Der Name Muhammad," thinks that Muhammad, like Ahmad, was previously a theophoric name, abbreviated from *Muḥammadʾīl*, "Praised be God." He also mentions (p. 26) that on some early Kufic tombstones from Fustat, even the feminine form *Muḥammada* is found. The form itself is perfectly sound, but it seems that it was no longer possible to use it in later times, when the respect for the Prophet's name had become a major concern of the faithful Muslims. See also Jurji, "Pre-Islamic Use of the Name Muḥammad."

5. Tapish, *Gulzār-i naʿt*, fol. 13b.

6. Naziri, *Dīwān*, p. 484.

7. Naziri, *Dīwān*, p. 486, *qaṣīda* no. 36.

8. Padwick, *Muslim Devotions*, p. 75; see also Razi, *The Path of God's Bondsmen*, p. 91, about the "laud" connected with the Prophet.

9. Sanaʾi, *Dīwān*, p. 363.

10. Padwick, *Muslim Devotions*, p. 43.

11. Baihaqi, *Dalāʾil an-nubuwwa*, pp. 121 ff.

12. Baihaqi, *Dalāʾil an-nubuwwa*, p. 121.

13. Baihaqi, *Dalāʾil an-nubuwwa*, p. 122; cf. Tirmidhi, *Shamāʾil al-Muṣṭafā* with commentary of Bajuri, pp. 286–88.

14. Baihaqi, *Dalāʾil an-nubuwwa*, 69; Abu Nuʿaim, *Dalāʾil an-nubuwwa*, pp. 26–27.

15. Rumi, *Mathnawī*, vol. 1, lines 726 ff.; Watt, "His Name is Aḥmad," states by means of statistics that Ahmad as a proper name occurs very rarely in early Islam, and discusses the problem of the Paraclete, refuting an article by A. Guthrie and E. F. F. Bishop, "The Paraclete, Almunhamama and Ahmad," which appeared in *MW* 41 (1951).

16. Goldziher, "Himmlische und irdische Namen."

17. Razi, *The Path of God's Bondsmen*, p. 249.

18. Canteins, *La voie des lettres*, chap. v: "Ṭâhâ."

19. Massignon, "La philosophie orientale d'Avicenne," p. 11, about *Yāsīn*.

20. M. Khaqani, *Ḥilya*, p. 7. In ʿUthman al-Mirghani's devotional poetry, the name Taha is very frequently used; it seems to appear often in connection with Muhammad's role as intercessor and is an important ingredient of popular songs in honor of the Prophet; it is then also combined with Yasin. See Bannerth, "Lieder ägyptischer *meddâḥîn*":

> You are, O Taha, for me my beloved,
> You are, O Taha, my intercessor!

Very similar verses occur in Sindhi folk poetry; see Baloch, *Maulūd*, pp. 151 ff. A charming expression of a popular poet's love for Taha is a poem by the Hausa poet Ibrahim Niass, quoted in Hiskett, "The 'Community of Grace,'" p. 117:

My heart does not crave for beautiful girls—
What are beautiful girls? Consider them a mirage beside
Taha [Muhammad], the Trustworthy, the holy one.
I have forgotten Laila and Maila and Tandami
Because of Taha, the trustworthy one of God, my known love . . .

One wonders whether line 332 in Ibn al-Farid's *Tā'iyya* contains an allusion to the Prophet's name Taha. It reads:

No wonder that I lord over all who lived before me,
Since I grasped the firmest stay in Taha.

Nicholson, *Studies in Islamic Mysticism*, p. 231, refers this to Sura 20, "Taha," verse 7, but a double meaning cannot be excluded.

21. Amir Khusrau, *Majnūn Lailā*, p. 10; he combines the letters *yā-sīn* with the teeth, because *sīn* stands metaphorically—because of its shape, س —for "teeth."

22. My colleague Georg Buddruss, of the University of Mainz, kindly sent me this *na't* in Shina with his explanations; he mentions that it is sung to a very sweet melody. It was published in Rawalpindi in 1974.

23. Tapish, *Gulzār-i na't*, fol. 12b, changes the participles *muṣṭafā*, *murtaḍā*, and *mujtabā* into the related verbal nouns: the Prophet, as Muṣṭafā, is "the cypress of the garden of *iṣṭifā*, selection"; as Murtaḍā he is "the boxtree of the orchard of *irtiḍā*, of being pleased"; and as Mujtabā, "the root of the branch of *ijtibā*, election"; and on the whole, he is "the origin of the twigs of the *Panjtan*," that is, Muhammad, 'Ali, Fatima, Hasan, and Husain. (Tapish was a Shia poet.)

24. Baljon, *Modern Muslim Koran Interpretation*, p. 99, mentions the way the Pakistani modernist Ghulam Parvez explains the divine address to the Prophet *Ya mudaththir!* He derives the word from *daththara*, *tadthīr*, in the special meaning "to arrange one's nest," which he then interprets as "setting one's house in order," so that *mudaththir* would be, in modern terms, the "world reformer," who is addressed by God: *Qum*, "Rise!" That is, he is called to start preaching world revolution.

25. Fischer, "Vergöttlichung und Tabuisierung der Namen Muhammads," p. 328. Becker, *Islamstudien*, 2:104, speaks of the tendency for "the names of Muhammad [to be] treated in the *Dalā'il al-khairāt* analogous to the names of God," when the *Dalā'il* and related works were used in East Africa.

26. One says therefore, when introducing a *ḥadīth* without mentioning Muhammad's name: "He—may God bless him and give him peace!—said . . . ." A Koranic quotation begins with "He—Great is His Majesty [or, Most High]—said . . . ."

27. Jami, *Dīwān*, p. 73, no. 47, in a *Salām*, "Greeting," for the Prophet. The *salām* became a very common poetic form in the later Persian and especially the Urdu traditions. See the small, modern collection by Siddiqi and Asi, *Muntakhab salām*, in Urdu.

28. The list is taken from my copy of the Koran (Lahore: Taj Company), which contains $17 \times 6 = 102$ names, among them twice *Rasūl ar-raḥmat*, plus *nabī ar-raḥmat*, while his *kunya* Abu'l-Qasim is not mentioned.

29. S. B. Bukhari, *Jawāhir al-auliyā*, pp. 221 ff.

30. Staples, "Muhammad, A Talismanic Force," describes a golden amulet with the ninety-nine names of the Prophet (without, however, realizing that Taha and Yasin are here his names and not, as he thinks, the names of Suras 20 and 36).

31. S. B. Bukhari, *Jawāhir al-auliyā*, pp. 223–24.

32. Edier and Young, "A List of the Appellations of the Prophet Muhammad," lists 201 names, found in an Arabic manuscript dated 1268 (A.D. 1851–2), now preserved in Leeds.

33. Horten, *Die religiöse Vorstellungswelt des Volkes*, p. 15. ʿAbdul Haqq Muhaddith Dihlawi, *Madārij an-nubuwwa*, pp. 293–308, enumerates more than four hundred names.

34. Nizami, "Makhzan al-asrār," *naʿt* no. 3, in *Kulliyāt-i Khamsa*, p. 23. Yemenite striped cloth was highly prized among the Arabs. Jami, *Dīwān*, p. 177, no. 117. In folk poetry, the appellations connected with the Prophet's Arab background appear frequently; thus in *Sīḥarfī* the letter *q* can stand for *Quraishi*, the *ʿain* for *ʿarab*; this word is sometimes lengthened, *ʿārab*, for the sake of the meter. A good example of such distortions appears in Baloch, *Ṭih akharyūñ*, 2:190.

35. Jami, "Salamān u Absāl," in *Haft Aurang*, p. 454.

36. Jami, "Iskandarnāma," in *Haft Aurang*, p. 915. Muhammad is, as the Urdu poet Tapish sang in the early nineteenth century (*Gulzār-i naʿt*, fol. 11b), not only "the sweet-singing nightingale of the rosegarden of Divine manifestation" but also "the twig of the rose of the rose parterre of Batha and Medina."

37. Jami, "Tuḥfat al-aḥrār," fifth *naʿt*, in *Haft Aurang*, p. 381.

38. A good survey of mystical epithets of the Prophet is the index of Baqli's *ʿAbhar al-ʿāshiqīn*; among the dozens of poetical addresses and attributes one finds, for example, "the lord of the lovers," "the falcon of the garden of Reality," "the sun of the prophets and full moon of the saints," "the lion of the meadow of the paradise of Intellect," "the bride of the palace of Unity," "the traveler in the deserts of isolation, *tajrīd*," etc.

39. Fischer, "Vergöttlichung und Tabuisierung der Namen Muhammads," deals in detail with these topics.

40. Busiri, *Die Burda*, ed. Ralfs, line 146.

41. Nabhani, *Al-majmūʿa an-nabhāniyya*, 3:232–35. For other poems of al-Burʿi (d. 1058) see Andrae, *Die person Muhammads*, pp. 337, 389.

42. Fischer, "Vergöttlichung und Tabuisierung der Namen Muhammads," pp. 332 ff.

43. Birge, *The Bektashi Order of Dervishes*, p. 268.

44. Nicholson, *Studies in Islamic Mysticism*, p. 105, from Jili's Perfect Man: "His original name is Muhammad, his name of honor Abu'l-Qasim, his description ʿAbdallah, and his title Shamsuddin."

45. Eaton, *Sufis of Bijapur*, p. 171.

46. Quoted in Siddiqi and Asi, *Armaghān-i naʿt*, p. 49.

47. Ghalib, *Kulliyāt-i fārsī*, 5:16–27, *naʿt* no. 3; see Schimmel, "Ghalib's *qaṣīda* in Honor of the Prophet."

48. Hallaj, "Ṭāsīn as-sirāj," in *Kitāb aṭ-ṭawāsīn*, p. 14.

49. Jurji, *Illumination in Islamic Mysticism*, pp. 84 ff.

50. Deladrière, *La Profession de Foi d'Ibn ʿArabī*, p. 128.

51. Jurji, *Illumination in Islamic Mysticism*, p. 86.
52. Baloch, *Maulūd*, p. 12, no. 23.
53. Cachia, "The Prophet's Shirt."
54. Nizami, "Makhzan al-asrār," in *Kulliyāt-i Khamsa*, p. 16.
55. ʿAttar, *Muṣībatnāma*, p. 20.
56. Jami, "Tuḥfat al-aḥrār," in *Haft Aurang*, p. 376, *naʿt* no. 1.
57. Miskin, "Risāla-i sulūk," in *Ladhdhat-i Miskīn*, 2:84.
58. ʿAttar, *Manṭiq uṭ-ṭair*, p. 24; cf. *Muṣībatnāma*, p. 22.
59. ʿAttar, *Ushturnāma*, p. 95, chap. 12, para. 7.
60. See Karahan, *Islam-Türk edebiyatînda Kîrk hadis*.
61. Jami, "Iskandarnāma," in *Haft Aurang*, p. 915.
62. Ramakrishna, *Panjabi Sufi Poets*, p. 99. The speculations with the *m* go back to early Islamic times: a sect called Muhammadiyya or Mīmiyya claimed divinity for Muhammad; their leader was executed between 892 and 902 (*Handwörterbuch des Islam*, s.v. Muḥammadiyya). At the same time, attempts at giving Muhammad's name a cabalistic interpretation are found in Hallaj, *Kitāb aṭ-ṭawāsīn*, "Ṭāsīn as-sirāj," p. 14.
63. Amir Khusrau, *Dīwān*, p. 596.
64. Rumi, *Dīwān*, no. 1578.
65. Arberry, *Discourses of Rumi*, p. 226.
66. Further examples are given in Schimmel, "Ghalib's *qaṣīda* in Praise of the Prophet," p. 209 n. 32: Shabistari, *Gulshan-i Rāz*, uses the *ḥadīth qudsī*, as does Naziri, *Dīwān*, p. 11, *ghazal* no. 15 (in combination with *qāba qausain*). See also Baloch, *Ṭih akharyūñ*, 1:41. A little Urdu poem from the Deccan by Qazi Mahmud of Gogi plays skillfully with this *ḥadīth qudsī*:

> If Muhammad becomes our help,
> then solve the riddle of the monotheist, O Mahmud:
> All our grief and pain will be refuted
> When for us *Aḥmad* becomes *Aḥad*, "One."

Interestingly, the poem consists exclusively of undotted letters, for the real names of the Prophet are not "blackened" by the use of diacritical marks (see chapter 7 below). Sayed, "Dīwān Qazi Maḥmūd Baḥrī of Gogi," no. 5, stanza 5. The importance of the letter *mīm* in the relation between *Aḥmad* and *Aḥad* also plays a role in Bengali Muslim creation epics. See Roy, *Islamic Syncretistic Tradition*, p. 124: one *mīm* gave birth to three names in the three worlds: "The name Aḥmad was remembered in heaven, that of Muḥammad on earth, and that of Maḥmūd by the snakes in hell." The tradition *Anā Aḥmad bilā mīm* is even found in some of the Ismaili *ginān*s, thus in the *Būjh Niranjan* (information kindly supplied by Ali S. Asani).
67. Jami, "Yūsuf u Zulaikhā," in *Haft Aurang*, p. 583. According to Jili, the floor of the eighth paradise is the roof of the Divine Throne; it is the "lauded station," *al-maqām al-maḥmūd*, which is promised to Muhammad (Sura 17:79). See Nicholson, *Studies in Islamic Mysticism*, p. 136.
68. Jami, "Silsilat adh-dhahab," in *Haft Aurang*, p. 9.
69. Deladrière, *La Profession de Foi d'Ibn ʿArabi*, pp. 136–37.
70. Jami, "Silsilat adh-dhahab," in *Haft Aurang*, p. 9.

71. Miskin, "Ramz al-maḥbūb," in *Ladhdhat-i Miskīn*, 2:86, combines the *alif-lām-mīm* at the beginning of Sura 2 with the three groups of seekers: *alif* are those, young and old, who worship God in His Oneness (*waḥdāniyya*) according to Hafiz's verse:

> There is nothing on my heart's tablet but the *alif* of my beloved's stature—
> What can I do? My teacher did not teach me any other letter.

Lām are those who, although they accept the *waḥdāniyya*, that is, the state of absolute Unity, yet accept the prophets as well, "for the sheer acceptance of the *waḥdāniyya* without the acceptance of the offices of prophethood does not lead to salvation." But *mīm* are "those beloved ones who accept Muhammad in his being God's beloved," *maḥbūbiyyat-i khudā*. The Indian Naqshbandi mystic here clearly points to the high rank of those who believe in Muhammad's unique position, and ranks them higher than the pure "believers in God's Unity," which category also comprises non-Muslims.

72. An interesting modern explanation of the letter *mīm* is given in Canteins, *La voie des lettres*, pp. 35 ff., where he describes the *m*, which in its isolated form looks somewhat like a bell, as "la chute vers l'abîme"; it is the letter connected with the revelation that reached Muhammad "like a bell," while the upright *alif* points to his *miʿrāj*, the upward way to the Divine Unity. The idea is taken over from Schuon, *Le Soufisme*, p. 144, where the word *rasūl*, "Messenger," is explained as pertaining to God's descent into the world in the Night of Might (*lailat al-qadr*), which corresponds to man's being elevated toward God in the night of the Heavenly Journey, *miʿrāj*.

73. Friedmann, *Shaykh Aḥmad Sirhindī*, p. 15.

74. Deladrière, *La Profession de Foi d'Ibn ʿArabī*, p. 14.

75. Mustaqimzade, *Tuḥfa-i khaṭṭāṭīn*, p. 4.

76. Ghalib, *Kulliyāt-i Fārsī*, vol. 5, *naʿt* no. 3; Schimmel, "Ghalib's *qaṣīda* in Praise of the Prophet."

77. Deladrière, *La Profession de Foi d'Ibn ʿArabī*, p. 136.

78. Iqbal, *Bāng-i Darā*, p. 231.

79. Siddiqi and Asi, *Armaghān-i naʿt*, p. 64.

80. ʿAbd Rabb an-nabī in Egypt (d. 1397), mentioned by Mustaqimzade, *Tuḥfa-i khaṭṭāṭīn*, p. 64.

81. Ghawwasi, *Saiful Mulūk wa Badīʿul Jamāl*, pp. 4–5.

CHAPTER SEVEN

1. For the concept of light in the history of religion see Andrae, *Die person Muhammads*, pp. 319–21.

2. Allusions to the "light" occur very frequently in titles of books dealing with the Prophet or with *ḥadīth*, from the collection of *ḥadīth* entitled *Mishkāt al-maṣābīh*, "The Niche for Lamps," to ʿAqqad's *Maṭāliʿ an-nūr*, "The Places Where the Light Rises"; from Busiri's *Al-kawākib ad-durriyya*, "The Radiant Planets . . . ," to Kīsakürek's modern Turkish poetry with the title *Çöle inen nur*, "The Light That Descended into the Desert."

3. Ikram, *Armaghān-i Pāk*, p. 128.

4. Hassan ibn Thabit, *Dīwān*, no. 5, line 18.

5. Hassan ibn Thabit, *Dīwān*, no. 34, line 8: cf. also no. 9, line 21. Ibn ʿArabi attributes to Muhammad's companion Ibn ʿAbbas an ode which, however, contains the whole theosophical terminology of later times; the author—whoever he may be—describes the light of the Prophet that illuminated the earth at his birth, etc. See Deladrière, *La Profession de Foi d'Ibn ʿArabī*, p. 125. Ibn al-Farid, too, sings in his poem "Ṭih ḍalālan":

The people of Badr were in a cavalcade in which thou didst
journey by night;
Nay, rather they traveled by day in the glow of thy luminousness . . .

Cited by Arberry, *Aspects of Islamic Civilization*, p. 66, and Nicholson, *Studies in Islamic Mysticism*, p. 174.

6. Hassan ibn Thabit, *Dīwān*, no. 131, line 9.

7. Cf. also the interpretation given to the Light verse in Aflaki, *Manāqib al-ʿārifīn*, p. 287, chap. 3, para. 200.

8. See Hallaj, "Ṭāsīn as-sirāj," in *Kitāb aṭ-ṭawāsīn*, p. 12, who also combines this epithet with the appellation *Makkī*, "because he is steadfast in His proximity," and *ḥaramī*, "belonging to the [Meccan] sanctuary," "because of his immense bounty."

9. Padwick, *Muslim Devotions*, p. 212; M. Smith, *Readings from the Mystics of Islam*, no. 47. Though it has survived only through a weak chain of transmission, the prayer nevertheless occurs in most mystical works, particularly fittingly in Dard, "Shamʿ-i maḥfil," in *Chahār Risāla*, no. 341, where it forms the last chapter and also Dard's last words; he died shortly after repeating the Prophet's favorite prayer.

10. Böwering, "The Prophet of Islam," pp. 49–50.

11. Böwering, "The Prophet of Islam," pp. 51–52.

12. Böwering, "The Prophet of Islam," p. 54.

13. Deladrière, *La Profession de Foi d'Ibn ʿArabī*, p. 130.

14. Hallaj, "Ṭāsīn as-sirāj," in *Kitāb aṭ-ṭāwāsīn*, pp. 9, 11. See also his poem (Shaibi, *Sharḥ Dīwān al-Ḥallāj*, p. 188, no. 24), with the beginning *ʿIlm an-nubuwwa miṣbāḥun min an-nūr*, "The knowledge of prophethood is a lamp from light. . . ."

15. Furuzanfar, *Aḥādīth-i Mathnawī*, no. 342.

16. Furuzanfar, *Aḥādīth-i Mathnawī*, nos. 44, 87.

17. Sarraj, *Kitāb al-lumaʿ*, p. 209.

18. Deladrière, *La Profession de Foi d'Ibn ʿArabī*, pp. 122, 124–25.

19. Jili, quoted in Nicholson, *Studies in Islamic Mysticism*, p. 122.

20. According to Thaʿlabi, Muhammad's essence was blended from paradisiacal clay and water from the paradisiacal fountain Tasnim, and looked like a white pearl which, overawed by God's loving gaze, began perspiring. From here, the connection with the epithet *durra yatīma*, the "orphaned," that is, unique, pearl could easily be made, which became even more meaningful because Muhammad was an orphan, *yatīm*. For Thaʿlabi see Goldziher, "Neuplatonische und gnostische Elemente im *ḥadīth*." Roy, *Islamic Syncretistic Tradition*, pp. 121 ff., esp. 127 ff. dwells extensively on these stories, which he apparently regards as an indigenous

Bengali tradition. See also ibid., p. 176: *nūr Muḥammad* is hidden in a white pearl in a lotus in the *amrit-kunda* (water of life) located in the second-highest area, the *ʿālam-i jabarūt*. See further Razi, *The Path of God's Bondsmen*, p. 61. Interestingly, a modern version of the old Sufi myth is found in ʿAbd ar-Rahim, *Islamic Book of the Dead*, pp. 20–22. There, not only the "white pearl like the peacock" and the creation from the sweat of the primordial messenger is mentioned but also the ranks of men that differ according to the part of the preexistent form of Muhammad on which their eyes fell: whoever saw his head became a caliph and sultan among creatures, whoever saw his left hand became a scribe, whoever saw his shadow became a singer, and so forth; those who saw nothing became Jews, Christians, Magians, or simply unbelievers.

21. M. Khaqani, *Ḥilya*, pp. 5–6, gives an almost identical description in Turkish verse.

22. ʿAttar, *Manṭiq uṭ-ṭair*, p. 18. See also Amir Khusrau, *Mathnawī Nuh Sipihr*, *naʿt*, pp. 13–18.

23. Yunus Emre, *Divan*, p. 577, no. CCLIII.

24. Enamul Haq, *Sufiism in Bengal*, p. 94.

25. Baloch, *Madāḥūñ*, p. 2, line 10.

26. Rumi, *Dīwān*, no. 1137; *Mathnawī*, vol. 4, line 1861.

27. Jami, *Dīwān*, p. 56, no. 35 (should be 34).

28. Rumi, *Dīwān*, no. 1705.

29. Furuzanfar, *Aḥādīth-i Mathnawī*, no. 134.

30. Paret, *Die legendäre Maghāzī-Literatur*, p. 174.

31. Razi, *The Path of God's Bondsmen*, p. 156.

32. Mustaqimzade, *Tuḥfa-i khaṭṭāṭīn*, pp. 614–15.

33. Qazi Abdal Mannan, *Heritage of Bangladesh*, p. 11.

34. For the whole development see Goldziher, "Neuplatonische und gnostische Elemente im *ḥadīth*," as well as the second half of Andrae, *Die person Muhammads*. See also Nyberg, *Ibn al-ʿArabī*, and Nicholson, *Studies in Islamic Mysticism*.

35. ʿAttar, *Tadhkirat al-auliyā'*, 1:67; cf. Nicholson, *The Idea of Personality*, pp. 86–87.

36. Qushairi, "Bāb al-maḥabba," in *Risāla*, p. 147; for more examples of this attitude see Meier, *Abū Saʿīd-i Abūʾl Ḫayr*, pp. 314 ff.

37. Qushairi, *Risāla*, p. 17.

38. Hujwiri, *Kashf al-maḥjūb*, p. 283.

39. Furuzanfar, *Aḥādīth-i Mathnawī*, no. 301; Abū Nuʿaim, *Dalā'il an-nubuwwa*, pp. 16 ff.; Goldziher, "Neuplatonische und gnostische Elemente im *ḥadīth*," pp. 324 ff. In the Shiite tradition, this includes the luminous preexistence of ʿAli, Fatima, Hasan, and Husain.

40. Razi, *The Path of God's Bondsmen*, p. 78.

41. Furuzanfar, *Aḥādīth-i Mathnawī*, no. 546.

42. Baloch, *Ṭih akharyūñ*, 1:30, 36 offers particularly good examples.

43. Furuzanfar, *Aḥādīth-i Mathnawī*, no. 70.

44. Furuzanfar, *Aḥādīth-i Mathnawī*, no. 163, from Bukhari and Muslim. In Suyuti's *Al-Jāmiʿ aṣ-ṣaghīr*, quoted by Furuzanfar, the *ḥadīth* occurs with the

addition *la yatazayyā bī*, "for Satan does not put on my form"; that is, to see the Prophet in a dream or a vision is really to see him. However, the interpretation of *ḥaqq*, "truth," as Divine Truth became common at least from Hallaj's days: he interprets this saying as referring to Muhammad in the state of absolute union with God, *ʿain al-jamʿ* (*Kitāb aṭ-ṭawāsīn*, p. 80, commentary on "Ṭāsīn as-sirāj"). Rumi has the Prophet say "When you have seen me you have seen God," and Iqbal takes up the idea in his late verse, *Armaghān-i Ḥijāz*, p. 71. It was widely accepted in this meaning among the Sufis.

45. The short treatises of the Indian Naqshbandi Sufi Miskin in the nineteenth century contain long paragraphs about the *jamāl-i Muḥammadī*, "the Muhammadan beauty," such as: "The True Beloved [God] has taken the mirror of the Muhammadan Essence before His face and said 'I was a hidden treasure . . .' " ("Risāla-i sulūk," in *Ladhdhat-i Miskīn*, 2:74; cf. ibid., 2:88, 96 and the "Ṭarīq-i maḥbūb," ibid., 2:100; and "Dīdar-i yār," ibid., 2:104).

46. M. Khaqani, *Ḥilya*, p. 11.

47. Siddiqi and Asi, *Armaghān-i naʿt*, p. 78.

48. Aflaki, *Manāqib al-ʿārifīn*, p. 379, chap. 3, para. 311.

49. For the idea of the Muhammadan Tree see Jeffery, "Ibn al-ʿArabī's *Shajarat al-kawn*"; Razi, *The Path of God's Bondsmen*, pp. 92, 159, 390.

50. White, "Sufism in Medieval Hindi Literature," pp. 128–29.

51. Miskin, "Shān-i maḥbūb," in *Ladhdhat-i Miskīn*, 2:91–93.

52. Nicholson, *Studies in Islamic Mysticism*, pp. 253–54; Ibn al-Farid's *Tāʾiyya*, line 616. See also Andrae, *Die person Muhammads*, p. 353.

53. Jami, "Salamān u Absāl," in *Haft Aurang*, p. 452.

54. According to Aflaki, *Manāqib al-ʿārifīn*, p. 614, chap. 4, para. 3, even Rumi remarked: "The external scholars know the stories, *akhbār*, of the Prophet; Maulana Shamsuddin knows the mysteries, *asrār*, of the Prophet, and I am the locus of manifestations of the lights, *anwār*, of the Prophet."

55. A. S. Husain, *Al-adab aṣ-ṣūfī*, pp. 230 ff.

56. Deladrière, *La Profession de Foi d'Ibn ʿArabī*, Introduction, pp. 16–18.

57. Aflaki, *Manāqib al-ʿārifīn*, p. 676, chap. 4, para. 77.

58. Deladrière, *La Profession de Foi d'Ibn ʿArabī*, p. 49. See also Nicholson, *Studies in Islamic Mysticism*, chap. 2, about Muhammad's "single nature," *fardiyya*. See also S. Q. A. Husain, *The Pantheistic Monism of Ibn al-ʿArabī*, p. 58.

59. Dard, *ʿIlm ul-kitāb*, p. 505; for a full translation of the passage see Schimmel, *Mystical Dimensions of Islam*, pp. 377–78.

60. Gätje, *Koran und Koranexegese*, p. 306, according to the *tafsīr* of Ibn ʿArabi's commentator, Kashani. See also Aflaki, *Manāqib al-ʿārifīn*, p. 665, chap. 4, para. 67.

61. Schuon, *Le Soufisme*, p. 113.

62. Rumi, *Dīwān*, no. 1793. Cf. also Nizami's well-known line in "Makhzan al-asrār" (*Kulliyāt-i Khamsa*, p. 2):

Ahmad the Messenger, before whom intellect is dust—
Both worlds are bound by his saddle-string (*fitrāk*).

63. Rumi, *Mathnawī*, vol. 7, commentary, p. 87.

64. Andrae, *Die person Muhammads*, pp. 338–39, citing Shattanaufi's *Bahjat al-asrār*, p. 36. *Nāmūs* is the Greek *nomos*, but is used here as an angelic or spiritual power. See *EI*, 1st ed., vol. 3, s.v. *nāmūs*.

65. Nasr, *Ideals and Realities of Islam*, p. 88.

66. Ghalib, *Kulliyāt-i Fārsī*, *naʿt* no. 3, line 52.

67. Hallaj, *Kitāb aṭ-ṭawāsīn*, commentary, p. 160, based on Sulami's *Tafsīr*.

68. Jami, "Iskandarnāma," in *Haft Aurang*, p. 915.

69. Gairdner, *Al-Ghazzālī's "Mishkāt al-anwār,"* translates and analyzes the treatise. See also Nicholson, *Studies in Islamic Mysticism*, p. 111; Nyberg, *Kleinere Schriften des Ibn al-ʿArabī*, p. 106; Andrae, *Die person Muhammads*, p. 335.

70. Translated in Nicholson, *Studies in Islamic Mysticism*, pp. 86–87.

71. For this development see Schaeder, "Die islamische Lehre vom Vollkommenen Menschen."

72. Gurbaxshani, *Luñwāria jā lāl*, p. 96.

73. Daudpota, *Kalām-i Girhōrī*; see Schimmel, "Sindhi Translations and Commentaries of the Qur'ān."

74. All these ideas are of course not new; the novelty is their use in the Sindhi language. See for instance Jami, *Dīwān*, p. 195, *ghazal* no. 157:

O bright one! "By the Morning light" (Sura 93:1) is your forehead,
"By the Night!" (Sura 92:1) is your ambergris-colored veil;
Ṭāhā (Sura 20) is a leaf from your tale,
Yāsīn (Sura 36) is a border on your sleeve;
Paradise is a result of your overflowing grace;
Hell is a spark from the flame of your wrath.

In the Sindhi tradition, a modern *Sīḥarfī* by Kamal Faqir (d. 1927) expresses the same ideas very clearly: not only do the prophets appear as Muhammad's disciples, but the Torah and Gospels as his commentary; in Baloch, *Ṭih akharyūñ*, 1:294–303.

75. Enamul Haq, *Sufiism in Bengal*, p. 94 n. 2. In December 1982 a Turkish lady who used to frequent a Sufi master in Istanbul told me, full of horror, that his disciples had claimed that Muhammad was indeed identical with Allah—how could she as a *sharīʿa*-minded Muslim deal with such people?

76. Qazi Abdal Mannan, "Sufi Literature in Bengal," p. 11. The idea is reminiscent of the *Puruśa śakta* in the Vedic tradition, though some may prefer to see influences of the Gnostic Adam Qadmōn myths. But in Bengal, Indian influence is more likely than that of Near Eastern mythology.

77. See Nicholson, *Studies in Islamic Mysticism*, pp. 115–16.

78. S. B. Bukhari, *Jawāhir al-auliyā*, pp. 474–91; the litany "By the Honor of Muhammad" occupies pp. 485–86. But much earlier, Qadi ʿIyad wrote in his *Shifā'* (1:137, quoted by Andrae, *Die person Muhammads*, p. 274) that "Adam in Paradise asked for forgiveness *bi-ḥaqq Muhammad*, "for Muhammad's sake."

79. Examples in Miskin, *Ladhdhat-i Miskīn*, 3:65–74. On the following pages, the same formulations occur with the names of the leaders of the great Sufi orders, always interrupted by the invocation of the Prophet.

80. Watanmal, *Life of Shah Abdul Latif*, pp. 37–38.

CHAPTER EIGHT

1. Kocatürk, *Tekke Şiiri Antolojisi*, p. 375; the poet is Vali (d. 1697). For literature on the *mīlād* see Hamadeh, "Muhammad the Prophet," nos. 1313–34.

2. Hadj-Sadok, "Le *mawlid* d'après le mufti-poète d'Alger, Ibn ʿAmmār'."

3. Abu Nuʿaim, *Dalāʾil an-nubuwwa*, p. 110, tells that the Prophet's birth, his entrance into Mecca, and his date of death happened all on a Monday, 12 Rabīʿ al-awwal. See also Zayyat, "The Month of Rabīʿ al-awwal in the Life of the Prophet." Mittwoch, "Muhammads Geburts- und Todestag," claims Jewish influences for the combination of the Prophet's birthday with the day of his death.

4. Snouck Hurgronje, *Verspreide Geschriften*, 5:406, about the customs in Terim in Hadramaut.

5. Maqrizi, *Kitāb al-mawāʿiẓ . . . al-khiṭaṭ*, 1:433, 466.

6. Ibn Khallikan, *Wafāyāt al-aʿyān*, 1:525–32: Hafiz ibn Dihya (trans. de Slane), 2:539–41.

7. Memon, *Ibn Taimiyya's Struggle against Popular Religion*, p. 243 and Introduction.

8. Enamul Haq, *Sufiism in Bengal*, p. 345.

9. It is called *Ḥusn al-maqṣid fī ʿamal al-maulid*, "The good intention in celebrating the *maulid*"; see Brockelmann, *GAL*, 2:157.

10. Koelle, *Mohammad and Mohammadanism*, p. 242.

11. Nowaihi, "Towards a Re-evaluation of Muhammad." I lately heard the same argument from high-ranking Arab diplomats and devout Turkish Muslims.

12. Paret, *Die legendäre Maghāzī-Literatur*, p. 146 n. *a*, mentions (1930) that one Dr. Fuchs was working on the history of the *maulid*, using the material collected by Erich Graefe, who was killed in 1914 during World War I (see his obituary in Becker, *Islamstudien*, 2:466–69). To my knowledge, he never published a comprehensive study of the subject, only the article "Mawlid" in the *Shorter Encyclopedia of Islam*.

13. Shinar, "Traditional and Reformist *maulid* Celebrations in the Maghrib." Paquignon, "Le Mouloud au Maroc," also emphasizes the Hamadsha and Issawiyya presence. For some customs in East Africa in the early twentieth century see Becker, "Materialien zur Kenntnis des Islam in Deutsch-Ostafrika," in *Islamstudien*, 2:101 ff.

14. Schimmel, "Sufismus und Heiligenverehrung im spätmittelalterlichen Ägypten," p. 276. Once, in 1462, the *maulid* was celebrated on 13 Rabīʿ al-awwal.

15. Qalqashandi, *Ṣubḥ al-aʿshā*, 1:160, a model for such a letter of congratulation.

16. Lane, *Manners and Customs of the Modern Egyptians*, pp. 436 ff.

17. The following information was kindly supplied by Dr. Ziauddin Ahmad Shakeb, of Hyderabad and London, from his forthcoming book on Golconda.

18. Badaoni, *Muntakhab at-tawārīkh*, 2:368 (trans. 2:380), mentions that one of Akbar's amīrs had cooked food for distribution on 12 Rabiʿ al-awwal.

19. *Dawn Overseas*, Karachi, 6 January 1983, p. 2, with numerous photographs showing garlanded people carrying banners.

20. *Muslim Digest*, Ramadan Annual 32, no. 12–33, no. 1 (July–August 1982),

pp. 185–93. The topic of the *mīlād an-nabī* was treated extensively in an earlier issue (32, nos. 6–7). The Ramadan issue contains an inquiry by a South African industrialist, Hajee A. M. Kalla, which is answered by a long *fatwā* by Mufti M. A. Awwary. Questions 1–4 pertain especially to the *maulūd*: first, whether it is permissible to hold it at all; secondly, whether it is permissible to stand while sending salutations upon the holy Prophet during the *maulid* gatherings; then, importantly, whether it is permissible to address the Prophet in the familiar second person; and whether it is permissible to prepare food for *mīlād an-nabī* and feed Muslims or distribute food among them. The *mufti* judges that "from the enlightened period of the four caliphs there is sufficient and strong proof that the esteemed companions of the holy Prophet Muhammad had established in their homes and in their gathering *mīlād an-nabī*." In fact "if someone rejects the above mentioned actions, then doubtless such a person, in the view of the *ahl-e-sunnat wa'l-jamaat* is lost, astray, leads astray, and there is fear of disbelief" (p. 9). The *mufti* brings seventy-one proofs for the necessity of celebrating the *mīlād*, and of standing up, and for the normal practice of addressing the Prophet in the second person. His proofs are taken from classical Arabic works, especially those used in the Deoband school, but also largely from Persian and, especially, Urdu devotional poetry. The *fatwā* is a fine compendium of modern prophetology and contrasts sharply with the attitude of the Saudi authorities, who follow the verdict of Ibn Taimiyya against such celebrations.

21. Enamul Haq, *Sufiism in Bengal*, pp. 344–45.

22. Mubarak, *Al-madā'iḥ an-nabawiyya*, p. 206.

23. Hassan ibn Thabit, *Dīwān*, no. 131, line 9.

24. Yunus Emre, *Divan*, p. 574, no. CCXLIX.

25. Andrae, *Die person Muhammads*, p. 64; Abu Nuʿaim, *Dalā'il an-nubuwwa*, pp. 88–100.

26. Nabhani, *Al-majmūʿa an-nabhāniyya*, 1:480.

27. Andrae, *Die person Muhammads*, pp. 62–63; Abu Nuʿaim, *Dalā'il an-nubuwwa*, pp. 221 ff.

28. Knappert, *Swahili Islamic Poetry*, 1:45. Most of the third volume of this useful publication is devoted to *maulids*.

29. Baihaqi, *Dalā'il an-nubuwwa*, p. 103; Sana'i, *Dīwān*, p. 363, and then generally in Persian poetry.

30. Bajuri, *Ḥāshiya ʿalā maulid . . . ad-Dardīr*, p. 3.

31. The oldest manuscript is preserved in the Aya Sofya Library; it was published, in Roman letters, as *Yaşayan mevlidi şerif* (The Living Noble *maulid*) in Istanbul in 1964. For translations, see MacCallum, *The Mevlidi Sherif*, and E. J. W. Gibb, *History of Ottoman Poetry*, pp. 241–48. See also Engelke, *Sülejman Tschelebis Lobgedicht auf die Geburt des Propheten*.

32. Knappert, *Swahili Islamic Poetry*, 1:107 (*maulid* rhyming in *-da*, line 21).

33. Shinar, "Traditional and Reformist *maulid* Celebrations in the Maghrib," p. 387.

34. About the celebrations in various countries see Çağatay, "The Tradition of *maulid* Recitations in Islam, Particularly in Turkey"; Cerbella, "Il natale del Profeta"; Nakhli, "Le moulid en Tunisie"; Paquignon, "Le mouloud au Maroc."

35. As moths fly around the candle thus the sun itself resembles a tiny moth compared to the Divine light.

36. Algar, "Some Notes on the Naqshbandi *ṭarīqat* in Bosnia," mentions the Serbo-Croatian translation by Hafiz Salih Gašovič.

37. My own copy, printed in Istanbul ca. 1912, contains a prayer for the Ottoman sultan Reshad.

38. Knappert, *Swahili Islamic Poetry*, 1:107.

39. Kocatürk, *Tekke Şiiri Antolojisi*, p. 375.

40. Yunus Emre, *Divan*, p. 575, no. CCL.

41. Knappert, *Swahili Islamic Poetry*, 1:100–131, 3:276 ff. For Barzanji see Brockelmann, *GAL* 2:384, S2:517.

42. Knappert, *Swahili Islamic Poetry*, 1:43; the Algerian mufti Ibn ʿAmmar, in his *Nikhat al-labīb bi-akhbār ar-riḥla ilāʾl-ḥabīb* (an account of his pilgrimage) describes the festivities of the *maulid* in Algiers in 1756 and quotes numerous poems by North African poets, including a *maulid muwashshaḥ* (strophic poem) of 217 verses; see Hadj-Sadok, "Le *mawlid* d'après le mufti poète d'Alger."

43. Serjeant, *Poetry and Prose from Hadramaut*, p. 36, no. 13.

44. Qazi Abdal Mannan, "Sufi Literature in Bengal," pp. 11–12. Dr. Ghulam Mustafa, an authority on and author of religious poetry, told me in Dacca in 1962 that good Bengali *maulids* were an innovation.

45. Baloch, *Maulūd*: the work contains poems by 175 poets from the early eighteenth century to our day. See Schimmel, "Neue Veröffentlichungen zur Volkskunde von Sind."

46. Baloch, *Munāqibā*, along with the companion volume *Muʿjizā*, gives the best survey of popular Sindhi expressions of the various events of the *sīra*, from the Prophet's birth to his first miracles.

47. Thus ʿAbdal ʿAli, *Guldasta-i Ḥāfiẓ Jhāndā*, pp. 7–9.

48. Dar, "Gujarat's Contribution to Gujari and Urdu," p. 33.

49. Baloch, *Munāqibā*, pp. 47–50.

50. It is quoted earlier in Aflaki, *Manāqib al-ʿārifīn*, p. 530, chap. 3, para. 519.

51. Siddiqi and Asi, *Armaghān-i naʿt*, p. 107.

CHAPTER NINE

1. Baloch, *Maulūd*, p. 10, no. 18 (ʿAbdur Raʾuf Bhatti).

2. Horovitz, "Miʿrāj"; for the literature on the subject see Hamadeh, "Muhammad the Prophet," nos. 1145–80, to which quite a few articles can be added.

3. Thus the sixteenth-century Egyptian mystical writer Najmuddin al-Ghaiti elaborated the story of the *miʿrāj* in his *Kitāb al-isrāʾ waʾl-miʿrāj*, which has largely influenced the Swahili versions of the legend. See Knappert, *Swahili Islamic Poetry*, 3:241. Ghaiti's work is translated in Jeffery, *Reader on Islam*, pp. 621 ff.; Waugh, in his article "Following the Beloved," largely relies on Jeffery's translation. For a traditionalist account see ʿAbdul Haqq Dihlawi, *Madārij an-nubuwwa*, 1:179–98.

4. Guillaume, "Where Was *al-masjid al-aqṣā*?"

5. Andrae, *Die person Muhammads*, pp. 41 ff., citing Ibn Hisham, *Sīra*, 1.200

ff. McKane, "A Manuscript on the *miʿrāj* in the Bodleian," speaks of an Arabic version of the *miʿrāj* legend with some unusual features; the unknown author, who emphasizes the element of light, seems to rely on Sufi sources.

6. Bukhari, *Ṣaḥīḥ*, 8:1:1.

7. See Affifi, "The Story of the Prophet's Ascent (*miʿrāj*) in Sufi Thought and Literature"; Azma, "Some Notes on the Impact of the Story of the *miʿrāj* on Sufi Literature"; Bevan, "Muhammad's Ascension to Heaven"; Blochet, "Études sur l'histoire religieuse de l'Iran, II"; Hartmann, "Die Himmelsreise Muhammads und ihre Bedeutung in der Religion des Islam"; Horovitz, "Muhammads Himmelfahrt"; Schrieke, "Die Himmelsreise Muhammads"; Porter, "Muhammad's Journey to Heaven"; Waugh, "Following the Beloved"; Widengren, *Muhammad: The Apostle and His Ascension*. Archer, *Mystical Elements in Muhammad*, discusses the subject rather extensively. As early as 1785, one J. Morder published in Frankfurt a "Fragment" under the title "Mohammeds Reise ins Paradies." As it was not unusual in the late nineteenth century to regard Muhammad as an epileptic, one even finds an attempt to explain the *miʿrāj* as a true experience of an epileptic. Dostoevski writes: "All you clever fools are convinced that he was simply a liar and impostor. But no! He really was in Paradise in the fit of epilepsy, which he suffered from, like I do. I don't know whether that bliss lasts for seconds, or hours, or months, but believe me, I wouldn't take all the joys that life can offer for it." Futrell, "Dostoyevsky and Islam," p. 22.

8. Cf. Scholem, *Major Trends in Jewish Mysticism*, pp. 44 ff. The *merkabah* mysticism offers interesting parallels with the *miʿrāj* legend, for instance, the wayfarer's examination at the gate; the "staying upright"; the idea that the angels, contrary to the perfected seeker, are not allowed into the Divine Presence; and the symbolism of the Divine Throne, which appears so prominently in poetical descriptions of the *miʿrāj*, especially in the Persianate tradition.

9. Baihaqi, *Dalāʾil an-nubuwwa*, p. 118.

10. Zimmer, *Maya*, pp. 27 ff. The story was applied to one Shaikh Shihabuddin, in Petis de la Croix, *Mille et un jours* (Paris 1710–12); it has been used by Amir Khusrau of Delhi in the *Ayina-i Iskandarī*, and in Egypt folk tradition claims that Shaikh ʿAbdul Qadir ad-Dashtuti (d. 1523) convinced the doubting Mamluk sultan of the reality of the *miʿrāj* by immersing his head in a bowl of water (Kriss and Kriss-Heinrich, *Volksglaube im Bereich des Islam*, 1:78). In Sindhi folktales, it forms the subject of the story of Eflatun the Magician; see Schimmel, *Märchen aus Pakistan*, pp. 133–39. It has also appeared in the German poetical tradition in Agnes Miegel's ballad "Die Mär vom Ritter Manuel."

11. Gätje, *Koran und Koranexegese*, pp. 105–8, citing Zamakhshari's commentary on Sura 17:1.

12. Tabari, *Tafsīr* on Sura 17:1. The Turkish critic Işik, "Shocking Writings," pp. 36–37, and his South African commentators violently attack Hamidullah's remark that "the *miʿrāj* is a state of mood. It was done when he forgot about his body and when his soul was dominant." Quoting Muhaddith Dihlawi, according to whom "he who does not believe that [Rasulallah was taken from Mecca to Masjid-i Aqsa] becomes an unbeliever," Işīk states that Hamidullah might even be a

"Batini or Ismaili," "for the Batinis believe in spiritual *mi'rāj* and this word of theirs is *kufr* and deviation."

13. Ahmad Khan, *Maqālāt-i Sir Sayyid*, 13:593–804: "Wāqi'a-i mi'rāj kī ḥaqīqāt u aṣliyyat" (The Truth and Origin of the *mi'rāj*). See also ibid., 11:711–65, his remarks against the acceptance of a bodily ascension, which culminate in the sentence: "We Muslims do not want to make our Prophet 'God's son,' and we are not desirous to make him 'sit at God's right hand.'"

14. Archer, *Mystical Elements in Mohammad*, p. 50. His entire chapter about the heavenly journey deserves careful study.

15. For the interpretation of "him" in Sura 53:13 by Sahl at-Tustari see Deladrière, *La Profession de Foi d'Ibn 'Arabi*, p. 124.

16. See Andrae, *Die person Muhammads*, pp. 80–81, citing Qastallani's *Al-mawāhib al-laduniyya*, 6:137.

17. Rumi, *Dīwān*, no. 1758.

18. Sana'i, *Dīwān*, p. 376.

19. Ikram, *Armaghān-i Pāk*, p. 158.

20. Hujwiri, *Kashf al-maḥjūb*, trans. Nicholson, p. 186: "Our apostle was sober; he beheld the same glory continuously, with ever increasing consciousness, all the way from Mecca, until he stood at the space of two bows' length from the divine presence."

21. J. N. Bell, *Love Theories in Later Hanbalite Islam*, p. 176.

22. Andrae, *Die person Muhammads*, p. 70, citing Tabari, *Tafsīr*, 32:26.

23. For this whole problem see Ritter, *Das Meer der Seele*, pp. 445 ff.

24. Arberry, *Discourses of Rumi*, pp. 211, 78.

25. Iqbal, *Six Lectures*, p. 124.

26. Ibn al-Farid, *Tā'iyya*, line 454, in Nicholson, *Studies in Islamic Mysticism*, p. 239.

27. Qushairi, "Bāb al-'ubūdiyya," in *Risāla*, p. 92.

28. Andrae, *Die person Muhammads*, p. 84.

29. B. A. Hashmi, "Sarmad," *Islamic Culture* 7 (1933): 670.

30. Andrae, *Die person Muhammads*, p. 83, citing Qastallani, *Al-mawāhib al-laduniyya*, 6:10.

31. Thus *Tuḥfa-i Raḥīm Yār*, pp. 7–8; the *munkir-i mi'rāj*, "the denier of the heavenly journey," is often attacked in Sindhi and Pashto verse too.

32. 'Attar, *Ilāhīnāma*, pp. 14–19.

33. In Rumi's version of this story, it is seventy thousand mysteries (thus Aflaki, *Manāqib al-'ārifīn*, p. 599, chap. 3, para. 589). The Prophet also recited the Koran seventy times in the Divine Presence, ibid., p. 490, chap. 3, para. 474.

34. Furuzanfar, *Aḥādīth-i Mathnawī*, nos. 26, 445.

35. Ghanizade, in Köprülüzade, *Eski Şairlerimiz*, p. 356. Cf. also Thabit's *Mi'rājiyye*, in E. J. W. Gibb, *History of Ottoman Poetry*, 4:22–23.

36. Usually it is said that Gabriel resembled the handsome Meccan Dihya al-Kalbi. Paret, *Die legendäre Maghāzī-Literatur*, p. 175, shows that in later legends Gabriel appears generally as a messenger to the Prophet, not so much in his heavenly glory. This remark is corroborated by the manner in which the mighty angel is

depicted in popular poetry, where he clearly appears to be subordinate to the Prophet (see chapter 10 n. 83).

37. Yunus Emre, *Divan*, p. 303, no. CLIX.

38. Furuzanfar, *Aḥādīth-i Mathnawī*, no. 100.

39. Furuzanfar, *Aḥādīth-i Mathnawī*, no. 48.

40. Arberry, *Discourses of Rumi*, p. 24. See Schimmel, *The Triumphal Sun*, pp. 352–66.

41. Rumi, *Mathnawī*, vol. 4, lines 3755 ff., esp. 3805; and vol. 1, line 1066:

Intellect says, like Gabriel, "O Ahmad!
If I should advance one step, He will burn me."

42. Longworth Dames, *Popular Poetry of the Baloches*, 1:158. This idea also occurs in a Panjabi poem in honor of Pir Piran ʿAbdul Qadir, the "wonderful flower in the Prophet's garden" on "whose neck the Prophet put his foot." I read this in a manuscript (ca. late nineteenth-century) in the possession of Syed Zulfiqar Ali Bokhari, Jhang.

43. Aflaki, *Manāqib alʿārifīn*, p. 365, chap. 3, para. 299.

44. Nizami, "Makhzan al-asrār," in *Kulliyāt-i Khamsa*, pp. 17–20; "Lailā Majnūn," ibid., pp. 433–36; "Haft Paikar," ibid., p. 606.

45. Jami, "Yūsuf u Zulaikhā," in *Haft Aurang*, pp. 584–85; cf. "Silsilat adh-dhahab," ibid., p. 10.

46. Molla Nusrati (d. 1684), the court poet of ʿAli ʿAdilshah of Bijapur and his successors, wrote a *miʿrājnāma*, and so did Sayyid Bulaqi in the Deccan in 1694. See Syed Naimuddin, "Sayyid Bulaqi's Mirājnāma," with some examples.

47. Jami, *Dīwān*, p. 289, no. 307; cf. Naziri, *Dīwān*, p. 47, *qaṣīda* no. 32. The sky "used the dust of the Prophet's road as antimony for its eyes and became radiant." Antimony not only embellishes the eyes but also enhances the sight; but the term *chashm raushan*, "may your eye be brightened" also means "Congratulations!" That means, the skies, which used the dust of the Prophet's road for their eyes, are to be congratulated that they were blessed by the touch of his feet. This idea occurs frequently in later Persian and Turkish poetry.

48. Ghanizade, in Köprülüzade, *Eski Şairlerimiz*, pp. 353–57.

49. The *rafraf* as the last vehicle for the Prophet appears in Nizami's *miʿrāj* poems and, following his example, also in the chapter on *miʿrāj* in Süleyman Chelebi's *mevlût*. Similarly, Naziri sings in his *naʿt* (*Dīwān*, p. 486):

His high ambition, *himmat*, put the foot from the skies on a *rafraf*.

50. Buraq—sometimes, as in Bulaqi's *Miʿrājnāma*, called *Barrāq*, "very radiant, lightning-like"—is sometimes confused by folk poets with ʿAli's famous white mule Duldul; see Darmesteter, *Chants populaires des Afghans*, no. 110, stanza 10. For a medieval Jewish distortion of the *miʿrāj* legend in connection with Buraq see Altmann, "The Ladder of Ascension."

51. First published by Pavet de Courteille in 1882 as *Mirâdj-nâme*; the facsimile edition by Séguy, *The Miraculous Journey of Mahomet*, contains excellent reproductions, although the text is not fully satisfying. For the topic see Ettinghausen, "Persian Ascension Miniatures of the Fourteenth Century."

52. Baloch, *Maulūd*, p. 334.

53. S. C. Welch, *Wonders of the Age*, plate 63. A good postcard of this miniature is available in the British Museum.

54. Now and then, in popular paintings, one sees the Prophet mounting Gabriel, not Buraq.

55. Yunus Emre, *Divan*, p. 575, no. CCLIV.

56. Sarraj, *Kitāb al-lumaʿ*, pp. 382–87; ʿAttar, *Tadhkirat al-auliyāʾ*, 1:172–76; see Nicholson, "An Early Arabic Version of the *miʿrāj* of Abū Yazīd al-Bisṭāmī"; and Ritter, "Die Ausspri̇̈che des Bāyezīd Bisṭāmī."

57. Aflaki, *Manāqib al-ʿārifīn*, p. 666, chap. 4, para. 67.

58. See Corbin, *Avicenna and the Visionary Recital*; Meier, "Der Geistmensch bei dem persischen Dichter ʿAṭṭār"; Ibn ʿArabi deals with the mystical *miʿrāj* in his book *Kitāb al-isrāʾ ila maqām al-asrāʾ*, analyzed by Azma, "Some Notes on the Impact of the Story of the *miʿrāj*."

59. Gölpĭnarlĭ, *Tasavvuftan dilimize geçen deyimler*, p. 235.

60. Buraq as an equivalent of Love occurs in Rumi's work in the following places: *Dīwān*, nos. 3, 288, 1313, 1426, 1595, 1741, 1997; in *Mathnawī*, vol. 5, line 4133, the gallows on which the lovers are killed is compared to Buraq because death leads the lover into the Divine presence. Folk poetry liked the rhyme *Ḥallāj–miʿrāj*, for Hallaj performed his "ascension" while on the gallows.

61. Rumi, *Dīwān*, nos. 1295, 1296; see Schimmel, *The Triumphal Sun*, pp. 289–90, for more examples of the "ladder."

62. Asín Palaćios, *Islam and the Divine Comedy*.

63. Cerulli, *Il "Libro della Scala" e la questione delle fonte arabo-spagnole della "Divina Commedia."*

64. Nicholson, "The 'Risālat al-Ghufrān' by Abū'l-ʿAlāʾ al-Maʿarrī."

65. Brockelmann, *GAL*, S3:487, first published in 1931 in the magazine *ad-Duhūr*.

66. Iqbal, *Jāvīdnāma*; trans. in English (Arberry; Ahmad), French (Meyerovitch), German (Schimmel), Italian (Bausani), Turkish (Schimmel). For Iqbal's use of the imagery of the *miʿrāj* see Schimmel, *Gabriel's Wing*, pp. 301–6.

67. He may have thought of Iqbal's verse (*Bāl-i Jibrīl*, p. 44):

I have learned this lesson from Mustafa's *miʿrāj*,
That the heaven is in the grasp of the world of humanity.

CHAPTER TEN

1. Sana'i, *Dīwān*, p. 365.
2. Ghulam Imam Shahid, in Siddiqi and Asi, *Armaghān-i naʿt*.
3. Siddiqi and Asi, *Armaghān-i naʿt*, p. 127.
4. Nabhani, *Al-majmūʿa an-nabhāniyya*, 1:8.
5. Nabhani, *Al-majmūʿa an-nabhāniyya*, 1:4; cf. Tapish, *Gulzār-i naʿt*, fol. 2b.
6. Nabhani, *Al-majmūʿa an-nabhāniyya*, 1:8.
7. Nabhani, *Al-majmūʿa an-nabhāniyya*, 1:7, quotes Busiri's *Hamziyya*.
8. Tapish, *Gulzār-i naʿt*, fol. 11b.
9. Baloch, *Madāḥūñ*, introduction p. 14.

10. Rasheed, "The Development of *naʿtia* Poetry," p. 56.

11. Rasheed, "The Development of *naʿtia* Poetry," p. 58.

12. In a lecture in the Arabic Seminar of Columbia University, 27 January 1983, Professor Abdul Karim Rafeq discussed the different *ṭāʾifa*, "professional organisations," in eighteenth- and nineteenth-century Syria and mentioned the *ṭāʾifa maddāḥīn ar-rasūl wa ḥakkāʾīn as-sīra an-nabawiyya*.

13. Hassan ibn Thabit, *Dīwān*, no. 89.

14. Kister, "A New Edition of the *Dīwān* of Ḥassān ibn Thābit," p. 285.

15. Hassan ibn Thabit, *Dīwān*, no. 19.

16. Utas, *Ṭarīq at-taḥqīq*, line 375.

17. For this development see Schimmel, *As Through a Veil*, pp. 14, 216–17 nn. 11–12. Grunebaum, "The Early Development of Islamic Religious Poetry," p. 24, has pointed out that the religious element is not among the recognized motives in Arabic literary theory.

18. Ed. Lette (Leiden, 1748). An excellent German version of this poem by Friedrich Rückert was published in the 1830s, but unfortunately there is no equally artistic rendering of the *Bānat Suʿād* in English; for an impression one may turn to Hidayat Hosain, "Bānat Suʿād," which is, however, a very pedestrian translation.

19. Paret, "Die Legende von der Verleihung des Prophetenmantels."

20. Baloch, *Madāḥūñ*, introduction p. 8.

21. Jami, "Yūsuf u Zulaikhā," in *Haft Aurang*, p. 587, and often in his work.

22. Quoted in Mubarak, *Al-madāʾiḥ an-nabawiyya*, p. 50.

23. Brockelmann, *GAL* 1:264, S1:467, with extensive bibliography. Nicholson, in his *Literary History of the Arabs*, mentions Busiri only in passing.

24. Baloch, *Ṭih akharyūñ*, 1:200, quotes a Sindhi poet who sings:

O Lord, to say the blessings for you
Is the medicine for all ailing people!

25. See Basset, *La Bordah du Cheikh al-Bousiri*, introduction.

26. Becker, *Islamstudien*, 2:105, mentions that in East Africa certain lines of the *Dalāʾil al-khairāt* and the *Burda* "are next in sanctity to certain verses of the Koran." Badaoni, *Muntakhab at-tawārīkh*, 2:384 (trans. 2:397), tells that in times of utter distress he used to repeat the *Burda*.

27. Most libraries own beautifully calligraphed copies of the *Burda*. A particularly fine copy with the interlinear Persian translation by Jami, written in 1477 by Sultan-ʿAli Mashhadi in Herat, is in the Chester Beatty Library; see Arberry, *Catalogue of the Persian Manuscripts*, no. 154. For other Persian paraphrases see Ahlwardt, *Verzeichnis der arabischen Handschriften*, nos. 7804–6; Ethé, *Catalogue of Persian Manuscripts*, nos. 170, 2647, 2650. A study of the manuscripts from the viewpoint of calligraphy and illumination would be worthwhile. See Schimmel, *Calligraphy and Islamic Culture*, pp. 59, 86, 118.

28. Kokan, *Arabic and Persian in Carnatic*, pp. 64–65.

29. Muhammad ad-Din Naqshbandi, *Qaṣīda-i Burda, maʿ sharḥ Panjābī*, is a skillful Panjabi verse rendering of the poem, which maintains the original rhyming letter *m*, adding to it the genitive ending *-dī*.

30. Knappert, *Swahili Islamic Poetry*, vol. 2, contains "The Two Burdas."

31. Drewes, *Een zestiende eeuwse Maleise vertaling van de Burda.*

32. Knappert, *Swahili Islamic Poetry*, 2:223.

33. S. S. Khusro Husaini kindly arranged such a recitation of the *Burda* for me at his house in Hyderabad/Deccan.

34. S. B. Bukhari, *Jawāhir al-auliyā*, pp. 444–45. One should repeat the *taṣliya* whenever the Prophet is mentioned in this poem; that can be done 41 times, 144 times, or, if possible, 1,001 times for each occurrence of his name.

35. J. W. Redhouse, in W. A. Clouston, *Arabian Poetry for English Readers* (Glasgow: privately printed, 1881), pp. 310–41.

36. Jeffery, *Reader on Islam*, pp. 605–20.

37. Mustaqimzade, *Tuḥfa-i khaṭṭāṭīn*, mentions that Busiri was also a calligrapher and had some disciples in calligraphy, pp. 411–12.

38. For Safiuddin al-Hilli see Brockelmann, *GAL* 2:194, S2:199: Nabhani, *Al-majmūʿa an-nabhāniyya*, 1:16 ff., discusses the *badīʿiyya*, the complicated "novel" style of later medieval poets.

39. Nabhani, *Al-majmūʿa an-nabhāniyya*, 1:564; cf. ibid., 1:173, the poem by ʿAbdul ʿAziz az-Zamzami al-Makki (d. 1556), which elaborates this form in even more complicated style.

40. In Witri's *naʿt*s the lines of each poem begin with the rhyming letter, thus the *Tāʾiyya* with *t*, the *Khāʾiyya* with *kh*, and so on. See Nabhani, *Al-majmūʿa an-nabhāniyya*, 1:11, 510, 589, 612, and others.

41. Kokan, *Arabic and Persian in Carnatic*, pp. 61–63: the Qadiri Sufi, Shaikh Sadaqatallah (d. 1703) wrote a *takhmīs* and *tadhyīl* of *al-qaṣīda al-witriyya*, that is, cinquains in alphabetical order plus eight *mukhammas* for each letter.

42. Nabhani, *Al-majmūʿa an-nabhāniyya*, 1:156, Shamsuddin an-Nawaji (d. 1455). Cf. Mustaqimzade, *Tuḥfa-i khaṭṭāṭīn*, pp. 720–21, about Muhammad Hilali ibn Najmuddin ad-Dimashqi (d. 1603): "he has eulogies for the Prophet arranged according to the letters."

43. Nabhani, *Al-majmūʿa an-nabhāniyya*, 3:321–23, Al-Hazim al-Andalusi al-Qartajani; pp. 324–26, ash-Shihab al-Mansuri.

44. Nabhani, *Al-majmūʿa an-nabhāniyya*, 1:34.

45. Nabulusi, *Dīwān al-ḥaqāʾiq*; for example, 1:50, 52, with the metaphor of light, 2:72, as a kind of greeting, *salām*, where one verse reads:

> Blessings and greetings from nearby
> For the excellent leader,
> The one of high range,
> For whom the trees walked,
> When he called them,
> While he was protecting [them?] with his general generosity.

A. S. Husain, *Al-adab aṣ-ṣūfī*, pp. 282 ff., discusses how the ideas about the *ḥaqīqa muḥammadiyya* were reflected in popular poetry from the thirteenth century, especially with the growth of the Sufi orders.

46. Muid Khan, *The Arabian Poets of Golconda*, pp. 102–8, about the *naʿt* of Sayyid ʿAli at the Qutbshahi court in Golconda.

47. Kokan, *Arabic and Persian in Carnatic*, p. 66: Shaikh Muhyiddin ibn

Shaikh ʿUmar Kayalpatam, *Al-qaṣīda al-muḥammadiyya*, composed ca. 1815.

48. A reproduction of the beginning of the *Sīra Purānam* appears in Schimmel, *Islam in India and Pakistan*, pl. XXXb.

49. Nicholson, *Studies in Islamic Mysticism*, p. 181.

50. Andrae, *Die person Muhammads*, p. 256; cf. p. 286.

51. Ibn Taimiyya considered that a pilgrimage whose purpose was exclusively the visit of the Prophet's tomb was "rebellion," *maʿṣiya*. See Memon, *Ibn Taimiyya's Struggle against Popular Religion*, pp. 15, 286, 292, and passim.

52. A. S. Husain, *Al-adab aṣ-ṣūfī*, pp. 218 ff.

53. Thus Jami, *Dīwān*, p. 289, no. 307.

54. ʿAbdul Latif, *Risālō*, "Sur Khanbhāt," canto 2, stanza 5.

55. Fine examples are Jami, *Dīwān*, p. 73, no. 47; p. 83, no. 56. The topic is very common in Urdu *naʿtiyya*.

56. Her book also contains good photographs of the Rauda and the entire sacred precincts; see plates 73–74, 79–83. The article "Madīna" in *EI*, 1st ed., vol. 3, gives an extensive description of the area of the Prophet's tomb and the history of the building.

57. Padwick, *Muslim Devotions*, p. 223.

58. Yunus Emre, *Divan*, p. 567, no. CXXXIX; cf. p. 565, no. CCXXVI.

59. Jami, *Dīwān*, pp. 88–89, no. 61; cf. "Silsilat adh-dhahab," in *Haft Aurang*, p. 11.

60. ʿAbdul Latif, *Risālō*, "Sur Ḍahar," canto 2, stanzas 1–3.

61. Baloch, *Maulūd*, p. 23, no. 54.

62. Siddiqi and Asi, *Armaghān-i naʿt*, p. 132.

63. *Mīlād Aḥmad*, p. 2.

64. *Mīlād Aḥmad*, p. 12.

65. *Mīlād Aḥmad*, p. 63.

66. Siddiqi and Asi, *Armaghān-i naʿt*, p. 140.

67. Jami, "Salamān u Absāl," in *Haft Aurang*, p. 454.

68. Nabhani, *Al-majmūʿa an-nabhāniyya*, 1:487.

69. Schimmel, *Zeitgenössische arabische Lyrik*, p. 95. Faituri's poem is printed in *ʿĀshiq min Ifrīqīya* (Beirut: Dār al-adab, 1964).

70. Cf. Baloch, *Ṭih akharyūñ*, 2:338–43: "May I see Medina's towers," a very repetitious poem with numerous alliterations in each verse.

71. Spies, "Sechs tunesische Arbeitslieder," p. 288.

72. Ghiyath Matin, *Zīna zīna rākh*, p. 11.

73. "To kiss the Prophet's tomb with one's eyes" and related expressions are standard formulas in Indo-Muslim poetry. See Baloch, *Ṭih akharyūñ*, 1:206.

74. S. B. Bukhari, *Jawāhir al-auliyā*, p. 222. The same story is told about Sayyid ʿAli Shirazi, who is buried on Makli Hill near Thatta, Sind, in Aʿzam Tattawi, *Tuḥfat aṭ-ṭāhirīn*, pp. 17–20. Similarly, Ahmad ar-Rifaʿi tells that he was concentrating upon the Prophet in the hope that he would extend his hand so that he might kiss it, and "at that moment his noble hand appeared [from the tomb] and I kissed it." Sindhi, *Inbāʾ al-anbāʾ*, p. 40.

75. *Mīlād Aḥmad*, p. 25.

76. Qaniʿ, *Maqālāt ash-shuʿarā*, p. 592.

77. Sana'i, *Dīwān*, pp. 34 ff.

78. Nizami, "Sharafnāma-i Iskandarī," in *Kulliyāt-i Khamsa*, p. 845: "In one hand he had a pearl, in the other hand the sword." This juxtaposition continues in *naʿtiyya* poetry to our day, and Iqbal's description of the true believer, the *mard-i momin*, is influenced by it, for the true believer should follow the Prophet in every respect. See also note 138 below.

79. Gesudaraz, *Dīwān Anīs al-ʿushshāq*, p. 17.

80. Zajączkowski, *Poezje stroficzne ʿĀšïq-paša*, p. 13, stanza 6. The refrain of the poem is *Ver ṣalāwat Muḥammad'a*, "Give blessings for Muhammad."

81. Siddiqi and Asi, *Armaghān-i naʿt*, p. 96.

82. See Razi, *The Path of God's Bondsmen*, p. 433: "I have two ministers in heaven and two upon earth; they are Gabriel and Michael, and Abu Bakr and ʿUmar." Nizami, in the *naʿt* of "Lailā u Majnūn," *Kulliyāt-i Khamsa*, p. 432, uses the same *ḥadīth* as basis.

83. Sana'i, *Dīwān*, p. 364; see also p. 167. In Sindhi *sīḥarfīs*, the enumeration of the four archangels as the Prophet's servants is a common topic; see Baloch, *Ṭih akharyūñ*, 1:34, 55 (1869), 207 (1918): "Gabriel is always the doorkeeper at your door, Michael is attached to you and sweeps your floor; ʿAzra'il is present, and Israfil is your special servant," and similar formulations. Ghalib, in his *mathnawī* in honor of the Prophet, "Abr-i Gauharbār," even says that "Gabriel's wing is a flywhisk for the Prophet's table" (*Kulliyāt-i Fārsī*, 5:96).

84. Darmesteter, *Chants populaires des Afghans*, no. 30.

85. Thus Bulaqi in his *Miʿrājnāma*; Syed Naimuddin, who discusses his poem, ascribes the existence of some verse with special praise for ʿAli to the (unknown) Persian model on which Bulaqi based his poem. That seems farfetched.

86. Sana'i, *Dīwān*, p. 167; cf. Jami, *Dīwān*, p. 74, no. 48.

87. Sana'i, *Dīwān*, pp. 374, 363. The oath is Sura 15:72, where God addresses the Prophet, *la-ʿumrik*, "By your life!" This idea, to which Razi, *The Path of God's Bondsmen*, p. 406, also alludes, was often taken up by the Sufi poets to highlight Muhammad's very special place.

88. Sana'i, *Ḥadīqat al-ḥaqīqa*, chap. 3, p. 209.

89. Sana'i, *Dīwān*, p. 44.

90. Sana'i, *Dīwān*, p. 363.

91. Sana'i, *Dīwān*, p. 374.

92. Nabhani, *Al-majmūʿa an-nabhāniyya*, 1:584.

93. Sana'i, *Dīwān*, p. 36; cf. the similar argument, p. 374.

94. Sana'i, *Dīwān*, p. 43.

95. For Avicenna's mystical aspects see Corbin, *Avicenna and the Visionary Recital*.

96. Jami, *Nafaḥāt al-uns*, p. 427; see also the unfriendly remarks about the philosophers in the work of Majduddin's disciple, Najm Razi Daya, passim. See further Jami, *Dīwān*, p. 140, no. 35.

97. ʿAttar, *Muṣībatnāma*, p. 54. The Divine order *qul*, "Speak!" in addressing the Prophet occurs more than three hundred times in the Koran. Shamsuddin Tabrizi, attacking those who believe that they can reach God without acknowledging the Prophet (as the philosophers allegedly do) made the statement: "You say, 'I

do not need Muhammad any more, for I have reached God!' But God *az Muḥammad mustaghnī nīst* [cannot do without him]. How could He? He has said, 'If We had willed We would have sent a warner in every village' [Sura 25:51]; now He did not do that and He did not want *lau shi'nā* [If We had willed]." Aflaki, *Manāqib al-ʿārifīn*, p. 665, chap. 4, para. 67. The meaning seems to be that if God had really had need for any other messenger, He would have sent him, but Muhammad was enough for his purposes.

98. Rumi, *Mathnawī*, vol. 1, line 3280.

99. Rumi, *Dīwān*, no. 1793.

100. Iqbal, *Payām-i Mashriq*, pp. 119, 122, juxtaposes the bookworm that lives in a manuscript of Avicenna's works, and the moth that experiences the fire of love. In *Żarb-i Kalīm*, p. 11, he says in classical style:

Bind your heart to the word of Muhammad, O son of ʿAli!
How long [will you deal] with Bu ʿAli [Avicenna]?

101. ʿAttar, *Muṣībatnāma*, p. 20.

102. ʿAttar, *Manṭiq uṭ-ṭair*, p. 18.

103. ʿAttar, *Ilāhīnāma*, p. 11; see Schimmel, *As Through a Veil*, p. 193.

104. ʿAttar, *Muṣībatnāma*, p. 20.

105. Rumi, *Dīwān*, no. 792.

106. Rumi, *Dīwān*, no. 409.

107. Rumi, *Dīwān*, no. 2010.

108. Rumi, *Dīwān*, no. 462.

109. Rumi, *Mathnawī*, vol. 5, line 2734; in *Dīwān*, no. 2400, Love is "Mustafa's coming in the midst of the infidels."

110. Rumi, *Dīwān*, no. 2.

111. Rumi, *Dīwān*, no. 1142.

112. Rumi, *Dīwān*, no. 1732.

113. Rumi, *Dīwān*, no. 1966.

114. Rumi, *Dīwān*, no. 1135.

115. Rumi, *Mathnawī*, vol. 4, lines 990–91.

116. Rumi, *Dīwān*, no. 2118.

117. Rumi, *Mathnawī*, vol. 6, lines 165–71.

118. Rumi, *Dīwān*, no. 490.

119. Aflaki, *Manāqib al-ʿārifīn*, p. 281, chap. 3, para. 193.

120. Arberry, *Discourses of Rumi*, p. 232.

121. Arberry, *Discourses of Rumi*, p. 117.

122. Arberry, *Discourses of Rumi*, pp. 211–12.

123. Arberry, *Discourses of Rumi*, p. 78.

124. Heper, *Mevlevi Ayînleri*, pp. 1–4, text and melody of the *naʿt-i sharīf*.

125. ʿIraqi, *Kulliyāt*, p. 74. Another, extremely high-soaring ode by ʿIraqi is found in a calligraphy in the Freer Gallery of Art (48.20 B), reproduced here on p. 136. It abounds in allusions to Muhammad's primordial light and his role as the "mirror of the Divine Truth [God] Most High."

126. Khaqani, "Tuḥfat al-haramain," in *Dīwān*, pp. 368 ff.

127. Hadi Hasan, "Qāsim-i Kāhī," p. 185.

128. Saʿdi, *Būstān*, p. 5.

129. Amir Khusrau, *Majnūn Lailā*, p. 14; see chapter 6 n. 21 above.

130. Amir Khusrau, *Majnūn Lailā*, p. 15. Later, Jami in his *Salām* (*Dīwān*, p. 73, no. 47) compares the Prophet to the ocean of mercy out of whose generosity the ocean (of this world) is but a dewdrop.

131. Amir Khusrau, *Dīwān*, p. 601.

132. Amir Khusrau, *Dīwān*, p. 596.

133. See for instance Nizami, "Khusrau u Shīrīn," *Kulliyāt-i Khamsa*, p. 127. The combination occurs then in many of the major *na*ʿ*t* poems in the Persian tradition.

134. Iqbal, *Asrār-i khudī*, lines 415–17.

135. Jami, *Dīwān*, pp. 95–100.

136. Saʿdi, *Qaṣāʾid*, p. 17.

137. ʿUrfi, *Kulliyāt*, *qaṣīda* no. 10. Also published in Abdul Ghani, *Persian Language and Literature at the Moghul Court*, 3:119, but that translation misses some essential points.

138. Naziri, *Dīwān*, p. 487, *qaṣīda* no. 36. Bedil, in the introductory *na*ʿ*t* of his *Chahār* ʿ*unṣur* (*Kulliyāt*, 4:4–5), similarly confronts the two aspects of the Prophet: his kind remark "I am a human being like you!" gives him the courage to call the Prophet, while the glory of *Anā Aḥmad bilā mīm* makes him feel that it would be bad manners to draw close to this luminous spiritual being. Cf. n. 78 above.

139. Ikram, *Armaghān-i Pāk*, p. 219.

140. Waliullah, *At-Tafhīmāt*, 2:246. One may mention in this connection that in the Indian environment a *ḥadīth qudsī* was known in which the Lord says *Anā* ʿ*arab bilā* ʿ*ain*, "I am the Arab (i.e., Muhammad), without the (letter) ʿ*ain*," or "without the essence" or "the eye," that is, *Rabb*, "Lord." This saying occurs in Sindhi folk poetry, but has never been popular in other Islamic countries, as far as I know.

141. Baloch, *Maulūd*, p. 2, no. 2, refrain.

142. Ramakrishna, *Panjabi Sufi Poets*, p. 73: ʿAli Haidar in his *sīḥarfī* under the letter *m*.

143. ʿAndalib, *Nāla-i* ʿ*Andalīb*, 2:104.

144. A typical example is Nefʿi's *na*ʿ*t* in Köprülüzade, *Eski Şairlerimiz*, pp. 397–99.

145. Kokan, *Khānwāda-i Qāżī Badruddaula*, pp. 191–94.

146. Furuzanfar, *Aḥādīth-i Mathnawī*, no. 228. Horten, *Die religiöse Vorstellungswelt des Volkes*, p. 150, calls the chapter about Muhammad's personality "Der mystisch lebende Muhammad als Vater seiner Gemeinde."

147. See chapter 11 n. 25 below.

148. *Mi*ʿ*rāj al-*ʿ*āshiqīn* is attributed to Gesudaraz, but the authorship is not undisputed. There are various editions: by Maulvi ʿAbdul Haq (1922); Khaliq Anjum (Delhi, 1956); Gopichand Narang (1967).

149. Shefta, in Siddiqi and Asi, *Armaghān-i na*ʿ*t*, p. 97.

150. Mahabbat Khan in Siddiqi and Asi, *Armaghān-i na*ʿ*t*.

151. Darmesteter, *Chants populaires des Afghans*, p. 104, no. 42.

152. Siddiqi and Asi, *Armaghān-i na*ʿ*t*, p. 106.

153. Numerous examples in Baloch, *Maulūd*. The *miṭṭā mīr* occurs frequently and is often expanded: for example, *mujtabā mukhtār mursal—māṛṛ kar yā Muḥammad*, "Elect, chosen, messenger—give support, O Muhammad!" and similar alliterations with *m*.

154. Sana'i, *Dīwān*, p. 35.

155. Jami, *Dīwān*, p. 289, no. 307.

156. Knappert, *Swahili Islamic Poetry*, 1:40.

157. Mirghani, *An-nūr al-barrāq*, pp. 1–31. *Abjad* is the traditional Semitic sequence of the alphabet in Arabic, as it is used for counting.

158. For the form see Vaudeville, *Bārahmāsa, les chansons des douze mois*.

159. Baloch, *Maulūd*, p. 6, no. 3. Compare also the verse by the eighteenth-century Deccani poet Firaqi Bijapuri, who emphasizes the love of the Prophet:

> Hey, Majnun! You have become disgraced because you gave your
> heart to Laila—
> What would have happened, had you given your heart to my Prophet?

Siddiqi and Asi, *Armaghān-i naʿt*, p. 67.

160. Baloch, *Maulūd*, p. 334.

161. Hussaini, "Bund-samāʿ."

162. Yunus Emre, *Divan*, p. 568, no. CCXLI.

163. Hickman, *Eshrefoghlu Rūmī: Reconstitution of His Divan*, letter M7.

164. Kocatürk, *Tekke Şiiri Antolojisi*, p. 402; the poet is Sezayi (d. 1738).

165. Bannerth, "Lieder ägyptischer *meddâhîn*," p. 12, no. 1.

166. Baloch, *Madāḥūñ*, p. 279, by Yusuf Athar.

167. Razi, *The Path of God's Bondsmen*, p. 157.

168. Rumi, *Dīwān*, no. 463. Jami, in "Lailā u Majnūn," *Haft Aurang*, p. 754, goes so far as to state that even Muhammad's "red-haired camel made both worlds 'red-faced,'" that is, "honored."

169. Iqbal, "Tarāna-i millī," in *Bāng-i Darā*, p. 172: "Our caravan leader is the Prince of Hijaz."

170. Muhammad is not only the boatman but can also be seen as the saving ark, as Rumi makes him say (*Mathnawī* vol. 4, line 3358): "I am the ark in this ocean of the universe."

CHAPTER ELEVEN

1. Schimmel, "The Golden Chain of 'Sincere Muhammadans,'" discusses the development in Indo-Pakistan in greater detail and gives the relevant source material in the notes.

2. Peacock, *Purifying the Faith: The Muhammadiyyah Movement in Indonesian Islam*.

3. About him see Friedmann, *Shaykh Aḥmad Sirhindī*.

4. Cf. chapter 2 nn. 3–4.

5. Jahangir, *Tuzuk-i Jahāngīrī*, 2:93.

6. The term *qayyūm* (absolutely used for God as The One Subsisting through Himself) is interpreted by Shah Waliullah, *Lamaḥāt*, p. 5, as (among other things)

"the one who upholds (*al-qayyūm bi-*) the contingent realities," or "the breath of the Merciful," or "the seal of the Divine names."

7. For the development see Schimmel, *Pain and Grace*, part 1.

8. Dard, *'Ilm ul-kitāb*, p. 432.

9. Dard, *'Ilm ul-kitāb*, p. 504; full translation in Schimmel, *Pain and Grace*, pp. 78–80.

10. Mazhar, "At-tanbīhāt al-khamsa," in *Makātīb-i Mirzā Maẓhar*, p. 214.

11. Baljon, *A Mystical Interpretation of Prophetic Tales by an Indian Muslim*, p. 58.

12. Iqbal, *Six Lectures on the Reconstruction of Religious Thought in Islam*, p. 124. The main part of chapter 5 of Iqbal's book deals with this problem.

13. Shah Waliullah, *At-Tafhīmāt*, 2:19.

14. Shah Waliullah, *Alṭāf al-quds*, p. 95, quoted in Jalbani, *Shāh Walīullāh ain hunajō falsafō*, p. 114.

15. Nyberg, *Kleinere Schriften des Ibn al-'Arabī*, Arabic text of "Al-tadbīrat al-ilāhiyya," p. 216, lines 133 ff.

16. *At-Tafhīmāt*, 1:28. More than nine centuries before Shah Waliullah, the Muʿtazilite al-Jahiz in Baghdad had developed a theory about the character of the prophets' message that resembles, in a certain way, Waliullah's idea that every prophet is sent with the equipment that fits his "material." Jahiz says in his *Kitāb ḥujaj an-nubuwwa* that God sent Moses at a time when Pharaoh believed in the power of magic; hence his miracle was to overcome the magicians. Jesus was sent when the art of healing was highly appreciated, and excelled therefore in healing miracles. Muhammad was sent when highest importance was given to beautiful language, and so his true miracle is the inimitable Koran. See Pellat, *Arabische Geisteswelt*, p. 80. In the late nineteenth century, the Indian modernist Shibli Nuʿmani also expressed similar ideas; see Murad, *Intellectual Modernism of Shibli Nuʿmānī*, pp. 44, 70–72.

17. Furuzanfar, *Aḥādīth-i Mathnawī*, no. 42. For the history of this *ḥadīth qudsī*, a favorite with the Sufis, see Graham, *Divine Word and Prophetic Word*, pp. 98, 173, saying no. 49.

18. Razi, *The Path of God's Bondsmen*, p. 151.

19. Dard, *'Ilm ul-kitāb*, p. 61.

20. For this development see *History of the Freedom Movement*, prepared by a board of editors, vols. 1–2 (Karachi, 1957). The most extensive study of Ahmad Brelwi is Mehr, *Sayyid Aḥmad Shahīd*. For the later development see Hunter, *Our Indian Musulmans*.

21. Padwick, *Muslim Devotions*, p. 150.

22. Padwick, *Muslim Devotions*, pp. 150–51.

23. Padwick, *Muslim Devotions*, pp. 164–65.

24. Padwick, *Muslim Devotions*, p. 147.

25. Ghalib, *Kulliyāt-i Fārsī*, 5:49–59, esp. 57; see Rahbar, "Ghālib and a Debatable Point of Theology."

26. *Iqbālnāma*, 1:117 (1922).

27. Troll, *Sayyid Ahmad Khan*, is the best modern study; see also Baljon, *The*

Reforms and Religious Ideas of Sayyid Ahmad Khan.

28. H. A. R. Gibb, *Whither Islam?*, p. 199.

29. Iqbal, letter of 20 January 1925; see Schimmel, *Gabriel's Wing*, p. 74.

30. Troll, *Sayyid Ahmad Khan*, pp. 322–24, translates his most important statement: "The belief in the prophethood of Muhammad."

31. Being the first book of its kind, Sayyid Ahmad's *Essays* aroused some comment in England; see Mountfort, "Mohammad: A Mohammadan Apologist in London."

32. Watt, "Carlyle and Muhammad." The chapter "The Hero as Prophet" was translated into Arabic by Muhammad Sibaʿi in 1934.

33. Irving's *Life of Muhammad* was soon translated into the major European languages, and as early as 1892 also into Urdu.

34. Troll, *Sayyid Ahmad Khan*, p. 43.

35. Ahmad Khan, *Maqālāt-i Sir Sayyid*, vol. 13, deals largely with the problem of miracles; see esp. pp. 92–103.

36. Troll, "Reason and Revelation in the Theology of Mawlānā Shiblī Nuʿmānī," p. 25.

37. Troll, "Sayyid Ahmad Khan and Islamic Jurisprudence," p. 9.

38. Troll, *Sayyid Ahmad Khan*, p. 235, a translation of the passage.

39. See chapter 2, n. 21.

40. W. C. Smith, *Modern Islam in India*, p. 52 (1969 ed.).

41. Professor Nowaihi's speech to the Harvard Islamic Society in 1968, "Towards a Reevaluation of Muhammad: Prophet and Man," emphasizes exactly the same viewpoint. Almost identical words were used by the officials of the Pakistan Embassy in Bonn, when I asked them about the arrangements for the *maulid* celebrations in the embassies of Islamic countries in December 1982.

42. Hourani, *Arabic Thought in the Liberal Age*, p. 135.

43. See Rahman, "*Sīrat an-nabī* of Allamah Shibli." The *Sīra* was translated into Sindhi by Lutfullah Badawi in 1935.

44. Jagtiani, *Muḥammad Rasūl Allāh*. Hamadeh, "Muhammad the Prophet," no. 730, mentions with approval a Hindustani work on the *Sīra* by Pandit Sundarlal, which was translated into Gujarati. This contrasts with the disgusting picture of the Prophet as given in a highly debated "*purāṇa*"; see Meyer, "Moses und Zarathustra, Jesus und Muhammad in einem Purāṇa." This *Bhavishyapurāṇa* was declared "a literary fraud" in 1903 by the German indologist Theodor Aufrecht because it contains information about the great Western religions, mentions the names of the Moghul emperors, and gives a most vicious description of *Mahāmada* (Muhammad). The age of this *purāṇa* is difficult to assess, but to a nonspecialist it looks indeed quite recent.

45. In the foreword to his *Sīrat an-nabī* (Life of the Prophet) Fath Muhammad Sehwani in 1914 attacked his colleagues in Sind: "By writing novels and plays they have made ashamed the Sindhi language and spoiled the taste of men; they have written exaggerated and untrue stories about the honored saints, but alas! they have not thought of writing about the benign state of the lord of the prophets!"

46. Thus the West African Sufi master Shaikh Ibrahim Niass sings in his collection of praise poems (*Nuzhat al-asmāʾ waʾl-afkār fī madīḥ al-amīn*, Zaria, n.d.):

Muhammad, the Servant of God, is beyond being compared with anyone . . .
The Merciful God has begotten no son, but [Muhammad] is his dear little servant.

Hiskell, "The 'Community of Grace,'" p. 116. See also the relevant statement in Schuon, *Le Soufisme*, p. 55. On 16 December 1982 the Pakistani paper *Dawn Overseas* published in its weekly column "Islam—Religion of Man" a contribution by Professor Qamaruddin Khan, the regular columnist for this field, entitled "Prophet a Human Being," which closes with the following paragraph: "There, however, exists a strong tendency in Islamic literature to portray the Prophet as a superhuman, to deify him, and in popular thinking, preaching and songs he is painted as an incarnation of God, and is shown to possess a higher divinity than Christ. This tendency has done great harm to Islam and to the personality of the Prophet. Therefore, a new effort must be made to give the true image of the Prophet to the world, and show him as the truest servant of God on earth." It is surprising that the author uses the word "incarnation"; it seems to me that this danger has been avoided in Islam despite the high-soaring mystical descriptions of the Prophet.

47. W. C. Smith, *Modern Islam in India*, p. 70.

48. W. C. Smith, *Modern Islam in India*, p. 71.

49. W. C. Smith, *Modern Islam in India*, p. 75. Good examples of the deep veneration of the Prophet in the theological school of ʿAli Riza Barelwi in Indo-Pakistan appear in Metcalf, *Islamic Revival in British India*, pp. 303–5.

50. Siddiqi and Asi, *Armaghān-i naʿt*, p. 133.

51. Gairdner, "Muhammad without Camouflage," pp. 53, 57. Cf. W. C. Smith, *Modern Islam in India*, p. 75 (1969 ed.), the quotation from W. Wilson Cash, *The Moslem World in Revolution*, that Muhammad "has been painted in colours drawn from a Christian paint box." The feeling that many trends in mystical and popular Islam were influenced by Christian customs and thought had been clearly expressed as early as the Middle Ages by critics like Ibn Taimiyya; see Memon, *Ibn Taimiyya's Struggle against Popular Religion*, introduction.

52. Hourani, *Arabic Thought in the Liberal Age*, p. 114.

53. Hourani, *Arabic Thought in the Liberal Age*, p. 129.

54. Hourani, *Arabic Thought in the Liberal Age*, p. 136.

55. Hourani, *Arabic Thought in the Liberal Age*, pp. 186–87.

56. Hourani, *Arabic Thought in the Liberal Age*, p. 190.

57. Wielandt, *Offenbarung und Geschichte*, p. 53.

58. Jeffery, *Muhammad and His Religion*, p. 3.

59. For these more or less poetical attempts see the critique in Khurshid and Zaki, *Muḥammad fīʾl-adab al-muʿāṣir*, part 2.

60. The very titles of Ahmad Amin's great trilogy about Islamic civilization once again evoke the traditional imagery of light: *Fajr al-Islām*; *Ḍuḥā al-Islām*; *Ẓuhr al-Islām*—the Dawn, Morning Light, and Noon of Islam.

61. Brockelmann, *GAL*, S3:209–10. Johansen, *Muḥammad Ḥusain Haikal*, pp. 16–70. Hamadeh, "Muhammad the Prophet," p. 84, thinks that Haikal's biography was influenced by Dermenghem's *La Vie de Mahomet*.

62. Qasimi, *Naqd kitāb Ḥayāt Muḥammad.*

63. ʿAqqad also wrote many books about the *ʿabqariyya*, "genius," of early Muslims.

64. ʿAqqad, *ʿAbqariyyat Muḥammad*, introduction.

65. Brockelmann, *GAL* S3:299–301. Khurshid and Zaki, *Muḥammad fīʾl-adab al-muʿāṣir*, pp. 17–34.

66. Thus one finds books by one Muhammad Faraj: *Al-ʿAbqariyyat al-ʿaskariyya fī ghazawāt ar-rasūl* (The Military Genius in the Wars of the Prophet), and *Muḥammad al-Muḥārib* (Muhammad the Warrior), published in Cairo, 1958, n.d. (ca. 1956), respectively.

67. Wielandt, *Offenbarung und Geschichte*, p. 89.

68. Wessels, "Modern Biographies of the Life of the Prophet in Arabic," p. 102.

69. W. C. Smith, *Modern Islam in India*, pp. 136–37.

70. In *Pensée Chiite*, no. 5 (1960).

71. Samancĭgil, *Hazreti Muhammad Türk mi idi?*

72. Rasheed, "The Development of *naʿtia* Poetry," p. 68.

73. Brockelmann, *GAL*, S3:244–45.

74. See Khurshid and Zaki, *Muhammad fīʾl-adab al-muʿāṣir*, pp. 37–51.

CHAPTER TWELVE

1. *Jāvīdnāma*, line 608.

2. *Payām-i Mashriq*, pp. 151–52.

3. Quoted in Andrae, *Die person Muhammads*, p. 187.

4. Siddiqi and Asi, *Armaghān-i naʿt*, p. 124.

5. *Bāl-i Jibrīl*, p. 61.

6. "Islam as a Moral and Political Ideal," *Hindustan Review* 20 (July–December 1909); reprinted in *Speeches and Statements.*

7. *Iqbālnāma*, 2:93.

8. *Pas che bāyad kard*, p. 69.

9. *Asrār-i khudī*, line 383.

10. *Rumūz-i bēkhudī*, pp. 193–94.

11. Cf. *Iqbālnāma*, 1:414.

12. *Pas che bāyad kard*, pp. 64 ff.

13. Allusions to the *Burda* in *Rumūz-i bēkhudī*, pp. 116, 118, 195; *Bāl-i Jibrīl*, p. 151.

14. *Iqbālnāma*, 1:248, letter to Sayyid Mahfuz ʿAli Badayuni.

15. *Pas che bāyad kard*, p. 49; cf. *Bāl-i Jibrīl*, p. 130.

16. *Payām-i Mashriq*, p. 221.

17. Cf. *Armaghān-i Ḥijāz*, p. 71.

18. *Iqbālnāma*, 1:404.

19. *Musāfir*, pp. 29 ff.

20. Jami, *Dīwān*, p. 83, no. 56.

21. Cf. *Iqbālnāma*, 2:36 (1911).

22. *Bāng-i Darā*, p. 156.
23. Cf. *Iqbālnāma*, 1:222 (1937), 382 (1937), 232 (1938).
24. *Bāng-i Darā*, p. 219.
25. *Iqbālnāma*, 2:397.
26. *Bāl-i Jibrīl*, p. 151.
27. *Pas che bāyad kard*, p. 29.
28. *Bāng-i Darā*, p. 232.
29. *Asrār-i khudī*, lines 343, 350.
30. *Bāng-i Darā*, p. 231.
31. *Asrār-i khudī*, lines 355–58.
32. Good examples in *Bāl-i Jibrīl*, pp. 110–11, 213; *Pas che bāyad kard*, pp. 23–31.
33. Furuzanfar, *Aḥādīth-i Mathnawī*, no. 54.
34. Cf. *Musāfir*, p. 3; *Pas che bāyad kard*, pp. 23 ff.
35. *Asrār-i khudī*, lines 362–63.
36. *Pas che bāyad kard*, pp. 12 ff.
37. *Rumūz-i bēkhudī*, p. 130.
38. *Jāvīdnāma*, "Sphere of Jupiter."
39. *Asrār-i khudī*, line 189.
40. *Iqbālnāma*, 1:153 (1922 to Sayyid Sulaiman Nadwi).
41. *Żarb-i Kalīm*, p. 53.
42. *Jāvīdnāma*, "Sphere of the Moon," *Ṭāsīn* of Zarathustra.
43. *Bāng-i Darā*, p. 281.
44. *Six Lectures on the Reconstruction of Religious Thought in Islam*, p. 124 (hereafter *Reconstruction*).
45. *Reconstruction*, p. 190.
46. Goldziher, *Muhammedanische Studien*, 1:23.
47. *Jāvīdnāma*, "Sphere of the Moon," *Ṭāsīn* of Muhammad.
48. *Stray Reflections*, no. 19; cf. *Reconstruction*, p. 146.
49. *Bāng-i Darā*, p. 173.
50. *Bāng-i Darā*, p. 174.
51. *Speeches and Statements*, p. 120.
52. *Pas che bāyad kard*, p. 66.
53. Ibn Khaldun, *Muqaddima*, book 1, part 3.
54. *Asrār-i khudī*, lines 395–96; cf. *Payām-i Mashriq*, "Lāla-i Ṭūr," p. 83.
55. *Musāfir*, p. 32.
56. *Payām-i Mashriq*, p. 161; about his attitude toward Turkey and Ataturk see Schimmel, *Gabriel's Wing*, pp. 240 ff.
57. *Żarb-i Kalīm*, p. 44.
58. *Speeches and Statements*, p. 238.
59. *Rumūz-i bēkhudī*, pp. 116–17.
60. *Bāng-i Darā*, p. 155.
61. *Rumūz-i bēkhudī*, p. 116.
62. *Bāl-i Jibrīl*, p. 97; cf. pp. 117, 119.
63. *Rumūz-i bēkhudī*, p. 163.

64. *Reconstruction*, p. 126.

65. *Reconstruction*, p. 17; Iqbal regrets that the interpreters have never properly assessed the importance of this story.

66. *Reconstruction*, p. 3.

67. *Payām-i Mashriq*, p. 6.

68. Baljon, *Modern Muslim Koran Interpretation*, p. 73.

69. Baljon, *Modern Muslim Koran Interpretation*, p. 73.

70. Khalid, "A Terrorist Looks at Islam."

71. "Open Letter to Pandit Nehru," in *Speeches and Statements*, pp. 111–44, this quotation pp. 108, 120.

72. *Armaghān-i Ḥijāz*, p. 81.

73. *Bāl-i Jibrīl*, p. 155.

74. *Bāng-i Darā*, p. 172.

75. *Armaghān-i Ḥijāz*, p. 29.

76. *Rumūz-i bēkhudī*, p. 190.

BIBLIOGRAPHY

Abbott, Nabia. *Aishah: The Beloved of Mohammad*. Chicago: University of Chicago Press, 1942. Reprinted 1982.

ʿAbdal ʿAlī Ḥāfiẓ Jhāndā. *Guldasta-i Ḥāfiẓ Jhāndā*. Lahore: Allāhwālē kī qaumī dukān, n.d.

Abdal Mannan, Qazi. "Sufi Literature in Bengal." Heritage of Bangladesh, Medieval Period. New York: Learning Resources in International Studies, n.d. [ca. 1975]. (One of a series of mimeographed articles.)

ʿAbd ar-Rahim ibn Ahmad al-Qadi. *Islamic Book of the Dead*. Norwich and San Francisco: Diwan Press, 1977.

Abdul Ghani, Muhammad. *History of Persian Language and Literature at the Mughal Court*. 3 vols. Allahabad: Indian Press, 1929. Reprinted 1972.

ʿAbdul Ḥaqq Dihlawī, Muḥaddith. *Madārij an-nubuwwa*. 2 vols. Delhi, 1281h/1864–5.

ʿAbdul Laṭīf of Bhit, Shāh. *Shāh jō Risālō*. Edited by Kalyān B. Adwānī. Bombay: Hindustān Kitābghar, 1958.

ʿAbdur Razzāq, Qāzī. *Asānjō piyārō nabī*. Karachi: Madīna dār ul-ishāʿat, 1959.

Abel, Armand. "Le caractère sociologique des origines du 'culte' de Mahomet dans l'Islam tardif." In *Mélanges Smets*, pp. 43–45. Brussels, 1952.

Abou Shama. "Origine du 'Mawlid' ou fête de la naissance du Prophète." *BEA* 5 (1945): 147.

Abū'l-Maḥāsin Ibn Taghrībirdī. *Annals, entitled An-nujūm az-zāhira fī ta'rīkh Miṣr wa'l-Qāhira*. Edited by William Popper. 8 vols. Berkeley: University of California Press, 1920–36.

Abun-Nasr, Jamil M. *The Tijaniyya: A Sufi Order in the Modern World*. London, New York, and Toronto: Oxford University Press, 1965.

Abū Nuʿaim al-Iṣbahānī. *Dalā'il an-nubuwwa*. Rev. ed. Hyderabad/Deccan: Dairatul Maarif, 1950.

Affifi, Abu'l-Aʿla. *The Mystical Philosophy of Muḥyīd'Dīn Ibnul-ʿArabī*. Cambridge: Cambridge University Press, 1936. Reprinted Lahore: Ashraf, n.d.

———. "The Story of the Prophet's Ascent (*miʿrāj*) in Sufi Thought and Literature." *Islamic Quarterly* 2 (1955): 23–29.

Aflākī, Aḥmad ibn Muḥammad. *Manāqib al-ʿārifīn*. Edited by Tahsin Yazĭcĭ. 2 vols. Ankara: Ankara Üniversitesi yayĭnlarĭndan, 1959–61. Translated into Turkish by Tahsin Yazĭcĭ as *Ariflerin menkibeleri*. Ankara: Milli Eğitim

Yayĭnevi, 1964. Abridged French translation by Clément Huart as *Les saints des dervishes tourneurs*. Paris: E. Leroux, 1918–22.

Ahlwardt, Wilhelm. *Verzeichnis der arabischen Handschriften*. Berlin: A. W. Schade. Vols. 7–9 and 16–20 of *Die Handschriften-Verzeichnisse der Königlichen Bibliothek zu Berlin*. Reprinted Hildesheim and New York: Olms, 1980–81.

Ahmad, Barakat. *Muhammad and the Jews: A Re-examination*. Delhi: Vikas, 1979.

Ahmad Khan, Sayyid. *Maqālāt-i Sir Sayyid*. Edited by Maulānā Muḥammad Ismāʿīl Panīpatī. 13 vols. Lahore: Majlis-i taraqqī-i adab, 1963.

———. *A Series of Essays on the Life of Mohammed, and Subjects Subsidiary Thereto*. London: Trübner & Co., 1870.

Ahrens, Karl. *Muhammad als Religionsstifter*. Abhandlungen für die Kunde des Morgenlandes, 19.4. Leipzig: Brockhaus, 1935.

Ajabnama: A Volume of Oriental Studies presented to E. G. Browne. Cambridge: Cambridge University Press, 1922.

Akseki, Ahmet Hamdi. *Peygamberimiz*. Ankara: Diyanet Işleri Reisliği, n.d. [after 1950].

ʿAlāyilī, ʿAbdallāh al-. *Mathaluhunna al-aʿlā* ("Their Loftiest Model," i.e., Khadija). Beirut: Dār al-ḥikma, 1956.

Algar, Hamid. "Some Notes on the Naqshbandi *ṭarīqat* in Bosnia." *WI*, n.s. 13, 3–4 (1971): 168–203.

———. See also Rāzī.

Ali, Mrs. Meer Hasan. *Observations on the Musulmauns of India*. 2 vols. London, 1832. Reprinted Karachi and New York: Oxford University Press, 1974.

Ali, Maulana Muhammad. *A Manual of Hadith*. Lahore: The Ahmadiyya Anjuman-i Ishaat-i Islam, n.d. [ca. 1960].

Ali, Ummed. *Mohammed in the Ancient Scriptures*. Agra: S. R. & Brothers, 1936.

Altmann, Alexander. "The Ladder of Ascension." In *Studies in Mysticism and Religion Presented to Gerschom Scholem*, pp. 1–32. Edited by E. E. Urbach et al. Jerusalem: Magnus Press, 1967.

Alwaya, Mohiaddin. "The Life of the Prophet Is the Exemplary Pattern of Conduct." *Majallat al-Azhar* 47, no. 3 (1975): 1–5.

Ameer Ali, Syed. *The Life and Teachings of Muhammad, or The Spirit of Islam*. London, 1897. Numerous later editions.

Amīr Khusrau. *Dīwān-i kāmil*. Edited by Maḥmūd Darwīsh, preface by Saʿīd Nafīsī. Tehran: Intishārāt-i jāwīdān, 1344sh/1965.

———. *Majnūn Lailā*. Edited by T. A. Magerramov. Moscow: Nauk, 1964.

———. *Mathnawī Nuh Sipihr*. Edited by M. Waheed Mirza. Calcutta: Baptist Mission Press, 1948.

ʿAndalīb, Nāṣir Muḥammad. *Nāla-i ʿAndalīb*. 2 vols. Bhopal, 1309h/1891.

Andrae, Tor. *Mohammad. Sein Leben und sein Glaube*. Göttingen: Vandenhoek und Ruprecht, 1932. Reprinted 1977. Translated by Theophil Menzel as *Mohammed: The Man and His Faith*. London: Allen and Unwin, 1956; New York: Harper Torchbook, 1960. Translated by Jean Gaudefroy-Demombynes as *Ma-*

homet, sa vie et sa doctrine. Paris: Adrien-Maisonneuve, 1945; 2nd ed., as Initiation à l'Islam, 2, 1979.
———. *Die person Muhammads in lehre und glaube seiner gemeinde*. Stockholm: P. A. Vorstedt og söner, 1918.
Antes, Peter. *Das Prophetenwunder in der frühen Aš'arīya bis al-Ghazālī*. Freiburg: Klaus Schwarz, 1970.
Anwarī, Auḥaduddīn. *Dīwān*. Edited by Saʿīd Nafīsī. Tehran: Pīrūz, 1337sh/1958.
ʿAqqād, ʿAbbās Maḥmūd al-. *ʿAbqariyyat Muḥammad*. Cairo: Dār al-hilāl, 1961.
———. *Dāʿī as-samāʾ: muʾadhdhin an-nabī Bilāl ibn Rabāḥ*. Cairo: Dār Saʿd liʾn-nashr, 1945.
Arberry, Arthur John. *Aspects of Islamic Civilization*. London: Allen & Unwin, 1964; Ann Arbor: University of Michigan Press, 1967.
———. *Discourses of Rumi*. London: John Murray, 1961.
———. *Sufism: An Account of the Mystics of Islam*. London: Allen and Unwin, 1950. Often reprinted.
———, et al. *The Chester Beatty Library: A Catalogue of the Persian Manuscripts and Miniatures*. 3 vols. Dublin: Hodges Figgis, 1959–62.
Archer, John C. *Mystical Elements in Mohammad*. Yale Oriental Series 11.1. New Haven, 1924. Reprinted 1980.
Arnold, Sir Thomas. *Painting in Islam*. Oxford: Clarendon Press, 1928. Paperback ed. New York, 1965.
Asad ibn Mūsā. *Kitāb az-zuhd*. Nouvelle édition . . . par R. G. Khoury. Wiesbaden: Steiner, 1976.
Asín Palaćios, Miguel. *La Escatologia Musulmana en la Divina Commedia*. 2 vols. Madrid and Granada, 1919.
———. *Islam and the Divine Comedy*. Translated and abridged by Harold Sutherland. London: Frank Cass, 1926. Reprinted 1968.
Aṣlaḥ, Muḥammad. *Tadhkirat-i shuʿarā-i Kashmīr*. Edited by Sayyid Hussamuddin Rashdi. 5 vols. Karachi: Iqbal Academy, 1967–68.
ʿAṭṭār, Farīduddīn. *Ilāhīnāma*. Edited by Helmut Ritter. Istanbul and Leipzig: Brockhaus, 1940. See also Boyle.
———. *Manṭiq uṭ-ṭair*. Edited by M. Jawād Shakūr. Tehran: Kitābfurūsh-i Ṭehrān, 1341sh/1962.
———. *Muṣībatnāma*. Edited by N. Wiṣāl. Tehran: Zawwār, 1338sh/1959. Translated by Isabelle de Gastines as *Le livre de l'épreuve*. Paris: Flammarion, 1981.
———. *Tadhkirat al-auliyāʾ*. Edited by Reynold A. Nicholson. 2 vols. London: Luzac; Leiden: Brill, 1905–7. Reprinted 1959.
———. *Ushturnāma*. Edited by Mehdī Muḥaqqiq. Tehran: University, 1339sh/1960.
Ayoub, Mahmoud. *Redemptive Suffering in Islam*. The Hague, Paris, and New York: Mouton, 1978.
Āzād Bilgrāmī, Ghulām ʿAlī. *Khizāna-yi ʿāmira*. Cawnpore, 1871.
Aʿẓam Tattawī, Muḥammad. *Tuḥfat aṭ-ṭāhirīn*. Edited by Aghā Badruddīn

Durrānī. Karachi: Sindhi Adabi Board, 1956.
Aziz Ahmad. *Islamic Modernism in India and Pakistan*. London and New York: Oxford University Press, 1967.
———, and Gustave E. von Grunebaum, eds. *Muslim Self-Statement in India and Pakistan 1857–1960*. Wiesbaden: Harrassowitz, 1970.
Azma, Nazeer el-. "Some Notes on the Impact of the Story of the *miʿrāj* on Sufi Literature." *MW* 63 (1973): 93–104.
ʿAzzām, ʿAbdar Raḥmān. *Baṭl al-abṭāl au abraz ṣifāt an-nabī Muḥammad*. Cairo: Maṭbaʿa dār al-kitāb al-ʿarabī, 1946. 2nd ed. 1954.
———. *The Eternal Message of Muhammad*. Translated from the Arabic by Caesar E. Farah. New York: The Devin-Adair Company, 1964.
Bābū Čilasī. *Zād-i safar*. Abbottabad, n.d. [ca. 1974]. (Shina poetry.)
Badaoni, ʿAbdul Qadir. *Muntakhab at-tawārīkh*. Edited by W. Nassau Lees, Maulwī Kabīruddin, and Maulwī Aḥmad Alī. Calcutta, 1864–69. Translated by G. Ranking (vol. 1), W. H. Lowe (vol. 2), and T. W. Haig (vol. 3). Calcutta, 1884–1925. Reprinted Patna: Academia Asiatica, 1973.
Baihaqī, Abū Bakr Aḥmad al-. *Dalāʾil an-nubuwwa*. Edited by ʿAbdur Raḥmān Muḥammad ʿUthmān. Madina: Al-maktaba as-salafiyya, 1389h/1969.
Bājūrī, Ibrāhīm al-. *Ḥāshiya ʿalā ash-shamāʾil al-muḥammadiyya (liʾt-Tirmidhī)*. Bulaq: Dār aṭ-ṭabāʿa al-ʿāmira, 1276h/1859–60.
———. *Ḥāshiya ʿalā maulid Ibn al-Barakāt Sīdī Aḥmad ad-Dardīr*. 2nd ed. Cairo: Al-maṭbaʿa al-khairiyya, 1326h/1908.
Baljon, Jon M. S. *Modern Muslim Koran Interpretation (1880–1960)*. Leiden: Brill, 1961.
———. *A Mystical Interpretation of Prophetic Tales by an Indian Muslim: Shāh Walī Allāh's taʾwīl al-aḥādīth*. Leiden: Brill, 1973.
———. *The Reforms and Religious Ideas of Sayyid Ahmad Khan*. 2nd ed. Lahore: Ashraf, 1953.
Baloch, Nabibakhsh A., ed. *Madāḥūñ ain munājātūñ*. Karachi: Sindhi Adabi Board, 1959.
———. *Maulūd*. Hyderabad/Sind: Sindhi Adabi Board, 1961.
———. *Muʿjizā*. Hyderabad/Sind: Sindhi Adabi Board, 1960.
———. *Munāqibā*. Hyderabad/Sind: Sindhi Adabi Board, 1960.
———. *Ṭih akharyūñ*. 2 vols. Hyderabad/Sind: Sindhi Adabi Board, 1960–61.
Bannerth, Ernst. "Lieder ägyptischer *meddâḥîn*." *WZKM* 56 (1960): 9–20.
Baqi, Fazlur Rahman. "*Kitāb faḍāʾil ar-ramy fī sabīl Allāh*." *IC* 34 (1960): 195–207.
Baqlī, Rūzbihān. *ʿAbhar al-ʿāshiqīn: Le jasmine des fidèles d'amour*. Edited by Henry Corbin. Tehran and Paris: Adrien-Maisonneuve, 1958.
———. *Sharḥ-i shaṭḥiyāt: Les paradoxes des Soufis*. Edited by Henry Corbin. Tehran and Paris: Adrien-Maisonneuve, 1966.
Barnett, Lionel D. *Panjabi: Printed Books in the British Museum*. London: British Museum, 1961.
Bārūdī, Maḥmūd Sāmī al-. *Kashf al-ghumma fī madḥ sayyid al-umma*. Cairo, 1909.
Basset, René. *La Bânat Soʿâd*. Algiers, 1910.

———, trans. *La Bordah du Cheikh al-Bousiri*. Paris, 1894.
Bbārānā gīta. Hyderabad/Sind: Sindhi Adabi Board, 1981. (Collection of Sindhi children's songs.)
Becker, Carl Heinrich. *Islamstudien*. 2 vols. Leipzig: Quelle und Meyer, 1932.
Bēdil, Mirzā ʿAbdul Qādir. *Kulliyāt*. 4 vols. Kabul: D'Pohnī Wizārat, 1344sh/1965.
Bēdil Rōhrīwārō. *Dīwān*. Edited by ʿAbd al-Ḥusain Mūsawī. Karachi: Sindhi Adabi Board, 1954.
Bell, Joseph N. *Love Theories in Later Hanbalite Islam*. Albany: SUNY Press, 1979.
Bell, Richard. "Muhammad and Previous Messengers." *MW* 24 (1934): 330–40.
———. "Muhammad's Visions." *MW* 24 (1934): 145–54.
Bevan, Anthony A. "Muhammad's Ascension to Heaven." *Zeitschrift für Alttestamentliche Wissenschaft*, Beiheft 27 (1914): 49–61.
Bijlefeld, Willem A. "A Prophet and More than a Prophet? Some Observations on the Qur'ānic Use of the Terms 'Prophet' and 'Apostle.'" *MW* 49 (1959): 1–28.
Bint ash-Shāṭī'. *Āmina bint Wahb*. Cairo: Dār al-hilāl, 1953.
———. *Banāt an-nabī*. Cairo: Dār al-hilāl, 1956.
———. *Nisā' an-nabī*. Cairo: Dār al-hilāl, 1960.
Birge, John K. *The Bektashi Order of Dervishes*. London: Luzac, 1937. Reprinted 1965.
Birkeland, Harris. *The Legend of the Opening of Muhammad's Breast*. Oslo: Nordske Videnskaps Academi, in commission J. Dywood, 1955.
Bismil, Ḥāfiẓ ʿAbdullāh Ṭhikurāʾī. *Mathnawī Muḥammadī*. Hyderabad/Sind: Islāmiyya Dār al-ishāʿat, 1957.
Bisṭāmī, ʿAbdur Raḥmān ibn Muḥammad al-. *Kitāb fi'l-kalām ʿalā ḥurūf ismi Muḥammad*. Princeton University, Jehuda Collection no. 4522, fols. 42b–52b.
Blachère, Regis. *Le problème de Mahomet: essai de biographie critique du fondateur de l'Islam*. Paris: Presses Universitaires de France, 1952.
———, Frédérique Duran, and Helena Delattre. *Dans les pas de Mahomet*. Paris: Librairie Hachette, 1956.
Blochet, Edgard. "Etudes sur l'histoire religieuse de l'Iran, II: l'ascension au ciel du Prophète Mohammad." *RHR* 40 (1899): 1–25, 203–236.
Blumhardt, James Fuller, and D. N. MacKenzie. *Catalogue of Pashto Manuscripts in the Libraries of the British Isles*. London: British Museum, 1965.
Bodley, R. V. C. *The Messenger: The Life of Mohammad*. New York: Doubleday, 1946. 2nd rev. ed. Lahore: Orientalia, 1954.
Boulainvilliers, Henri Comte. *La vie de Mahomet, avec des reflexions sur la religion Mahométane, et sur les coutumes des musulmans*. 2nd ed. Amsterdam, 1731. English translation, London, 1731.
Bousset, Wilhelm. "Die Himmelsreise der Seele." *ARW* (1901): 136–69, 229–73.
Böwering, Gerhard. *The Mystical Vision of Existence in Classical Islam: The Qur'ānic Hermeneutics of the Sufi Sahl at-Tustarī (d. 283/896)*. Berlin: de Gruyter, 1979.
———. "The Prophet of Islam: The First and the Last Prophet." In *The Message of the Prophet*, pp. 48–60. Islamabad: Government of Pakistan, 1979.

Boyle, John A., trans. *The Ilāhīnama "Book of God" of Farīduddīn ʿAṭṭār*. Manchester: Manchester University Press, 1976.

Braune, Walther. *Die Futūḥ al-ġaib des ʿAbd ul-Qādir*. Berlin and Leipzig: de Gruyter, 1933.

Bravmann, Meir M. "The Origin of the Principle of *ʿiṣmah*." *Muséon* 88 (1975): 221–25.

Brockelmann, Carl. *Geschichte der arabischen Literatur* (*GAL*), 3 vols. with supplements (S). Leiden: Brill, 1898, 1937, 1943–49.

Broomfield, G. W. "The Psychology of Mohammed." *MW* 16 (1926): 37–58.

Brunel, René. *Le monachisme errant dans l'Islam: Sidi Heddi et les Heddâwa*. Paris: Larose, 1955.

Buddruss, Georg. *Aus den Anfängen der Shina-Literatur*. In preparation.

———. *Khowar-Texte in arabischer Schrift*. Wiesbaden: Steiner, 1982.

Buhl, Frants. "The Character of Mohammad as a Prophet." *MW* 1 (1911): 356–64.

———. "Fasste Muhammad seine Verkündigung als eine universelle, auch für Nichtaraber bestimmte Religion auf?" *Islamica* 2 (1926): 135–49.

———. *Das Leben Muhammads*. Enlarged translation from the Danish edition of 1903 by Hans Heinrich Schaeder. Heidelberg: Quelle und Meyer, 1930. 2nd ed. 1955.

Bukhārī, Abū ʿAbdallāh Muḥammad. *Kitāb jāmiʿ aṣ-ṣaḥīh*. Edited by Ludolf Krehl and W. Juynboll. 4 vols. Leiden: Brill, 1862–1908. Translated by M. M. Khan as *Sahih al-Bukhari*. 6 vols. Lahore: Ashraf, 1978–80.

Bukhārī, Sayyid Bāqir ibn Sayyid ʿUthmān. *Jawāhir al-auliyā*. Edited by Dr. Ghulām Sarwar. Islamabad: Iran–Pakistan Institute of Persian Studies, 1976.

Burney, Mohd. Elias. *Mishkaat us-salawaat: A Bouquet of Blessings on Muhammad the Prophet (Peace be on Him)*. Transliterated into roman script and translated into English by M. A. Haleem Eliasi. Hyderabad/Deccan, 1978.

Burton, Richard. *Sindh, and the Races That Inhabit the Valley of the Indus*. London, 1851. Reprinted Karachi: Oxford University Press, 1973.

Būṣīrī, Abū ʿAbdallāh Muḥammad al-. *Die Burda*. Edited and translated into German by C. A. Ralfs, with metrical Persian and Turkish translations. Vienna, 1861.

———. *Nafḥ al-warda fī sharḥ al-burda*. With the Persian verse translation by Jāmī and the Urdu verse translation by Fayyāżaddīn Niẓāmī. Hyderabad/Deccan, 1969. English translation by Shaikh Faizullah-bhai as *A Moslem Present, Part I: The Poem of the Scarf*. Bombay, 1893. See also Basset.

Cachia, Pierre. "The Prophet's Shirt: Three Versions of an Egyptian Narrative Ballad." *Journal of Semitic Studies* 26, no. 1 (1981): 79–106.

Çağatay, Neşet. "The Tradition of *maulid* Recitations in Islam, Particularly in Turkey." *SI* 28 (1968): 127–33.

Cameron, A. J. *Abū Dharr al-Ghifārī*. London: Luzac, for the Royal Asiatic Society, 1973.

Canteins, Jean. *La voie des lettres*. Paris: Albin Michel, 1981.

Carlyle, Thomas. *On Heroes and Hero Worship, and the Heroic in History*. London: Chapman & Hall, 1840. Numerous later editions. Part translation (the lectures on Muhammad) into Arabic by Muḥammad Sibāʿī as *Muḥammad rasūl al-hudā wa'r-raḥmat*. Beirut: Al-maktaba al-ahliyya, 1934.

Cerbella, G. "Il natale del Profeta." *Libia* 4 (1954): 21–31.

Cerulli, Enrico. *Il "Libro della Scala" e la questione delle fonte arabo-spagnole della "Divina Commedia."* Vatican City, 1949.

Chelkowski, Peter J., ed. *Taʿziyah: Ritual and Drama in Iran*. New York: New York University Press, 1979.

Chester Beatty Library. See Arberry; Minorsky.

Chew, Samuel C. *The Crescent and the Rose: Islam and England during the Renaissance*. New York: Oxford University Press, 1937.

Corbin, Henry. *Avicenna and the Visionary Recital*. Translated by W. R. Trask. New York and London: Pantheon Books, 1960.

Cordt, Hartwig. *Die Sitzungen des ʿAlāʾ ad-dawla as-Simnānī*. Zurich: Juris Druck und Verlag, 1977.

Dailami, ʿAli ibn Aḥmad ad-. *Sīrat Abī ʿAbdillāh Ibn al-Khafīf ash-Shīrāzī in the Persian Translation of Junaid-i Shīrāzī*. Edited by Annemarie Schimmel. Ankara: Ilâhiyat Fakültesi, 1955.

Damīrī, Kamāladdīn Muḥammad. *Kitāb al-ḥayawān*. 2 vols. Cairo: 1305h/1887. Reprinted Beirut, n.d. [ca. 1955].

Dammann, Ernst. *Dichtungen in der Lamu-Mundart des Suaheli*. Hamburg: Friedrichsen, de Gruyter & Co., 1940.

Daniel, Norman. *Islam and the West: The Making of an Image*. Edinburgh: Edinburgh University Press, 1958.

Dar, M. J. "Gujarat's Contribution to Gujari and Urdu." *IC* 27 (1953): 18–36.

Dard, Khwāja Mīr. *ʿIlm ul-kitāb*. Delhi, 1310h/1892–3.

———. *Chahār Risāla*. Bhopal, 1309h/1891–2.

Dardīr. See Bājūrī.

Darmesteter, James. *Chants populaires des Afghans*. 2 vols. Paris, 1888–90. Reprinted Amsterdam: Philo Press, n.d.

Darwāzah, Muḥammad ʿIzzat. *Sīrat ar-rasūl, Ṣūra muqtabasa min al-qurʾān al-karīm*. Cairo: Maṭbaʿat al-istiqāma, 1948. (Biography of the Prophet based exclusively on the Koran.)

Daudpota, ʿUmar Muhammad. *Kalām-i Girhōrī*. Karachi: Maṭbaʿa al-ʿarab, 1956.

Dawud, ʿAbdul Ahad. *Mohammad in the Bible*. Allahabad: The Abbas Manzil Library, 1952.

Deladrière, Roger. *La Profession de Foi d'Ibn ʿArabī*. With an introduction, translation, and commentary. Paris: Michel Allard, 1978.

Dermenghem, Émile. *Mahomet et la tradition islamique*. Paris: Éditions du Seuil, 1955. Translated by Jean M. Watt as *Muhammad and the Islamic Tradition*. New York: Harper, 1958. Translated into German as *Mohammad in Selbstzeugnissen und Bilddokumenten*. Berlin: Rowohlt, 1960.

———. *La vie de Mahomet*. Paris: Plon, 1929. Translated by Arabella York as *The Life of Mahomet*. London: George Routledge & Son, 1939. A Turkish translation appeared in 1930, an Arabic one in 1949.

Donaldson, D. M. "Salmān the Persian." *MW* 19 (1929): 338–52.
Drewes, Gerardus W. J. *Een zestiende eeuwse Maleise vertaling van de Burda van al-Busiri, Arabisch lofdicht op Muhammad*. The Hague: Nijhoff, 1955.
Durrani, F. K. Khan. *The Great Prophet*. Tabligh Literature Co., 1931. Often reprinted.
Eaton, Richard M. *Sufis of Bijapur*. Princeton: Princeton University Press, 1978.
Edier, R. Y., and M. J. L. Young. "A List of the Appellations of the Prophet Muhammad." *MW* 66 (1976): 259–62.
Eliade, Mircea. "Le symbolisme du 'vol magique.'" *Numen* 3 (1956): 1–13.
Enevoldsen, Jens. *O Måne! Skynd dig! Stig op og skin!* Herning: Poul Kristensen for Dansk Pathanmission, 1967.
Engelke, Irmgard. *Sülejman Tschelebis Lobgedicht auf die Geburt des Propheten*. Halle: Niemeyer, 1926.
Esin, Emel. *Mecca the Blessed, Medinah the Radiant*. New York: Crown Publishers, 1963.
Ess, Joseph van. *Der Wesir und seine Gelehrten*. Wiesbaden: Steiner, 1981.
Ethé, Hermann. *Catalogue of the Persian Manuscripts in the India Office Library*. London: India Office Library and Records, 1903. Reprinted 1980.
Ettinghausen, Richard. "Persian Ascension Miniatures of the Fourteenth Century." In *L'Oriente e l'Occidente nel Medieaevo*, pp. 360–83. Roma: Accademia dei Lincei, 1956.
Fānī Murādābādī. *Hindū shuʿarā kā naʿtiya kalām*. Lyallpur, 1962.
Farid, A. H., comp. and trans. *Prayers of Muhammad*. Lahore: Ashraf, 1969. Reprinted 1974.
Fatḥ Muḥammad Sehwāṇī, Ḥakīm. *Sīrat an-nabī*. Karachi, 1916. 2nd ed. Hyderabad/Sind: Sindhi Adabi Board, 1978.
Fischer, August. *Muḥammad und Aḥmad*. Leipzig: Sächsische Akademie der Wissenschaften, 1932.
———. "Vergöttlichung und Tabuisierung der Namen Muhammads." In *Beiträge zur Arabistik, Semitistik und Islamkunde*, pp. 307–39. Edited by Richard Hartmann and Helmuth Scheel. Leipzig: Harrassowitz, 1944.
Foster, Frank H. "An Autobiography of Muhammad." *MW* 26 (1936): 130–52.
Friedmann, Yohanan. "Qiṣṣat Shakarwātī Farmāḍ." *Israel Oriental Studies* 5 (1975): 233–58.
———. *Shaykh Aḥmad Sirhindī: An Outline of His Thought and a Study of His Image in the Eyes of Posterity*. London and Montreal: McGill University Press, 1972.
Fück, Johann. "Muhammad—Persönlichkeit und Religionsstiftung." In J. Fück, *Arabische Kultur und Islam im Mittelalter*, pp. 152–75. Edited by Manfred Fleischhammer. Weimar: Hermann Böhlau's Nachf., 1981.
———. "Die Originalität des arabischen Propheten." In Fück, *Arabische Kultur und Islam im Mittelalter*, pp. 142–52.
Furati, Mewlâ. *Das Buch der vierzig Fragen*. Translated from the Turkish by Joachim Hein. Leiden: Brill, 1960.
Furūzānfar, Badīʿuzzamān. *Aḥādīth-i Mathnawī*. Tehran: University, 1334sh/1955.

Futrell, Michael. "Dostoyevsky and Islam (and Chokan Valikhanov)." *SEER* 57, no. 1 (1979): 16–31.

Fuzuli. *Divan*. Edited by Abdulbaki Gölpĭnarlĭ. Istanbul: Inkilâb, 1948.

Gabrieli, Francesco. *Mahomet: présentation de Mahomet*. Textes de Mahomet, Ibn Ishak, Tabari, Maçoudi, Ibn Al-Kalbi, Dante, Napoléon, Victor Hugo. Paris: A. Michel, 1965.

Gairdner, W. H. Temple. *Al-Ghazzālī's "Mishkāt al-anwār": The Niche for Lights*. Royal Asiatic Society Monographs, 19. London, 1924. Reprinted Lahore: Ashraf, 1952.

______. "Mohammad without Camouflage: Ecce Homo Arabicus." *MW* 9 (1919): 25–57.

Gätje, Helmut. *Koran und Koranexegese*. Zurich and Stuttgart: Artemis, 1971. (Especially important is chapter 2: "Mohammad.") Translated by Alford Welch as *The Koran and Its Exegesis*. Berkeley and Los Angeles: University of California Press, 1976.

Gaudefroy-Demombynes, Maurice. *Mahomet*. Paris: A. Michel, 1957. 2nd ed. 1969.

Geiger, Abraham. *Was hat Muhammad aus dem Judentum aufgenommen?* Bonn, 1833. 2nd ed. Leipzig: M. W. Kaufmann, 1902.

Gēsūdarāz, Sayyid Muḥammad Ḥusainī. *Dīwān Anīs al-ʿushshāq*. Hyderabad/Deccan: 1369h/1941.

Ghaiṭi, Muḥammad ibn Aḥmad. *Kitāb al-isrāʾ waʾl-miʿrāj*. Cairo: Maṭbaʿa Dār iḥyāʾ al-kutub al-ʿarabiyya, n.d.

Ghālib, Mirzā Asadullāh. *Kulliyāt-i Fārsī* (Persian Works). 17 vols. Lahore: University of the Punjab, 1969.

Ghawwāṣī, Mollā. *Saiful Mulūk wa Badīʿul Jamāl*. Edited by Mīr Saʿādat ʿAlī Riżwī. Hyderabad/Deccan: Majlis-i ishāʿat-i dakhnī makhṭūṭāt, 1357h/1938.

Ghazzālī, Abū Ḥāmid al-. *Iḥyāʾ ʿulūm ad-dīn*. 4 vols. Bulaq, 1289h/1872.

Ghiyath Matin, Sayyid. *Zīna zīna rākh*. Hyderabad/Deccan: Ḥalaf, 1980.

Gibb, Elias John Wilkinson. *A History of Ottoman Poetry*. 6 vols. London: Luzac, 1900–1909. Reprinted London: 1958–63.

Gibb, Sir Hamilton A. R. *Whither Islam?* London: Gollancz, 1932.

Gilsenan, Michael. *Saint and Sufi in Modern Egypt*. Oxford: Clarendon Press, 1973.

Goergens, E. P. *Mohammad, ein Charakterbild. Auf Grund der Darstellung Termidī's*. Berlin: C. Habel, 1878.

Goethe, Johann Wolfgang von. *West-Östlicher Divan*. Unter Mitwirkung von Hans Heinrich Schaeder herausgegeben und erläutert von Ernst Beutler. Leipzig: Dieterichsche Verlagsbuchhandlung, 1943. First published 1819; numerous other editions available.

Goldziher, Ignaz. "The Appearance of the Prophet in Dreams." *JRAS* (1912): 503–6.

______. "Chatm al-Buchârî." *Der Islam* 6 (1915–16): 214.

______. "Himmlische und irdische Namen." In *Ajabnama*, pp. 157–62.

______. "Influences chrétiennes dans la littérature religieuse de l'Islam." *RHR* 18 (1888): 180–99.

———. *Muhammedanische Studien*. 2 vols. Halle: Niemeyer, 1889–92. Translated by C. R. Barber and S. M. Stern as *Muslim Studies*. Edited by S. M. Stern. Chicago: Aldine, 1966, 1971.

———. "Neuplatonische und gnostische Elemente im *ḥadīth*." *Zeitschrift für Assyriologie* 22 (1908): 317–44.

Gölpīnarlī, Abdulbaki. *Tasavvuftan dilimize geçen deyimler ve atasözleri*. Istanbul: Inkilap ve Ata, 1977.

Graham, William A. *Divine Word and Prophetic Word in Early Islam*. The Hague: Mouton, 1977.

Gramlich, Richard. "Mystical Dimensions of Islamic Monotheism." In *We Believe in One God*, pp. 136–48. Edited by Annemarie Schimmel and Abdoljavad Falaturi. London: Burns & Oates, 1980.

———, trans. *Die Gaben der Erkenntnisse des ʿUmar as-Suhrawardī (ʿAwārif al-maʿārif)*. Wiesbaden: Steiner, 1978.

Grimme, Hubert. *Muhammad*. 3 vols. Münster i. W.: Aschendorff, 1892–95.

———. "Der Name Muhammad." *Zeitschrift für Semitistik* 6 (1928): 24–26.

Grunebaum, Gustave E. von. "The Early Development of Islamic Religious Poetry." *Journal of the American Oriental Society* 60 (1940): 23–29.

———. *Muhammadan Festivals*. Leiden: Brill; New York: Schuman, 1958.

———. "Von Muhammads Wirkung und Originalität." *WZKM* 44 (1937): 29–50.

Guillaume, Alfred. *The Life of Muhammad*. A translation of Ibn Isḥāq's *Sīrāt rasūl Allāh*. London: Oxford University Press, 1970.

———. "Where Was *al-masjid al-aqṣā*?" *Andalus* 18 (1935): 323–36.

Gurbaxshani, Hotchand M. *Luñwāriya jā lāl*. Karachi: Educational Pub. Co., 1934. Reprinted Hyderabad/Sind, 1978.

Haas, Hans. *Das Bild Muhammads im Wandel der Zeiten*. Berlin: Hutten-Verlag, 1916.

Hadi Hasan. "Qāsim-i Kāhī, His Life, Time, and Works." *IC* 27 (1953): 99–131, 161–94, 199–224.

Hadj-Sadok, Mahammed. "Le *mawlid* d'après le mufti-poète d'Alger Ibn ʿAmmār'." In *Mélanges Louis Massignon*, 2:269–92. Damascus: Institut français de Damas, 1956–57.

Haikal, Muhammad Husain. *Ḥayāt Muḥammad*. Cairo: Maṭbaʿa Dār al-kutub al-miṣriyya, 1935.

Ḥallāj, al-Ḥusain ibn Manṣūr al-. *Kitāb aṭ-ṭāwāsīn, texte arabe avec la version persane d'al-Baqlī*. Edited and translated by Louis Massignon. Paris: Geuthner, 1913.

Hamadeh, Muhammad Maher. "Muhammad the Prophet: A Selected Bibliography." Ph.D. dissertation, University of Michigan, 1965.

Hamadhānī, Badīʿuzzamān. *Maqāmāt*. Translated by Gernot Rotter as *Vernunft ist nichts als Narretei*. Tübingen: Erdmann, 1982.

Hamdi, ʿAbd al-Hamid, and ʿAli Abdar Raziq. "The Mohammad of the Newspapers." *MW* 18 (1928): 167–72.

Hamidullah, Muhammad. "Ce que pensait Lénine de Muhammad?" *Pensée Chiite* 5 (1960).

______. "La date de naissance du Prophète Muhammad." *France–Islam* 28–29 (June–July 1969).
______. *The Earliest Extant Work on the ḥadīth: Ṣaḥīfat Hammām ibn Munabbih*. 5th ed. Hyderabad/Deccan, 1961.
______. *The First Written Constitution in the World*. 2nd rev. ed. Lahore: Ashraf, 1968.
______. *Le Prophète de l'Islam*. 2 vols. Paris: Vrin, 1959.
Handwörterbuch des Islam. Edited by Arend J. Wensinck and J. H. Kramers. Leiden: Brill, 1941. English edition: *Shorter Encyclopaedia of Islam*. Edited by Hamilton A. R. Gibb and J. H. Kramers. Leiden: Brill, 1953.
Haq, Muhammad Enamul. *Sufiism in Bengal*. Dacca: Asia Society of Bangladesh, 1975.
Hartmann, Richard. "Die Himmelsreise Muhammads und ihre Bedeutung in der Religion des Islam." *Vorträge des Bibliothek Warburg*, 1928–29, pp. 42–65. Leipzig and Berlin: De Gruyter, 1930.
______. *Die Religion des Islam*. Berlin: E. S. Mittler & Sohn, 1944.
Hāshim, Makhdūm Muḥammad. *Dharīʿat al-wuṣūl ilā janāb ar-rasūl (durūd sharīf)*. Facsimile ed. with introduction by Maulānā Ghulām Muṣṭafā Qāsimī. Hyderabad/Sind: Mihran Arts Council, n.d. [1982].
Hashmi, Bashir Ahmad. "Sarmad, His Life and Quatrains." *IC* 7 (1933): 663–73, 8 (1934): 92–104.
Hāshmī, Sayyid Jahāngīr. *Mathnawī Maẓhar al-āthār*. Edited by Sayyid Hussamuddin Rashdi. Karachi: Sindhi Adabi Board, 1955.
Hāshmī, Ṭayyib. *Muʿjizāt-i sarwar-i kāʾināt*. Lahore: Shuʿāʿ-i adab, 1966.
Ḥassān ibn Thābit. *Dīwān*. Edited by Walid N. Arafat. GMS, n.s. 21. 2 vols. London: Luzac, 1971.
Heiler, Friedrich. *Erscheinungsformen und Wesen der Religion*. Stuttgart: Kohlhammer, 1961.
Heper, Sadettin. *Mevlevi Ayĭnleri*. 2nd ed. Konya: Turizm Derneği, 1978.
Hickmann, William. "Eshrefoghlu Rumi: Reconstitution of His Diwan." Ph.D. dissertation, Harvard University, 1972.
Hidayat Hosain, Muhammad. "Bānat Suʿād of Kaʿb ibn Zuhair." *IC* 1 (1927): 67–84 (translation and interpretation).
______. "Translation of ash-shamāʾil of Tirmizi." *IC* 7 (1933): 395–409, 561–72; 8 (1934): 46–54, 273–89, 364–86, 531–49.
Hiskett, Mervyn. "The 'Community of Grace' and Its Opponents, the 'Rejecters': A Debate about Theology and Mysticism in Muslim West Africa with Special Reference to Its Hausa Expression." *African Language Studies* 17 (1980): 99–140.
Holland, R. "Zur Typik der Himmelfahrt." *ARW* 23 (1925): 207–20.
Horovitz, Josef. "The Earliest Biographies of the Prophet and Their Authors." *IC* 1 (1927): 535–59, *IC* 2 (1928): 22–50, 164–82, 495–562.
______. "Miʿrāj." *EI*, 1st ed., 3:505–8.
______. "Muhammads Himmelfahrt." *Der Islam* 9 (1919): 159–83.
______. "Die poetischen Einlagen der *Sīra*." *Islamica* 2 (1926): 308–12.

———. "Salmān al-Fārisī." *Der Islam* 12 (1922): 178–83.
———. "Zur Muhammadlegende." *Der Islam* 5 (1914): 41–55. Translated as "The Growth of the Mohammad Legend." *MW* 10 (1920): 49–58.
Horten, Max. *Muhammedanische Glaubenslehren*. Bonn, 1916.
———. *Die religiöse Gedankenwelt der gebildeten Muslime*. Halle: Niemeyer, 1916.
———. *Die religiöse Vorstellungswelt des Volkes im Islam*. Halle: Niemeyer, 1917.
Hourani, Albert. *Arabic Thought in the Liberal Age*. London and New York: Oxford University Press, 1970.
Huart, Clément. "Selmân de Fârs." In *Mélanges Hartwig Derenbourg*, pp. 297–310. Paris: Leroux, 1909.
Huitema, Taede. *De Voorspraak (shafāʿa) in den Islam*. Leiden: Brill, 1936.
Hujwīrī, ʿAlī ibn ʿUthmān al-Jullabī al-. *Kashf al-maḥjūb*. Translated by Reynold A. Nicholson. GMS, 17. London: Luzac; Leiden: Brill, 1911. Reprinted 1959 and often thereafter.
Hunter, W. W. *Our Indian Musulmans*. London, 1871.
Ḥusain, ʿAlī Ṣafī. *Al-adab aṣ-ṣūfī fī Miṣr fīʾl-qarn as-sābiʿ al-hijrī*. Cairo: Dār al-maʿārif, 1964.
Husain, S. Q. A. *The Pantheistic Monism of Ibn ʿArabi*. Lahore: Ashraf, 1970.
Ḥusain, Ṭāhā. *ʿAlā hāmish as-sīra*. 3 vols. Cairo: Dar al-maʿārif, 1943.
Hussaini, Seyid Shah Khusro. "Bund samāʿ." *IC* 44 (1970): 177–85.
Ibn al-Jauzī, ʿAbdur Raḥmān. *Talbīs Iblīs (naqd al-ʿilm waʾl-ʿulamā)*. Cairo: Aṭ-ṭabāʿat al-munīriyya, n.d.
Ibn ʿArabī, Muḥyīʾddīn. *Fuṣūṣ al-ḥikam*. Edited by Abūʾl-Aʿlā ʿAffīfī. Cairo: ʿIsā al-bābī al-ḥalabī, 1946. Translated by R. W. J. Austin as *Ibn al-Arabi: The Bezels of Wisdom*. Preface by Titus Burckhardt. New York: Paulist Press, 1980.
———. *Al-Futūḥāt al-makkiyya*. 4 vols. Cairo, 1329h/1911.
———. *La Profession de Foi*. See Deladrière.
Ibn Ḥazm, Abū Muḥammad ʿAlī. *Al-faṣl fīʾl-milal waʾl-ahwāʾ waʾn-niḥal*. 4 vols. Cairo 1317–21h/1899–1903.
Ibn Isḥāq. *Sīrat rasūl Allāh. Das Leben Muhammads bearbeitet von ʿAbd el-Malik ibn Hishâm*. Edited by Ferdinand Wüstenfeld. 2 vols. in 3. Göttingen, 1858–60. Reprinted 1961. Translated by Gernot Rotter as *Das Leben des Propheten*. Tübingen: Erdmann, 1976. See also Guillaume.
Ibn Iyās. *Badāʾiʿ az-zuhūr fī waqāʾiʿ ad-duhūr*. Edited by Paul Kahle and Mohammed Mostafa. 3 vols. Istanbul and Leipzig: Brockhaus, 1931–36.
Ibn Kathīr, ʿImāduddīn Ismāʿīl. *Maulid Rasūl Allāh*. Edited by Dr. Ṣalāḥuddīn al-Munajjid. Beirut: Dār al-kutub al-jadīda, 1961.
Ibn Khaldun. *The Muqaddima*. Edited by Étienne Quatremère. Prologèmes d'Ibn Khaldun. 3 vols. Paris: Académie des Inscriptions et Belles Lettres, 1858. Translated from the Arabic by Franz Rosenthal as *Ibn Khaldūn: The Muqaddimah*. Bollingen Series, 43. 2nd ed. 3 vols. Princeton: Princeton University Press, 1967.
Ibn Khallikān, Aḥmad ibn Muḥammad. *Wafāyāt al-aʿyān*. Edited by Muḥammad Muḥyīʾddīn ibn ʿAbdil Ḥamīd. 5 vols. Cairo: Maktabat an-nahḍa al-

miṣriyya, 1958. Translated by Baron MacGuckin de Slane. 4 vols. Paris, 1842–71.

Ibn Qayyim al-Jauziyya, Shamsuddīn Muḥammad. *Aṭ-ṭibb an-nabawī*. Edited by ʿAbdal Ghanī ʿAbdal Khāliq, with medical explanations by Dr. ʿAdil al-Azharī, and elucidation of the *ḥadīth* by Maḥmūd Faraj al-ʿUqda. Mecca: Maktabat an-nahḍa al-ḥadītha, n.d. [ca. 1958].

Ibn Saʿd, Muḥammad Kātib al-Wāqidī. *Kitāb aṭ-ṭabaqāt al-kubrā: Biographien Muhammads, seiner Gefährten und der späteren Träger des Islams*. Edited by Eduard Sachau et al. 11 vols. Leiden: Brill, 1904–40. New ed. Beirut, 1960–68.

Ibn Taghrībirdī. See Abū'l-Maḥāsin.

Ibn Taimiyya, Aḥmad. *Aṣ-ṣārim al-maslūl ʿalā shātim ar-rasūl*. Edited by Muḥammad Muḥyī'ddīn ibn ʿAbdil Ḥamīd. Tanta: Maktaba Tāj, 1379h/1960.

Ibrahim, Ezzeddin, and Denys Johnson-Davies. *An-Nawawi's Forty Hadith*. Damascus: The Holy Koran Publishing House, 1976. 2nd ed. 1977.

Ibrāhim, Ṣābir ʿAbduh. *Bilāl ibn Rabāḥ*. Baghdad: Ash-shirka al-islāmiyya, 1957.

Ibrāhīm Tattawī. *Takmilat Maqālāt ash-shuʿarā*. Edited by Sayyid Hussamuddin Rashdi. Hyderabad/Sind: Sindhi Adabi Board, 1961.

Ikrām, Shaikh Muḥammad. *Armaghān-i Pāk*. Karachi: Idāra-i maṭbūʿāt-i Pākistān, 1953.

Ikramullah, Shayeste S. *From Purdah to Parliament*. London: The Cresset Press, 1963.

Inal, Ibnülemin Mahmud Kemal. *Son Hattatlar*. Istanbul: Devlet Matbaasĭ, 1954.

Iqbal, Sir Muhammad. *Armaghān-i Ḥijāz*. Lahore: n.p., 1938.

———. *Asrār-i khudī*. Lahore: n.p., 1915. Translated by Reynold A. Nicholson as *The Secrets of the Self*. London: Macmillan, 1920.

———. *Bāl-i Jibrīl*. Lahore: n.p., 1935.

———. *Bāng-i Darā*. Lahore: n.p., 1924.

———. *Iqbālnāma (Makātīb-i Urdū)*. Edited by Shaikh Muḥammad ʿAṭā. 2 vols. Lahore: Ashraf, n.d.

———. *Jāvīdnāma*. Lahore: n.p., 1932. Translated by Arthur John Arberry as *Javidnama*. London: George Allen & Unwin, 1966. Translated by Shaikh Mahmud Ahmad as *The Pilgrimage of Eternity*. Lahore: Institute of Islamic Culture, 1961. Arabic, German, French, Italian, and Turkish translations are also available.

———. *Musāfir*. Lahore: n.p., 1934.

———. *Pas che bāyad kard*. Lahore: n.p., 1936.

———. *Payām-i Mashriq*. Lahore: n.p., 1923. Translated by Annemarie Schimmel as *Botschaft des Ostens*. Wiesbaden: Harrassowitz, 1963.

———. *Rumūz-i bēkhudī*. Lahore: n.p., 1917.

———. *Six Lectures on the Reconstruction of Religious Thought in Islam*. Lahore: Ashraf, 1930. Often reprinted.

———. *Speeches and Statements*. Compiled by Shamloo. Lahore: al-Manar Academy, 1945. 2nd ed. 1948.

———. *Stray Reflections*. Edited by Javid Iqbal. Lahore: Ashraf, 1961.

———. *Żarb-i Kalīm*. Lahore: n.p., 1937.
ʿIrāqī, Fakhruddīn. *Kulliyāt*. Edited by Saʿīd Nafīsī. Tehran: Sanāʾī, 1138sh/1959.
Irving, Washington. *The Life of Muhammad*. Leipzig: Tauchnitz, 1850. Translated as *Das Leben Mohammeds*. Leipzig, 1869. Arabic, French, Italian, Swedish, Turkish, and Urdu translations are also available.
Isik [Işîk], Huseyn Hilmi. "Shocking Writings of Dr. Hamidullah on Prophet Muhammad and Islam Revealed." *Muslim Digest* 34, nos. 3–4 (1983): 27–38.
ʿIyāḍ, al-Qāḍī. *Kitāb ash-shifāʾ fī riʿāyat ḥuqūq al-Muṣṭafā*. Istanbul, 1312h/1895. With the commentary of Maulānā Aḥmad Shihābuddīn al-Khafājī, *Nasīm ar-riyāḍ fī sharḥ al-qāḍī ʿIyāḍ*; at the margin ʿAlī al-Qārī's *Sharḥ ash-shifāʾ*. 4 vols. Beirut: Dār al-kitāb al-ʿarabiyya, n.d.
Jackson, Paul. "Shaikh Sharafuddin Maneri's Vision of Muhammad." *Vidyajyoti* 46, no. 8 (1982).
Jaʿfarī, Raʾīs Aḥmad. *Iqbal aur ʿashq-i rasūl*. Lahore: Ashraf, 1956.
Jagtiāṇī, Lālchand. *Muḥammad Rasūl Allāh*. Hyderabad/Sind, 1911.
Jahangir, Emperor. *Tuzuk-i Jahāngīrī*. Translated by A. Rogers and H. Beveridge. 2 vols. London, 1909–14. Reprinted 1978.
Jairazbhoy, Alhaj Qassim Ali. *Muhammad: A Mercy to All the Nations*. London: Luzac, 1937.
Jalbānī, Ghulām Ḥusain. *Shāh Walīullāh ain hunajō falsafō*. Hyderabad/Sind: Shah Waliullah Academy, 1961.
Jamāluddīn, Dr. Muḥsin. *Iḥtifālāt al-mawālīd an-nabawiyya fīʾl-ashʿār al-andalusiyya waʾl-maghribiyya waʾl-mahjariyya*. Baghdad: Dār al-Baṣrī, 1967.
Jāmī, ʿAbdur Raḥmān. *Dīwān-i kāmil*. Edited by Hāshim Riżā. Tehran: Pīrūz, 1341sh/1962.
———. *Haft Aurang*. Edited by Aqā Murtazā and Mudarris Gīlānī. 2nd ed. Tehran: Saʿdī, 1351sh/1972.
———. *Nafaḥāt al-uns min ḥaḍarāt al-quds*. Edited by Mahdī Tauḥīdīpūr. Tehran: Saʿdī, 1336sh/1957.
Jazūlī, Muḥammad ibn Sulaimān. *Dalāʾil al-khairāt*. Numerous manuscripts.
Jeffery, Arthur. "Ibn al-ʿArabī's *Shajarat al-kawn*." *Islamic Studies* (1959): 43–77. Separately published, Lahore: Aziz Publishers, 1980.
———. *Muhammad and His Religion*. Indianapolis: Bobbs-Merrill, 1958.
———. "The Quest for the Historical Mohammad." *MW* 16 (1926): 327–48.
———. *Reader on Islam*. The Hague: Mouton, 1962.
———. "Was Muhammad a Prophet from His Infancy?" *MW* 20 (1930): 226–34.
Johansen, Baber. *Muḥammad Ḥusain Haikal*. Wiesbaden: Steiner, 1967.
Jurji, Edward J. *Illumination in Islamic Mysticism*. Princeton: Princeton University Press, 1937.
———. "Khadīja, Mohammad's First Wife." *MW* 26 (1936): 197–99.
———. "Pre-Islamic Use of the Name Muḥammad." *MW* 26 (1936): 389–91.
Juynboll, G. H. A. *The Authenticity of Tradition Literature: Discussions in Modern Egypt*. Leiden: Brill, 1969.
———. "Dyeing the Hair and Beard in Early Islam: A *ḥadīth*-analytical study." Manuscript in author's files.

Kaʿb ibn Zuhair. *Bānat Suʿād (Carmen panegyricum in laudem Muhammadis)*. Edited by G. J. Lette. Leiden, 1748.
Kahle, Paul. *Der Leuchtturm von Alexandrien. Ein arabisches Schattenspiel aus dem mittelalterlichen Ägypten*. Stuttgart: Kohlhammer, 1930.
Karahan, Abdulkadir. "Aperçu général sur les "quarante *ḥadīth*" dans la littérature islamique." *SI* 4 (1955): 39–55.
———. *Islam-Türk edebiyatǐnda Kǐrk hadis*. Istanbul: Istanbul Üniversitesi Edebiyat Fakültesi yayǐnlarǐndan no. 587, 1954.
———. "Un nouveau *mathnawī* de la littérature turque-ottomane: le *Mevlid Haticetül-Kubrā*, ou la description du mariage de Khadija avec le Prophète." *Turkologischer Anzeiger* 4 (1972): 230–35.
Karīmullāh, Muḥammad. *Maulūd*. London, India Office Library, MS Urdu 145 (Delhi Arab 319A).
Khafājī. See ʿIyāḍ.
Khalid, Detlev. "A Terrorist Looks at Islam." Review of N. R. Roy, *Historical Role of Islam* (Lahore: Sindh Sagar Academy, 1972). *Outlook*, 9 December 1972.
Khāqānī, Afḍaluddīn Badīl. *Dīwān*. Edited by Żiāʾuddīn Sajjādī. Tehran: Zawwār, 1338sh/1959.
Khāqānī, Mehmet Bey. *Ḥilya-i sharīf*. N.p. [Istanbul], 1264h/1847.
Khūrshīd, Fārūq, and Aḥmad Kamāl Zakī. *Muḥammad fīʾl-adab al-muʿāṣir*. Cairo: Al-maktab al-fannī liʾn-nashr, 1959.
Kidwai, Shaikh M. H. *The Miracles of Muhammad*. London: Luzac, 1906.
Kienberg, Leah, ed. "The Book of Dreams by Ibn Abīʾd-Dunyā." Ph.D. dissertation, University of Michigan, 1977. To be published in the Max Schloesinger Memorial Series, The Hebrew University, Jerusalem.
Kǐsakürek, Necip Fazǐl. *Çöle inen nur*. Istanbul: Büyük Doğu Yayǐnlarǐ, 1974.
———. *Es-selâm: Mukaddes Hayattan Levhalar*. Istanbul: Büyük Doğu Yayǐnlarǐ, 1973.
Kister, Meir J. "On a New Edition of the Dīwān of Ḥassān ibn Thābit." *BSOAS* 39 (1976): 255–86.
Knappert, Jan. "The Figure of the Prophet Muhammad According to the Popular Literature of the Islamic Peoples." *Swahili*, no. 32 (1961): 24–31.
———. *Swahili Islamic Poetry*. 3 vols. Leiden: Brill, 1971.
Kocatürk, Vasfī Mahir. *Tekke Şiiri Antolojisi*. Ankara: Buluş Kitabevi, 1955.
Koelle, S. W. *Mohammad and Mohammadanism, Critically Considered*. London: Rivington, 1889.
Kokan, Muhammad Yousuf. *Arabic and Persian in Carnatic, 1710–1960*. Madras: Hafiza House, 1974.
———. *Khānwāda-i Qāżī Badruddaula*, vol. 1. Madras: Dār at-taṣnīf, 1963.
Köprülüzade, Mehmet Fuat. *Eski Şairlerimiz: Divan Edebiyati Antolojisi*. Istanbul: Ahmet Halit Kitabevi, 1931.
Krenkow, Fritz. "The Tārīkh Baghdād of the Khaṭīb Abū Bakr Aḥmad ibn ʿAlī ibn Thābit al-Baghdādī." Appendix: "The Appearance of the Prophet in Dreams." *JRAS* (1912): 77–79.

Kriss, Rudolf, and Hubert Kriss-Heinrich. *Volksglaube im Bereich des Islam*. 2 vols. Wiesbaden: Harrassowitz, 1960–62.
Kritzek, James. *Peter the Venerable and Islam*. Princeton: Princeton University Press, 1964.
Lammens, Henri. *Fatima et les filles de Mahomet: notes critiques pour l'étude de la sīra*. Rome: Pontificio Istituto Biblico, 1912.
———. "Was Muhammad Sincere?" *MW* 5 (1915): 262–67.
Lane, Edward William. *Manners and Customs of the Modern Egyptians*. London 1846. Several reprintings.
Lazarus-Yafeh, Hava. *Some Religious Aspects of Islam*. Leiden: Brill, 1981.
Lehmann, Edvard, and Johan Pedersen. "Der Beweis für die Auferstehung im Koran." *Der Islam* 5 (1914): 54–61.
Leszynski, Rudolf. *Mohammedanische Traditionen über das Jüngste Gericht*. Gräfenhainichen, 1909.
Levi della Vida, Giorgio. "Sīra." *EI*, 4:440 ff.
Lings, Martin. *Muhammad*. London: George Allen & Unwin, and Islamic Text Society, 1983.
———. *A Sufi Saint of the Twentieth Century*. 2nd ed. London: George Allen & Unwin, 1971.
Littmann, Enno. *Mohammad im Volksepos*. Det Kgl. Danske Videnskapernes Selkab, Historisk-filologiske meddedelser, 33, no. 3. Copenhagen: Ejnar Munksgaard, 1950.
Longworth Dames, M. *Popular Poetry of the Baloches*. 2 vols. London: Royal Asiatic Society, 1907.
Lubis, Haji Muhammad Bukhari. "Qaṣīdas in Honor of the Prophet: A Comparative Study between Al-Būṣīrī's *Al-Burdah* and ʿAṭṭār's *naʿt* in his *Ilāhīnāma*." M.A. thesis, University of Chicago, 1980. Published under the same title, Bangi: Penerbit Universiti Kebangsaan Malaysia, 1983.
Lüling, Günther. *Die Wiederentdeckung des Propheten Muhammad. Eine Kritik am 'christlichen' Abendland*. Erlangen: Lüling, 1981.
Luṭf, Muḥammad Luṭf ʿAlī Khān. *Sarāpā sarwar al-anbiyā*. Cawnpore, 1869.
MacCallum, Lyman. *The Mevlidi Sherif by Suleyman Chelebi*. The Wisdom of the East Series. London: John Murray, 1943.
Mach, Rudolf. *Catalogue of Arabic Manuscripts (Yahuda Section) in the Garrett Collection, Princeton University Library*. Princeton: Princeton University Press, 1977.
Maḥmūd, Dr. ʿAbdul Qādir. *Al-fikr aṣ-ṣūfī fī's-Sūdān*. Cairo: Dār al-fikr al-ʿarabī, 1968–69.
Maqqarī, Aḥmad ibn Muḥammad al-Maghribī al-. *Fatḥ al-mutaʿāl fī madḥ an-niʿāl*. Hyderabad/Deccan: Dairatul Maarif, 1334h/1916.
Maqrīzī, Aḥmad al-. *Kitāb al-mawāʿiẓ wa'l-iʿtibār bi-dhikri' l-khiṭaṭ wa'l-āthār*. Bulaq: Dār aṭ-ṭabāʿat al-miṣriyya, 1853. Reprinted 1951.
Margoliouth, David. "Relics of the Prophet Mohammad." *MW* 27 (1937): 20–27.
Massignon, Louis. "L'homme parfait en Islam et son originalité eschatologique." *Eranos-Jahrbuch* 15 (1947): 287–314.

———. "Les origines de la méditation Shiite sur Salmân et Fâtima." In *Mélanges H. Massé*, pp. 264–66. Tehran: Institut Français, 1963.

———. *La Passion d'Al-Ḥosayn ibn Manṣour al-Ḥallāj, martyre mystique de l'Islam*. 2 vols. Paris: Geuthner, 1922. 2nd ed. 4 vols. Paris: Gallimard, 1975. Translated by Herbert Mason as *The Passion of al-Hallaj, Mystic and Martyr of Islam*. Bollingen Series, 98. 4 vols. Princeton: Princeton University Press, 1982.

———. "La philosophie orientale d'Avicenne." In *Mémorial Avicenne*. Cairo: Institut Français d'Archéologie Orientale, n.d. [1959?].

———. "La Rawḍa de Medine, cadre de la méditation musulmane sur la destinée du Prophète." *BIFAO* 59 (1960): 241–72.

———. "Salmân-i Pak et les prémices spirituelles de l'Islam iranien." In Massignon, *Parole Donnée*, pp. 91–128. Edited by Vincent Monteil. Paris, 1962.

Maẓhar Jānjānān. *Makātīb-i Mirzā Maẓhar*. Edited by ʿAbdur Rāziq Quraishī. Bombay: ʿAlawi Book Depot, 1966.

McAuliffe, Jane D. "Chosen of All Women: Mary and Fāṭima in Qurʾānic Exegesis." *Islamo-Christiana* (1981): 19–28.

McCarthy, Richard, ed. *Al-Bāqillānī, Abū Bakr Muḥammad ibn al-Ṭayyib (d. 1013): Miracle and Magic, a Treatise on the Nature of Apologetic Miracle*. Beirut: Librairie Orientale, 1958.

McKane, William. "A Manuscript on the *miʿrāj* in the Bodleian." *Journal of Semitic Studies* 2 (1957): 366–76.

McPherson, Joseph W. *The Moulid of Egypt*. Cairo: M. N. Press, 1941.

Meier, Fritz. *Abū Saʿīd-i Abū l-Ḫayr. Wirklichkeit und Legende*. Acta Iranica, 4. Teheran and Liège: Bibliothèque Pahlavi; Leiden: Brill, 1976.

———. "Der Geistmensch bei dem persischen Dichter ʿAṭṭār." *Eranos-Jahrbuch* 13 (1946): 283–353.

Mēmon, Dr. Abdul Majīd Sindhī. *Naʿtiyya Shāʿirī*. Larkana: Sindhi Adabī Academi, 1980.

Memon, Muhammad Umar. *Ibn Taimiyya's Struggle against Popular Religion*. The Hague and Paris: Mouton, 1976.

Metcalf, Barbara Daly. *Islamic Revival in British India: Deoband, 1860–1900*. Princeton: Princeton University Press, 1982.

Meyer, J. J. "Moses und Zarathustra, Jesus und Muhammad in einem Purāṇa." *WZKM* 43 (1936): 1–18.

Mez, Adam. *Die Renaissance des Islam*. Heidelberg: Carl Winter, 1922. Translated into English by S. Khudabakhsh and David Samuel Margoliouth. Patna, 1937.

———. "Geschichte der Wunder Muhammads." *Verhandlungen des 2. Internationalen Kongresses für Allgemeine Religionsgeschichte*. Basel: Helbing & Lichtenhahn, 1905.

Mīlād Aḥmad, yaʿnī Anwār-i Aḥmadī. Hyderabad/Deccan: Minar Bookshop, n.d. (A collection of Urdu *naʿt*.)

Minorsky, Vladimir. *The Chester Beatty Library: A Catalogue of the Turkish*

Manuscripts and Miniatures. Dublin: Hodges Figgis, 1958.
Mīr Taqī Mīr. *Kulliyāt*. Edited by Dr. Ebadet Brelwi. Lahore: Urdu Dunyā, 1958.
Mīrghānī, Sayyid Muḥammad ʿUthmān al-. *Majmūʿ aurād aṭ-ṭarīqa al-khatmiyya*. Cairo: Maṭbaʿa Muṣṭafā al-bābī al-ḥalabī, 1344h/1925–26. Numerous later editions.
———. *Maulid an-nabī*. Cairo: Maṭbaʿa Muṣṭafā al-bābī al-ḥalabī, 1348h/1929–30. Numerous later editions.
———. *An-nafaḥāt al-madīniyya fī'l madā'iḥ al-muṣṭafawiyya*. Cairo: Maṭbaʿa Muṣṭafā al-bābī al-ḥalabī, 1351h/1936.
———. *An-nūr al-barrāq fī madḥ an-nabī al-miṣdāq*. Cairo: Maṭbaʿa Muṣṭafā al-bābī al-ḥalabī, 1351h/1936.
Miskīn Shāh. *Ladhdhat-i Miskīn*. Hyderabad/Deccan: Maṭbaʿ Mufīd, 1312h/1894–95.
Mittwoch, Eugen. "Muhammads Geburts- und Todestag." *Islamica* 2 (1926): 397–401.
Moinul Haq, S. "Prophet Muhammad: The Advent of a New Religio-social Order." *Journal of the Pakistan Historical Society* 20 (1972): 1–33.
Mountfort, William. "Mohammad: A Mohammadan Apologist in London." *The Religious Magazine* 47 (March 1872): 244–50. (Discusses Sir Sayyid's *Essays on the Life of Muhammad.*)
Mouradjan, J. "Note sur les altérations du nom de Mohammad chez les noirs islamisés de l'Afrique Occidentale." *Bulletin du Comité français Afrique Occidentale Française* (1938): 459–62.
Mubārak, Zakī. *Al-madā'iḥ an-nabawiyya fī'l-adab al-ʿarabī*. Cairo: Muṣṭafā al-bābī al-ḥalabī wa aulāduhu, 1943.
Muḥammad ad-dīn, Ḥājjī Maulānā. *Qaṣīda-i Burda maʿ sharḥ Panjābī*. Lahore: Allāhwālē kī qaumī dukān, n.d. (no. 87).
Muḥarram, Aḥmad. *Dīwān majd al-Islām au al-Iliyād al-islāmiyya*. Cairo: Maktaba Dār al-ʿurūba, 1383h/1963.
Muḥsin Kākōrawī. *Kulliyāt-i naʿt-i Maulwī Muḥammad Muḥsin*. Edited by Maulwī Muḥammad Nūr ul-Ḥasan. Lucknow: an-Nāẓir Press, 1324h/1904.
Muid Khan, Muhammad A. *The Arabian Poets of Golconda*. Bombay: University Press, 1963.
Muir, William. *The Apology of al-Kindi*. London, 1887.
———. *The Life of Mahomet*. With introductory chapters on the original sources for the biography of Mahomet and on the pre-Islamic history of Arabia. 4 vols. London: Smith, Elder & Co., 1858–61. New editions until 1923. Numerous reprints.
Munāwī, Sharafuddīn ʿAbdallāh al-. *Al-maulid al-jalīl*. Būlāq, 1904.
Murad, Mehr Afroz. *Intellectual Modernism of Shibli Nuʿmani*. Lahore: Institute of Islamic Culture, 1976.
Muslim Digest. Monthly. Durban, South Africa: Makki Publications.
Muslim ibn al-Ḥajjāj, Abū'l-Ḥusain. *Ṣaḥīḥ*. Cairo: Dār iḥyā' al-kutub al-ʿarabiyya, 1955.
Mustaqīmzāde, Sulaimān Saʿduddīn. *Tuḥfa-i khaṭṭāṭīn*. Edited by Ibnul Emin Mahmud. Istanbul: Devlet Matbaasī, 1928.

Nabhānī, Yūsuf ibn Ismāʿīl an-. *Al-majmūʿa an-nabhāniyya fī'l-madā'iḥ an-nabawiyya*. 4 vols. Beirut: Al-maṭbaʿa al-adabiyya, 1903. Reprinted in 4 vols., Beirut, n.d.

———. *Wasā'il al-wuṣūl ilā shamā'il ar-rasūl*. Beirut: Al-maṭbaʿa al-adabiyya, 1310h/1892. Reprinted 1970.

Nābulusī, ʿAbdul Ghanī an-. *Dīwān al-ḥaqā'iq wa majmūʿa ar-raqā'iq*. Damascus: ʿAbdul Wakīl ad-Dāribi, n.d. [ca. 1957].

Naimuddin, Syed. "Sayyid Bulaqi's Mirājnāma." *Nagpur University Journal* 9 (1943): 101–5.

Nakhli, Mohammed. "Le moulid en Tunisie." *IBLA* 3 (1939): 155–60.

Nāṣir-i Khusrau. *Dīwān ashʿār Ḥakīm Nāṣir-i Khusrau Qūbādābādī*. Edited from the corrected manuscript of the late Taqizadah. Tehran: Nashr Chakāma, 1341sh/1962.

Nasr, Seyyed Hoseyn. *Ideals and Realities of Islam*. London: Allen & Unwin, 1966.

Nath, R. *Monuments of Delhi: Historical Study*. New Delhi: Indian Institute of Islamic Studies, 1979. (Based on Sayyid Ahmad, *Athār as-sanādīd*.)

Nawawī. See Ibrahim and Johnson-Davies.

Naẓīrī Nishāpūrī. *Dīwān*. Edited by Maẓāhir Muṣaffā. Tehran: Amīr Kabīr, 1340sh/1961.

Nicholson, Reynold Alleyne. "An Early Arabic Version of the *miʿrāj* of Abū Yazīd al-Bisṭāmī." *Islamica* 2 (1926): 402–15.

———. *The Idea of Personality in Sufism*. Cambridge: Cambridge University Press, 1923.

———. *A Literary History of the Arabs*. Cambridge: Cambridge University Press, 1907. Reprinted 1966.

———. "The 'Risālat al-Ghufrān' by Abū'lʿAlā' al-Maʿarrī, Summarized and Partially Translated." *JRAS* (1900): 637–720, (1902): 75–101.

———. *Studies in Islamic Mysticism*. Cambridge: Cambridge University Press, 1921. Reprinted 1967.

———. "An Unknown Biography of Muhammad Entitled *Kitābu man ṣabara ẓafira*." In *Orientalische Studien Theodor Nöldeke gewidmet*, pp. 16–32. Edited by Carl Bezold. Giessen: Töpelmann, 1906.

Niẓāmī Ganjawī, Ḥakīm Ilyās. *Haft Paikar*. Edited by Hellmut Ritter and Jan Rypka. Istanbul: Devlet Matbaasī, 1934.

———. *Kulliyāt-i Khamsa*. 3rd ed. Tehran: Amīr Kabīr, 1351sh/1972.

Nowaihi, Mohamed al-. "Towards a Re-evaluation of Muhammad: Prophet and Man." *MW* 60 (1970): 300–13.

Nurbakhsh, Dr. Jawad. *Traditions of the Prophet*. New York: Khanqah-i Nimatullahi, 1981.

Nwyia, Paul. *Exégèse coranique et langage mystique*. Beirut: Dār el-mashreq, 1970.

Nyberg, Hendrik Samuel. *Kleinere Schriften des Ibn al-ʿArabī*. Leiden: Brill, 1919.

Öten, Mehmet. *Peygamberimizin mucizeleri*. Konya, 1977.

Padwick, Constance E. *Muslim Devotions*. London: SPCK, 1960.

Paquignon, Paul. "Le mouloud au Maroc." *RMM* 41 (1911): 525—36.
Paret, Rudi. *Die legendäre Maghāzī-Literatur. Arabische Dichtungen über die muslimischen Kriegszüge zu Mohammads Zeit*. Tübingen: J. C. B. Mohr (Paul Siebeck), 1930.
______. "Die Legende von der Verleihung des Prophetenmantels (*burda*) an Kaʿb ibn Zuhair." *Der Islam* 17 (1928): 9–14.
______. *Mohammad und der Koran. Geschichte und Verkündigung des arabischen Propheten*. 5th ed. Stuttgart: Kohlhammer, 1980.
Pavet de Courteille, Abel. *Mirâdj-nâme: Récit de l'ascension de Mahomet au ciel, composé A.H. 840 (1436–37)*. Paris, 1882. Reprinted Amsterdam: Philo, 1975.
Peacock, James L. *Purifying the Faith: The Muhammadiyah Movement in Indonesian Islam*. Menlo Park, Calif.: The Benjamin/Cummings Publishing Company, 1978.
Pearson, James Douglas. *Index Islamicus*. Cambridge: W. Heffner, 1906–55. Supplements, 1956–60, 1961–65, 1966–70, 1971–75, 1976–80, 1981–.
Pellat, Charles. *Arabische Geisteswelt. Ausgewählte und übersetzte Texte von Al-Ǧāhiẓ (777–869)*. Translated from the French by Walter W. Müller. Zurich: Artemis, 1967.
Porter, J. R. "Muhammad's Journey to Heaven." *Numen* 21 (1974): 64–80.
Qalqashandī, Aḥmad al-. *Ṣubḥ al- aʿshā fī ṣanāʿat al-inshāʾ*. 14 vols. Cairo: Maṭbaʿa Dār al-kutub al-miṣriyya, 1918–22.
Qāniʿ, Mīr ʿAlī Shīr. *Maqālāt ash-shuʿarā*. Edited by Sayyid Hussamuddin Rashdi. Karachi: Sindhi Adabi Board, 1956.
Qāsimi, ʿAbdallāh ibn ʿAlī. *Naqd kitāb Ḥayāt Muḥammad li-Muḥammad Haikal*. Cairo: al-Maṭbaʿa ar-raḥmāniyya, 1935.
Qasṭallānī, Aḥmad ibn Muḥammad al-. *Al-mawāhib al-laduniyya fīʾl-minaḥ al-muḥammadiyya*. Bulaq, 1864. Commentary by az-Zurqānī, Bulaq, 1278h/1861. Synopsis by Yūsuf an-Nabhānī, *Al-anwār al-muḥammadiyya min al-mawāhib al-laduniyya*. Beirut 1310–12h/1892–94; Cairo 1320h/1902–3.
Qushairī, ʿAbdul Karīm al-. *Kitāb al-miʿrāj*. Edited by ʿAlī Ḥusain ʿAbdul Qādir. Cairo: Dār al-kutub al-ḥadītha, 1964.
______. *Ar-risāla fī ʿilm at-taṣawwuf*. Cairo: Dār al-kutub al-ʿarabiyya al-kubrā, 1330h/1912.
Raḍwān, Fatḥī. *Muḥammad ath-thāʾir al-aʿẓam*. Cairo: Dār al-hilāl, 1954.
Rahbar, Daud. "Ghālib and a Debatable Point of Theology." *MW* 56 (1966): 14–17.
Rahman, Fazlur. *Islam*. London: Weidenfels & Nicolson, 1966.
______. *Prophecy in Islam*. London and New York: Allen & Unwin, 1958.
______. "*Sīrat an-nabī* of Allamah Shibli." *Journal of the Pakistan Historical Society* 8 (1960): 167–83, 260–70.
Rahnema, Zeinolabedin. *Payambar: The Messenger*. Translated from the Persian into English by Laurence Elwell-Sutton. Lahore: Ashraf, 1964. French translation, Paris, 1967.
Ramakrishna, Lajwanti. *Panjabi Sufi Poets*. London and Calcutta: Oxford University Press, 1938. Reprinted Delhi, 1975.

Rasheed, Ghulam Dastgir. "The Development of *naʿtia* Poetry in Persian Literature." *IC* 39 (1965): 53–69.

Rasslan, Wassel. *Mohammad und die Medizin nach den Ueberlieferungen*. Berlin: Dr. E. Ebering, 1934.

Rāzī Dāyā, Najm al-Dīn. *The Path of God's Bondsmen from Origin to Return*. Translated from the Persian by Hamid Algar. Persian Heritage Series, 35. Boulder, Colo.: Westview Press, 1980.

Rice, David Talbot. *The Illustrations to the "World History" of Rashīd al-Dīn*. Edited by Basil Gray. Edinburgh: Edinburgh University Press, 1976.

Riḍā, Muḥammad Rashīd. *Khulāṣat as-sīra al-muḥammadiyya wa ḥaqīqat ad-daʿwā al-islāmiyya*. 2nd ed. Cairo: Maṭbaʿat al-Manār, 1345h/1927.

Ritter, Hellmut. "Die Aussprüche des Bāyezīd al-Biṣṭāmī." In *West-Östliche Abhandlungen, Festschrift für Rudolf Tschudi*, pp. 231–43. Edited by Fritz Meier. Wiesbaden: Harrassowitz, 1954.

———. *Das Meer der Seele. Gott, Welt und Mensch in den Geschichten Farīduddin ʿAṭṭārs*. Leiden: Brill, 1955. 2nd ed. 1977.

Riyāshī, Labīb ar-. *Nafsiyyat ar-rasūl al-ʿarabī Muḥammad ibn ʿAbdillāh, as-sūbarmān al-ʿālamī al-awwal*. Beirut: Dār ar-raiḥāni liʾn-nashr, 1935.

Robson, James. "Blessings on the Prophet." *MW* 26 (1936): 365–71.

———. "Does the Bible Speak of Mohammad?"*MW* 25 (1935): 17–26.

———, trans. *Tabrīzī, Mishkāt al-Maṣābīḥ*. 4 vols. Lahore: Ashraf, 1964–65.

Rodinson, Maxime. "A Critical Survey of Modern Studies on Muhammad." In *Studies on Islam*, pp. 23–84. Translated and edited by Merlin L. Swartz. Oxford and New York: Oxford University Press, 1981. Originally published as "Bilan des études mohammediennes." *Revue historique* 229 (1963).

———. *Mahomet*. Editions du Seuil, 1961. 2nd ed., 1968. English translation by Anne Carter. New York: Pantheon Books, 1971.

Rosenzweig-Schwannau, Vincenz von. *Funkelnde Wandelsterne zum Lobe des besten der Geschöpfe*. Vienna, 1824. (German translation of Būṣīrī's *Burda*.)

Roy, Asim. *The Islamic Syncretistic Tradition in Bengal*. Princeton: Princeton University Press, 1983.

Royster, James E. "The Study of Muhammad: A Survey of Approaches from the Perspective of the History and Phenomenology of Religion." *MW* 62 (1972): 49–70.

Rūmī, Maulānā Jalāluddīn. *Dīwān-i kabīr yā kulliyāt-i Shams*. Edited by Badīʿuzzamān Furūzānfar. 10 vols. Tehran: University, 1336sh/1957–.

———. *Fīhi mā fīhi*. Tehran: Shirkat-i sihāmī-i nāshirīn-i kutub-i Irān, 1338sh/1959.

———. *Mathnawī-i maʿnawī*. Edited and translated, with commentary, by Reynold A. Nicholson. Vols. 1, 3, 5 text; 2, 4, 6 translation; 7 and 8 commentary. GMS, n.s. 4. London: Luzac, 1925–40. Reprinted, translation only.

Saʿadeh, Mounir R. "Why Not Canonize Mohammad?" *MW* 27 (1937): 294–97.

Sadarangani, H. J. *Persian Poets of Sind*. Karachi: Sindhi Adabi Board, 1956.

Saʿdī, Muṣliḥuddīn. *Būstān–Gulistān–Ghazaliyāt–Qaṣāʾid*. Edited by Muḥd. ʿAlī Furūghī. 4 vols. Tehran: Eqbāl, 1342sh/1963.

Saḥḥār, ʿAbdul Ḥamīd Jauda as-. *Bilāl muʾadhdhin ar-rasūl*. Cairo: Maktabat Miṣr, n.d. [1944].

St. Elie, Anastase Marie de. "Le culte rendu par les Musulmans aux sandales de Mahomet." *Anthropos* 5 (1910): 363–66.

Samancĭgil, Kemal. *Hazreti Muhammad Türk mi idi?* Istanbul: Mesa Yayĭnlarĭ, 1958.

Samarrāʾī, Dr. Ibrāhīm. *Al- aʿlām al-ʿarabiyya*. Baghdad: Al-maktabat al-ahliyya, 1964.

Sanāʾī, Abūʾl-Majd Majdūd. *Dīwān*. Edited by Mudarris Rażawī. Tehran: Ibn-i Sīnā, 1341sh/1962.

———. *Ḥadīqat al-ḥaqīqa wa sharīʿat aṭ-ṭarīqa*. Edited by Mudarris Rażawī. Tehran: Tahuri, 1320sh/1941.

Sardar, Ziauddin. *Muhammad: Aspects of His Biography*. London: The Islamic Foundation, 1978.

Sarrāj, Abū Naṣr as-. *Kitāb al-lumaʿ fīʾt-taṣawwuf*. Edited by Reynold A. Nicholson. GMS, 21. London: Luzac; Leiden: Brill, 1914. Several reprintings.

Saunders, J. J. "Mohammed in Europe." *History: The Journal of the Historical Association*, n.s. 39 (February–June 1954): 14–25.

Schacht, Joseph. "Sur l'expression 'sunna du Prophète.'" *Mélanges H. Massé*, pp. 361–65. Tehran: Institut Français, 1963.

Schaeder, Hans Heinrich. "Die islamische Lehre vom Vollkommenen Menschen, ihre Herkunft und dichterische Gestaltung." *ZDMG* 79 (1925): 192–268.

Schariati, ʿAli. *Fatima ist Fatima*. Bonn: Informationsabteilung der Botschaft der islamischen Republik Iran, 1981.

Schimmel, Annemarie. *As Through a Veil: Mystical Poetry in Islam*. New York: Columbia University Press, 1982.

———. *Calligraphy and Islamic Culture*. New York: New York University Press, 1984.

———. *A Dance of Sparks: Studies in Ghalib's Imagery*. New Delhi: Ghalib Academy, 1978.

———. *Gabriel's Wing. A Study into the Religious Ideas of Sir Muhammad Iqbal*. Leiden: Brill, 1963.

———. "Ghalib's *qaṣīda* in Praise of the Prophet." In *Islam: Past Influence and Present Challenge*, pp. 188–209. Edited by Pierre Cachia and Alford Welch. Edinburgh: Edinburgh University Press, 1979.

———. "The Golden Chain of 'Sincere Muhammadans.'" In *The Rose and the Rock*, pp. 104–34. Edited by Bruce B. Lawrence. Durham: Duke University Program, 1979.

———. *Al-Halladsch, Märtyrer der Gottesliebe*. Cologne: Hegner, 1969.

———. *Islam in India and Pakistan*. Iconography of Religions, 22.9. Leiden: Brill, 1982.

———. *Märchen aus Pakistan*. Translated from the Sindhi. Cologne: Diederichs, 1980.

———. *Mystical Dimensions of Islam*. Chapel Hill: University of North Carolina Press, 1975.

———. "Neue Veröffentlichungen zur Volkskunde von Sind." *WI*, n.s. 9 (1963): 237–59.
———. *Die Orientalische Katze*. Cologne: Diederichs, 1983.
———. *Pain and Grace: A Study of Two Mystical Writers of Eighteenth-Century Muslim India*. Leiden: Brill, 1976.
———. "The Place of the Prophet of Islam in Iqbal's Thought." *Islamic Studies* 1, no. 4 (1962): 111–30.
———. "Der Regen als Symbol in der Religionsgeschichte." In *Religion und Religionen. Festschrift für Gustav Mensching*, pp. 178–89. Bonn: Röhrscheidt, 1966.
———. "Sindhi Translations and Commentaries of the Qur'ān." *Oriens* 16 (1963): 224–43.
———. "Some Glimpses of Religious Life in Egypt during the Later Mamluk Period." *Islamic Studies* 4, no. 4 (1965): 353–92.
———. "Some Notes on the Cultural Activities of the First Uzbek Rulers." *Journal of the Pakistan Historical Society* (1960): 149–66.
———. "The Sufis and the *Shahāda*." In *Islam's Understanding of Itself*. Edited by Richard Hovanassian and Speros Vryonis, Jr. Malibu: Udena Publications, 1983.
———. "Sufismus und Heiligenverehrung im spätmittelalterlichen Ägypten." In *Festschrift Werner Caskel*, pp. 274–89. Edited by Erwin Graefe. Leiden: Brill, 1968.
———. *The Triumphal Sun: A Study of the Works of Jalāloddin Rumi*. London: Fine Books; The Hague: East–West Publications, 1978.
———. *Und Muhammad ist Sein Prophet. Die Verehrung des Propheten in der islamischen Frömmigkeit*. Cologne: Diederichs, 1981.
———. "The Veneration of the Prophet Muhammad, as Reflected in Sindhi Poetry." In *The Saviour God: Comparative Studies in the Concept of Salvation*, pp. 129–43. Edited by S. G. F. Brandon. Manchester: Manchester University Press, 1963.
———. *Zeitgenössische arabische Lyrik*. Tübingen: Erdmann, 1975. (German verse translations of contemporary Arabic poetry.)
———, and Abdoljavad Falatori, eds. *We Believe in One God: The Experience of God in Christianity and Islam*. London: Burns & Oates, 1979.
Scholem, Gershom. *Major Trends in Jewish Mysticism*. 2nd ed. New York: Schocken, 1954.
Schroeder, Eric. *Muhammad's People*. Portland, Me.: Wheelwright, 1955.
Schuon, Frithjof. *Islam and the Perennial Philosophy*. Translated by J. Peter Hobson. Preface by S. H. Nasr. London: World of Islam Festival Pub. Co., 1976.
———. *Le soufisme, voile et quintessence*. Paris: Dervy-Livres, 1980.
Séguy, Marie Rose, ed. *The Miraculous Journey of Mahomet: Mirâj-Nâmeh (Bibliothèque Nationale, Paris, Ms. Suppl. Turc 190)*. New York: Braziller, 1977. German translation, Munich: Prestel, 1977.
Sellheim, Rudolf. "Das Lächeln des Propheten." In *Festschrift für Adolf E. Jensen*, 2:621–30. Munich: Renner, 1964.

Serjeant, Robert. *South Arabian Poetry, 1: Poetry and Prose from Hadramaut.* London: Taylor's Foreign Press, 1951.
Shafi, Muhammad. "A Description of the Two Sanctuaries of Islam." *Ajabnama*, pp. 416–37.
Shahidullah, Mohammad, and Abdul Hai. *Traditional Culture in East Pakistan.* Dacca: Dept. of Bengali, University of Dacca, 1963.
Shaibi, Kamil M. al-, ed. *Sharḥ Dīwān al-Ḥallāj.* Beirut and Baghdad: Al-Nahda Bookshop, 1973.
Shakūr Beg, Mirzā. *Madīna kā ṣadaqa.* Hyderabad/Deccan, n.d.
Shalabī, Maḥmūd. *Ishtirākiyya Muḥammad* (Muhammad's Socialism). Cairo: Maṭbaʿa al-qāhira al-ḥadītha, 1962.
Sharabāṣī, Aḥmad al-. *Maulid al-hudā. Masraḥiyya islāmiyya.* Cairo: Kutub thaqāfiyya, 1962.
Sharqāwī, ʿAbdur Raḥmān ash-. *Muḥammad rasūl al-ḥurriyya.* Cairo: ʿĀlam al-kutub, 1962.
Shinar, Pesah. "Traditional and Reformist *maulid* Celebrations in the Maghrib." In *Studies in Memory of Gaston Wiet*, pp. 371–413. Edited by Miryam Rosen-Ayalon. Jerusalem: Hebrew University, 1977.
Ṣiddīq Ḥasan Khān, Nawwāb. *Ḥusn al-uswa bimā thubita min Allāh wa rasūlihi fīʾn-niswa.* Beirut, n.d.
Ṣiddīqī, Sājid, and Walī Āsī. *Armaghān-i naʿt.* Lucknow: Maktaba-i dīn ū adab, 1962.
———. *Muntakhab salām.* Lucknow: Maktaba-i dīn ū adab, 1965.
Siddiqui, ʿAlī Muḥsin. *Burda al-madīḥ, sharḥ qaṣīda-i Burda.* Karachi: Maktaba-i isḥāqiyya, 1977.
———. *Kaʿb ibn Zuhair or Qaṣīdat Bānat Suʿād.* Karachi: Maktaba-i isḥāqiyya, 1968.
Siddiqui, Mohammad ʿAbdul Majid. *Ziarat-e Nabi, ba Halat-e Bedari* (Visits by the Prophet in Wakeful State). Lahore: Marhaba Publications, 1983.
Sindhī, Abūʾl-Ḥasan al-Madanī as-. *Inbāʾ al-anbāʾ fī ḥayāt al-anbiyāʾ.* Edited by Ghulām Muṣṭafā al-Qāsimī. Hyderabad/Sind: Shah Waliullah Academy, 1978.
Smith, Margaret. *Readings from the Mystics of Islam.* London: John Murray, 1950.
Smith, Wilfred Cantwell. *The Faith of Other Men.* New York: Mentor Books, 1965.
———. *Islam in Modern History.* Princeton: Princeton University Press, 1957; New York: Mentor Books, 1959.
———. *Modern Islam in India.* 2nd ed. Lahore, 1947. Another ed., Lahore: Ashraf, 1969, based on the London ed. of 1946.
Snouck Hurgronje, Christian. *Verspreide Geschriften.* 6 vols. Leipzig: K. Schroeder, 1923–27.
———. "Zur Dichtkunst der Bâ ʿAṭwah in Hadhramaut." In *Orientalische Studien Theodor Nöldeke gewidmet*, 1:97–107. Edited by Carl Bezold. Giessen: Töpelmann, 1906.
Söderblom, Nathan. *The Living God.* The Gifford Lectures. London: Oxford University Press, 1930.

Spies, Otto. "Sechs tunesische Arbeitslieder aus Gabes." In *Festschrift für Fritz Meier*, pp. 285–91. Edited by Richard Gramlich. Wiesbaden: Steiner, 1967.

Sprenger, Aloys. *A Catalogue of the Arabic, Persian and Hindustạny Manuscripts in the Libraries of the King of Oudh*. Calcutta, 1854. Reprinted 1977.

______. *The Life of Mohammad from Original Sources*. Allahabad: Presbyterian Mission Press, 1851.

Staples, W. E. "Muhammad, A Talismanic Force." *Journal of Semitic Languages and Literatures* 57 (January–October 1940): 63–70.

Stieglecker, Hermann. *Die Glaubenslehren des Islam*. Paderborn: Schöningh, 1962.

Storey, C. A. *Persian Literature: A Bio-bibliographical Survey*, vol. 1, part 2. London: Luzac, 1953.

Suhrawardi. See Gramlich.

Süleyman Chelebi. *Mevlûd-i şerif*. Istanbul, n.d. [ca. 1921]. New ed., *Yaşayan Mevlidi şerif*. Edited by Şevket Rado. Istanbul: Doğan Kardes, 1964.

Syed, Dr. Muhammad Hafiz. "Dīwān Qāzī Maḥmūd Baḥrī of Gogi, translated and edited." *Allahabad University Studies* 13 (1937): 149–222.

Tabataba'i, ʿAllamah Sayyid Muhammad Husain. *Shiite Islam*. Translated and edited by Seyyed Hoseyn Nasr. London: George Allen & Unwin, 1975.

Tabrīzī, Walīud-Dīn Moḥammad al-Khaṭīb al-. *Mishkāt al-maṣābīḥ*, vol. 1. Translated and annotated by ʿAbdul Hameed Siddiqui. New Delhi: Kitab Bhavan, 1980. See also Robson.

Ṭapish, Raḥmat ʿAlī. *Gulzār-i naʿt*. London, India Office Library, MS Urdu 154.

Thomsen, William. "Muhammad, His Life and Person." *MW* 34 (1944): 96–133.

Tirmidhī, Abū ʿĪsā. *Shamāʾil al-Muṣṭafā*. With the commentary of Ibrāhīm al-Bājūrī. Bulaq: Dār at-ṭabāʿa al-ʿāmira, 1276h/1859–60.

Trimingham, J. Spencer. *The Sufi Orders in Islam*. Oxford: Clarendon Press, 1971.

Troll, Christian W. "The Fundamental Nature of Prophethood and Miracle: A Chapter from Shibli Nuʿmani's *Al-Kalām*, Introduced, Translated and Annotated." *Islam in India: Studies and Commentaries* 1 (1982): 86–115.

______. "Reason and Revelation in the Theology of Mawlānā Shiblī Nuʿmānī (1857–1914)." *Islam and the Modern Age* 13, no. 1 (1982): 19–32.

______. *Sayyid Ahmad Khan: A Reinterpretation of Muslim Theology*. Delhi: Vikas, 1978.

______. "Sayyid Ahmad Khan and Islamic Jurisprudence." *Islamic and Comparative Law Quarterly* 2, no. 1 (March 1982): 1–16.

Tuḥfa-i Raḥīm Yār. Lahore: Allāhwālē kī qaumī dukān, 1960.

ʿUrfī Shīrāzī, Muḥammad. *Kulliyāt*. Edited by Ghulāmḥusain Jawāhirī. Tehran: n.p., 1336sh/1957.

Üsküdārī, ʿAzīz ibn Faḍlallāh. *Risāla fi'ṭ-ṭarīqa al-muḥammadiyya*. Princeton University, Jehuda Collection no. 2841.

Utas, Bo. *Ṭarīq at-taḥqīq: A Critical Edition of a Sufi Mathnavi*. Lund: Curzon Press, 1973.

Vaudeville, Charlotte. *Bārahmāsa, les chansons des douze mois dans les littératures indo-aryennes*. Pondicherry: Institut Français d'Indologie, 1965.

Vidyarti, Abdul Haque, Maulana. *Buddha Foretells the Advent of Prophet of Islam*. N.p. [Lahore?], 1955.
———. *Mohammad in World Scriptures*. Dar ul-kutub islāmiyya, 1940.
———, and Umed Ali. *Muhammad in Parsi, Hindoo and Buddhist Scriptures*. Allahabad: Abbas Manzil Library, 1955.
Vocke, Harald. "Der Prophet Mohammad als 'Imam des Sozialismus.'" *Frankfurter Allgemeine Zeitung*, 17 August 1966.
Wagner, Ewald. *Abū Nuwās. Eine Studie zur arabischen Literatur der frühen Abbasidenzeit*. Wiesbaden: Steiner, 1965.
Wahab, Syed Abdul. *The Shadowless Prophet of Islam*. Lahore: Ashraf, ca. 1949.
Walīullāh, Shāh. *Lamaḥāt*. Edited by Ghulām Muṣṭafā Qāsimī. Hyderabad/Sind: Shah Waliullah Academy, 1966.
———. *At-Tafhīmāt al-ilāhiyya*. Edited by Ghulām Muṣṭafā Qāsimī. 2 vols. Hyderabad/Sind: Shah Waliullah Academy, 1967–70.
Walker, J. "Asiya: The Wife of Pharaoh." *MW* 18 (1928): 45–48.
Wāqidī, Muḥammad al-. *Kitāb al-maghāzī*. Edited by M. Jones. 3 vols. London: Oxford University Press, 1966.
Watanmal, Lilaram. *The Life of Shah Abdul Latif*. Hyderabad/Sind, 1889. Reprinted Hyderabad/Sind: Sindhi Adabi Board, 1978.
Watt, William Montgomery. "Carlyle and Muhammad." *Hibbert Journal* 53 (1954–55): 247–54.
———. "His Name is Ahmad." *MW* 43 (1953): 110–17.
———. *Muhammad at Mecca*. Oxford: Clarendon Press, 1953.
———. *Muhammad at Medina*. Oxford: Clarendon Press, 1956.
———. *Muhammad, Prophet and Statesman*. Oxford: Oxford University Press, 1961.
Waugh, Earle. "Following the Beloved: Muhammad as Model in the Sufi Tradition." In *The Biographical Process*, pp. 63–85. Edited by Frank E. Reynolds and Donald Capps. The Hague and Paris: Mouton, 1976.
Welch, Anthony. *Calligraphy in the Arts of the Muslim World*. Austin: University of Texas Press, 1979.
Welch, Stuart Cary. *Wonders of the Age: Masterpieces of Early Safawid Painting*. Cambridge, Mass.: Fogg Art Museum, 1979.
Wessels, Antonie. "Modern Biographies of the Life of the Prophet in Arabic." *IC* 49 (1975): 99–105.
White, Charles S. J. "Sufism in Medieval Hindi Literature." *History of Religions* 5, no. 1 (1965–66): 114–32.
Widengren, Geo. *Muhammad: The Apostle and His Ascension*. Uppsala: Lundquist, 1955.
Wielandt, Rotraut. *Offenbarung und Geschichte im Denken moderner Muslime*. Wiesbaden: Steiner, 1971.
Yunus Emre. *Divan*. Edited by Abdülbaki Gölpĭnarlĭ. Istanbul: Ahmet Halid Kitabevi, 1943.
Yusuf Ali, A. *The Personality of Muhammad the Prophet*. Lahore: Ashraf, 1931.
Zafrulla Khan. *Islam: Its Meaning for Modern Man*. New York and Evanston: Harper & Row, 1962.

Zahāwī, Jamīl Ṣidqī az-. "Thaura fī jahannam." *Ad-Duhūr* 1, no. 6. Beirut, 1931. German translation by G. Widmer, *WI* 17 (1935): 50–72.
Zajączkowski, Ananiasz. *Poezje stroficzne ʿAšïq-paša*. Warsaw, 1967.
———. "Poezje stroficzne (*muvaššaḥ*) mameluckiego sultan Qanṣūh (Qanṣauh) Gavri." *Rocznic orientalistyczny* 27 (1964): 82–84.
Zayyat, Ahmad az-. "The Month of Rabīʿal-awwal in the Life of the Prophet." *Majallat al-Azhar* 32 (1960–61): 1–4.
———. "Muhammad the Messenger of God: The First to Declare Human Rights." *Majallat al-Azhar* 31 (1959–60): 185–88.
Zimmer, Heinrich. *Maya. Der indische Mythus*. Zurich: Rascher, 1957.
Zolondek, Leo. *Book XX of Ghazzālī's Iḥyāʾ ʿulūm ad-dīn*. Leiden: Brill, 1963. (This is the central chapter of the *Iḥyāʾ*, dealing with the Prophet.)
Zwemer, Samuel M. "Hairs of the Prophet." *Goldziher Memorial Volume*, 1: 48–54. Edited by Samuel Löwinger and Joseph Somogyi. Budapest, 1948.
———. "The 'Illiterate' Prophet: Could Mohammad Read and Write?" *MW* 11 (1921): 344–63.

INDEX OF KORANIC QUOTATIONS

INDEX OF PROPHETIC TRADITIONS

ḤADĪTH

ḤADĪTH QUDSĪ

ḤADĪTH AN-NAWĀFIL

INDEX OF PROPER NAMES

(nn. 66, 67), 305 (n. 78), 309 (n. 12), 310 (n. 29)
Iran, 20, 48, 63, 89, 116, 117, 148, 149, 161, 171, 173, 195, 196, 204, 205, 251; eastern, 3, 136, 199
Iraq, 20, 42, 65, 145, 146; Iraqi, 125
ʿIrāqī, Fakhruddīn (d. 1289), 63, 136, 203, 204, 306 (n. 125)
Irving, Washington, 229, 310 (n. 33)
ʿĪsā, 107, 114, 263 (n. 7). *See also* Jesus
Işīk, H. H., 298 (n. 12)
Ishmael (Ismāʿīl), 14, 92, 102, 160
Ishtirākiyya Muḥammad (Fatḥī Riḍwān), 237
Islam (Zafrulla), 255
Ismāʿīl, angel, 160
Ismāʿīl ibn Mūsā (d. 760), 20
Ismailis, 20, 283 (n. 34), 289 (n. 66), 299 (n. 12)
Ismāʿīl Meeruthi (Mīraṭī) (d. 1917), 64, 277 (n. 34)
Ismāʿīl Shahīd, Muḥammad (d. 1831), 222, 225, 227
Israel, 16, 50, 117
Isrāfīl, angel of resurrection, 140, 305 (n. 83)
Isrāʿīl, 102
Issawiyya (ʿĪsāwiyya) order, 147, 295 (n. 13)
Istanbul, 39, 83, 294 (n. 75), 296 (n. 31), 297 (n. 37)
Italian, 226
Ithnāʾ ʿashariyya, "Twelver" Shia, 20
ʿIyāḍ ibn Mūsā, Qāḍī (d. 1149), 33, 46, 58, 60, 65, 70, 73, 105, 150, 276 (nn. 14, 21), 278 (n. 8), 284 (n. 58), 294 (n. 78)

Jacob, 35, 64
Jaʿfar aṣ-ṣādiq, sixth *imām* (d. 765), 113
Jagtiānī, Lālchand, 231
Jahāngīr, Salīm, Moghul emperor (r. 1605–27), 217, 264 (n. 4)
Jāḥiẓ, ʿAmr ibn Bahr al- (d. 869), 309 (n. 16)
Jaisalmer, 83
Jalāʾ al-ʿuyūn (Majlisī), 266 (n. 35)
Jamālī Kanbōh (d. 1535), 163
Jāmī, ʿAbdur Raḥmān (d. 1492), 28, 40, 63, 71–73, 76, 78, 79, 81, 87, 110, 112, 116–18, 128, 131, 133, 137, 139, 170, 180, 183, 191, 193, 197, 205–9, 212, 216, 243, 268 (n. 10), 270 (n. 43), 271 (n. 60), 280 (n. 55), 302 (n. 27), 307 (n. 130), 308 (n. 168)
Jāmiʿ aṣ-ṣaghīr, al- (Suyūṭī), 292 (n. 44)
Jāmiʿ at-tawārīkh (Rashīduddīn), 271 (n. 51)
Jauharat al-kamāl, prayer, 100
Jāvīdnāma (Iqbāl), 174, 227, 239, 240, 246, 247, 249, 251
Jawāb-i Shikwā (Iqbāl), 121, 244
Jawāhir al-auliyāʾ (Sayyid Bāqir Bukhārī), 92, 110
Jawāhir al-biḥār (Nabhānī), 270 (n. 39)
Jazūlī, Abū ʿAbdallāh Muḥammad al- (d. ca. 1465), 86, 95, 188, 285 (n. 67)
Jeffery, Arthur, 3, 7, 185, 234, 263 (n. 6), 297 (n. 3)
Jerusalem, 14, 42, 159, 160, 244, 268 (n. 6), 284 (n. 59)
Jesus, 5, 6, 16, 49, 57, 62–64, 74, 84, 117, 139, 146, 151, 167, 186, 196, 245, 264 (n. 7), 280 (n. 57), 309 (n. 16); in fourth heaven, 160. *See also* Christ; ʿĪsā
Jews. *See* Judaism
Jhang, 300 (n. 42)
Jīlī, ʿAbdul Karīm al- (d. ca. 1408), 127, 137, 140, 288 (n. 44), 289 (n. 67), 291 (n. 19)
Job, 48, 64
Jonah (Yūnus), 63, 276 (n. 21)
Joseph (Yūsuf), 16, 35, 39, 63, 139
Judaeo-Christian, 6, 12, 16, 17, 212
Judaism, 12, 56; Jews, 39, 65, 71, 265 (n. 25), 292 (n. 20); Jewish, 12, 16, 48, 75, 161, 253, 295 (n. 3), 300 (n. 50); settlements, 12; community, 14, 15
Junaid, Abūʾl-Qāsim al- (d. 910), 269 (n. 26)
Juraij, monk, 51

Kaʿb ibn Mālik (d. ca. 673), 179
Kaʿb ibn Zuhair (d. after 632), 179–81
Kaʿba, 12, 14, 15, 92, 151, 153, 160, 192, 198, 204, 208, 215, 249
Kaifī, Pandit Brijmohan Datatrich (d. 1954), 90, 193
Kakōrawī, Muḥsin (d. 1905), 91, 117, 211
Kalhora dynasty (r. 1720–86 over Sind), 128

Ṣāḥibdinā, 284 (n. 64)
Ṣaḥīḥ (Bukhārī), 27, 28
Ṣaḥīḥān (Bukhārī and Muslim), 27, 274 (n. 125)
Sahl at-Tustarī (d. 896), 125–27, 130, 132, 200, 299 (n. 15)
Saʿīd ibn Zaid (d. ca. 670), 268 (n. 55)
Saiful Mulūk (Ghawwāṣī), 98, 121
Ṣāliḥ Gašovič, Ḥāfiẓ, 297 (n. 36)
Salīm. *See* Jahāngīr
Sālimiyya school, 279 (n. 27)
Salmā, 207
Salmān al-Fārisī (d. after 656), 14, 22, 267 (nn. 51, 53)
Sāmī al-Bārūdī, Maḥmūd (d. 1904), 235
Sanāʾī, Abūʾl-Majd Majdūd (d. 1131), 21, 70, 107, 118, 138, 174, 176, 195–200, 212, 221
Sanūsiyya, 57, 276 (n. 6)
Sanūsiyya order, 225, 226
Sarāpā sarwar al-anbiyā (Luṭf), 271 (n. 57)
Sarfarāz Khān Kalhōrō (d. 1775), 128
Ṣārim al-maslūl, aṣ- (Ibn Taimiyya), 66
Sarmad Shahīd (d. 1661), 165
Ṣarṣarī, Yaʿqūb ibn Yūsuf as- (d. 1258), 187
Sarwar, 232
Sassui, 213
Satan, 39, 58, 61, 68, 79, 247, 269 (n. 11), 293 (n. 44)
Saudi Arabia, 149, 271 (n. 51), 296 (n. 20)
Sazāyī (d. 1738), 214, 308 (n. 164)
Scharīʿatī, ʿAlī, 266 (n. 35)
Schuon, Frithjof, 32
Semitic, 6, 308 (n. 157)
Serbo-Croatian, 155, 297 (n. 36)
Seven Sleepers, 209
Shabistarī, Maḥmūd (d. 1320), 289 (n. 66)
Shādhilī, Abūʾl-Ḥasan ash- (d. 1258), 281 (n. 63)
Shādhiliyya order, 94, 181, 219
Shāfiʿī, Muhammad ibn Idrīs ash- (d. 820), 280 (n. 49)
Shāh-Maḥmūd Nīshābūrī, calligrapher (d. 1564 or later), 269 (n. 10)
Shaibānī Khān Uzbek (r. 1501–10), 117
Shaikh Chānd (15th cent.), 129, 140
Shakēb, Żiāuddīn Aḥmad, 295 (n. 17)
Shakīl Badāyūnī, 87
Shakrawati Farmāḍ, King, 70
Shalabī, Maḥmūd, 237
Shamʿ-i maḥfil (Dard), 291 (n. 1)
Shamāʾil al-Muṣṭafā (Tirmidhī), 33, 270 (n. 36)
Shamsuddīn, epithet of Muḥammad, 288 (n. 44)
Shamsuddīn of Tabrīz (d. 1248), 24, 61, 134, 173, 201–3, 293 (n. 54), 305 (n. 97)
Sharābāsī, Aḥmad ash-, 156
Sharqāwa order, 41
Sharqāwī, ʿAbdur Raḥmān ash-, 237
Shauqī, Aḥmad (d. 1932), 188, 234
Shawāhid an-nubuwwa (Thanāʾī), 282 (n. 69)
Sheba, Queen of, 63
Shēfta, Nawāb ʿAẓīmuddaula (d. 1869), 210, 307 (n. 149)
Shia, 18–21, 42, 118, 170, 197, 219, 240, 266 (n. 35), 274 (n. 119), 287 (n. 23); Shiites, 11, 18, 20, 47, 59, 66, 113, 130, 219, 220, 266 (n. 41), 292 (n. 39)
Shiblī, Abū Bakr ash- (d. 945), 126, 217, 130, 229
Shiblī Nuʿmānī (d. 1914), 94, 231, 309 (n. 16)
Shifāʾ (Avicenna), 199
Shihāb al-Manṣūrī, ash-, 303 (n. 43)
Shihābuddīn, Shaikh, 298 (n. 10)
Shikwā (Iqbāl), 244
Shilha-Berber, 183
Shina language, 109, 287 (n. 22)
Shīrāz, 50, 79, 207
Shīvprasād Dōhī (19th cent.), 176
Sibāʿī, Muḥammad as-, 310 (n. 32)
Siberian shamans, 161
Sibi (Sind), 89
Ṣiddīq, as-, 197. *See also* Abū Bakr
Ṣiddīq Ḥasan Khān (d. 1890), 275 (n. 133)
Ṣiddīqī, family name, 266 (n. 37)
Sijelmasi, Mohamed, 41
Sidrat al-muntahā, the Lote Tree of the Boundary, 125, 161, 167, 168, 171
Sikhs, 221, 225
Sinai, Mount, 42
Sind, 82, 83, 88, 89, 128, 138, 139, 157, 188, 195, 212, 215, 231, 270 (nn. 33, 34), 284 (n. 66), 304 (n. 74), 310 (n. 44). *See also* Indus Valley
—Sindhi, 11, 32, 39, 70, 77, 79, 82, 89,

INDEX OF TECHNICAL TERMS AND CONCEPTS

a, *alif*, first letter of the Arabic alphabet, numerical value 1, cipher for God (*Allāh*) the One, and for the beloved, 73, 116, 118, 217, 290 (nn. 71, 72); of Adam, 72

a-l-m (*alif-lām-mīm*) (Sura 2:1), 118, 290 (n. 71)

abābīl birds (Sura 105), 265 (n. 7)

ʿabasa, "he frowned" (Sura 80:1), 273 (n. 105)

ʿabd, "servant, slave"; its use should be restricted in nomenclature to "God's servant," 121

ʿabduhu, "His servant" (Suras 17:1, 53:10), epithet of Muḥammad during his most sublime experience, 108, 142, 165, 246

abjad, the Arabic alphabet in the old Semitic order as used for chronograms and magical purposes, 212, 308 (n. 157)

abtar, "without issue" (Sura 108:3), 139

Adam qadmon, the primordial man, 294 (n. 76)

āfrīn, "praise," and *āfrīnish*, "creation," 205

aḥad, "One" (cf. Sura 112); God as, 116–18, 200, 212, 217, 289 (n. 66)

ahl al-bait (Sura 33:33), the members of Muḥammad's immediate family, 19

ahl al-kisāʾ, the members of Muḥammad's family who were taken under his cloak, 19

ahl al-kitāb, "People of the Book," members of those religious communities that have a Divinely inspired scripture, 65

ahl as-sunna waʾl-jamāʿa, "the followers of the Prophetic tradition and the community," i.e., the Sunnites, 20, 296 (n. 20)

ʿain al-jamʿ, "absolute union" between man and God, 293 (n. 44)

akhbār (plur. of *khabar*), "news, stories," 293 (n. 54)

akhlāq-i muḥammadī, the noble qualities of the Prophet, which the believer is expected to imitate, 228

ʿālam, "world," 116; *ʿālam al-malakūt al-aʿlā*, the world of supreme sovereignty, 115; *ʿālam al-mulk*, world of the kingdom, 115; *ʿālam-i jabarūt*, the second highest spiritual plane, 292 (n. 20); *al-ʿālamīn*, "the worlds," 265 (n. 27)

alif. See *a*

Allāhu akbar, "God is greater (than anything)," 268 (n. 54)

amāna, "trustworthiness," quality of a prophet, 57

amrit-kunda, "Water of life" in Hindu mythology, 292 (n. 20)

ʿamūd, "column (of light)," 125

anāʾl-ḥaqq, "I am the Truth": *anāʾl-ḥaqq muḥammadī*, the realization of true Muslimhood according to Shams-i Tabrīz, 25

anwār (plur. of *nūr*), "lights," 293 (n. 54)

ʿaql al-akbar, al-, "the Greatest Intellect," 115

ʿaql-i kull, "Universal Intellect," 199

arbaʿīn, "forty": *ḥadīth*, 28; days of seclusion, 117. See also *m*

arwāḥ (plur. of *rūḥ*), "spirits," 127

ʿaṣabiyya, "esprit de corps, close cooperation among individuals, strengthened by religion," 250

ʿashara al-mubashshara, al-, "the Ten who were promised Paradise," 23, 111, 268 (n. 55)

ʿāshiq, "lover": God is Muḥammad's, 127; man is Muḥammad's, 210

INDEX OF TECHNICAL TERMS AND CONCEPTS